The Holy Places of Jerusalem in Middle East Peace Agreements

The Holy Places of Jerusalem in Middle East Peace Agreements

The Conflict between Global and State Identities

Enrico Molinaro

BRIGHTON • PORTLAND

Copyright © Enrico Molinaro, 2009, 2010.

The right of Enrico Molinaro to be identified as Author of this work has been asserted in
accordance with the Copyright, Designs and Patents Act 1988.

2 4 6 8 10 9 7 5 3

First published in 2009, reprinted in paperback 2010, in Great Britain by
SUSSEX ACADEMIC PRESS
P.O. Box 139
Eastbourne BN24 9BP

and in the United States of America by
SUSSEX ACADEMIC PRESS
920 NE 58th Ave.   Suite 300
Portland, Oregon 97213–3786

All rights reserved. Except for the quotation of short passages for the purposes
of criticism and review, no part of this publication may be reproduced,
stored in a retrieval system or transmitted in any form or by any
means, electronic, mechanical, photocopying, recording or
otherwise, without the prior permission of the publisher.

British Library Cataloguing in Publication Data
A CIP catalogue record for this book is available from the British Library.

Library of Congress Cataloging-in-Publication Data
Molinaro, Enrico.
  The holy places of Jerusalem in Middle East peace agreements : the conflict between global
    and state identities / Enrico Molinaro.
       p. cm.
  Includes bibliographical references and index.
  ISBN 978-1-84519-404-8 (p/b : alk. paper)
 1. Jerusalem—International status. 2. Arab–Israeli conflict—1993– —Religious aspects.
 3. Arab–Israeli conflict—1993– —Peace. 4. Sacred space—Jerusalem. 5. Sacred
 space—Political aspects—Palestine. I. Title.
 DS109.95.M64 2009
 956.05′3—dc22
                                                                                    2009002321

Typeset and designed by SAP, Brighton & Eastbourne.
Printed by TJ International, Padstow, Cornwall.
This book is printed on acid-free paper.

Contents

Preface ix
Acknowledgments x

Introduction 1
   I   Purpose of the research 1
   II Methodology and limits of the research 3
   III Sources 4

1 The Holy Places of Jerusalem in the Middle East Peace Agreements 5

   1.1 The Declaration of Principles on Interim Self-Government Arrangements (DoP) of September 13, 1993 5
      1.1.1 The secret negotiations held in Oslo leading to the DoP 5
      1.1.2 The reference to Jerusalem in the DoP provisions 7
      1.1.3 The territorial–political status quo in Jerusalem after the DoP 8
   1.2 The letter sent on October 11, 1993, by Israeli Foreign Minister Peres to Norway's Foreign Minister Holst 10
   1.3 The Israeli–Jordanian Peace Treaty of October 26, 1994 13
      1.3.1 The Status Quo/Modus Vivendi on the Har Ha Bait/Al Sharif Haram
      1.3.2 The competition between Jordan and the PLO on the Jerusalem *Waqf* 15
   1.4 Agreements concluded by the Holy See mentioning the Status Quo 18
      1.4.1 Fundamental Agreement with Israel (December 13, 1993) 18
      1.4.2 Basic Agreement with the PLO (February 15, 2000) 22

2 Personal Jurisdiction in the Ottoman Empire and the Origin of the inter-Christian Status Quo 25

   2.1 Personal and territorial criteria for organizing Political authority: A historical overview 25
      2.1.1 Roman Empire until the Middle Ages 25
      2.1.2 Legal–historical background of the term sovereignty and its three different aspects: Independence, authority and title 26
      2.1.3 Functional, personal and territorial jurisdiction in international practice: The limits of the European state model 29

vi | Contents

    2.2 The principle of personal jurisdiction in the Ottoman Empire   31
        2.2.1 The application of personal jurisdiction in the Millet system   31
        2.2.2 The Capitulations and the consular jurisdiction applied to foreign and protected persons   32
    2.3 The origin of the Status Quo in the Christian Holy Places under Ottoman rule   36
        2.3.1 The Ottoman Firmans and the guarantees towards the Christian population of the Empire in the Paris Treaty of 1856   36
        2.3.2 The Berlin Treaty's new attitude of protecting all Christendom   39
        2.3.3 The introduction of the state model to the Middle East and the origin of Arab nationalism   42

3   The Status Quo in the Holy Places during the British Mandate   46

    3.1 The concept of the Holy Places' inviolability for all religions   46
        3.1.1 Theodor Herzl's and Herbert Samuel's plans for a Jewish role in Palestine   46
        3.1.2 The Sykes–Picot Agreement and the Husayn–McMahon correspondence   49
        3.1.3 The negotiations with the World Zionist Organisation and the Balfour Declaration   52
    3.2 British steps towards Holy Places' international protection at Peace Conferences   54
        3.2.1 Priority of world interest in the Holy Places at the Paris Peace Conference   54
        3.2.2 The King–Crane Commission and the San Remo conference   57
    3.3 The terms of the mandate in Palestine approved by the League of Nations   58
        3.3.1 The British policy towards the Muslim, Christian and Jewish communities   58
        3.3.2 The development of the Palestinian-Arab and the Jewish-Zionist national movements   62
        3.3.3 The 1929 disturbances and the Jewish–Muslim Status Quo/Modus Vivendi   64
    3.4 Settlement of disputes on rights and claims in connection with the Holy Places   67
        3.4.1 Immunity from ordinary jurisdiction according to the 1924 Palestine Holy Places Order in Council   67
        3.4.2 The competent body to settle the Holy Places' disputes   68
        3.4.3 A critique of the erroneous interpretation of the local government's authority according to the Paragraph 3 of the 1924 Order-in-Council   70
    3.5 The proposals of a special regime for Jerusalem from 1937 to 1947   71
        3.5.1 The Peel and Woodhead Commissions' partition plans   71
        3.5.2 The 1939 White Paper, President Truman's policy and the termination of the British Mandate   74
        3.5.3 The United Nations Special Committee on Palestine (UNSCOP)   76
        3.5.4 The Partition Resolution's special regime for Jerusalem and the status of the General Consuls in the city   78

4	**The Status Quo/Modus Vivendi of the Holy Places in the Arab–Israeli Conflict**	81
	4.1 The Jordanian–Israeli Armistice Agreement of April 3, 1949	81
	4.1.1 The partition of Jerusalem between Israel and Jordan	81
	4.1.2 Israeli position on the protection of the Holy Places	84
	4.1.3 The Israeli Draft Resolution on Jerusalem submitted to the General Assembly on November 25, 1949	88
	4.1.4 The position of the United States on the partition of the city	90
	4.2 Jordan's practice until 1967	91
	4.2.1 Jordanian position on the administration of the divided city	91
	4.2.2 Jordanian practice in the Holy Places	93
	4.3 Israeli practice in the Holy Places since 1967	95
	4.3.1 Israeli Jurisdiction over East Jerusalem	95
	4.3.2 The preservation of the Status Quo in the Christian Holy Places	97
	4.3.3 The new Modus Vivendi in the Muslim–Jewish Holy Places	101
5	**The Legal Regime Applied to the Holy Places of Jerusalem**	105
	5.1 Legal–empirical criteria to define the Holy Places	105
	5.2 The Status Quo in the Christian Holy Places	107
	5.3 Procedural and material norms of the Status Quo system of law	110
	5.4 The relationship between the Status Quo/Modus Vivendi and the principles of freedom of religion and worship	112
	5.5 The broader cultural–religious status quo in Jerusalem	114
	5.6 Hypothesis of an international local custom (objective regime) and the binding effects of unilateral declarations	117
	5.7 The partial suspension of the principles applied to the Holy Places in times of war	120

Conclusions and Suggestions for Further Research   123

A. The Status Quo/Modus Vivendi and the Quartet's Road Map in the perspective of the global and state identity models   123
B. Suggestions for further research   126
    B.1 The competition between the two identity models and the cycles of Western history   126
    B.2 Legal implications of the three alternative definitions of sovereignty   129
C. Israeli–Palestinian meetings behind closed doors on Jerusalem and its Holy Places   130

Annexes   133

Annex I: The Palestine (Holy Places) Order in Council, 1924   133
Annex II: Provisions included in international documents adopted in the context of the Middle East Process mentioning Jerusalem or the Holy Places (in chronological order)   134
(a) Letter sent on October 11, 1993 by Israeli Foreign Minister Peres to Norway's Foreign Minister Holst   134

(b) Fundamental Agreement between Israel and the Holy See, signed on December 13, 1993 134
(c) Section 3 of the Washington Declaration, signed by Israel and Jordan on July 25, 1994 134
(d) Article IX of the Peace Treaty between Israel and Jordan, signed on October 25, 1994, titled "Places of Historical and Religious Significance and Interfaith Relations" 135
(e) Basic Agreement between the Holy See and the Palestine Liberation Organization, concluded on February 15, 2000 135

Annex III: Principles governing the cultural and religious status quo in Jerusalem 135
(a) Preamble: special objectives of the authorities administering the city 136
(b) Principles applying to the Holy Places, religious buildings and sites 136
(c) Religious and cultural rights of the local communities 137
(d) Religious and cultural rights applying to all visitors and residents 137

Annex IV: Glossary of key terms related to sovereignty and status quo 138
(a) Different meanings of the term sovereignty 138
1. Independence 138
2. Title 138
3 Authority 138

(b) Different meanings of the expression status quo in Jerusalem 138
1. The Status Quo (capitalized) in the Holy Places between the recognized communities 138
2. The cultural/religious status quo (not capitalized) between the recognized communities and the territorial authorities 139
3. The political/territorial status quo (not capitalized) between the Israelis and the Palestinians 139

Notes 140

References 176
1. Books 176
2. Journals 180
3. Unpublished material 181
4. Official documentation (in chronological order) 181
5. United Nations documentation 183
6. International jurisprudence (in chronological order) 183
7. Newspaper articles 184

Index 185

Preface

This book is based on a doctoral thesis approved by the Hebrew University of Jerusalem in 2006. However, my perspective on the symbolic value of Jerusalem has evolved over many years. It arose, initially, out of my desire to contribute to the conflict analysis between Israelis and Palestinians. In the early nineties, when I first envisioned this project, the idea was to put together a multidisciplinary research that would develop into a thorough study of the Arab–Israeli political and religious contention. The pivotal point of this research was to observe objectively the relationship between diplomats, politicians, academics, intellectuals and religious leaders, while being fully aware of my own Western social and cultural prejudices.

After having lived ten years in Jerusalem, I realized that I needed to deepen my understanding of the struggle between the two powerful Western elite groups. This discovery changed the focal point of my book, which now revolves around the competition between two parallel interpretations of the socio-political reality: on the one hand, the state/territorial approach and on the other, the global/transnational one. With this magnifying lens to hand, the yet undefined concept of *Jerusalem* appears to be the crossroad of many debates about national and religious identity, including the controversial theory of *Clash of Civilizations*.

I sincerely wish that my work will open up a constructive debate on the intricate issue of Jerusalem and its Holy Places, leading upcoming generations to an innovative way of understanding international politics.

Acknowledgements

No book is ever the product of one person's efforts, and certainly this one is no exception. It would never have become reality without the help and suggestions of many supportive friends and colleagues.

I would like to acknowledge the debt I owe to students, friends and colleagues at the Israeli, Italian and Palestinian Universities as well as the members of the association I have the honor to chair, "Mediterranean Perspectives".

I am particularly grateful to my Doctoral thesis' supervisors, Prof. Raymond Cohen and Dr. Esther Cohen, as well as my Master thesis' supervisor, Prof. Luigi Ferrari Bravo, for their thoughtful and creative comments, and for exploring with me the boundaries of professional friendship.

I would like to also thank Blythe Liebgott, Christine Fillion, Elizabeth Farren, Giuliana Mammucari, Judy Cohen, Steve Odero Ouma and Viviana Colombini for putting up with me during the extensive editing process. Additional gratitude goes to Steve for the arduous task of proofreading.

The Holy Places of Jerusalem in Middle East Peace Agreements

The Conflict between Global and State Identities

Introduction

1 Purpose of the research

Throughout history, members of various communities around the world have associated a particularly significant event — either real or allegorical — with a specific site. Such a site was regarded as holy and was venerated in shared rituals and traditions that were passed on from generation to generation.

In Jerusalem, certain places are culturally and spiritually the locus of devotion for different groups. This explains why members of the local recognized communities[1] have long been competing for their possession, conditions of access, as well as worship rights.

Jerusalem and its Holy Places have seen many regimes come and go. Over the years, various communities have raised fierce controversies over worship rights, such as the Holy Sepulchre inter-Christian disputes and the Har Ha Bait/Haram Al Sharif (Temple Mount/Noble Sanctuary)[2] Israeli-Jewish/Palestinian-Muslim disputes.

Presently, no major controversies exist between the Jewish and the Christian denominations regarding the Holy Places of Jerusalem. Until 1967, large numbers of Israelis had neither heard of the Christian sanctuaries, nor had they a clear notion of their significance. Additionally, "Judaism does not lay any special claim to the sites of the Holy Sepulchre or the Basilica of the Nativity."[3]

But the compound in the Old City of Jerusalem, sacred to both Jews and Muslims, has long been the object of heated discussions between Israelis and Palestinians. Both parties have bitterly argued over the name of the city where this compound is located: the Hebrew version is *Yerushalayim*, while the Arabs call it *Al Quds*.

Additional terminological controversies have arisen over the name of the compound, whose Hebrew denomination is *Har ha-Bayit*, the *Temple Mount*. Most Jews consider it to be the exact location of Mount Moriah, where the two Jewish Temples stood.

King Solomon built and inaugurated the First Temple in approximately 950 BCE, the Babylonians destroyed it in 568 BCE, and the Second Temple was rebuilt in 515 BCE. In 18 BCE, King Herod restored the temple that was once again destroyed by the Romans in 70 CE.

The rectangular walled compound, with unequal sides at the southeastern corner of the Old City of Jerusalem, contains the holiest Jewish memories, the exact spot where religious Jews believe "the Divine Presence dwells"[4] permanently. Most of the Israeli Chief Rabbis maintain that when the Messiah comes, they will rebuild their temple and restore traditional rituals.

However, until that event occurs, the Jewish Orthodox establishment has prohibited the entry of their congregations into the area for fear of its desecration. This explains why after the destruction of the temple, the Western Wall, which is the western section of the wall that once surrounded the temple compound (also called *Wailing Wall* by many non-Jews), has, since the twelfth century,[5] been the most important Holy Place for the Jews, and their main center of worship.

On the other hand, the Muslims believe that the Prophet Mohammed ascended to Heaven from the same place. Therefore, towards the end of the seventh century,[6] they began interpreting the Koranic verses about the Prophet Mohammed's night journey from Mecca on his flying horse *al-Buraq*, lightning, to *al Aqsa*, the extreme mosque. Thus, the Muslims commemorated these events by building two major shrines on the compound: in Arabic, *al-Haram al-Sharif*, the *Noble Sanctuary*.

In 691 CE, the Muslims constructed the Dome of the Rock, *qubbat al-sakhra*, whose name comes from the rock on which Mohammed allegedly left his footprint. Then in 705 CE, they constructed the *al-Aqsa* Mosque.

While the former is a structure that glorifies the "holy rock,"[7] as well as a place for private prayer, the latter is "a mosque, a place officially designated for public prayer on Fridays and holidays."[8]

In light of the controversy over the entitlement to raise legitimate claims concerning the Holy Places, an international legal perspective is needed. This legal perspective may also be helpful in highlighting the state/territorial and global/transnational approaches to Jerusalem, later described in this research.

A study of these two competing approaches can shed new light on the broader international legal and diplomatic aspects of the Jerusalem issue. Jerusalem and its Holy Places are historically symbolic issues charged with emotional meaning for the collective identities and interests of the corresponding groups.

According to the state/territorial perspective, the relevant groups would be the Israelis and the Palestinians, whereas according to the global/transnational interpretation, such groups would be labeled as Jews, Christians, and Muslims.

In the state/territorial perspective, the symbolic value of Jerusalem and its Holy Places is related to the development of the conflicting national Israeli and Arab — later Palestinian — collective identities. This state/territorial model was introduced to the area during Napoleon's expedition to Egypt, and developed more intensively after the 1930s.

On the contrary, in the global perspective, millions of people identify themselves as Jews, Christians and Muslims. This definition is based on a global/trans-territorial rather than state/territorial approach. These people, who are mostly living outside of Jerusalem and the Israeli–Palestinian areas, consider the city and its Holy Places to be a locus for worship and spiritual devotion.

In order to regulate the relationship between the competing Christian communities claiming rights over the same sites, during the eighteenth and the nineteenth centuries, the Ottoman Empire developed a set of rules known since then as the *Status Quo*.

Hereinafter, both terms *Status Quo* and *Holy Places* will be capitalized as a conventional way to avoid possible confusion with other polysemous meanings in different contexts, in which such terms will not be capitalized.[9] Hence, in this book, the expression *Holy Places* of Jerusalem defines those sites regulated by the *Status Quo*.

This study is multidisciplinary in nature and intends to provide an overview and original interpretation of the relevant provisions included in the international documents adopted in the Middle East Peace Process, and to answer the following questions:

1 Under which conditions and to what extent does international law regulate and protect the interests of the various recognized communities in the Holy Places?
2 Which types of collective identities and which representative communities are entitled to raise claims on these places?
3 What is the exact definition of the Holy Places' *Status Quo* (capitalized), as opposed to the other meanings of the Latin expression in Jerusalem?

II Methodology and limits of the research

The methodology of this work combines inductive and deductive research. Adopting a multidisciplinary perspective helps to determine and explain the different meanings of the expressions *Holy Places* and *Status Quo*, as well as the equally controversial and often manipulated term *sovereignty*. This study examines the relevant available documents in order to ascertain the terminological, semantic and legal implications of such terms and expressions when used in different contexts.

A detailed analysis of all manifestations of international practice relating to the Holy Places in Jerusalem would go far beyond the scope of this study. The fulcrum of the present study is limited to the most controversial issues surrounding the legal regime applied to them. In particular, this study is focused on an analysis of the international documents so far adopted in the context of the current Middle East Peace Process that have incorporated provisions related to this issue.

From a legal perspective, a comprehensive research on this topic should take into account all the legal systems related to the subject at hand: Ottoman, British Mandatory, United Nations, Jordanian, Egyptian, Israeli, Palestine Liberation Organization, Palestinian Authority, Muslim, Jewish and Canon law. Additionally, Jerusalem Christian communities have their own autonomous legal systems applicable to their members.

In order to adequately undertake such ambitious research, an institutional framework for a team of scholars and experts in the different fields of law is needed. Moreover, this type of institutional framework is also necessary if one wants to consider the subject of the Holy Places of Jerusalem in its full significance through multiple perspectives such as anthropology, comparative religion, history, international relations, law, political sciences and sociology.

A wider research plan could also meticulously describe all the specific locations that labeled as *Holy Places*, as well as draft a detailed list of every substantial right claimed by the various Christian communities under the Status Quo legal regime.

However, the object of the present study is limited to the relevant procedural and formal aspects of the legal regime applied to the Holy Places together with its historical–diplomatic background, from its origin to the present. Various problems indirectly related to this topic are excluded from this research since they are not essential to the issues discussed.

For example, one of the major issues not considered in this study is whether the law of belligerent occupation should apply to the area of Jerusalem that came within Israel's municipal borders after the 1967 War.[10] Another issue not specifically dealt with in this work is the status of other Holy Places located outside the present municipal boundaries of Jerusalem, namely in Bethlehem.

The interim peace agreements concluded between Israel and the Palestine Liberation Organization, as well as the permanent status negotiations that have developed between the parties, have substantially influenced the international legal status of these areas.

III Sources

This study is the result of an extensive and in depth investigation conducted over several years, through meetings with diplomatic, religious and political authorities, who have provided me with exclusive insights, personal feedback and unpublished documents commonly not accessible to the greater public.

The intertwined combination of inductive and deductive methodology applied to the significant amount of documents examined makes it impossible to mention all the sources used to construct the main hypothesis of this study.

As a result, the references quoted in the notes include only a selected number of primary sources and a limited number of scholarly publications. Additionally, a number of selected documents have been attached to the main study in order to allow the reader to better understand some specific aspects of the issue at hand.

Although some of the quoted documents are accessible, this study attempts to interpret them in an innovative way, and illustrates how either state/territorial or global/transnational discourses have influenced the various local governments' decisions. The same reasoning applies to the choice of secondary sources and the scholarly literature quoted in the footnotes.

Thus, a limited number of scholarly references have been selected, in order to provide the reader with an overview of the main events relating to the developments in the Holy Places. These references include the *Foreign Relations of the United States* (*FRUS*) and other available collections of documents edited by Ora Ahimeir, Jacob Coleman Hurewitz, Ruth Lapidoth, Meron Medzini. Other main references include the works by Eugene Bovis, Yitzhak Sergio Minerbi, Shlomo Slonim and Walter Zander.

This selection of authors was made to provide the reader with a consistent and homogeneous narrative of the relevant events. This allows the reader to verify the main findings of the study without engaging in additional scholarly debates on issues not essential to this book.

1 The Holy Places of Jerusalem in the Middle East Peace Agreements

1.1 The Declaration of Principles on Interim Self-Government Arrangements (DoP) of September 13, 1993

1.1.1 The secret negotiations held in Oslo leading to the DoP

From the Madrid Peace Conference of October 1991 to the present day, the parties involved in the Peace Process have mentioned *the Holy Places of Jerusalem* in various diplomatic documents, referring in different ways, to a set of rules, which confirm some sort of status quo in these places. Other diplomatic developments which occurred before 1991 have been briefly reviewed in this book, since they did not significantly impact upon the subject matter under examination.

The United Nations Security Council Resolution 242,[11] adopted in November 1967 in the wake of the June War, laid down the basic principles referred to in many of the peace agreements arrived at so far between Israel and the Palestine Liberation Organization.

This resolution, which was subjected to differing interpretations by the parties involved,[12] neither includes any express reference to Jerusalem nor is Jerusalem mentioned in the United Nations Security Council Resolution 338 of October 22, 1973, which reaffirmed the guidelines of Resolution 242 and was adopted in the wake of the October 1973 War.

In a similar vein, no reference to Jerusalem was ever made in the Camp David "Framework for the Middle East Peace Accords," signed at the White House on September 17, 1978 by then Egyptian President Muhammad Anwar Al-Sadat and the then Israeli Prime Minister Menachem Begin and witnessed by the then President of the United States, James E. Carter Jr.[13]

Since no agreement was ever reached, the parties to the treaty decided to avoid any reference to this sensitive subject in the text of their agreements but chose to express their respective opinions in the accompanying letters exchanged at the conclusion of the Camp David agreements.[14]

Whereas Begin's letter did not specifically refer to the subject of the Holy Places, Sadat's letter to Carter shows the Egyptian attitude vis-à-vis the principles to be applied to the Holy Places:

5. All peoples must have free access to the City and enjoy the free exercise of worship and the right to visit and transit to the holy places without distinction or discrimination.
6. The holy places of each faith may be placed under the administration and control of their representatives.[15]

For practical purposes the current peace process is usually regarded as having begun with the Madrid Conference for Peace in the Middle East, convened by the United States and the former Soviet Union in October 1991.[16]

According to the latter country's letter of invitation to the Madrid Conference, Israel and the Palestinians (invited as part of the joint Jordanian–Palestinian delegation) would conduct their negotiations in phases, beginning with talks aimed at reaching interim self-government arrangements.

Once agreed upon, these interim self-government arrangements were to last for a period of five years and in the course of the third year after the establishment of the self-governing authority, negotiations on the permanent status of West Bank and Gaza were to start, thereby creating a timetable similar to the one included in the 1978 Egyptian–Israeli Camp David Framework.

The term *West Bank* used in this work corresponds to the area known in Israel with the Hebrew biblical name of Judea and Samaria. The State of Israel currently controls the broader area of both the former Palestine Mandate within the armistice green line of 1948–1949 and, since the War of 1967, officially defined as the administered territories. The latter definition includes the areas formerly controlled by Jordan on one hand and the Gaza Strip, formerly controlled by Egypt, on the other. However, the expression became more controversial or obsolete since the implementation of the Oslo accords, with the beginning of the administration of the Palestinian Authority in the area, analyzed below in this book.

Bilateral and multilateral negotiations took place after the Madrid conference ended. The text of the invitation did not explicitly refer to Jerusalem, but the city was certainly a central element of the negotiations that preceded the Conference and in drafting the letter of assurance that the United States sent to the Palestinians, where their belief was expressed that "no party should take unilateral actions that seek to predetermine issues that can only be reached through negotiations,"[17] and explicitly mentioned *East Jerusalem*.

The official post-Madrid bilateral meetings took place between Israel and a Palestinian delegation that did not formally include representatives of the Palestine Liberation Organization (hereinafter, *the PLO*), upon Israel's demand. However, Israel conducted simultaneous secret negotiations in Oslo with the PLO under the auspices of Norway's Minister of Foreign Affairs Johan Jorgen Holst.

The PLO was founded by 422 Palestinian personalities, chaired by Ahmed Shuqeiri, in May 1964 in Jerusalem, following an Arab League decision. When Fateh (Arabic for *conquest*), led by Yasser Arafat, took over the PLO in 1969, it became an umbrella organization for various Palestinian factions. United Nations General Assembly's Resolution 3210 of 14 October 1974 recognized the PLO as the representative of the Palestinian people and granted it observer status.[18]

This unofficial "Oslo channel" was created following a meeting held in London in December 1992 between two Palestinian delegates, Afif Safieh and Ahmed Qureia, and the Israeli representative Yair Hirschfeld. The latter is a scholar from the Israeli University of Haifa; current PLO representative in Washington Safieh was the

PLO's representative in Britain and at the Holy See, while current chief Palestinian negotiator Qureia, also known as Abu Ala, was at that time the Fatah's financial affairs chief.[19]

As a result, a Declaration of Principles on Interim Self-Government Arrangements — hereinafter the *DoP* — also known as the *Oslo Declaration* or the *Oslo Agreement*,[20] was initialed in Oslo by the Israeli government and the PLO on August 19, 1993 and signed in Washington, D.C. a few weeks later, on September 13.

Shimon Peres, on behalf of the Government of Israel, and current Palestinian Authority Chairman Mahmoud Abbas "for the PLO team (the Jordanian–Palestinian Delegation to the Middle East Peace Conference) and representing the Palestinian people" signed the DoP. The document was also witnessed by representatives of the United States and the Russian Federation.

1.1.2 The reference to Jerusalem in the DoP provisions

Article V of the DoP, titled "Transitional Period and Permanent Status Negotiations" is devoted to the timetable of the two phases of negotiations. According to Section 3 of the same article, the "permanent status negotiations" between the Government of Israel and the Palestinian people's representatives would cover "remaining issues, including: *Jerusalem*, refugees, settlements, security arrangements, borders, relations and cooperation with other neighbors, and other issues of common interest."[21] With these provisions, Israel agreed for the first time to include *Jerusalem* in the negotiations' agenda.

A document published in March 1999 on the website of the Israeli Foreign Ministry gives a number of explanations as to why "Israel has agreed to address Jerusalem-related issues in the permanent status phase of the current peace negotiations."[22] The on-line document states that "the status of Jerusalem is unique," as it plays a significant role "in the religious identity of hundreds of millions of believers in the monotheistic faiths" and "many Palestinian Arabs also call the city their home."

As to the Palestinian concessions, the PLO agreed to exclude the municipal area of Jerusalem from the jurisdiction of the Palestinian Interim Self-Government Authority, defined in the agreement as "the Council."

Article IV Paragraph B, titled "Specific Understanding and Agreements" of the "Agreed Minutes to the Declaration of Principles on Interim Self-Government Arrangements" states that the "agreed powers, responsibilities, spheres and authorities transferred to" the Palestinian Council's jurisdiction "will cover West Bank and Gaza Strip territory, except for issues that will be negotiated in the permanent status negotiations." The list of such issues, slightly different from the list in Article V of the DoP, includes: "*Jerusalem*, settlements, military locations, and Israelis."[23]

A similar but not identical provision included in the Israeli–Palestinian Interim Agreement on the West Bank and the Gaza Strip, hereinafter defined as *the Interim Agreement*, confirms that "in accordance with the DoP, the jurisdiction of the Council will cover West Bank and Gaza Strip territory as a single territorial unit."

It also mentions the following list of "permanent status" issues: "*Jerusalem*, settlements, specified military locations, Palestinian refugees, borders, foreign relations and Israelis" and any "powers and responsibilities not transferred to the Council."[24]

The Interim Agreement was signed in Washington, D.C., on September 28, 1995 by Prime Minister Yitzhak Rabin and Foreign Minister Shimon Peres for the

Government of the State of Israel and by Chairman Yasser Arafat "for the PLO, the representative of the Palestinian people."

The United States President Bill Clinton and Secretary of State Warren Christopher together with representatives of the Russian Federation, the Arab Republic of Egypt, the Hashemite Kingdom of Jordan, the Kingdom of Norway and the European Union witnessed the signature.

In the DoP, an additional reference to Jerusalem can be found in Annex 1 Paragraph 1, of the Protocol on the Mode and Conditions of Elections, according to which "Palestinians of Jerusalem who live there will have the right to participate in the election process" for the Interim Self-Government Authority for the West Bank and Gaza, following an agreement between the two sides.

These provisions neither clarify the meaning of the term *Jerusalem*,[25] nor specify the limits of the city implied in the term. Such city limits could be those that existed under the British Mandate or those recommended in the 1947 United Nations General Assembly partition resolution,[26] those established by Israel and Jordan in the wake of the 1949 Armistice Agreement[27] or those adopted by Israel after 1967.[28]

Moreover, since the 1967 limits were slightly changed in 1993,[29] mainly in relation to the western boundary of the city, it is not clear whether this controversial term refers only to the territory occupied as a result of the June 1967 war, namely *East Jerusalem*, or to the whole area included in the present municipal boundaries.

The former legal adviser of the Israeli foreign ministry Ruth Lapidoth believes that the parties had in mind *East Jerusalem*. However, various "matters of interest to the Palestinians about west Jerusalem" may also have come into consideration,[30] which may include "the rights of the refugees who left those areas," or matters of common interest involving both parts of the city, such as "the question of freedom of access."

The negotiators may have intentionally left unclear the borders of the area defined by the term *Jerusalem*, thus keeping more flexible the permanent status negotiations not only in relation to the various aspects of the Jerusalem question but also concerning the definition of the issue.

Lapidoth maintains that in finalizing the agreement, Israel used certain terms "with the meaning that they have in her internal legislation." Although the term *Jerusalem* should relate "to the area included in the municipal jurisdiction of the city under Israeli law,"[31] "with the agreement of the parties, the negotiations on Jerusalem could also encompass a larger area."

Such an enlargement could help in making decisions "for demographic, technical and economic purposes as well as for planning in the spheres of communication and transportation" and "could perhaps facilitate the achievement of a compromise with regard to the national aspirations of the parties."[32]

The question of "territorial delimitation" does not influence the issue at hand in this work, namely the legal status of the Holy Places, "since most of those are situated in the Old City, which under any definition is included in 'Jerusalem.'"[33]

1.1.3 The territorial–political status quo in Jerusalem after the DoP

In diplomatic as well as political documents and discourses, the expression *status quo* refers to several different aspects of the Jerusalem question. Diplomats and journalists tend to use this expression to also characterize the political and territorial situation as frozen since 1967 due to the outcome of the Arab–Israeli conflict, pending a final solution to be negotiated by the interested parties. In other words, the expression may in certain instances *not* refer to the Holy Places or to the religious dimension of the city.

DoP's Section 4, Article V incorporates the agreement between the two parties where "the outcome of the permanent status negotiations should not be prejudiced or preempted by agreements reached for the interim period." Should this provision be interpreted as an international obligation on the parties to refrain from any act involving a change of the situation on the ground, possibly defined as the territorial–political status quo? Certainly, as in all agreements of this kind, the parties must act according to the principle of good faith.

In the opinion of former Israeli Ambassador to the United Nations Yehuda Blum, a pattern of "constant Palestinian attempts to change the existing *status quo*, by creating *faits accomplis* on the ground to enhance the PLO's bargaining posture in the projected permanent status negotiations concerning the future of Jerusalem,"[34] has marked the period since the signing of the DoP.

One example mentioned by Blum was the "New Orient House" located "in the eastern part of the city, which had once served as the office locale of the Palestinian contingent in the Jordanian–Palestinian delegation to the Madrid conference and to the subsequent Washington talks prior to the signing of the DoP."[35]

Blum explains that the building had been transformed into a *de facto* PLO Mission in Jerusalem. The PLO flag flew over the building, and official visitors to Israel had been hosted there as if they were entering exterritorial "Palestinian" soil.[36]

Blum considers the appointment of the Grand Mufti of Jerusalem as another PLO attempt to change the political status quo in Jerusalem. On October 15, 1994, on the wake of the death of the incumbent Mufti Suleiman Ja'abari chosen by Jordan in the summer of 1994, the Government of Jordan appointed his successor the then chief justice of the Islamic courts, Sheik Abdul Kader Abdeen.

This selection followed a practice that had started in 1948 and continued to 1967. Similarly, the appointment of the late Ja'abari, "scion of a well known pro-Jordanian family,"[37] was not an exception since, according to Musallam, he was selected "without due consultation with the PLO."[38]

One day after Abdeen's appointment, a member of the Palestinian Authority in charge of *Waqf* Affairs, Hassan Tahboub immediately made a counter-appointment on behalf of Chairman Arafat and called to the post the Imam of al-Aqsa Mosque, Sheik 'Ikrima Sabri.[39]

Musallam described Sheik Sabri as "a man known for his strong personality, (. . .) was the Imam who led the prayers at al-Aqsa when President Sadat of Egypt visited Jerusalem and prayed at the Mosque in 1979."[40] On the wake of his appointment as Mufti, Sheikh Sabri succeeded in accompanying the Turkish Prime Minister on her tour and prayer in al-Aqsa Mosque and attended meetings with her at the Orient House.[41]

According to Blum, agents of the Jericho-based Palestinian preventive security service headed by Jibril Rajoub, were posted on the Har ha Bait/Haram al-Sharif Compound in order "to isolate the Jordanian-appointed mufti and to prevent him from functioning."[42]

As a result, when Sheikh Abdeen finally retired in 1998, "Jordan did not appoint a replacement and made do with appointing a young sheik, Abd al-A'Zim Silhab, to be responsible for two Sharia courts in Jerusalem that had been under Abdeen's supervision."[43]

On December 26, 1994, in view of the intense competition about the preservation of the political–territorial status quo in the city, the Israeli Knesset adopted the "Gaza/Jericho Agreement Implementation (Limiting of Activities) Law" by 56 to 6 votes, with 32 abstentions.[44]

This law distinguishes the status in Jerusalem of the Palestinian Authority and the PLO, namely, only the former needs a written permit from the Government of Israel to open or operate any representation in Israel, including any institution, office or agency, or to hold any type of meetings, including marches, either on its behalf or under its auspices. On the other hand, any representation or meeting convened by the PLO can be canceled by the Israeli government.

Thus, the 1994 law bars any activity in Israel by the PLO or the Palestinian Authority "of a political or governmental nature or other similar activity within the area of the State of Israel which does not accord with respect for the sovereignty of the State of Israel without the agreement of the State of Israel."[45]

These provisions were introduced together with parallel legislation intended to incorporate into Israel's legal system,[46] the May 1994 Cairo Agreement between Israel and the PLO on the Gaza Strip and the Jericho Area.

Several decisions made by the Government of Israel have also been considered attempts to change the political and territorial status quo in the city. A recent example is the reaction by several members of United Nations Security Council to the recommendations made by the Israeli Cabinet at a meeting on June 21, 1998 chaired by the then Prime Minister Benyamin Netanyahu, regarding a plan to expand westward the Jerusalem's jurisdiction and the creation of an umbrella municipality, officially aimed at streamlining services in the Jerusalem region.

On June 30, 1998, the Russian Federation representative in the United Nations Security Council defined such decisions as "unilateral actions aimed at changing the demographic composition and borders of Jerusalem in violation of the status quo,"[47] and the representatives of China and France claimed that the Israeli decisions would "change" or "clearly alter the existing status quo"[48] in Jerusalem.

As Klein pointed out, in practice, "both sides have been acting to establish facts in preparation for the decisions on the future of East Jerusalem."[49] These facts have altered the territorial–political status quo in Jerusalem, while different, although related, facts have influenced the cultural–religious status quo in the city.

1.2 The letter sent on October 11, 1993 by Israeli Foreign Minister Peres to Norway's Foreign Minister Holst

A short time elapsed from the initialing of the Oslo Accord on August 19, 1993, and the signing of the DoP in Washington D.C. on September 13, 1993, between Israel and the PLO. According to Musallam, during this period "three letters were to have been exchanged between the two sides through the late Norwegian Minister of Foreign Affairs, Johann Jørgen Holst, forming an integral part of the peace agreement. (. . .) Without the exchange of these letters, the DoP would most probably not have been signed."[50]

Musallam underlines that all three letters "originally carried the same date"[51] of

September 9, 1993, that is, four days prior to the signing of the DoP. Only two letters were actually signed during Holst's shuttle mission between Jerusalem and the PLO headquarters in Tunis. Therefore, the third letter, hereinafter *the Peres Letter*, must have been signed and exchanged on October 11, 1993, less than one month after the signing of the DoP.[52]

According to Klein, Peres's letter to Holst was signed "on October 10 or 11, after the Knesset had approved the declaration of principles and Rabin had declared that there were no secret commitments supplementary to it."[53] Meanwhile, on September 29, 1993, the head of the Political Department of the PLO, Farouq Qaddoumi had met Holst at the United Nations Headquarters in New York. According to Musallam, Qaddoumi, "delivered a draft of the said letter to an astonished Holst, who promised to work on the issue with the Israeli side."[54] In a letter addressed to the Norwegian Foreign Minister summing up their discussion in New York, Qaddoumi warned that up to that point Israel had "failed to sign and deliver the letter about Jerusalem,"[55] thus making the Oslo agreement "incomplete."[56]

According to Klein, Peres's promise to preserve the existing situation in the Palestinian institutions of Jerusalem, including the Orient House, was formulated "only after long wrangling (. . .) in exchange for Arafat giving in to his demand to remove the city from the jurisdiction of the Palestinian Authority."[57] Initially, Peres, instructed by Prime Minister Rabin, had retracted his previously given consent, explaining that the move was in view of the "fear of Israeli public outrage that would topple the government." Peres did eventually send the letter to Holst[58] who, Musallam maintains, "was to convey its content to its real destination, Chairman Arafat."[59]

The Palestinian side agreed that the letter would not even be brought to the knowledge "of the PLO's supreme institutions, which would be called on to ratify the Palestinian decisions."[60] Accordingly, the letter was kept secret until June 6, 1994, when the Israeli Foreign Minister, in the wake of demands of members of the Likud opposition in the Israeli Parliament, and following Arafat's allusion to reveal its contents, felt compelled to make the letter public.

In his letter, Peres confirmed that "the Palestinian institutions of East Jerusalem and the interests and well being of the Palestinians of East Jerusalem are of great importance and will be preserved"[61] and stated that "all the Palestinian institutions of East Jerusalem, including the economic, social, educational and cultural, and the holy Christian and Muslim places, are performing an essential task for the Palestinian population." In the same letter, Peres gave assurance that the Israeli Government would not hamper their activity but would, on the contrary, encourage the fulfillment of their "important mission."

On the occasion of the inauguration ceremonies for President Nelson Mandela, in May 1994, Chairman Arafat made the first PLO public allusion to the existence of the letter while visiting a mosque in Johannesburg to meet representatives of the Muslim community, in order to discuss with them the agreement between the PLO and Israel signed five days earlier in Cairo.[62]

During this visit, Arafat gave a speech which was later labeled as "The Sermon on Jihad," mainly because of the following phrase: "You have to come and to fight and to start a Jihad to liberate Jerusalem, the first shrine."[63] An unidentified person recorded the statement and the Israeli organization "Women in Green" made it available to Israel Radio, which broadcast it on May 17, 1994.[64] Musallam believes that Arafat made such comment in the course of a speech that represented the "strongest defense ever in front of a foreign audience"[65] of the aforementioned Cairo Agreement. He maintains that Arafat, in fact, "(. . .) was mobilizing support for the agreement, calling on this Muslim audience and the entire Muslim *Umma* [community] to support the agreement."[66]

Klein, on the contrary, maintains that Arafat's speech was "exceptional in the sharpness of the language he used". It was "also exceptionally inaccurate — to say the least — in explaining why he had participated in the Madrid conference, and why he had, in view of the whole world, refused to sign a part of the Cairo accords."[67]

In his Johannesburg speech, Arafat referred to Jerusalem as "the first shrine of the Muslims," explaining why he had insisted on receiving the Peres–Holst letter from the Israeli side "before signing" the Oslo Agreements, emphasizing Jerusalem as one of the items "under discussion" in the negotiations. In Arafat's opinion, Peres's letter accorded the Palestinians the responsibility "for all the Christian and the Muslim and the Islamic holy sacred places", highlighting the fact that he had mentioned the Christian before the Islamic ones. He explained this insistence on his being "faithful to the Agreement" between the Khalif Omar Ibn Al Khattab and the Patriarch Sophronius, urging for "the support of the Islamic Umma."[68]

This letter by Peres represents, to the best of my knowledge, the only Israeli diplomatic document on the ongoing Middle East peace negotiations which expressly mentions *East Jerusalem* although the reference appears without further explanations as to the precise geographical borders of the area in question.[69]

An indirect Israeli official interpretation of the letter, or at least of the intention that lies behind its language, is found in the document "The Status of Jerusalem" on the Israeli Foreign Ministry Internet site,[70] which states that the "civil right of Palestinian Arabs to maintain their own non-political humanitarian, educational and social institutions was reiterated by Israel during the Israeli–Palestinian negotiations."[71] Although Peres's letter seemed to include "the holy Christian and Muslim places," among "all the Palestinian institutions of East Jerusalem" that are "performing an essential task for the Palestinian population," a different reading of the text would exclude this conclusion.[72]

Klein maintained that "later Israeli attempts to portray the commitments in the letter" as solely related to the operation of non-governmental "institutions (such as those that offer health, education, charity, and welfare services) were forced not to say pathetic."[73] He stated that for the first time, through Peres' letter Israel recognized "not only Muslim and Christian religious institutions, but also the Palestinian institutions in the eastern part of the city and their importance to the population,"[74] Therefore, Israel also promised to preserve the territorial–political status quo therein.

As to the international legal nature of this document, Lapidoth expresses the opinion that the letter should be considered a mere statement of policy and not a binding unilateral declaration. Its "lack of clarity" and "its blurred syntax," in particular, makes it "impossible to ascertain the contents of what was promised."[75] According to the then legal adviser of the Israeli Foreign Ministry Joel Singer, the Peres letter was intended to "preserve the status quo in Jerusalem."[76] Hirsch maintained that only after "Israel concluded some compromise regarding Jerusalem"[77] in the 1993 DoP, were the Palestinians "ready to sign the agreement." Without such linkage with the Israeli concessions on Jerusalem "the likelihood of such an agreement would have been slight."[78]

From this perspective, one possibility is that Peres's letter, although not directly a part of the 1993 DoP, may be considered as a part of the *context* in which they should be interpreted and have some legal effect under the customary law rules of interpretation codified in the Vienna Convention on the Law of Treaties of 1969.[79] According to Article 31 of the Vienna Convention:

> 1. The context for the purpose of the interpretation of a treaty shall comprise, in addition to the text, including its preamble and annexes: (. . .)
> (b) Any instrument which was made by one or more parties in connection with the conclusion of the treaty and accepted by the other parties as an instrument related to the treaty (. . .)

Contrary to this opinion, Lapidoth maintains that since the contents of the Peres letter do not deal with the same subject matter of the Declaration,[80] it cannot serve to interpret the DoP. As to the addressee of the letter, even though Norway passed the letter on to Arafat, Lapidoth doubts whether a third party can rely on the letter as a binding unilateral declaration or a valid element for the purpose of interpretation.[81]

1.3 The Israeli–Jordanian Peace Treaty of October 26, 1994

1.3.1 The Status Quo/Modus Vivendi on the Har Ha Bait/Haram Al Sharif

On July 25, 1994, Israel and Jordan signed a joint Declaration in Washington D.C. (hereinafter the *Washington Declaration*).[82] The Washington Declaration was followed on October 26, 1994 by a Treaty of Peace,[83] whose Article IX is entitled "Places of Historical and Religious Significance and Interfaith Relations." Whereas in Paragraph 1 of Article IX, the parties undertake to guarantee "freedom of access to places of religious and historical significance" in general, in its Paragraph 3, the parties undertake to "act together to promote interfaith relations among the three monotheistic religions, with the aim of working towards religious understanding, moral commitment, freedom of religious worship, and tolerance and peace."[84]

Similarly, Paragraph 3 of the Washington Declaration states that "(. . .) the two sides have agreed to act together to promote interfaith relations among to three monotheistic religions (. . .)." Paragraph 2 of the Treaty refers more specifically to Jerusalem and includes two provisions: one concerning the present, the other the future, almost identical in their contents to the parallel provisions which were included in Paragraph 3 of the Washington Declaration.

In the provision regarding the present, Israel declares that it *respects* Jordan's *present role* at the Muslim *holy shrines*, a reference presumably to the main Holy Places in Jerusalem located in the area under the responsibility of the Islamic *Waqf*, namely, the Har ha Bait/Haram al-Sharif compound.

In Lapidoth's viewpoint, the expression *holy shrines* used in this provision has a narrower connotation than *Holy Places*,[85] while according to Musallam, the provision contains "a statement of fact"[86] concerning the respect for "the already existing role of Jordan,"[87] that is, a confirmation of the Status Quo/Modus Vivendi similar to the one included in Peres's letter to Holst mentioned in the previous section. Such confirmation could also be interpreted from some provisions of the Fundamental Agreement between Israel and the Holy See as well as in the Basic Agreement between the PLO and the Holy See.[88] "Thus there seems to be an emerging consensus among the parties that the *status quo* in some form or another must be part of any agreement on the permanent status of Jerusalem."[89]

The present study examines the progressive extension of the inter-Christian Status Quo legal regime as applied to the Israeli-Jewish/Palestinian-Muslim Holy Places. To this end, this study analyzes the extent to which international law has taken into consideration this progressive phenomenon. The extension of the inter-Christian procedural rules of the Status Quo to the Jewish/Muslim Holy Places began during the period of the British Mandate:[90]

> The British Mandatory authorities in Palestine extended the principles of the Status quo [sic] [mentioned in the 1878 Treaty of Berlin] also to the Western (Wailing) Wall in Jerusalem and to Rachel's Tomb (near Bethlehem).[91]

In this legal–historical context, Cust, a British Mandatory officer, listed the following Holy Places under the Status Quo in his Memorandum, a sort of confidential account of practice on this subject, well known to all experts:

> The Holy Sepulchre with all its dependencies.
> The Deir al Sultan.
> The Sanctuary of the Ascension.
> The Tomb of the Virgin (near Gethsemane).
> The Church of the Nativity.
> The Grotto of the Milk and the Shepherds' Field near Bethlehem are also in general subject of the Status Quo, but in this connection there is nothing on record concerning these two sites.
> The Wailing Wall and Rachel's Tomb, of which the ownership is in dispute between the Muslims and the Jews, are similarly subject to the Status Quo.[92]

The cautious wording of the British document clearly shows that the list is only indicative. Cust's list is not the irreversible result of a historical development and may for this reason change under unpredictable circumstances, such as new controversies between the recognized communities over their respective rights and claims. The Status Quo legal regime, for example, might also be applied to new controversies, such as the dispute between Christian communities and a section of the Muslim communities concerning the area in front of the Nazareth Basilica.[93] Similarly, the Status Quo procedural norms might be extended, by analogy, to another possible Modus Vivendi regulating the conflicts between the Jewish and Muslim recognized communities over worship and possession rights of the Cave of Machpela/Ibrahimi Mosque in Hebron and other Jewish/Muslim sanctuaries.

A careful examination of the specific contents of the mutual obligations arising out of the Israeli–Jordan Treaty's provisions included in Article IX paragraph 2 reveals that Israel undertook not to take any action inconsistent with the Status Quo/Modus Vivendi in the sharing of the administration and jurisdiction vis-à-vis the Holy Places located in this area, under the autonomous administration of the *Waqf* and controlled by the Jordanian authorities.

Klein maintains that with this provision "Israel officially recognized for the first time Jordan's special status in regard to the Islamic holy shrines in Jerusalem."[94] He further explains this attitude by saying that "Israel claims that its paramount interest is to guarantee its political sovereignty over the eastern city, and that management of the Islamic Holy Places and their religious status is not part of their political sovereignty."[95]

In other words, Klein emphasizes that the terms of the quoted provisions "suggest that Israel has relinquished any claim to actualize sovereignty over the Islamic Holy Places in Jerusalem, and has surrendered the Temple Mount as a religious site"[96] and that "Jordan received from Israel a foothold in the Islamic Holy Places in Jerusalem by excluding Israel from them, while Israel strengthened its position that the existence of Islamic Holy Places in East Jerusalem does not in itself eviscerate Israel's political sovereignty over the City."[97]

The very fact that this provision focuses exclusively on the *shrines* might indirectly exclude any Jordanian claim for territorial jurisdiction or control of part of Jerusalem or of a right of administration there. Even if the term *respect* used in the treaty's provision may involve a bilateral obligation upon Israel towards Jordan, this commitment may be considered as a further confirmation of the attitude of all the interested parties vis-à-vis the present Status Quo/Modus Vivendi in the Holy Places. In fact, the late King Hussein himself had personally invested considerable sums in the restoration of the Dome of the Rock edifice, linking its financial responsibility in the holy sites and its right to religious custodianship.[98]

However, the Secretary General of the Arab League Ahmad Issmat Abdul Majid issued a press communiqué at the end of a meeting of the permanent representatives of the Arab League held on July 28, 1994 (three days after the signature the Washington Declaration), to further stress that its paragraph 3, identical to the corresponding provision included in Article IX of the Israeli–Jordanian Peace Treaty signed three months later, "confirms a right and does not establish that right."[99]

Interestingly enough, Jordan as well, by accepting these principles, seemed to agree on the present Status Quo/Modus Vivendi since there is neither a reference in the text of the agreement to any claim formally raised to change or alter the present situation, nor does the agreement include a request to go back to the situation existing before 1967, when the present *plaza* did not exist and the Jewish prayer area in front of the Western Wall of the Har ha Bait/Haram al-Sharif was much smaller.[100]

1.3.2. The competition between Jordan and the PLO on the Jerusalem Waqf

As previously mentioned, the commitments on the respect of the Status Quo/Modus Vivendi refer only to the relationship between the two parties, and thus the expression "negotiations on the permanent status" included in the last paragraph of the aforementioned Paragraph 2 might refer to the negotiations foreseen in the bilateral agreements between Israel and the PLO.[101]

According to Lapidoth, "the lack of reference to the parties to the negotiations on the permanent status" might have been "intended to leave the door open to a claim by Jordan that it should participate in those negotiations, at least with regard to Jerusalem."[102] She further maintains that Israel's commitment to give "high priority to the Jordanian historic role" at the Muslim holy shrines in those negotiations does not necessarily imply that this role corresponds with the Jordanian "present role," mentioned Article IX. In other words, Israel only committed itself to adopt a certain attitude in the negotiations, without specifying the meaning of its commitment. This is the reason why Lapidoth considers the provision in the Jordan–Israel Treaty compatible with the 1993 DoP.[103]

The question as to whether the letter sent by Israeli Foreign Minister Peres on October 11, 1993[104] ought to have any international legal value implies a possible conflict with the Peace Treaty provisions where the rules of general international law relating to conflicting agreements between different parties may apply.[105]

Both documents would indeed have been valid and Israel might have, then, implemented one preferred text over the other and incurred international responsibility towards the party whose agreement it did not implement.[106] Article 25 Paragraphs 2, 5 and 6 of the Israel–Jordan Treaty of Peace requires that its own provisions should prevail:

> 2. The Parties undertake to fulfill in good faith their obligations under this Treaty, without regard to action or inaction of any other Party and independently of any instrument inconsistent with this Treaty.
> (...)
> 5. The Parties undertake not to enter into any obligation in conflict with this Treaty.
> 6. Subject to Article 103 of the United Nations Charter, in the event of a conflict between the obligations of the Parties under the present Treaty and any of their obligations, the obligations under this Treaty will be binding and implemented (Article 25).

Lapidoth has pointed out the similarity between the provisions quoted above and the relevant provisions in the 1979 Treaty of Peace between Egypt and Israel.[107] Additionally, according to Klein, Prime Minister Rabin and King Hussein formulated the reference to Jordan's special role at the Muslim "holy shrines" in Jerusalem "in such a way that the Palestinians would not be able [to] make a legal claim that it contradicted Israel's undertakings"[108] to them.

In any case, these provisions both in the Washington Declaration and in the Peace Treaty, have aroused sharp criticism on the part of the Palestinians and created competition[109] between Jordan and the Palestinians so intense that it has led to the appointment of two new Muftis in charge of the prayers in the Muslim Holy Places in Jerusalem, one appointed by Jordan, the other by the Palestinians.

According to Ifrah Zilberman, the Palestinians also "wished to control the assets of the Islamic establishments and the Islamic Endowments, and thereby to reject Jordanian claims to have a role in managing Islamic affairs in Jerusalem."[110] For this reason, a Department of Islamic Endowments was established "by the Palestinian Authority in an effort to control Islamic courts in the Jerusalem area."[111]

On 9 September 29, 1994, the Jordanian government dissociated itself from the *Waqf* administration in the West Bank and transferred it to the Palestinian Minister of Religious Endowments, Hassan Tahboub, who also headed the Supreme Muslim Council, located in al-Haram al-Sharif. He received "all documents relevant to administering the *Waqf* in the West Bank, but not those dealing with the Jerusalem district."[112]

In Musallam's opinion, the *high priority* of Jordan's permanent status would exclude "from the outset any 'third party,' namely the PLO, from a particular role on religious supervision, no matter how important or peripheral that supervision might be."[113]

Musallam also noted the omission of any reference in the text of the Israeli–Jordanian agreements to the Christian Holy Places, since Jordan's role "is confined to the Islamic holy sites in Jerusalem."[114] By comparison, during the Oslo negotiations "the PLO insisted on including the Christian holy places as part of the commitment made by Israel in the aforementioned 'Peres Letter.'"[115]

On January 26, 1994, in an attempt to help solve the controversial issue of "Jerusalem's final political status," King Hussein himself went so far as to make a suggestion that would allow "Muslim, Jewish and Christian authorities to assume jurisdiction over sites the respective religions deemed holy in the city."[116] In this regard, Jordan's position was that it "only could recognize God's sovereignty over Jerusalem,"[117] or, in his own words, "sovereignty of the holy places belongs to the Almighty in heaven."[118] In his speech before the United States Congress, King Hussein stated:

> My religious faith demands that sovereignty over the holy places in Jerusalem resided with God and God alone. Dialogue between the faiths should be strengthened; religious sovereignty should be accorded to all believers of the three Abrahamic faiths, in accordance with their religions. In this way, Jerusalem will become the symbol of peace and its embodiment, as it must be for both Palestinians and Israelis when their negotiations determine the final status of Arab East Jerusalem.[119]

According to Klein, former Jordanian Prime Minister and King Hussein's "confidant"[120] Adnan Abu Odeh had anticipated Jordan's position in an article published in the Spring 1992:

> (. . .) The walled city, the true and holy Jerusalem, would belong to no single nation or religion. Rather, it would belong to the whole world and to the three religions: Muslims, Christian and Jewish. Thus no state would have political sovereignty over it (. . .) Over the walled city of Jerusalem (. . .) no flags would fly (. . .) The holy walled city of Jerusalem would be open to all (. . .) It would be governed by a council representing the highest Muslim, Christian and Jewish religious authorities. Each authority would be responsible for running and maintaining the holy sites of its faith (. . .).[121]

Adnan Abu Odeh held the positions of Chief of the Royal Court, Political Advisor to King Hussein, Minister of information and Jordan's permanent representative at the United Nations. In an article published in 1996 the same author expressed a similar position:

> So I propose that we should remove this less than one square kilometer from the city of Jerusalem, and make it a holy, sanctified area, with no flags flying over that area. In other words, there should be no political identity for that section of the City. It is the city of God, the spiritual basin. We should remove it from the political conflict among nations. Flags should fly only outside the wall.[122]

On this matter, Musallam quoted a phrase taken from a speech given by the Jordanian Prime Minister Majali at an official ceremony attended by the United States Secretary of State Christopher and Israeli Foreign Minister Peres: "Sovereignty over the holy places of Jerusalem is only for God, and in his name, we should respect and honour that right."[123] Furthermore, in an interview given to the editor of the Egyptian daily *Al-Ahram*, Ibrahim Nara, King Hussein stated:

(. . .) The issue of Jerusalem will be tackled with time in accordance with the Palestinian–Israeli accord. We will continue to carry out our duty toward the holy places until a satisfactory and accepted solution is reached. We only want to do our duty, nothing more nothing less. At the same time, my personal feeling regarding the Muslim, Christian, and even Jewish holy places is that they should not be placed under the sovereignty of this or that country, or any side. My personal feeling is that the holy places should unite all believers in God who should have the same rights. The Islamic holy places, for example, should belong to the entire Islamic world. Interfaith dialogue will turn Jerusalem, this small city and small land, as God wanted it to be, into a destination for all worshippers. Otherwise, tragedies will recur. I believe this view will be accepted by all people and all parties (. . .).[124]

Article B, Paragraph 3 of the Washington Declaration, reaffirmed in Article IX, Paragraph 2 of the Peace Treaty implies Jordanian–Israeli cooperation. However, the status of the Muslim holy shrines in Jerusalem is of concern to several other interested parties, namely Egypt, Morocco and Saudi Arabia, to mention only a few. In this respect, Klein maintains that such intensive Israeli–Jordanian cooperation "clearly would weaken the Palestinian position in their struggle to establish eastern Jerusalem as their capital."[125]

Referring to the PLO's position on this issue, Chairman Arafat stated: "(. . .) Let them [Israel and Jordan] decide whatever they want. Jerusalem will continue to remain an Islamic-Christian Palestinian city. We are the only owners of decision-making and of authority on all the holy places in it."[126] And "(. . .) No Arab or Israeli leader controls the holy shrines in eastern Jerusalem. This right is the Palestinians' alone"[127] and "let Hussein and Rabin hear me, Jerusalem is the capital of Palestine whether they like it or not, whether they will it or not, and those who do not like this, let them go and drink the water of the sea of Gaza."[128] As to the specific issue of "God's sovereignty," in a public speech in Gaza, Arafat stated:

Jurisdiction is for God all over the universe. His Chair engulfs all the heavens and earth and not only Jerusalem. Jurisdiction over the universe is God's, but sovereignty over Jerusalem and jurisdiction over Jerusalem is for the Palestinian people.[129]

An accurate analysis of the competition and controversies about the question of who represents the Muslim side does not challenge the existence and validity of the general principles applying to the Status Quo/Modus Vivendi in the Holy Places of Jerusalem[130] since both Jordan and Palestinian authorities seem willing to accept the current balance of interests with Israel in the management of the main shrines of the city. A detailed examination of the two provisions found in Article B, Paragraph 3 of the Washington Declaration and in Article IX of the Peace Treaty confirms this assumption vis-à-vis the Israeli position.

1.4 Agreements concluded by the Holy See mentioning the Status Quo

1.4.1 Fundamental Agreement with Israel (December 13, 1993)

The first instance where the expression *Status Quo* (capitalized) is mentioned in an international agreement concluded after the beginning of the Middle East Peace

Process is Article 4, Paragraph 1 of the Fundamental Agreement between Israel and the Holy See.[131]

The signing of the treaty on December 13, 1993, marks an important moment in the complex and controversial relations between the two parties. According to Rabbi David Rosen, "the normalization of relations between the Holy See and the State of Israel is indeed the culmination of a process — a process of reconciliation that began with the Second Vatican Council and the promulgation of *Nostra Aetate* (October 1965)."[132]

The first Israeli Ambassador to the Holy See Shmuel Hadas agrees that "Vatican II and its *Nostra Aetate* declaration thus became the foundations of a new theological edifice, built brick by brick, which gradually modified the Catholic Church's attitude towards the Jewish people and the State of Israel."[133] In his address on the occasion of the presentation of his credentials to Pope John Paul II on September 29, 1994, Ambassador Hadas defined the signing of the Agreement as "(. . .) a unique act, for its protagonists are unique."[134]

In an interview given in 1994, Pope John Paul II declared: "it must be understood that the Jews, who for thousands of years were dispersed among the nations of the world (. . .) decided to return to the land of their ancestors. This is their right!"[135] These considerations may explain the Agreement's "theological and historical rather than legal"[136] language adopted in the preamble, unusual for international diplomacy:

> MINDFUL of the singular character and universal significance of the Holy Land;
> AWARE of the unique nature of the relationship beween the Catholic Church and the Jewish people and of the historic process of reconciliation and growth in mutual understanding and friendship between Catholic and Jews (. . .)
> REALIZING that such an Agreement will provide a sound and lasting basis for the continued development of their present and future relations (. . .) AGREE upon the following (. . .)

Some observers have used historical and theological reasons to explain the Holy See's refusal to establish diplomatic relations with the State of Israel from the moment of its establishment in 1948. John T. Pawlikowski, for instance, believes that two tendencies whose roots lie "in the early centuries of Christianity" have played "a prominent role in shaping the Catholic outlook on the issues of the Jewish people and the land of Israel over the centuries:" the first was the "so-called theology of 'personal wandering' with respect to the Jewish people," according to which "Christians regarded Jews as forever relegated to the status of 'displaced persons' among the nations of the world;"[137] the second major theological tendency within Christianity has been a focus on efforts to supersede "a supposedly exclusive Jewish emphasis on 'earthly' Israel."[138]

Pawlikowski believes that the very emergence of the expression "Holy Land" in reference to this region was "part and parcel of this overall theological tendency"[139] and that it was Justin Martyr, in his Dialogue with Trypho in the second century AD, "the first major post-biblical work on Christian-Jewish relations, [who] introduced for the first time the term 'holy land' into the Christian vocabulary"[140]

The Dominican Stephan the Borbon claimed that the Christians were the "descendants of the Holy Land both according to the flesh and the spirit:"[141] "our father Adam was created here and like the other patriarchs is buried in this country" and from the "spirit's" point of view, "our father Christ and our mother the Holy Virgin were born, lived, died and were buried here." The same logic applies to "our father the apostles" and to the origin of "our mother the Church," thus, "the land is ours by the right of succession as far as we are the true children of God."

These claims to the land are all "derived from the Jewish past and based on the presumption that the Church had become the true Israel," and even though "no attempt has ever been made to find a scriptural basis for this claim," "this land belongs to us by the right of purchase and acquisition; for Christ bought it for us by his blood, has expelled the Jewish people from it by the might of the Romans and has handed it to Christendom."

Finally, since "Christ was the supreme feudal Lord" and the Crusaders "his vassals" the Holy Land became the *patrimonium Christi*, the inheritance of God." Accordingly, "the Christian knight" had the feudal duty "to fight for his Lord's restoration."[142]

These complex theological issues are only briefly mentioned in this work in order to explain the delay in the normalization of diplomatic relations between Israel and the Holy See. A far wider discussion would be required, which would go beyond the scope of this study, since reflections on these issues even among contemporary theologians "are still at an embryonic stage."[143]

The first Israeli Ambassador to the Holy See Shmuel Hadas asserted four problems hindering the normalization of relations which are more closely related to the political–diplomatic context: "the status of Jerusalem and the Holy Places", "the Palestinian problem", Israel's "absence of recognized borders", related to "the fate of the administered territories," and the "concern for the Catholic minorities in the Arab countries, given the fear of reprisals."[144]

In July 1992, in the wake of the Madrid Peace Conference, the Holy See and the State of Israel established a Permanent Bilateral Commission. This led to the signing of the Fundamental Agreement on December 30, 1993, a few months after the signature of the Oslo agreement which occurred on September 13, 1993, between Israel and the PLO.[145]

It may be safely assumed that the results of the Madrid Conference, where Arab states and a Palestinian delegation openly negotiated with Israel, had an influence on the Holy See.[146] Among others, the Holy See's spokesman Msgr. Joaquin Navarro-Valls made this connection clear at the press conference following the establishment of the Permanent Bilateral Commission.[147] Minerbi goes so far as to say that "for Israel, the signature of the Fundamental treaty was a kind of dividend of the peace process."[148]

The then Secretary for Relation with States of the Holy See Msgr. J.L. Tauran declared in Jerusalem: "If the Palestinian partners, supported by the Arab world, were seated around the negotiating table, who could blame the Holy See for pursuing a more formal dialogue with the Israeli authorities?"[149] This explains why the Fundamental Agreement between Israel and the Holy See, although not a formal "Middle East Peace Agreement," has herein been considered in the same broad diplomatic–political context.

Furthermore, as highlighted by Rosen, "it was to the evident advantage of the Holy See to be involved in the peace process, to both contribute to it as a whole and in order to protect its own interests. Israel made it clear to the Vatican that diplomatic normalization between them was an essential prerequisite to facilitate such participation."[150]

In other words, the Holy See "did not wish to remain on the fringes of the peace process now underway. The fears for the fate of the Catholic minorities in the region — mentioned above as an important reason for the Holy See to delay the normalization of its diplomatic relations with Israel — apparently disappeared."[151] The Pope's reference to Jerusalem in his reply to the new Israeli Ambassador's address is noteworthy:

> It is also to be hoped that the unique and sacred character of this Holy City will receive international guarantees that will also ensure its access to all believers.[152]

The negotiations of the Bilateral Commission were also affected by factors external to the bilateral agenda and more directly related to the complex and fluctuating Arab–Israeli relations. Among them "(. . .) the expulsion of the Hamas activists by Israel, which led to a suspension of talks for more than three months, even though this cause was not formally acknowledged as the reason for the hiatus."[153]

In this regard, both parties have declared "their respective commitment to the promotion of the peaceful resolution of conflicts among states and nations, excluding violence and terror from international life."[154] As for the Catholic side, "while maintaining in every case the right to exercise its moral and spiritual teaching-office, [the Holy See] deems it opportune to recall that, owing to its own character, it is solemnly committed to remaining a stranger to all merely temporal conflicts, which principle applies specifically to disputed territories and unsettled borders."[155]

According to Rosen, when the Permanent Bilateral Commission was established, the majority of the eleven items agreed upon in the agenda "concerned rights and privileges that the Church has enjoyed *de facto* since Ottoman times, but now sought to enshrine *de jure* under Israeli law."[156]

The Fundamental Agreement also includes provisions confirming the religious status quo in the broader sense,[157] as well as the principle of freedom of religion in general. Articles 1 and 2 of the Fundamental Agreement, for instance, recall the continued "commitment to uphold and observe the human right to freedom of religion and conscience," a commitment that should bind both parties of the Agreement in their respective spheres. Article 3, Paragraph 2 reaffirms the traditional "right of the Catholic Church to carry out its religious, moral, educational and charitable functions, and to have its own Institutions, and to train, appoint and deploy its own personnel in the said Institutions or for said functions to these ends."

As for the Status Quo in the Holy Places in its narrower sense as described in this study, Article 4, Paragraphs 1 and 2 of the Fundamental Agreement reads as follows:

> 1 The State of Israel affirms its continuing commitment to maintain and respect the "Status quo" in the Christian Holy Places to which it applies and the respective rights of the Christian communities there under. The Holy See affirms the Catholic Church's continuing commitment to respect the aforementioned "Status quo" and the said rights.
> 2 The above shall apply notwithstanding an interpretation to the contrary of any Article in this Fundamental Agreement.

It is notable that Paragraph 3 of the same article refers more specifically to "the obligation of continuing respect for and protection of the character proper to *Catholic sacred places*, such as churches, monasteries, convents, cemeteries and the like,"[158] whereas Paragraph 4 generally refers to "the continuing guarantee of the freedom of

Catholic worship," thereby establishing a clear distinction between the "Holy Places to which" the special regime of the Status Quo "applies" (Article 4.1) on one hand and the regime applied to other "places," qualified merely as "sacred" (Article 4.3), on the other.

The provision included in Article 4, Paragraph 2 establishes a different hierarchy in case of a conflict with other norms of the Agreement: "The above shall apply notwithstanding an interpretation to the contrary of any Article in this Fundamental Agreement."

The fact that such provision does not appear in any other article of the Agreement shows the outstanding importance given by the parties to the Status Quo and "the respective rights of the Christian communities thereunder," following Article 4.1 of the Agreement. At the same time, it offers a further confirmation of the autonomous legal nature of the Status Quo regime, regardless of any relation with other systems of law.[159]

It must be stressed that the parties, while stipulating an international agreement in which they adopted for the first time the expression *Status Quo* (capitalized), did not intend to introduce any new regime or to create any norm. In Article 4, Paragraph 1 of the Agreement "the State of Israel affirms its continuing commitment to maintain and respect" such a regime. Similarly, in the same provision, "the Holy See affirms the Catholic Church's continuing commitment to respect the aforementioned" regime.

As for the exact meaning of the expression *Status quo* referred to in Article 4, Paragraph 1 of the Agreement, it similarly must be stressed that neither an explanation is given in relation to the legal principles that such a regime would imply, nor does the interpreter have any hint as to their specific contents or scope derived from an analysis of the Agreement's provisions.[160]

This is in contrast with other expressions or definitions mentioned in the Agreement, such as "Catholic Church and the Church," "Communities of the Catholic Church," "The State of Israel and the State." Article 13, Paragraph 1 (subheadings a, b and c, respectively) is devoted to explaining and clarifying those terms.

However, no similar provision of the Agreement explains the exact meaning of the *Status Quo* expression and no other diplomatic texts or agreements by any of the two parties fulfill this task. This lack of statutory definition also characterizes the only other two agreements examined in this study that mention the Holy Places of Jerusalem, namely the Israeli–Jordanian Peace Treaty of 1994 and the PLO-Holy See Basic Agreement of 2000.

1.4.2 Basic Agreement with the PLO (February 15, 2000)

On February 15, 2000, the Holy See and the PLO concluded a Basic Agreement[161] which, among other issues, dealt with the status of Jerusalem and the Holy Places. Paragraph 8 (e) of the Preamble and Article 4 of the Agreement explicitly mention the Status Quo.

The wording of Article 4 of the Basic Agreement is almost identical to the parallel reference to the Status Quo in the corresponding Article 4 of the Fundamental Agreement: "(. . .) The regime of the "Status Quo" will be maintained and observed in those Christian Holy Places where it applies." Paragraph 8 (e) of the Basic

Agreement's Preamble includes a reference to the "Regime of the 'Status Quo.'"

This provision does not expressly state whether the Status Quo regime applies only to the Christian Holy Places. However, from the context of the expression, such a legal regime might encompass Muslim and Jewish Holy Places as well.

A careful reading of the whole paragraph leads one to formulate the hypothesis that the interests protected by this regime, in the places "where it applies," were those of "the three monotheistic religions," which are mentioned in Paragraph b of the Basic Agreement's Preamble. This hypothesis appears to be strengthened if one takes into account the tendency book towards an extension of the Status Quo/Modus Vivendi system to the Muslim and Jewish religious communities, as discussed in this study.

More generally, the whole Paragraph 8 of the Preamble calls "for a special statute for Jerusalem, internationally guaranteed, which should safeguard": "freedom of religion and conscience for all; the equality before the law of the three monotheistic religions and their institutions and followers in the City; the proper identity and sacred character of the City and its universally significant, religious and cultural heritage; the Holy Places and the freedom of access to them and of worship in them." The last principle to be safeguarded by this "special statute" is "the Regime of the "Status Quo" in those Holy Places where it applies."

Paragraph 7 of the Preamble refers to "an equitable solution for the issue of Jerusalem, based on international resolutions, (...) fundamental for a just and lasting peace in the Middle East" and considers the "unilateral decisions and actions altering the specific character and status of Jerusalem" as "morally and legally unacceptable."

However, these provisions neither seem to add particular legal value to the principles included in Article 8 nor alter the meaning of its provisions. According to Paragraph 2 of the Preamble, the parties are "deeply aware of the special significance of the Holy Land, which is inter alia a privileged space for inter-religious dialogue between the followers of the three monotheistic religions."

A reference to the "inter-religious dialogue" is reaffirmed also in paragraph 2 of the Agreement whereas Paragraphs 2 and 8 of the Preamble refer to "the three monotheistic religions." This terminology is interestingly similar to both the concluding provisions of Article 3 of the Washington Declaration and Article IX, Paragraph 3 of the Peace Treaty between Jordan and Israel, as discussed in the preceding section.

This consideration as well as the general reference in the Preamble to the "universally significant, religious and cultural heritage" of Jerusalem seems to confirm the conclusion suggested above, that the parties, by omitting the adjective "Christian" from the expression "Status Quo in the Holy Places" might have intended to refer to the Christian, Muslim as well as Jewish Holy Places.

The Basic Agreement between the Holy See and the PLO does not contradict the basic principles which apply to the Holy Places of Jerusalem included in the agreements agreed upon by Israel or the PLO. On the contrary, it represents a sort of logical conclusion of the evolution of their principles, which may be summarized as follows:

a. Peres's letter indirectly confirmed the Status Quo/Modus Vivendi in the Christian and Muslim Holy Places.
b. The Fundamental Agreement between Israel and the Holy See explicitly confirmed the Status Quo in the Christian Holy Places to which it applies and the respective rights of the Christian communities thereunder.

c. The Washington Declaration and the Peace Treaty between Israel and Jordan confirmed the present balance of rights and interests (Modus Vivendi) in the Muslim holy shrines in Jerusalem. These rights are currently exercised from the Muslim side through the special role of the Hashemite Kingdom of Jordan.
d. The Basic Agreement between the PLO and the Holy See explicitly confirmed the Status Quo in those Christian Holy Places where it applies. Additionally, in line with the historical trend described in this work, its provisions also confirmed the Status Quo/Modus Vivendi in the Holy Places of the three monotheistic religions.

Since none of the aforementioned documents includes provisions explaining the exact meaning of the expression *Status Quo* (capitalized), it has become necessary, in order to interpret these terms, to analyze the historical-legal background of this legal regime from its origin through the Ottoman rule to the present.

A thorough analysis of the context in which the agreement was made may help to interpret the meaning of the treaty's provision in question. The customary law rules of interpretation, as expressed in Article 31, Paragraph 1, 2 and 3 of the Vienna Convention on the Law of Treaties of 1969, state that the terms of a treaty must be interpreted "in their context and in the light of its object and purpose" and there shall be "taken into account, together with the context (. . .)":

> (b) any subsequent practice in the application of the treaty which establishes the agreement of the parties regarding its interpretation.[162]

These provisions may also help understand the meaning of the expression *Status Quo* included in the two treaties recently concluded by the Holy See. The Latin expression (Status Quo) appeared for the first time in 1878 in a multilateral treaty, whose Article LXII includes a provision stating that no alterations can be made in the Status Quo of the Holy Places. The subsequent practice in the application of the treaty from the Ottoman Empire until today included in this book is a necessary element, according to the above quoted Vienna Convention's provisions, of the context to take into account in order to understand the meaning of a treaty provisions.

Incidentally, the last Paragraph of Article 31 of the Vienna Convention states that:

> (c) A special meaning shall be given to a term if it is established that the parties so intended.

As previously stressed, in order to understand the proper meaning of the Latin expression *Status Quo* in relation to the Holy Places, special consideration ought to be granted to the peculiar historical-diplomatic background in which the terms were first adopted. The historical analysis of such expression's meaning used both in diplomatic and common terminology up until the present day has been a main focus of this study.

2 | Personal Jurisdiction in the Ottoman Empire and the Origin of the Inter-Christian Status Quo

2.1 Personal and territorial criteria for organizing political authority: A historical overview

2.1.1 Roman Empire until the Middle Ages

Over the centuries, changes have occurred in the distribution of administrative power corresponding to specific socio-economic and political needs. Since antiquity, the laws of the group, termed "personal laws,"[163] as well as the laws of the polity of residence, have governed the legal relationship among different groups in various instances in whole or part. The Roman Empire, at the time roughly corresponding to present-day Europe and most of the Middle East, adopted a dynamic combination of both territorial and personal jurisdiction for organizing political authority. These two main criteria were not mutually exclusive and the were adopted by the Roman Rulers on a case-by-case basis.

In Roman and Hellenistic antiquity, socio-political borders were defined following the identity of the ethnic group, the *ethnos*. The empire, the larger boundary of a local entity, coexisted with and overlapped the community's ethnic boundaries. In areas under its control, Rome did not exercise an absolute and exclusive authority over its subjects, but actually allowed various degrees of autonomy, particularly in the judicial sphere. The residents of the conquered areas had the status of foreigners allowed to use their own law, *peregrini qui suis legibus utuntur*, and thus lived in accordance with local law, *secundum propriae civitatis iura*. Romans gave such autonomy also to several areas of the Middle East, including Judaea, approximately modern Israel/Palestine.[164]

This attitude continued until the end of the Roman Empire, when Cassiodorus, a Roman politician and writer who favored cooperation between Romans and Gothics, became the secretary of the Ostrogothic King Theodoricus. In order to express the dynamic application of personal and territorial jurisdiction typical of Roman law, he used the following formula: *Romanis, Romanus judex erit; Gothis, Gothus; et sub diversitate judicum una justitia complectabatur*.[165]

From another perspective, the special notion of *res divini juris*, a thing under divine law, shows the complex way Romans organized authority: *divine law*, unlike ordinary private law, referred to special areas which belonged to none, *res nullius*, or to God, *res sacrae*. In places such as temples, churches and other separate areas with similar functions, Roman law prohibited any business activity related to them, classified as *res extra patrimonium* and *extra commercium*.

Ordinary judicial jurisdiction on substantive disputes did not apply to sanctuaries and neither did any ordinary law, *jus humanum*, since they were "set apart from ordinary use and dedicated to religious purpose."[166] In these particular areas, if a person took refuge within the precinct of a sanctuary, the authority of the local ruler was not fully applicable. The Romans recognized in their eastern provinces the right of *asylia*. This term brings to mind the pan-Hellenic custom of ancient Greece, which considered sanctuaries as properties of the gods, and therefore inviolable areas.

Although the precise function and motivations of *asylia* are still disputed, it is believed that the immunity of a certain place was granted in recognition of its particularly sacred character, in respect and veneration of a particular god or goddess. At various times during the Hellenistic and Roman periods, despite violence and war in the area, the city of Jerusalem was declared sacred and inviolable. Moreover, in the Byzantine period, individual churches based a trust-like relationship on a similar concept.

The wide-scale adoption of Roman law became part of Europe's legal heritage. However, after the barbarian invasions, European rulers ended the combination of both criteria in favor of either territorial or personal jurisdiction following their respective socio-political interests.

Medieval rulers applied Roman law principles in forging various political institutions according to criteria most suitable to them. The trans-territorial elites of the Empire and the Church generally favored personal jurisdiction and allegiance, while local sovereigns preferred to use their own geographical territory to define the boundaries of different polities. The mutable balance of power in Europe between these two elites eventually led to the prevalence of one of the two criteria, which over the centuries seemed to follow an apparent dichotomist cyclical process.

For centuries, these various forms of governments created a complex web of overlapping and asymmetrical allegiances. The European continent in the Middle Ages appeared like "an archetype of non-exclusive territorial rule."[167] In this context, "The notion of firm boundary lines between the major territorial formations did not take hold until the thirteenth century; prior to that date, there were only *frontiers*, or large zones of transition."[168]

The Franks, and later the Lombardians, applied the first large-scale personal laws' system to their conquered Italian territories,[169] mainly due to marked ethnic differences in the area. Gradually, however, such ethnic differences became less defined, thus weakening and undermining the system itself. As a result, "a process of mutual reaction between German customs and Roman law started to develop until both eventually came under the influence of canon law."[170] In this new socio-political context, the Emperor and the Pope respectively exercised their authority on a universal basis, through the Holy Roman Empire and the Church.

2.1.2 Legal–historical background of the term sovereignty and its three different aspects: independence, authority and title

As time progressed, local elites started challenging the prevailing trans-territorial global elites, who privileged the criterion of personal jurisdiction over the territorial one. Local rulers, on the contrary, gradually emphasized territorial jurisdiction as a criterion to define the scope of their political authority. This phenomenon further developed over the centuries, especially after the 1648 Peace of Westphalia, which ended the Thirty Years' War, under the pressure of territory-oriented European kings. The emerging modern state brought about a notion of an "ideal political community"[171] whose components at a later stage, particularly from the nineteenth century on, would eventually link together local residents as citizens with a common national identity.

At the end of the seventeenth century, the term *sovereignty* defined the king's supreme power within specified boundaries and became popular in European legal literature, thus giving moral and philosophical legitimation to a legal reality already influencing large parts of Europe. The term — originally, in its French version, *souverainité* — has its etymological origin in the word *souvre*, from the Latin *supra*, literally meaning *above/higher*, referring to the superior power of the local government vis-à-vis any other authority within the country's boundaries.

Jean Bodin first developed the legal meaning of this concept in public municipal law. Thomas Hobbes and Baruch Spinoza in their writings on political philosophy gave the term *sovereignty* its modern absolute character. Similarly, the absolute and exclusive features of private property in Roman law influenced the patrimonial concept of state territory.

The term *sovereignty*, as it appears in scholarly literature as well as in diplomatic documents and treaties, eventually made its way through to international law. This normative system corresponds to a different social and legal context, where the subjects, unlike in municipal law, are not individuals. In international law the subjects are mainly governments and international organizations, that is, entities having the capacity of exercising international rights and duties and maintaining their rights through international claims.[172] This implies a need to interpret international legal norms in their proper context thereby requiring a *vindicatio in libertatem* or a quest for consideration which is separate from other systems of law.

In modern times *sovereignty* has been used in reference to *states*, to the extent that these terms have been used to define two "twin concepts."[173] The term *state* is also common in international practice, including major multilateral treaties, such as Article 2, Paragraph 4 of the United Nations Charter and Article 34, Paragraph 1 of the Statute of the International Court of Justice.

Traditionally, international legal scholars as well as diplomats consider the delimitation of the exercise of authority within the territory of a state as one of the main purposes of international law. According to this view, any foreign penetration might be dangerous for the local order and the integrity of the state's life. Territorial jurisdiction has been defined as "the authority over a geographically defined portion of the surface of the earth and the space above and below the ground which a sovereign claims as his territory, together with all persons and things therein."[174] Consequently, any person or thing situated within or entering the territory of a state should *ipso facto* be subject to the state's authority.

A necessary link was hence established between the state's effective authority over an area and its exclusive right to exercise such authority along with the its ability to be an independent actor in the international arena. *Independence*, then, became a necessary corollary of territorial *authority* in relationships among states and of its legal source, or *title*. As a result, international legal scholars and diplomats, especially

European, began to use the term *sovereignty* to mean three different concepts: *independence*, *authority* and *title*.

I. Independence[175] has been adopted by international legal scholars as well as diplomats as a synonym for the term *sovereignty* to define an essential prerequisite for the states to be subjects of international law. Justice Dionisio Anzilotti has defined *independence* as (*external*) *sovereignty*, or *suprema potestas*, "by which is meant that the state has over it no other authority than that of international law,"[176] in relation to persons, things and relationships within its territory. Hence, a state must be independent of other legal orders, particularly foreign governments, and any external interference must be justified by a specific norm of international law.

II. Sovereignty is also a synonym for (full) *authority*, which each state is entitled to exercise within the limits of customary international law. The word *authority* is preferred here to alternative terms such as governmental *control, power* or *jurisdiction*[177] or other words borrowed from Roman law terminology, such as *imperium*. As explained in the section that follows, the term *jurisdiction* in this study defines the scope of the *powers* — *functional jurisdiction* — attributed to the state or any other subject of international law vis-à-vis a defined area of the globe and a group of people, from the perspective, respectively, of *territorial* and *personal jurisdiction*.[178]

Arbiter Max Huber of the Permanent Court of Arbitration, in his decision on the Island of Palmas, refers to the "facts showing the actual display of sovereignty."[179] Here the term has been used as a synonym for *authority*, and its "actual display" is nothing but its own exercise, or manifestation. Huber considered the principle of exclusive authority of the state over its own territory as the point of departure in settling most questions that concern international relations. He handed down his decision in 1928, when the idea of the absolute and exclusive powers of the nation-state prevailed in Europe.

As previously mentioned, the historical process of the territory-oriented state model, developed in Europe following the 1648 Peace of Westphalia. This led to the affirmation of the modern nation-state, and its ideological, philosophical and political characteristics started emerging in the nineteenth century. As an example, a U.S. Supreme Court decision issued in 1812 was quoted by the *ad hoc* judge designated by India Chagla, of the International Court of Justice, to confirm the fundamental principle of international law, according to which "a state exercises an exclusive competence on its own territory."[180] This political-historical context helps explain why the expression *territorial sovereignty* describes the *authority* of a state within its territorial boundaries[181] encompassing all possible rights, duties, powers, liberties, and immunities that a state may exercise.

III. Title from the Latin *titulus*, can also mean *sovereignty*, or the source of authority of any particular state in regard to a particular territory. Legal titles correspond to the vestitive facts, since the law recognizes them as creating rights, protecting corresponding vested interests, from which the state's authority flows.

Arbiter Huber explained that he felt bound to keep to the terminology employed in the Special Agreement establishing the arbitration, whose preamble referred to "sovereignty over the Island of Palmas."[182] Under Article I, Paragraph 2 of the agreement, Huber had to determine whether the Island of Palmas (or Mingias) formed a part of the territory of the Netherlands or of the United States. In determining to whom the territory belonged, the term *sovereignty* referred to the *title* over the Island. Even if this meaning of the term is different from the previously quoted actual display of *authority*, in Huber's decision the two meanings were related, since the latter served as proof of the existence of the former.

2.1.3 Functional, personal and territorial jurisdiction in international practice: The limits of the European exclusive state model

In international law the authority exercised by states, that is, their jurisdiction, is delimited by three major criteria: functional, territorial and personal. These three criteria refer, respectively, to the delimitation according to the contents of the various powers considered, *ratione materiae*, their scope in territorial space, *ratione loci*, and specific categories of people, *ratione personarum*.

A full discussion of these three dimensions of authority, plus the additional element of its delimitation over time, *ratione temporis*, would go beyond the limited scope of this work. Thus, only a brief description is given:

a) *Functional jurisdiction* refers to the range of powers that a state's authority implies. Additional distinctions may be drawn between legislative, executive, or judicial jurisdiction, depending upon the organization of a given state's constitutional system.
b) *Territorial jurisdiction* refers to the spatial dimension or scope of authority.
c) *Personal jurisdiction* refers to the categories of people — be they citizens or not — under the state's authority.

A person crossing into another state's border may at once be subject to that state's territorial jurisdiction, unless s/he is exempt from such jurisdiction by virtue of a special status, such as diplomatic immunity, and may be accountable for his/her conduct on its territory. Following a territory-oriented perspective, the local authority may demand that alien residents in a given state pay customs and taxes.

At the same time, an alien may remain under the personal jurisdiction of his/her state of citizenship, since territorial jurisdiction has never entirely superseded personal jurisdiction. In international legal practice, personal jurisdiction was enforced in Western and Northern Europe until the Middle Ages as the prevailing criterion,[183] to assert and delimit authority over individuals on grounds of allegiance or protection. The latter system allows members of different local communities to be governed by the laws of their own group, as defined by religious or ethnic criteria, and not by local laws.

Distinguishing between the functional, territorial and personal dimensions of a state's jurisdiction may be useful in describing various cases where a state's authority and ability to regulate its affairs within its territory are delimited. Territorial and personal jurisdiction may also overlap, regardless of the abstract theory that excludes the possible joint exercise of authority of two or more states over the same area. In principle, since various state systems are homogeneous, each state might extend its authority to a limit that may extend beyond the territorial or personal jurisdiction of the other. Consequently, state A might extend its legislative jurisdiction — for example, its private law — to regulate relations among subjects of state B's legal system, even though in principle states tend to limit the territorial scope of their law.[184]

States' systems of law delimit the territorial competence of various regional or municipal administrations within their boundaries. International law, on the contrary, simply determines whether or not an organized entity is a subject of the law, without distinguishing between different categories of subjects of international law.

The range of powers generally attributed by international jurisprudence and doctrine to the states has changed over the centuries. By implication, no subject of law is perfectly *sovereign*, in the sense that it can be outside and above the law. As a result, the latent contradiction between *sovereignty* and the very notion of subject of law questions the utility of this concept as a model of legal explanation, a "*Procédé d'explication valable*," to use Rousseau's words.[185] Procedural and other practical purposes may justify attempts to determine the powers that a state usually exercises in international law. In this limited perspective, the assumption is that a state possesses a specific power unless international law expressly excludes it, although in practice the state's powers may be limited in many ways.

An inherent consequence is that courts may give restrictive interpretation to treaty provisions limiting a state's authority. The well-known decision of the Permanent International Court of Justice in the Lotus case of 1927, for example, excluded the possibility of presuming possible restrictions on the independence of states. According to the Court, there is a general presumption in favor of exclusive territorial authority and only where a permissive rule exists is it possible for any state to exercise its powers in the territory of another. The Court justified this assumption by offering practical explanations and noting that even "the territoriality of criminal law," on which the quoted decision was based, "is not an absolute principle of international law."[186] In practice, this means that the courts may adopt the accepted pattern of state powers to decide on which party to place the burden of proof in case of claimed exceptions from full territorial authority.

This analysis helps understand how a thorough analysis of the issue of the Holy Places of Jerusalem, given the specific context of the Middle East Peace Agreements, is directly related to the way international law organizes territorial authority from a theoretical and political perspective. The term *sovereignty* particularly in the nineteenth century has been associated with the model of the modern nation-state and may represent the core political European heritage exported to the Middle East.

It is not within the scope of this work to outline the existing theories on the complex relationship between state and territory in international law or to suggest new ones. Nor is the purpose of this study to illustrate in detail the complex issues related to the problematic penetration of European cultural, political and economic influence in the Middle East in general. Rather, the limited goal of this analysis is to clarify, through a historical–hermeneutic approach, the main concepts involved in the European model of *territorial sovereignty* and to explain the different meanings of this misleading term in international law, with particular reference to Jerusalem and Holy Places therein.[187]

It is useful to stress that the political need to defend and strengthen the power of the state or the monarch in the face of obstacles and setbacks was behind the creation and gradual general adoption of the concept of sovereignty in Europe. Identifying the range of definitions of this term may help clarify ambiguous terminology as well as elucidate policy options available to the parties engaged in territorial conflict, particularly in the Middle Eastern and the Mediterranean regions. Avoiding narrow interpretations of the term, resulting from a typically European tradition exclusive approach of a nation state's authority, may facilitate a resolution of recent ethnic and religious conflicts in the area.

It is, then, evident that temporary socio-economic and political concerns of competing elites have often succeeded at influencing and shaping the organization of power following abstract models. These may be equivalent to the described ways of organizing political authority, according to principles of prevalently personal or territorial jurisdiction.

The territory-oriented approach suggests a model characterized by the full juxtaposition of three different aspects of state power defined as *sovereignty*: *independence*, *authority* and *title*. These terms, by replacing *sovereignty*, offer a clearer terminology, which may help describe the range of exceptions to the state/territorial-oriented approach, ultimately facilitating solutions to territorial conflicts. By learning the lessons of the past, one may succeed at shaping a more stable future by challenging the dominant Western models of identity in order to allow different levels of group identification to find suitable institutional representation.

2.2 The principle of personal jurisdiction in the Ottoman Empire

2.2.1 The application of personal jurisdiction in the Millet system

As considered above, the Roman Empire allowed a flexible combination of both territorial and personal jurisdiction to governments under their control. The Ottoman authorities adopted and expanded "the same system of recognition and assignment of self-government to each distinct nationality"[188] in the area previously controlled by Imperial Rome. This system, known by the Turkish term *Millet*, recognized "Armenians and other nationalities" living in this territory as "entitled to a large measure of self-government" and "accorded to foreign Christian nations" similar privileges.

This "led to the non-application to Turkey of the principles of territorial sovereignty generally recognized elsewhere." Non-Muslim communities had to pay taxes "for imperial purposes" but "they were, so far as concerns their own particular interests, to determine themselves the taxes which they were to bear" and "were entitled to have schools of their own."

This "system of diverse nationality recognized by ancient usage and essential to the existence of the Empire" applied "to the settlement of business disputes," regulated by the national courts of the non-Muslim litigants. A similar principle of separate jurisdiction was applied to religious disputes, assigned to the heads of given communities for their solution. Most members of the recognized communities living in the Ottoman Empire seemed to find this administrative arrangement acceptable, notwithstanding phenomena of discrimination and even persecution. The *Millet* system guaranteed their administrative autonomy, particularly in the spheres of worship and spiritual–religious organization as well as in personal status.

According to Judge Henry Eli Baker, "even if Islam was the official religion of the Ottoman Empire, the State protected the free exercise of all other religions recognized in the Empire; similarly, the various communities enjoyed all the traditional religious privileges", in accordance with the existing practice.[189]

Baker points out that "the practice of such communities should not have been contrary to public morals or conducive to the disturbance of the public order."[190] For a better understanding of the *Millet* system, it must be recalled that "the Koranic traditional norms apply only to Muslims; non-Muslims, so long as they remain unconverted to Islam, being permitted to continue to be governed by their former national and religious laws."[191]

The Ottoman legal system did not authorize "the interference of the authorities to prevent the holding of religious worship; on the contrary the laws and the treaties alike declare the exercise of religious worship to be the privilege of all."[192] The Muslim authorities in the Ottoman Empire rarely interfered with the worship in non-Muslim shrines and granted the Christian and Jewish population under their control a stable status of recognized minority, with established rights and duties "in accordance with the prescriptions of the Koran, as a 'people of the Book.'"[193]

The sections that follow will examine how Western political elites have overemphasized only one of the two intertwined criteria of territorial and personal jurisdictions, due to their respective political interests, to export and promote their corresponding model of collective identity, that is, state/territorial or global/trans-territorial in the Middle East and elsewhere, through a sophisticated political manipulation of the controversy over the legal status of the symbols *par excellence* of their ideological competition: Jerusalem and its Holy Places.

2.2.2 The Capitulations and the consular jurisdiction applied to foreign and protected persons

Long before 1517, when the Ottoman Empire included Jerusalem in its borders, intense competition developed among European powers which, at times, aggressively intervened under the pretext of disputes between the different Christian recognized communities in the Holy Places. Over centuries of its rule, the Sublime Porte, the official name of the Ottoman Government, and the Christian European powers concluded commercial bilateral agreements, known as *Capitulations*, whose provisions were divided into little chapters called *capitula*, term from which the expression originated. These accords, generally bilateral, regulated the trade relations between the Ottoman Empire and a given Christian Power but did not aim at a complete and systematic regulation of the interests of different recognized communities in the Holy Places, although international legal relevance was granted to those interests.

These agreements included clauses that granted a special legal, judicial and administrative treatment to those clergy members who were European citizens. The Capitulations gave a similar special status to those Christian clergymen who were protected by foreign powers although they were citizens of the Ottoman Empire. The Ottoman authorities "did indeed occasionally object to the granting of protection to its subjects who had never left Turkey."[194]

Nevertheless, this legal arrangement continued to apply to many "classes of persons, usually called 'protected persons' or 'protégés'" who, "acquiring a semi-naturalization,"[195] enjoyed Western elite rights and were subjects to Western states' liabilities and jurisdiction in Turkey. As an example, "the English Government, between 1839 and 1842, gave 'protection,' that is the right to be under English jurisdiction in Turkey and not under Ottoman jurisdiction, to many families of Jews who were suffering persecution at the hands of the Turks."[196]

According to the provisions of the Capitulations, European consuls, through consular courts, applied their own national laws to foreigners resident in the Empire.[197] Hence, those people were subjected not to the laws and the judicial authorities of the local government, namely the Ottoman Sublime Porte, but to those of their protecting European powers,[198] represented locally by the consuls.

It can be concluded that the described legal and administrative treatment of those protected persons followed the criterion of personal jurisdiction. The personal criterion of jurisdiction limited the application of the state/territorial European absolute and exclusive model, according to which any local government should have applied the same rules of the land to all citizens and residents.[199]

The legal opinion of an American lawyer on January 21, 1887 stated that "the treaties called Capitulations"[200] created the exceptional legal situation of "a series of *imperia in imperio*." This "doctrine of exterritoriality" created a "fiction of international law," according to which every Western "citizen resident in Turkey is supposed to be in" his/her country of nationality. The same American lawyer emphasized that "the existing system is the direct lineal representative in unbroken succession of a wider exterritoriality which existed during the middle ages and had been continued from Roman times."[201]

The Roman Empire had used a combination of territorial and personal jurisdiction, distinguishing between Roman citizens and foreigners: the citizens were subject of Roman civil law, *jus civile* or *jus Quiritium*, while a special magistrate, called *praetor peregrinus*, applied his own amalgam or *contaminatio* of Roman and foreign provincial law to the foreigners, *peregrini*. The new branch of law, *jus gentium*, filtered through the magistrate's authority, *imperium*, and tempered by considerations of equity was quite different from its original components. As a result, the full title given to this special magistrate, *praetor peregrinus qui inter peregrinos* or *inter cives et peregrinos jus dicit*, explained his function of creating law, in Latin: *jus reddere*, or *jus dicere*, from which the word *jurisdiction* originates. This travelling magistrate, through jurisprudential decisions, made law (for settling disputes) between (foreign) travelers and citizens on one side and between (foreign) travelers themselves on the other.

In this specific context, the term *jus gentium* should not be confused with other less used meanings of this Latin expression. *Jus gentium*, when referring to the law governing the relations of Rome with other polities, corresponded to the modern idea of international law. The same Latin expression could have an additional meaning: the natural law, *jus naturale*, or natural order, *naturalis ratio*, also defined as the law of "all peoples", *jus omnium gentium*, which included the Romans.

However, *jus gentium* was generally known as the law created by the *praetor peregrinus*, and represented the product of the political and economic interactions of Romans with foreign territories gradually conquered. This development related particularly to the Eastern areas of the Mediterranean basin, since the sea was the quickest and safest means of communication and exchange. In commercial relations with foreign political entities, the Roman courts used their legal customs for contractual transactions concluded in Rome, while the local law of family and succession remained untouched.[202] This Roman experience influenced the *Capitulations*, which referred not only to the aforementioned bilateral treaties but also to their contents, namely, the set of administrative special arrangements created by those treaties and applied to protected persons. The Treaty of Amity and Commerce signed in February 1535 by Suleiman the Magnificent for the Ottoman Empire, and Francis I, King of France, was in many respects a model for subsequent Capitulations and regulated the described arrangement.

In its provisions this agreement never mentioned Jerusalem, Bethlehem or the Holy

Places. Instead, what was clearly stated was the prohibition of forceful conversion to Islam of French subjects and a grant of "the right to practice their own religion".[203] The treaty's provisions quoted above were the only ones not directly applicable to commerce and business. Consequently, the principle of immunity from ordinary local jurisdiction was established in the sensitive field of religious issues, according to the criterion of personal jurisdiction.[204]

Although Genoa, Florence, and especially Venice had previously obtained Capitulations from the Sublime Porte,[205] the French treaty of 1535 set the precedent for a series of similar bilateral treaties concluded between European Powers and the Ottoman Empire. The 1535 treaty was indeed renewed and expanded in October 1569, July 1581, February 1597, May 1604, June 1673 and in perpetuity[206] on May 28, 1740 and finally terminated on August 6, 1924.[207]

The Capitulations of 1740 also confirmed the "supreme authority"[208] of the Emperors of France among other Christian leaders and the right to precedence at the Ottoman Court to the Ambassador of France, "according to ancient practice"[209] established in the capitulations of July 1581. This particular privilege played a dominant part in French policy in the area. Article 1 of the Capitulations of 1740 regarding the freedom to visit Jerusalem, prohibited any interference with the "members of religious orders who are in the Church of the Holy Sepulchre, called *Camamat*."[210] Article 28 incorporated basic principles relating to religious freedom, including the protection of "the bishops and religious persons under the jurisdiction of the Emperor of France".[211] Furthermore, it was stated that these persons should not be prevented "from the exercise of their religious rites according to their usage" in their places of worship, and grants them their right to visit and access such places, provided they do not exceed "the limits of their profession."[212]

The same Capitulations of 1740 also established the legal grounds for the rights of missionaries from other countries. One example was the United States "in their stipulations as to the rights and privileges of the members of religious bodies." Their status was "the same as that of the French missionaries and 'religieux,'" even "in the matter of receiving goods free of duty through the custom-house."[213]

However, the United States' claims on their own missionaries were not solely based on the French Capitulations since these claims were "maintained far more effectively under the treaties of Paris and Berlin,[214] under the Turkish decrees which preceded these treaties, and under the settled customs of the Porte."[215] The protection of interests such as the privileges of religious schools is "not merely a contemporaneous construction of the Turkish capitulations, treaties, and edicts, but a construction so continuous that it has the force of settled law."[216]

Moreover, the Capitulations of 1604 had already determined for the first time, that "the subjects of the Emperor of France and those of the Princes who are his friends or allies may visit under his [the Sultan's] protection freely the Holy Places of Jerusalem without any hindrance being put in their way."[217] The treaty had also introduced the principle "that the monks who live in Jerusalem and serve in the Church of the Holy Sepulchre of our Lord Jesus Christ, may stay there, come and go securely without any trouble or disturbance."[218] These provisions, in particular, represented the first instance where the expression "Holy Places" was mentioned in a treaty.[219]

Over the following centuries, various European powers competed with one another to establish their exclusive protectorate over Christian residents in the

Ottoman Empire. A few examples are: Article 11 of the Treaty of Peace of Belgrade between the Ottoman Empire and Russia, of September 7–18, 1739, which established a similar right of protection to all Orthodox Christians in the Empire, and Articles 6, 7 and 14 of the Treaty of Peace of Küçük Kaynarca on July 10–21, 1774 between the same countries.[220]

The provisions of some of the treaties concluded by these Western powers played a major role in determining the distinction between the protection of the right to visit or see the Holy Places and the right to worship therein. For example the treaty of 1612 concluded between the Netherlands and Turkey, only included the right to see described in the 1680 treaty as "*besichtigen*", or sightseeing.[221]

One of the sixty-four articles of this treaty regarding religion entitled the Dutch subjects and their servants to visit Jerusalem:

> Neither the monks in the Church of the Holy Sepulchre nor anyone else is to hinder them and to say: "You are Lutherans, we do not want to let you see the places!" But they must show them the places which is customary to see without any opposition or excuse.[222]

The Capitulations of 1740 made the French case particularly noteworthy since "France received the right to extend individual or group protection to all Latin-rite Catholics throughout the empire, regardless of nationality,"[223] which, then, broadened by custom to the Eastern-rite Catholics.[224]

Moreover, "in the absence of diplomatic relations between the Holy See and the Ottoman Empire, France took upon itself the representation of the Holy See before the Sublime Porte."[225] At the Congress of Berlin in 1878, France, contending against England, ultimately succeeded in being granted its rights with the Berlin Treaty.[226] Eventually, the Holy See formally recognized France's rights, and "in 1888 instructed all priests in the Levant to seek France's protection when needed."[227]

This shows how the Capitulations' regime played a unusual role in the competition between Western exclusive national interests in protecting Christian clergy in the Ottoman Empire and the Holy Places in particular. It must be emphasized that this regime was linked to a legal arrangement mainly based on personal jurisdiction enforced by consular courts.

All of the above treaties and provisions clearly show the complexity and contradictions of the regime in relation to the conflicting models of collective identity, state/territorial or global/trans-territorial, which became even more manifest on the occasion of the 1878 Berlin Treaty analyzed below.

The bilateral agreements concluded with the various Sultans included provisions dealing with freedom of religion, access and worship at the Holy Places, but while the Capitulations' provisions had given those interests international legal relevance, none of these treaties ever aimed at a complete and systematic regulation of the interests of the different recognized communities in the Holy Places.

This gives good reason for the present research which is aimed at studying the different rulers' administrative practice on the subject, in order to ascertain the existence of non-written norms regulating this complex matter.

2.3 The origin of the Status Quo in the Christian Holy Places under Ottoman Rule

2.3.1 *The Ottoman firmans and the guarantees towards the Christian population of the Empire in the Paris Treaty of 1856*

In 1841, the alliance between Austria, Prussia and Great Britain had defeated the Pasha of Egypt, Mohammed Ali and restored the Ottoman administration in Syria.[228] During the negotiations between the Ottoman Empire on one hand and Austria, Prussia and Great Britain on the other, King Frederick William IV, King of Prussia, submitted a memorandum including the "first suggestions in history for an international agreement on the Holy Places of Jerusalem, Bethlehem and Nazareth."[229]

From a historical perspective, the Prussian King's proposal of an international regime for the Holy Places was possible only after the three European multinational empires had defeated the secular Ali, who was spreading the idea of Arab identity and pride in the area. By extending the Capitulations' principle of personal jurisdiction, the Prussian proposal aimed at establishing the "personal exterritoriality" of the Christian population living there rather than a "territorial internationalisation" of the towns in question, consequently making the Christian residents no longer subjects of the Sultan while retaining their right of domicile against the payment of an annual tax. The Prussian proposal envisioned the formation of three independent communities — Catholic, Greek and Protestant — each following the personal jurisdiction criterion under a *Resident* who would lead his own community. Austria and France would appoint the Resident of the Catholics, while Russia would appoint the Greek leader, while the Protestant one would be appointed by Great Britain and Prussia.

"The ownership of the Holy Places in Jerusalem, Bethlehem and Nazareth — not the towns themselves — was to be transferred to the 'five Great Christian Powers, Austria, Russia, France, Great Britain and Prussia,' who would make special arrangements with those who were in their actual possession."[230] However, this proposal was not accepted because "Russia did not wish to see the Holy Places under a joint protection of the European Powers."[231] The Ottoman government promulgated a set of *firmans*, imperial decrees[232], in an attempt to impose a temporary truce to the Christian communities' repeated disputes and conflicting claims to respective rights and interests over several major venerated sites.[233] Nonetheless, these *firmans*, often times changed the complex web of substantial rights and privileges in the Holy Places in rather arbitrary ways which depended upon the temporary balance of powers between the recognized communities and their European protectors.[234]

Only as late as February 1852 did Sultan Habdul Mejid decide to freeze the situation which existed since 1757, by transmitting an important *firman* to the Vizier Hafiz Ahmed Pasha, governor of Jerusalem. According to Bovis, the 1852 *firman*, compared to the Status Quo established since 1757, embodied a few minor concessions to the Latins.[235] Zander asserts that this *firman* "was to become the last *firman* on the issue of the Christian Holy Places."[236] The Sultan's decree of 1852, which was the result of a careful examination conducted by a committee of lawyers appointed by the Porte, was meant "to serve constantly and forever as a permanent rule":[237]

> The disputes which from time to time arise between the Greek and Latin nations [Millets], respecting certain Holy Places which exist both within and without the City of Jerusalem, have now been again revived.

A Commission has in consequence been formed, composed of certain Muchirs and distinguished men of the law, and of other persons, to examine this question thoroughly; and this is the result of the research and of the investigations of that Commission, and of those of the Cabinet Councils held after the Commission.

The places in dispute between the two rites are — the great cupola of the Church of the Holy Sepulchre; the little cupola, which is above the spot called the Tomb of Jesus, on whom may the blessing of God rest, and which is in the church before-mentioned; the Hadjir el Moughtesil; Golgotha, which is also within the enclosure of the Church of the Holy Sepulchre; the Arches of the Holy Mary; the Great Church which is in the village of Bethlehem; as well as the Grotto, which is the true spot where Jesus — may the blessing of God be upon him — was born, and which is situated below that church; and the tomb of the blessed Mary, whom may God bless.[238]

Having defined the disputed places and investigated the conflicting claims, the *firman* determined "that all these places must be left in their present state."[239] Other similar expressions confirming the current situation appear throughout the document:

(. . .) That arrangement shall still continue. But as it does not follow from this that it is permitted to alter the existing state of things in that church (. . .) or in short, to make any new arrangement calculated to incommode other sects (. . .)." No change shall be made in the present state (. . .). As, according to ancient and modern documents, (. . .) they shall remain as at present. (. . .) It has been declared just to uphold and to confirm (. . .) the permission which they possess *ab antiquo* of exercising their worship in a spot where various nations [Millets] exercise theirs, but upon condition that they shall make no alteration either in the administration or in the present condition of that monument. As this decision confirms and consolidates the rights which have been granted (. . .) by my august ancestors, and confirmed by *firmans* invested with Hatti-Scherifs issued from my Imperial throne, it has accordingly obtained my sovereign assent, as I have much at heart to maintain the above-mentioned rights. None of the parties shall allow themselves to contravene this decision. (. . .) On condition that they make no alteration in the present condition.

The 1852 *firman* represented a confirmation and clarification of the shared rights of the various communities in the Holy Places, demarcating which areas were under whose control and maintaining the time schedules to officiate in areas shared with more than one community.[240]

Four years later, the Treaty of Paris signed on March 30, 1856, in marking the end of the Crimean War, made no specific mention of the Holy Places, although Article 9 confirmed the commitments undertaken on February 18, 1856 through various *firmans* of the same Sultan on various aspects of freedom of religion and worship:

Art. IX. His Imperial Majesty the Sultan, having, in his constant solicitude for the welfare of his subjects, issued a *firman* which, while ameliorating their condition without distinction of religion or of race, records his generous intentions towards the Christian population of his Empire, and wishing to give a further proof of his sentiments in that respect, has resolved to communicate to the Contracting Parties the said *firman*, emanating spontaneously from his sovereign will.

The Contracting Parties recognize the high value of this communication. It is clearly understood that it cannot, in any case, give to the said Powers the right to interfere, either collectively or separately, in the relations of His Majesty the Sultan with his subjects, nor in the internal administration of his Empire.[241]

A general interpretation of the quoted articles would create the notion that the 1856 *firman*, according the principle of equality and "without distinction of religion or of race," only briefly mentioned the Sultan's "generous intentions towards the Christian population of his Empire". However, in actual fact, the *firman* referred to "all the Christian communities or other non-Muslim persuasions, established in [the] Empire". For example, in paragraph 6 of the *firman*, the Sultan stated that:

> All the privileges and spiritual immunities granted by my ancestors *ab antiquo*, and at subsequent dates to all the Christian communities or other non-Muslim persuasions [rites], established in my Empire, under my protection, shall be confirmed and maintained.

Paragraphs 11, 12 and 13 of the 1856 *firman* made particular reference to "buildings set apart for religious worship" without expressly mentioning the Holy Places regulated by the *Status Quo*, where different communities shared rituals in the very same shrines:

> In the towns, small boroughs, and villages where the whole population is of the same religion, no obstacle shall be offered to the repair, according to their original plan, of buildings set apart for religious worship, for schools, for hospitals, and for cemeteries.
>
> The plans of these different buildings, in case of their new erection, must, after having been approved by the patriarchs or heads of communities, be submitted to my Sublime Porte, which will approve them by my imperial order, or make known its observations upon them within a certain time. Each sect, in localities where there are no other religious denominations, shall be free from every species of restraint as regards the public exercise of its religion.
>
> In the towns, small boroughs, and villages where different sects are mingled together, each community inhabiting a distinct quarter shall, by conforming to the above-mentioned ordinances, have equal power to repair and improve its churches, its hospitals, its schools, and its cemeteries. When there is question of their erection of new buildings, the necessary authority must be asked for, through the medium of the patriarchs and heads of communities, from my Sublime Porte, which will pronounce a sovereign decision according that authority, except in the case of administrative obstacles.[242]

In this respect, a possible interpretation of this last paragraph is that the "question" should include disputes between "different sects" over the very same "buildings set apart for religious worship." Such interpretation would imply a formal transfer from ordinary jurisdiction to central political authority to settle such disputes. Moreover, the *firman*, dealt extensively with the subject of freedom of religion Paragraphs 14 and 15, for example, clearly state:

> The intervention of the administrative authority in all measures of this nature [public exercise of religion, mentioned in the paragraphs quoted above] will be entirely gratuitous. My Sublime Porte will take energetic measures to insure to each sect, whatever be the number of its adherents, entire freedom in the exercise of its religion. Every distinction or designation pending to make any class whatever of the subjects of my empire inferior to another class, on account of their religion, language, or race, shall be forever effaced from administrative protocol. The laws shall be put in force against the use of any injurious or offensive term, either among private individuals or on the part of the authorities.
>
> As all forms of religion are and shall be freely professed in my dominions, no subject of my

empire shall be hindered in the exercise of the religion that he professes, nor shall he be in any way annoyed on this account. No one shall be compelled to change their religion.

2.3.2 The Berlin Treaty's new attitude of protecting all Christendom

In 1878, Prussian Chancellor Bismarck proposed that all signatories of the 1856 Treaty of Paris assemble to review its terms in the Congress of Berlin, from June 13 to July 13 of the same year. The main outcome[243] of the Berlin Treaty that was born out of this Congress, is the explicit mention of the Status Quo: "for the first time in history an agreement about the Christian Holy Places was reached among the major European Powers and the Ottoman Empire."[244]

Article LXII of the Berlin Treaty is the only provision dealing with the Holy Places, while Article LXIII states that the Treaty of Paris of 30 March 1856, dealing with similar subjects, is "maintained in all such of [its] provisions as are not abrogated or modified by the preceding stipulations":[245]

> LXII. The Sublime Porte having expressed the intention to maintain the principle of religious liberty, and give it the widest scope, the Contracting Parties take note of this spontaneous declaration.
>
> In no part of the Ottoman Empire shall difference of religion be alleged against any person as a ground for exclusion or incapacity as regards the discharge of civil and political rights, admission to the public employments, functions and honors, or the exercise of the various professions and industries.
>
> All persons shall be admitted, without distinction of religion, to give evidence before the tribunals.
>
> The freedom and outward exercise of all forms of worship are assured to all, and no hindrance shall be offered either to the hierarchical organization of the various communions or to their relations with their spiritual chiefs.
>
> Ecclesiastics, pilgrims, and monks of all nationalities traveling in Turkey in Europe, or in Turkey in Asia, shall enjoy the same rights, advantages, and privileges.
>
> The right of official protection by the Diplomatic and Consular Agents of the Powers in Turkey is recognized both as regards the above-mentioned persons and their religious, charitable, and other establishments in the Holy Places and elsewhere.
>
> The rights possessed by France are expressly reserved, and it is well understood that no alterations can be made in the *status quo* of the Holy Places.[246]

Zander maintains that with this provision "Turkish jurisdiction over the Christian Sanctuaries was no longer free but by international agreement suspended;" from this assumption he further draws the conclusion that "no investigation into substantive rights and claims concerning the Christian Holy Places was in future to take place"[247] Zander adds that the pledge embodied in the Treaty of Berlin to maintain the Status Quo "excluded any investigation as to whether the *status quo* was legally justified."[248]

However, this conclusion does not necessarily rule out a possible settlement of disputes on the actual contents of the Status Quo or, indirectly, of any dispute arising out of new and unpredictable changes in the Holy Places.[249]

Article LXII of the Berlin Treaty represents the first instance where "the term '*status quo*' appeared in an international convention."[250] This expression is not an

Ottoman creation, nor is it embodied in Ottoman decrees or documents. In fact, the expression is the result of European diplomatic influence, which adopted the expression to define an arrangement between the various powers towards the Ottoman Sultans and was used to refer to the complex arrangements in the relationship between the recognized local communities which were not consulted during the drafting of the Berlin Treaty.

It was the 1852 *firman* (the *Status Quo de jure*), as well as the immemorial practice of rituals in the Holy Places (the *Status Quo de facto*), that defined the specific rights and duties regulated by these arrangements.

According to the confidential Memorandum written on the subject during the British Mandatory period, the expression *Status Quo* also applies to the Ottoman *firmans*, regardless of whether the expression had ever been mentioned in those documents.[251] In fact, since the Ottoman period the interested Christian religious communities were unable to find a proper and equitable solution based on mutual consent or on an ordinary judicial settlement.

As a result, the expression Status Quo in the Holy Places has since defined this sort of truce which has frozen the situation until this very day,[252] by embodying a legal regime enacted to divide space and time for the use and possession of the Holy Places between Christian communities.

Properly understood, Article LXII of the Berlin Treaty contains an internal ambivalence in any attempt to codify the subject of the Status Quo in the Holy Places on the part of international bodies or other authorities influenced by Western approach.[253]

This provision grants that "the principle of religious liberty (. . .) should be maintained, that "the freedom and outward exercise of all forms of worship are assured to all" and that "Ecclesiastics, pilgrims, and monks of all nationalities" (. . .) "shall enjoy the same rights, advantages, and privileges," therefore affirming the principle on religious freedom without any form of discrimination.

Surprisingly, Article LXII also states that "the right of official protection by the Diplomatic and Consular Agents of the Powers in Turkey is recognized (. . .) in the Holy Places and elsewhere," while "the rights possessed by France are expressly reserved." Moreover, it determines that "no alterations can be made in the *status quo* of the Holy Places," in so doing reaffirming a regime which is discriminatory by definition, since it gives rights of worship and possession in the Holy Places only to the recognized religious communities, regardless of any criterion of equality.

In other words, it was precisely the Status Quo regime that recognized an element of discrimination between the various religious communities by entitling only some of them to maintain the traditional privileges and interests in the exercise of access and worship to the Holy Places. The aforementioned arrangements aimed at merely describing the situation in the land, were neither perfectly balanced nor impartial in the distribution of rights among the communities.

Furthermore, "the right of official protection" of the various European Powers, especially "the rights possessed by France," established a legal situation that proved to be discriminatory. Not all the recognized communities had a "Power" to refer to, and not all the "Powers" had the same ability or will to "protect" their respective communities.

During the Berlin Congress, the issue of "possessions, religious, charitable and other establishments of Russian ecclesiastics in the Holy Places,"[254] had inflamed the negotiations between the conflicting national claims raised by French and Russian delegates concerning their respective exclusive protectorates. Article XXII of the Preliminary Treaty of San Stefano of March 3, 1878 imposed by Russia after its victorious campaign of 1877/1878 against Turkey, had already referred to this issue.

At the Berlin Congress, the British delegation represented by Lord Salisbury, and strongly supported by Bismarck, tried to influence the text of Article LXII of the Berlin Treaty with a new attitude of substituting "all Christendom for a single nationality."[255] According to Zander, as a result, the Berlin Congress witnessed a clear trend towards the abolition of the aforesaid privileges over individual recognized Christian communities, to be replaced by "the rights of Christendom as a whole."[256]

The British representative, "as a Protestant and always preoccupied with humanitarian considerations, "denied any interest in exclusive religious protectorate, which, on the contrary, should be permanently abolished". In such a way he preceded any French-Russian competition over the Roman-Catholics and Orthodox privileges in the Holy Places in deliberations by the Congress.

According to the British position, total equality should be given "to all Christian denominations in the Holy Land and the protection of the different nationalities be left to their respective diplomatic representations and Consulates."

The British position certainly embarrassed France and directly challenged its claims to exclusive protection, with its inherent diplomatic, ceremonial, and liturgical privileges of all Latins regardless of their nationality. In fact, this position threatened France's centuries old source of prestige and political power in the East.[257]

It is interesting to see the contradictory ways in which the British and French representatives reported to their governments on the final text of the Berlin's agreement, reached after lengthy and difficult negotiations.

Lord Salisbury stressed "the equality of rights for all denominations which had been established,"[258] thereby entirely abandoning "the special protection" that "ecclesiastics of the Russian religion and for Russian monasteries on Mount Athos," included in the Preliminary Treaty of Peace of San Stefano. He concluded that "large provisions" of the new treaty secured "religious liberty to all persons, nations or foreigners, living within the Ottoman dominions, but no special privileges are created for the members of any single nation;"

French Foreign Minister Waddington claimed that France's long established exclusive privileges of national jurisdiction and "patronage religieux" had been successfully preserved. He added that for the first time all great powers of Europe had formally agreed to confirm such privileges in a treaty, at a time when they were so dangerously disputed.

This ambiguous agreement reached by the seven signatories of the treaty, namely, Great Britain, France, Germany, Austria-Hungary, Italy, Russia, the *protectors* of the communities involved, and the local authority of Turkey, exclusively concerned the Christian Holy Places.

Two main positions on the Holy Places had again confronted each other: the exclusive, state/territorial approach towards the conflict on one hand and the humanitarian, religious, and global/trans-territorial approach, supported by Britain, on the other. The compromise between the two conflicting Western approaches have produced far-reaching consequences into the present time.

Since the signing of the Berlin Treaty, competition among European Powers has time and again raised high levels of tension, under the pretext of the disputes between Christian communities over the Holy Places. Nevertheless, the compromise of the Status Quo between various national exclusive claims on one hand and the global, humanitarian, all-inclusive approach on the other has been broadly maintained.

Again on a British initiative, the all-inclusive approach, by implicit analogy, extended to non-Christian Holy Places, namely Jewish and Muslim, with the open support of an influential section of the United States establishment. At the end of the Ottoman Empire, a process began which complicated matters even further by adding a local state/territorial dimension. Indeed, the Holy Places became the object of a locally based struggle, with interference of powerful western advisers, between the Zionist and the Arab, later Palestinian, nationalist movements.

2.3.3 The introduction of the state model to the Middle East and the origin of Arab nationalism

European culture gradually influenced the Ottoman Empire in various ways. The purpose of this work is neither to offer a complete analysis of the various "definitions, arguments and hypothesis on the inception of the concept of nation and nationalism"[259] in Western history and thought, nor to take sides on whether such a notion is "constructed, as opposed to being a given" old primordial phenomenon, providing "communities with the social cohesion needed for survival."[260]

Scholars and politicians who support the global/trans-territorial model of identity defile national-state identity as a mere constructed notion, whereas supporters of the opposite approach take for granted the idea of national-state identity as an element of modern geopolitics in states' authority,[261] a notion that also in the Middle East has gained popularity since the nineteenth century.

Napoleon was the first one to openly encourage the development of Arab nationalism, or Arabism, using national-oriented arguments. On July 1, 1789, he started his stunning conquest of Egypt and Palestine in Alexandria to knock "a mortal blow at England."[262] The French General did not claim, as the Crusaders did, that his expedition aimed at recovering the Holy Places for the Christians.

On the contrary, when he reached Palestine on March 1, 1799, he declared: "Jerusalem does not lie on my line of march."[263] His instructions were clear: "The Roman Legions protected all religions. You will find here customs different from those of Europe; you must get used to them."[264] In religion Napoleon saw "the mystery of the social order".[265] This explains why he wanted to convince the ruled people that he was sharing, or at least respecting, their religion:

> It was by making myself a Catholic that I won the war in the Vendé, by making myself a Moslem that I established myself in Egypt (. . .) If I were to govern a nation of Jews I would rebuild the Temple of Salomon.[266]

In their fight against Napoleon, the Ottomans appointed Mohammed Ali as the Viceroy of Egypt. However, in 1831 he rebelled and with his son Ibrahim Pasha conquered Syria, which included modern Palestine, until the intervention in 1841 of European multinational empires.[267] His rule in the area introduced secular legislation, restricting the power of Sharia bureaucracy (the traditional religious Muslim legal system), replaced by public officers dependent on the salaries and rules of the secular central authority. He also initiated a drastic program of national education in Arabic language.

Additionally, Ali "sent students on scholarships to Europe in order to acquaint Arab youth with nationalist ideas and so as to thereafter challenge the traditional conception of Ottoman-Arab Muslim fraternity."[268] The contact of Arab societies with Western cultures, while highlighting the desire "to achieve social and economic justice, as well as to acquire the techniques of modern science and its application,"[269] contributed to the revival of "Arab heritage."[270]

Significantly the first document related to the dispute examined by the "Wailing Wall Commission" mentioned in the December 1930 Report was a decree issued in 1840[271] by Ibrahim Pasha concerning the Wailing Wall. In the 1830s and 1840s, mostly in Lebanon, American and French missionaries opened schools with instructions in Arabic and offered printing presses for the publishing of Arabic books.

Until 1869, no Ottoman law regulated the establishment of foreign schools, "and the carrying of such schools was regarded as one of the privileges belonging to the inmates of religious establishments."[272] Not only did the Ottoman authorities refrain from interfering for a long time "with the establishment of these schools or their unrestricted continuance to the present time, but it has repeatedly intervened to protect them against unlawful aggression on the part of ill-disposed persons."[273]

Articles 1, 32–36 and 82 of the French Capitulations of 1740 granted immunity, protection and special privileges to "religious organizations established in the Turkish Empire."[274] The Ottoman attitude "has always shown that the privileges anciently accorded to" the foreign religious bodies established within its boundaries "cover their right to conduct school without interference".[275]

By the eve of World War I, the influence of foreign religious bodies became increasingly political and spread to Syria, Mesopotamia (now Iraq) and Egypt. Many new nationalistic Arab thinkers sprouted from similar Western Christian educational institutions such as the University of St. Joseph, founded by the Jesuits in 1875.

The Syrian Protestant College in Beirut, later known as the American University of Beirut, was the first Christian educational institution to spread the use of Arabic presses and to manufacture a new Arabic type, *American Arabic*. This College created its own Arabic textbooks and supplied other state schools with Arabic texts.[276]

Butros al-Bustani, a student of the American missionary schools, compiled the first Arabic dictionary in over three centuries. He also translated the Bible into Arabic and started working on an encyclopedia. He expressed his devotion to Arab cultural revival and political unity through his newspaper *al-Jinan*, which "tried to bring the reader a sense of devotion to the homeland."[277]

Towards the end of the nineteenth century, the Ottoman authorities intensified their opposition to the publication and use on their territory of what they considered "subversive books pointed against the religion of the state or against public order."[278] This policy did not prevent in the decade before 1914, particularly after the Young Turks *coup d'état* of 1908, the foundation of a number of Arab nationalist societies, a few of them secret, with avowed political objectives.

These societies demanded no independence but political autonomy for the predominantly Arab districts and Arab representation in the Imperial government in Istanbul, and full equality with the Ottoman Turks. This emphasis is made manifest in the resolution adopted by an Arab-Syrian Congress held in Paris in June 18–24, 1913, which was attended by 24 official delegates who came from Lebanon and

Syria,[279] with the exception of three from the United States and two from Mesopotamia.

World War I brought about the end of the Ottoman Empire. In the Turkish core region of the Empire, as a result of the general development towards secular nationalism "the Kemalist revolution completely abolished both religious law and religious jurisdiction."[280] In the rest of the Empire, a parallel evolution towards the European secular state model[281] followed a slower path which came to completion only after the World War II.[282]

A general process of codification along the lines of the Napoleonic code took place in the area formerly under the Ottoman Empire. With the secularization of the law, there was a parallel reduction in the jurisdiction of the religious in favor of the civil courts."[283] Paradoxically, today, only Israel continues to apply most of the described principles of personal law to the various recognized communities, inherited from the Ottoman Empire through the British Mandate in Palestine, in this way representing quite a special case in the area.

Broadly speaking, the Western European legal concept of *territorial sovereignty*, which became a basic feature of nineteenth century international law, inevitably spread to the Middle East. The Ottoman Empire had already "started after the end of the Crimean War in 1856 to abandon the communal aspects of the Islamic system of international law and to adopt the modern rules prevailing among the European concert of nations to which the Sublime Porte became a fully-integrated party during the Berlin Congress of 1875."[284]

A clear example of Western influence can be found in Yemen's handling of its controversy with Eritrea before the Permanent Court of Arbitration, which had "introduced the doctrine of *uti possidetis*, according to which on the dismemberment of the Ottoman Empire (. . .) there is a presumption, both legal and political in character, that the boundaries of the independent states which replace it will correspond to the boundaries of its former administrative units."[285]

However, in a memorandum quoted in the same section of the arbitration, "sovereignty" — in the sense of *title* — "which the Ottoman Empire possessed over all these possessions" was "carefully distinguished" from "a right of jurisdiction over the African side, which had been conferred on the Khedive."[286]

Moreover, the Arbitral Court raised the question "whether this doctrine of *uti possidetis* (. . .) could properly be applied to interpret a juridical question arising in the Middle East shortly after the close of the First World War."[287] In other words, the Tribunal was hesitant to apply European notion of acquisition of territorial sovereignty in an area which had once been part of the Ottoman Empire where concepts of Islamic law had prevailed.

According to the Arbrital Court, the notion of territory in these areas, although very different from the one recognized in contemporary international law, was much in harmony with Middle Eastern socio-economic and cultural patterns. The "historic rights" which developed "through a process of historical consolidation as a sort of '*servitude internationale*'" are only another example of Ottoman practice "falling short of territorial sovereignty," and provide "a sufficient legal basis for maintaining certain aspects of a *res communis* that had existed for centuries."[288] Moreover, the Arbitral Court believed that only an appreciation of regional legal traditions would help "allow the re-establishment and the development of a trustful and lasting cooperation between the two countries."[289]

This idea appears again in the second phase of the award of 1998, where "The sovereignty that the Tribunal has awarded to Yemen over" the contested areas should respect, embrace and "be subject to the Islamic legal concepts of the region."[290] In this context, the Tribunal quoted the *Encyclopaedia of International Law*, in which it is written, "Islam is not merely a religion but also a political community — *umma* — endowed with a system of law designed both to protect the collective interest of its subjects and to regulate their relations with the outside world."[291]

In summary, supporters of the state national model have indeed tried to extend the political, legal and social features of the original Western paradigm to the Middle East, not just as a mere constructed notion, but as a solid reality. Napoleon, first in Egypt then in the rest of the Near East, promoted secular Arab nationalism, or Arabism. In his victorious military march he even bypassed Jerusalem, which later British rulers would consider as the symbol of global religious collective identity and the birth place of the three monotheistic faiths.

Not surprisingly Mohammed Ali in following the example set forth by Napoleon, whom he had once been appointed to fight, conquered Syria (then including modern Palestine), which remained under his control until the intervention by the European multinational empires in 1841. During his rule, Mohammed Ali and his son Ibrahim Pasha set up a secular centralized state system similar to its European continental model. The development of modern science techniques and their application brought about a revival of Arab national pride, particularly in the cultural and linguistic field.

3 | The Status Quo in the Holy Places during the British Mandate

3.1 The concept of the Holy Places' inviolability for all religions

3.1.1 Theodor Herzl's and Herbert Samuel's plans for a Jewish role in Palestine

Towards the end of the nineteenth century, simultaneous with the rise of Arab nationalism, Jews of various cultural, ethnic, ideological and spiritual affiliations escaped persecution in their home countries and migrated to Palestine in small numbers that increased over time to enlarge the *yishuv*, the local Jewish community. They found that most members of the old *yishuv* accepted the *Millet* system of the Ottoman Empire to some extent as a tolerant arrangement.

One example is the *firman* "issued by Sultan Abdul Hamid in the year 1889, which decreed that "there shall be no interference with the Jews' places of devotional visits and of pilgrimage that are situated in the localities which are dependent on the Chief Rabbinate, nor with the practice of their ritual."[292] This document was significant for the Jewish community which used it as a "Jewish Exhibit" in the Report of the Wailing Wall Commission appointed by Great Britain on December 1930.[293]

The late nineteenth-century new immigrants proved to be radically different from the original Jewish community in their determination to create an autonomous region in Palestine. The cultural and spiritual movement called *Hibbat Ziyyon*, "the Love of Zion," then newly founded by Leo Pinsker, promoted emigration from Russia to establish Jewish settlements in Palestine.[294] These Jewish immigrants assumed that in Palestine they would be free from the religious and racial persecution they had experienced in Russia, Poland and Romania.

A representation of Jewish immigrants committees in Palestine sought "assistance and support"[295] also from the United States' delegation in Constantinople on behalf of "oppressed coreligionists who are suffering under legal disabilities." "Owing to the daily recurrence of prosecution and disasters of the most fearful description," their Jewish "brethren," "living in a state of panic-stricken suspense," expected to find "peace and protection" in the Ottoman Empire "where they would thankfully become loyal and patriotic subjects of His Magnanimous Majesty the Sultan."[296]

This is the initial historical context in which the progressive development of both Arab and Jewish national movements in Palestine took place. At the same time, various

Western powers, particularly Anglo-Saxon, began proposing solutions to separate the Holy Places, mostly the ones located in Jerusalem, from the rest of the surrounding area and to give them a special legal regime. As the collapse of the Ottoman rule in the area unfolded, British officials formally raised a new proposal for the first time: the idea of internationalizing all of the Holy Places, without giving preference to any of the interested communities.

In his famous book *Der Judenstaat*, published in 1895, Theodore Herzl, the pioneer of political Zionism, presented the idea of "safeguarding" the Holy Places (only the Christian ones) from the jurisdiction of the local authorities in Palestine:

> The sanctuaries of Christendom would be safeguarded by assigning to them an extra-territorial status such as is well known to the law of nations. We should form a guard of honor about these sanctuaries, answering for the fulfillment of this duty with our existence. This guard of honor would be the great symbol of the solution of the Jewish Question after eighteen centuries of Jewish suffering.[297]

Minerbi's interpretation of Herzl's words is an arrangement that would exclude certain buildings and sites from civil ordinary jurisdiction. He believes that Herzl may have been influenced by the special extraterritorial status enjoyed by Great Britain in China following the treaties of 1842 to 1844. Minerbi quoted from Sir Francis Piggott's book on *Exterritoriality* of 1907:

> Exterritoriality is in essence the extension of jurisdiction beyond the borders of the state. It embodies certain rights, principles and immunities which are enjoyed by the citizens, subjects or protégés of the state within the boundaries of another, and which exempt them from local territorial jurisdiction and place them under the laws and judicial administration of their own state. Extraterritoriality is often confused with exterritoriality, but the latter refers only to the immunities accorded a diplomatic envoy and his suite in accordance with international law, while the former may be said to involve the establishment of an international servitude by elevating the nationality principle of jurisdiction over the territorial principle.[298]

In 1896, Herzl had learnt from the Austrian journalist Philip Michael de Newlinsky that the Ottoman Sultan "would have never given up Jerusalem" since the Sultan had reportedly stated, "the Mosque of Omar must remain forever in the hands of Islam."[299] Herzl's reply was that it was possible to "go around that difficulty," again proposing his plan for the Holy Places:

> We shall extraterritorialize Jerusalem, so that it will belong to nobody and yet everybody: and with it the Holy Places become the joint possession of all believers — a great condominium of culture and morality.[300]

In February 1899, the Zionist leader again stressed to the Pope's nuncio in Vienna, Monsignor Egidio Taliani, "that no takeover of the control of the Holy Places was ever intended. Jerusalem and Bethlehem would be given extraterritorial status, and the capital of the Jewish nation would be located elsewhere."[301] In August 1899, in his opening address to the Second Zionist Congress, Herzl pointed out the relationship between the Jewish Question and world politics and referred to the German Kaiser, who was planning his visit to the Holy Places, as "the most modern monarch of the inhabited earth."[302] He stressed that the "hidden anxiety, at times to the point of pure hatred," echoed in the "public opinion of all countries" because the "land cannot be, and indeed never shall be, the possession of one great Power." Herzl concluded that "(. . .) the return of the Jews to Palestine would solve this question for the world and for the Turks."[303] On September 10, 1899 Herzl sent a letter to Felice Ravenna, the chairman of the Zionist Federation in Italy, to whom he had previously asked to arrange for him audience with the Pope.

In his letter, Herzl reiterated his idea of "extraterritorial status" for the Holy Places in Palestine: "*res sacra extra commercium du droit des gens.*"[304] He further confirmed this formula of neutrality and respect for the Holy Places several times, most importantly on January 23, 1903 during his meeting at the Vatican with Pope Pius X, who expressed his concern about possible Zionist plans to rebuild the destroyed Temple in Jerusalem and "to renew the sacrificial services in the ancient way."[305]

A few years later, Sir Herbert Louis Samuel drafted a new plan. Samuel had taken part in various British governments, namely from 1909 to 1916 and again in 1931, serving also as the first High Commissioner in Palestine from 1920 to 1925. In his *Memoirs* he described himself as "the first member of the Jewish community ever to sit in a British Cabinet" given that, as he recalled, the father of former Prime Minister Disraeli withdrew his child from the community.

Herzl's idea to encourage Jewish settlement in the area was partly revised by Samuel's plan to neutralize the whole of Palestine, since the planned state "could not be large enough to defend itself."[306] His intention was to forestall any permanent exclusive national claims on the area. Samuel warned that "if Palestine, as was likely, were to be separated from Turkey, for it to fall under the control of any of the great Continental Powers would be a danger." On the contrary, "it was important that the new state should be founded under the auspices of the most progressive of the countries in which the Jews found themselves," such as Great Britain and the United States.

Moreover, "the free access of Christian pilgrims should be guaranteed." Samuel trusted that "the Jewish brain" was "rather a remarkable thing" and that "under national auspices, the state might become a fountain of enlightenment and a source of a great literature and art and development of science." However, he believed that the millions of Jews living in various countries of the world ought to have remained, for the most part "scattered since Palestine was too small to contain them."

On February 5, 1915, Foreign Secretary Sir Edward Grey positively replied to Samuel's plan and advanced a suggestion to neutralize Palestine "under international guarantee, and to place the control of the Holy Places in the hands of a Commission in which the European Powers, and the Pope, and perhaps the United States, would be represented."

Samuel recognized that "the more the situation was explored, the clearer it became that the idea of a Jewish State was impracticable." At that time, this conclusion changed his opinion "in favour of something in the nature of a British Protectorate." One month later, on March 16, 1915, the Military Secretary of the India Office Sir Edmund Barrow wrote that after the end of the war Palestine should be "neutralized and administered as an autonomous province by an international commission or corporation under the aegis of the Entente."[307]

A special committee appointed in April 1915, was chaired by the Assistant Undersecretary of State at the Foreign Office and former Minister in the British Embassy in Vienna Sir Maurice de Bunsen. Another member of the Committee, who would play an important role in the negotiations on behalf of the British Government was Sir Mark Sykes. In June 1915, De Bunsen presented a recommendation to the British cabinet where he stressed that "the sacred places of Palestine [were] a separate question"; the whole Palestinian region "must be recognized as a country whose destiny must be the subject of special negotiations."[308]

The subsequent sections of this chapter examine the relationship between the plans for a Jewish "national home" in the area and the idea of a separate status for Jerusalem's Holy Places; the way in which Samuel and other British leaders meant to handle these two ideas so as to avoid the danger of Palestine falling under the control of any of the great Continental Powers, namely, France and Germany, once separated from Turkey; and the consistent push for the planned Jewish polity and the guaranteed free access to the Holy Places to be under Anglo-Saxon auspices. Additionally, the development throughout the British Mandate's period and subsequent partial failure of such policy with the ousting of British rulers and the foundation of Israel in 1948 on a state-national basis, will be illustrated.

3.1.2 The Sykes–Picot Agreement and the Husayn–McMahon correspondence

During World War I, the British Government engaged in diplomatic discussions on one hand with its allied powers, Russia and France, and on the other hand with the leader of the Arab rebellion against the Ottoman Empire, Sharif Husayn.

Diplomatic exchanges between Russia, Great Britain, and France over a period of five weeks, from March 4 to April 10, 1915, produced the "Constantinople Agreement". In March 1915, the French Ambassador in Petrograd made known to the Russian Foreign Minister his country's intention "to annex Syria,"[309] which included Palestine. Russian diplomats were quick to remind the French Ambassador of "the presence in Jerusalem" of "an independent governor."[310] Subsequently, the Russian Foreign Minister informed the Russian Ambassador in Paris that his Imperial Government was "prepared largely to satisfy France's desires concerning Syria and Cilicia proper."[311] However, he stressed once again that the question of the possible inclusion of the Holy Places in the area under French control required special attention.

The diplomatic correspondence described above illustrates that the Russian government believed that the area surrounding the Holy Places should be considered separate from the rest of the Ottoman territory, due to the presence of these extraordinary sites. These Russian concerns were exploited by the British Government as a pretext to avoid a situation whereby a single European country, especially France, would gain exclusive control of Palestine.

While the negotiations with France were taking place, Lord Kitchener,[312] a British officer at that time Secretary of State for War in London (formerly British Agent and Consul General in Egypt), entered into a confidential agreement with Sharif of Mecca, Husayn, in which he promised him an Arab state in the very same area still under Ottoman rule, in return for an insurrection against the Sultan.

Over an eight-month period, from July 14, 1915 to March 10, 1916, Sharif Husayn and the first British High Commissioner for Egypt Sir Henry McMahon exchanged ten letters, the so-called Husayn–McMahon correspondence.

In a letter dated October 24, 1915, addressing the promise of an Arab state, the British officer stressed that "without prejudice to our existing treaties with Arab chiefs", the future state should exclude from its borders "the two districts of Mersina and Alexandretta and portions of Syria lying to the west of the districts of Damascus, Homs, Hama and Aleppo" since they "cannot be said to be purely Arab." Sir McMahon stated that "As for those regions lying within those frontiers wherein Great Britain is free to act without detriment to the interests of her ally France," Great Britain was "prepared to recognize and support the independence of the Arabs in all the regions within the limits demanded by the Sharif of Mecca" and clarified that "Great Britain will guarantee the Holy Places against all external aggression and will recognize their inviolability."[313]

In his letter of November 5, 1915, Husayn decided to accept the exclusion of the *vilayets* (Ottoman regions) of Mersina and Adana in the Arab Kingdom "in order to facilitate an agreement and to render a service to Islam." However, he took a firm stand stating that "the two *vilayets* of Aleppo and Beirut and their sea coasts are purely Arab *vilayets*, and there is no difference between a Muslim and a Christian Arab: they are both descendants of one forefather," emphasizing the Muslim commitment to "follow the footsteps of the Commander of the Faithful Omar Ibn Khattab, and other Khalifs succeeding him, who ordained in the laws of the Muslim Faith that Muslims should treat the Christians as they treat themselves."

Sharif Husayn responded to McMahon's comments quoting Omar's declaration: "They will have the same privileges and submit to the same duties as ourselves" and "will thus enjoy their civic rights in as much as it accords with the general interests of the whole nation."[314]

In his reply of December 14, 1915, McMahon noted "with great pleasure and satisfaction" Sharif's "assurances that the Arabs are determined to act in conformity with the precepts laid down by Omar Ibn Khattab and the early Khalifs, which secure the rights and privileges of all religions alike" but "with regard to the *vilayets* of Aleppo and Beyrut", underlined that "the question will require careful consideration"[315] in view of the French ally's interests. In the meantime, negotiations between Great Britain and France continued on the future of the Ottoman Empire, including the area around Jerusalem. On October 21, 1915, British Foreign Minister Sir Edward Grey disclosed the Hussayn-McMahon exchanges to the French Ambassador in London, Paul Cambon. Grey proposed a discussion to Cambon regarding their respective interests in Ottoman Asia.[316]

The details of the negotiations were entrusted to Sir Mark Sykes and Charles François George-Picot, respectively officers in the Foreign Service of Britain and France. In their first meeting on November 23, 1915, Sykes suggested a form of internationalization of the whole Palestine. After Lloyd George became British Prime Minister in December 1916, one of his goals was to obtain the annexation of Palestine or a British trusteeship thereof.

The historian Minerbi explains that a joint control with France seemed to be a real danger to the British because it could leave the door open to Germany. Sykes feared German ambitions in the Middle East, "for if the Germans were to gain control of Palestine, they would be able to exert pressure on the Pope, the Orthodox Church, and the Zionists."[317]

George Picot agreed to the British proposal, but requested that the planned separate enclave under an international regime be limited to an area around Jerusalem and Bethlehem. He was adamant that Syria, including the main part of Palestine, should be considered French.[318] In a joint memorandum of December 1915, Sykes and Picot explained their decision to set up an international regime. They claimed that "the Latin and Orthodox religions require equal consideration in Palestine," while "the members of the Jewish community throughout the world have a conscientious and sentimental interest in the future of the country" and furthermore that, "the mosque of Omar represents, next to Mecca, the most holy and venerable shrine in Islam, and it must be a *sine qua non* that the Mosque of Omar itself should be under the sole control of Muslims."[319]

In February 1916, Sykes and Picot visited French Ambassador Petrograd Maurice Paléologue for the final negotiations which established that Palestine would form "a special autonomous province under international control."[320] The Russian Minister of War solemnly confirmed that "Palestine will be put under the general protectorate of the European Powers."[321]

In a communication to Petrograd, Russian Foreign Minister Sazonov declared that "Russian interests covered all Holy Places and territories where Orthodox institutions existed." Therefore he recommended for all these towns and places, "an international administration, with free access to the harbours of the Mediterranean, since the Russian Government would never recognize exclusive sovereign rights of any Power in the country."[322]

Through an exchange of eleven letters commonly known as the Sykes–Picot Agreement, the tripartite understanding among Britain, France and Russia on the division of the Ottoman Empire, resulted in the French acceptance of internationalizing the whole central Palestine. Accordingly, a letter of May 16, 1916 stated that a specific agreement between Russia, France and Britain will determine "a view to securing the religious interests of the Entente Powers, Palestine, with the Holy Places as separated from Turkish territory and subjected to a special regime."[323]

In a letter sent to his French counterpart Cambon on May 16, 1916, British Foreign Minister Grey referred to the "international administration" to be established, whose formal structure would "be decided upon after consultation with Russia, and subsequently in consultations with the other Allies, and the representatives of the Sharif of Mecca."[324]

France, Great Britain and Russia planned to establish the "international administration" in an area simply colored in brown on the map attached to the agreement[325] which included Jerusalem, Bethlehem, Nazareth, and the shores of Lake Tiberias. The agreement stated, "The brown Zone includes: Palestine without Haifa and Acre."[326]

The main guidelines of the British policy as derived from the diplomatic documentation discussed above can be summarized as follows:

1 The areas in the Eastern Mediterranean coast of the Ottoman Empire, corresponding to Israel, Palestinian Authority[327] and Lebanon needed not be included in the borders of the Arab state-to-be because of the British claim that such areas were not purely Arab. Great Britain's reason for this exclusion had been the need to protect rights and privileges of all religions alike, in addition to previous agreements engaged with France. Consequently, the British claimed that an exclusive homogeneous nationalistic government would harm the interests of religious groups in the areas. Their official goal was to protect this universally recognized interest, in line with the global model of collective identity sponsored in all areas under British rule.
2 The Holy Places of all religions alike were to be were be a value in themselves,

regardless of which single specific religious community they belonged to. Therefore, their inviolability was to be considered a sacred trust.

3 Great Britain unilaterally assumed the responsibility to guarantee the inviolability of the Holy Places against all external aggression in the name and on behalf of the whole world even though, at the time, no one in the world had imposed such a burden on British shoulders.

3.1.3 The Negotiations with the World Zionist Organization and the Balfour Declaration

During the period March–June 1917, a Russian-born journalist and member of the Zionist Executive of the World Zionist Organization, Nahum Sokolow, visited the European continent to seek French and Italian official endorsements of the Zionist program of Jewish colonization in Palestine. French Foreign Minister Jules Cambon, the first one to acknowledge Sokolow's request, wrote in a letter that "it would be a deed of justice and of reparation to assist, by the protection of the Allied Powers, in the renaissance of the Jewish nationality in that Land from which the people of *Israel* were exiled so many centuries ago" and that the implementation of such commitment should occur once "the independence of the Holy Places" was safeguarded. Cambon's letter recalled that the goal of the French intervention in the war was to defend a people wrongfully attacked and "to assure the victory of right over might." The letter concluded by expressing "sympathy for" Mr. Sokolow's "cause, the triumph of which", the letter assured, "is bound up with that of the Allies."[328] Sokolow, a Russian-born professor of chemistry at the University of Manchester, had already traveled to England late in 1914, and succeeded in winning the interest of various members of the British Cabinet.

As a result, in February 1917, Sir Mark Sykes, on behalf of the British government, began discussions with Zionist leaders that culminated with the well-known letter sent by Foreign Minister Arthur James Balfour on November 2, 1917. The letter (ever since dubbed the Balfour Declaration) conveyed through Lord (Baron) Lionel Walter Rothschild the British Government's "sympathy with Jewish Zionist aspirations" to the Zionist Federation and viewed "with favour the establishment in Palestine of a national home for the Jewish people" pledging to work hard so as to facilitate the achievement of this object. Nonetheless, the Declaration stated "that nothing shall be done which may prejudice the civil and religious rights of existing non-Jewish communities in Palestine, or the rights and political status enjoyed by Jews in any other country."[329]

By clearly stressing that "nothing shall be done which may prejudice (. . .) the rights and political status enjoyed by Jews in any other country," the Balfour Declaration left open the question of the extent to which the Zionist "national home" would fully represent the world Jewish community, defined as Jewish "race" in the first version of the same Declaration.[330] This issue directly related to the problem of the potential representation of world Jewry by Zionist institutions.

In fact, Article 4 of the British Mandate approved in 1922 by the League of Nations' Council recognized the Zionist Organization as "the appropriate Jewish agency." The Palestine Zionist Executive, elected by the Jewish Congress, represented the agency in Palestine which was replaced by the Jewish Agency for Palestine in a joint conference of Zionists and non-Zionists held in Zurich in August 1929.[331]

Moreover, on September 21, 1922, the United States Congress adopted a resolution which favored in similar terms "the establishment in Palestine of a national home for the Jewish people."[332] In the Congress resolution, a significant difference is to be noted between the original draft where it was stated that the United States Government merely "pledges its support" to the establishment of the Jewish National Home and the final draft where the Government clearly "favors" such a development.[333] The resolution also agreed with the British explicit condition "that the holy places and religious buildings and sites in Palestine shall be adequately protected"[334] and that no action would be taken which may prejudice the civil and religious rights "of Christian and all other non-Jewish communities in Palestine."

Sir Herbert Samuel, in his Report to the Secretary of State for the Colonies as the first High Commissioner in Palestine, recalled the endorsement of the Balfour Declaration "by unanimous resolutions of both Houses of the Congress of the United Sates,"[335] stressing thereby the American resolution's legal and political importance.

Since "(. . .) outside Palestine, both among Jews and non-Jews, there was much uncertainty as to the real intentions of the British Government's policy,[336] Samuel felt obliged to clarify the meaning of "a National Home for the Jewish People" reported in the Balfour Declaration. His explanation made an essential clarification as to the meaning that ought to be given to the word "nationality." In areas of Europe, where global/trans-territorial models of collective identity prevail and the idea of nation-state is less developed, nationality is not equivalent to citizenship.

Samuel underlined examples of Eastern Europe, Russia, Austria and the Ottoman Empire, where people were accustomed to distinguish several distinct "nationalities" although they were members of the same polity. Conversely, residents of these areas were used to the idea of individuals that belong to a single Jewish "nationality," even though they were residents and even citizens of different other countries.

In the state/territorial approach, popular in western and continental Europe, the term "a national" is equivalent to "a citizen," in that all members of a given state belong to that "nationality whereas residents who do not belong to the same "nationality" are aliens[337] and nobody should be permitted to be a citizen of more than one state. In accordance with the global approach, Samuel explains that all Jews may be a "people" and entitled to a "national home," without belonging to the same nationality, that is, a Jew who is, for example, a national of Great Britain, France or the United States, would keep his citizenship unaffected. Bernard Lewis has expressed a similar opinion:

(. . .) In English, both British and American, the word commonly used is 'nationality' which basically means what is written on a passport. *Nationalité* in French and the equivalents in some other European languages are used in much the same way. But not in all. German *Nationalität* and Russian *natsional'nost* convey ethnic and cultural, not legal and political nationality. For these they use other words — *Staatsangehörikeit*, 'state-belonging' in German, *graždanstvo* 'citizenship' in Russian. English legal usage still has no accepted term to denote this kind of ethnic, cultural identity within a nationality. (. . .) Even within Europe, there are thus significant variations of terminology and usage. Variation — and the opportunity for confusion — becomes greater in regions where this whole terminology was sometimes borrowed, sometimes imposed, but remained alien to a large part of the population.[338]

For this reason, it appears evident that the Balfour Declaration did not intend to encourage a secular national movement aimed at building a Jewish national independent territorial entity outside British political and cultural control. On the contrary, the British have generally stressed the importance of religion in the local conflict, implicitly claiming to be the only ones who could guarantee the traditional Holy Places' Status Quo on behalf of the whole world.

The substantial difference between the British and the French approach is evident: whereas through the Balfour Declaration, Great Britain pledged the Allied Powers' assistance to the Zionist aspirations in Palestine provided that the civil and religious status quo in the area be maintained, Cambon's letter referred only to safeguarding the independence of the Holy Places in order to preserve French traditional interests and exclusive privileges.

3.2 British steps towards the Holy Places' international protection at Peace Conferences

3.2.1 Priority of world interests in the Holy Places at the 1919 Paris Peace Conference

On January 4, 1918, immediately after issuing the Balfour Declaration, the British government instructed Commander D. G. Hogarth of the Arab Bureau in Cairo to deliver a message to the Sharif of Mecca King Husayn of the Hijaz, on the occasion of his visit to Jeddah. Hogarth's message stressed the determination on the part of the Allied Powers "that the Arab race shall be given full opportunity of once again forming a nation in the world" and "that no people shall be subject to another." Hogarth added that in Palestine "there must be a special regime to deal with these places approved of by the world" based on the "fact that there are in Palestine shrines, Wakfs and Holy places, sacred in some cases to Muslims alone, to Jews alone, to Christians alone, and in others to two or all three." Further, this message stressed that "these places are of interest to vast masses of people outside Palestine and Arabia" while the Mosque of Omar (the Dome of the Rock) in Jerusalem "shall be considered as a Muslim concern alone and shall not be subjected directly or indirectly to any non-Moslem authority."

Moreover, His Majesty's Government supported the world "Jewish opinion" constantly favoring "a return of Jews to Palestine," and "the realisation of this aspiration," in so far as it "is compatible with the freedom of the existing population both economic and political." As a result, the message inherently suggested that the Arabs should accept the "friendship and cooperation"[339] that the leaders of the world Jewry's Zionist movement were determined to offer.

From the foregoing, it may be deduced that the main argument not to include Palestine in the territory allotted to the Arab "nation" was the presence of "shrines, Wakfs and Holy places." Additionally, the British stressed the basic concept that these places are of interest to vast masses of people outside Palestine and Arabia and should then be considered as a value in themselves, regardless of which local religious community they belong to.

So, the recommendation that there ought to be a universally approved special regime to deal with these places was stated in the quoted document. Eventually, this idea was incorporated into the British Mandate by the League of Nations, and its political and legal consequences have lasted until the present day. Some of these principles had already been expressed on the occasion of the conquest of Jerusalem by General E.H.H. Allenby, on December 9, 1917. British forces, under the General's control, took over the whole area, inhabited by an Arabic-speaking population, formerly under Ottoman rule and divided it into three districts: the North district comprised Lebanon and Western Syria; the East district consisted of Eastern Syria and Transjordan; the South district was officially defined for the first time in centuries, as "Palestine."

At the time of his official entry into the Old City of Jerusalem, on December 11, 1917, General Allenby "proceeded on foot into the Old City of Jerusalem, with a French colonel, Diepape, at his right and an Italian colonel, D'Agostino, at his left. A Franciscan monk read out a British proclamation, stressing that":[340]

> (...) since your City is regarded with affection by the adherents of three of the great religions of mankind, and its soil has been consecrated by the prayers and pilgrimages of multitudes of devout people of these three religions for many centuries, therefore do I make known to you that every sacred building, monument, holy spot, shrine, traditional site, endowment, pious bequest or customary place of prayer, of whatsoever form, of the three religions, will be maintained and protected according to the existing customs and beliefs of those to whose faiths they are sacred. [341]

The Proclamation, read in seven languages, stated that soldiers of Islamic faith had been placed to guard the tomb of Rachel and the tombs of the Patriarchs, and that both of these Holy Places were entrusted to exclusive Muslim control. Moreover, the Proclamation confirmed that the Muslim family that held the keys of the Basilica of the Holy Sepulchre, "in memory of the generous act by which the Caliph Omar intended to protect that church." [342]

In response to a formal inquiry by seven Arab spokesmen from Ottoman Asia, who then resided in Cairo, the High Commissioner for Egypt Sir Reginald Wingate explained the aims of the British war in the Arabian Peninsula and the Arab provinces to the north. The document, ever since dubbed "The Declaration to the Seven," delivered on June 16, 1918, was referred to by General Allenby as "the policy of His Majesty's Government," which promised that the future government of the areas occupied by allied forces "should be based upon the principle of the consent of the governed."[343]

At the same time, in claiming the area, Jewish and Arab local communities' representatives tried to reach an agreement based on a bilateral approach. Chairman of the Zionist Organization Dr. Chaim Weizmann and Emir Faysal of Hedjaz reached an agreement on January 3, 1919 that also dealt with the Holy Places and the free exercise of religion in general. The signatories made no reference to the solution envisaged in the British approach to internationalization to guarantee the arrangements on the Holy Places, and implicitly assigned such a task to the local authority of the respective parties:

> Article V. No regulation nor law shall be made prohibiting or interfering in any way with the free exercise of religion; and further the free exercise and enjoyment of religious profession and worship without discrimination or preference shall forever be allowed. No religious test shall ever be required for the exercise of civil or political rights.
> Article VI. The Mohammedan Holy Places shall be under Mohammedan control.[344]

Well aware of the attempts to find a bilateral compromise between the two local leaderships, the Intelligence Section of the American Delegation to the Peace Conference in Paris sent tentative recommendations for the Near and Middle East to President Wilson on January 21,1919. According to Hurewitz, "a pervasive (...)

British influence is manifest on the policy recommendations of the United States."[345]

Also, this document recommended the establishment of "a separate state of Palestine," whose separation "from Syria finds justification in the religious experience of mankind." However such a state should "be placed under Great Britain as a Mandatory of the League of Nations," since it needs "wise and firm guidance. Its population is without political experience, is racially composite, and could easily become distracted by fanaticism and bitter religious differences."

As far as the Jews were concerned, the document stated that they would "be invited to return to Palestine and settle there," until the League of Nations would "recognize Palestine as a Jewish state," assuring in any case "the protection of the personal — especially the religious — and the property rights of the non-Jewish population." Further, the document recommended "that the holy places and religious rights of all creeds in Palestine be placed under the protection of the League of Nations and its Mandatory." The basis for this recommendation was, according to the document, "self-evident."[346]

On February 3, 1919, the Zionist Organization, for its part, sent a Memorandum to the Supreme Council at the Peace Conference which included both the Balfour Declaration and the assurance that "there shall be forever the fullest freedom of religious worship for all creeds in Palestine" hence ruling out any "discrimination among the inhabitants with regard to citizenship and civil rights, on the grounds of religion or of race." Moreover, the Zionist Memorandum agreed to the insertion of specific provisions "relating to the control of the Holy Places."[347]

As for the British position, a memorandum on the Near East drawn up in February 1919 for the Peace Conference stated:

> The international interests in the straits [of the Dardanelles] or in the free access to the Holy Places in Palestine for all religions which have a legitimate interest in each of them, are so important, that they should, if necessary, receive priority to the wish of the inhabitants of the areas in which they are located.[348]
>
> (. . .) The Christian, Jewish and Moslem Holy Places in Palestine, like the waterway in the zone of the straits, constitute a world interest of such importance that it should take precedence, in case of conflict, over political aspirations of the local inhabitants.[349]

A "Sketch of a Draft Treaty of Peace between Turkey and the Allied Governments"[350] followed the principles laid down by previous documents of the British administration. The document stated that the Mandatory body should transfer the protection of the Sanctuaries to a "suitable religious organization" which was to be in exclusive charge of the total administration and jurisdiction.

A second draft, dated April 1919, laid down the following principles for the Holy Places:

> 14. The British Government will be responsible for providing that certain Holy Places, religious buildings or sites regarded with special veneration by the adherents of one particular religion, are transferred to the permanent possession and control of suitable bodies selected or appointed by it and representing the adherents of the religion concerned. The selection of the Holy Places, religious buildings or sites to be so transferred will be made by the British Government. Such transference shall, however, not affect the right and duty of the British Government to maintain order and decorum in the places so transferred, and the buildings and

sites will be subject to the provisions of such laws relating to public monuments as may be enacted by the Government of Palestine (. . .).[351]

3.2.2 The King–Crane Commission and the San Remo Conference

Upon President Woodrow Wilson's insistence, in 1919 the Supreme Council of the Allied Powers at the Paris Peace Conference, appointed the King–Crane Commission, whose main task was "to elucidate the state of opinion and the soil to be worked on by any Mandatory" in Syria and Palestine and "to come back and tell the Conference what they found with regard to these matters."[352] The proposal to place the Holy Places under the supervision of an international commission emerged once again in the Report which was completed on August 30, 1919. The document also stressed "the duty of the Mandatory" to ensure "complete religious liberty (. . .) in the constitution [and] in the practice of the state" and "jealous care" to be "exercised for the rights of all minorities" in the area.

In view of the creation of the "Jewish state, however gradually that may take place," the document emphasized that "Palestine is 'the Holy Land' for (. . .) millions of (. . .) Jews, Christians and Muslims alike" all over the world. The document dealt with the situation "in Palestine, especially with those conditions which touch upon religious feeling and rights," adding that "the relations in these matters in Palestine are most delicate and difficult." "The holy places" should be "cared for by an International and Inter-religious Commission," which should include Jewish representation. This document envisaged a situation which was "somewhat as at present, under the oversight and approval of the Mandatory [body] and of the League of Nations,"[353] regardless of any religious affiliation to the various local communities, in this way confirming the British approach.

Finally, at the international conference held in San Remo, Italy, in April 1920, the Allies granted the mandate to Great Britain for the whole of Palestine (including the Holy Places). And so, at first, the region came under Great Britain's control as an occupied territory, later as a Mandate under the supervision of the League of Nations and remained in this status until the Arab–Israeli War of 1948.[354]

The Mandate's[355] Terms incorporated several suggestions about the Holy Places taken from the King–Crane Commission. During the San Remo Conference, the Italian Prime Minister Francesco Saverio Nitti stated that "the historical necessity in the past of protecting Christian bodies under the Turkish regime had now come to an end." Nitti explained that the new reality of "a civilized nation," representing "the European religious communities," made it possible to "guarantee to the whole world the safeguarding of the interests of those communities."[356]

Two months later, on June 25, 1920, Herbert Samuel confirmed Nitti's expectations about Britain's role vis-à-vis those communities, to Pope Benedict XV and the Secretary of State Cardinal Gasparri. Samuel made his visit to the Vatican on his way to Jerusalem, where he was to begin his task as first British High Commissioner. He recalled that the Pope had read "with much satisfaction"[357] the statement of policy published when the announcement was made of his appointment to Palestine which had initially caused "some preoccupation" on the Pope's part, who now "felt reassured." In the meeting Samuel repeated the assurance "that an impartial attitude would be observed towards all religions and that there would be complete religious toleration and liberty in Palestine."[358]

These early assurances are particularly important in view of the policy in the area announced by the British government throughout World War I negotiations. As previously mentioned, over the centuries each European state has generally claimed to be the exclusive legitimate protector of a particular religious community in the Holy Places which would entitle each protector to guarantee and safeguard its own interests in the area. This attitude explains the "basic distinction between the Sanctuaries of the *rulers* of the country and those of the *ruled*":[359]

> (T)he former rarely present any difficulties: thus Catholic rights in the Christian Holy Places were not endangered in the Latin Kingdom of Jerusalem; Moslem shrines were well respected under the Turkish reign; and there are no complaints today from Jewish religious authorities about Jewish rights at the Western (Wailing) Wall. (. . .) Conversely the position of the Sanctuaries of the ruled will vary according to the attitudes of the rulers.[360]

On the contrary, the British introduced a new element of impartiality on behalf of the League of Nations, which represented at that time the interests of the international community at large. As soon as they became directly involved in the negotiations on the future of Palestine, the British expressed their attitude predicting an end of the Ottoman rule. With this in mind, they acknowledged the existence of the traditional Status Quo regime imposed during Ottoman rule, which became a pillar of their policy in the area.

According to Reiter, until 1937 the British officially refrained "from intervention in religious affairs, whether Muslim or not," including matters of the *Waqf*, the Islamic trust endowment in charge of the Muslim sites and properties. From the very start, so as to deal "with all religious communities on an equal footing" the British government curtailed privileges the Muslims had enjoyed in the Ottoman Empire. Their policy implied the preservation of "the status quo in religious affairs" and "only such changes were to be made as were indisputably necessitated by the change of regime." Generally, they introduced reforms "through indirect legislation, unlikely to conflict with the *shari'a*."[361]

In summary, immediately following World War I, British and United States élites advocated for the idea of an International and Inter-religious Commission for the Holy Places as well as the duty of the Mandatory body to ensure, impartially, complete religious liberty in the land sacred to millions of Jews, Christians and Muslims alike all over the world. This global/trans-territorial view went against the traditional continental Europe state/territorial approach, which protected Christian Holy Places and local communities in Jerusalem along exclusive national lines, constantly in competition with one another.

3.3 The Terms of the Mandate in Palestine approved by the League of Nations

3.3.1 The British policy towards the Muslim, Christian and Jewish communities

On August 10, 1920, the Allied Powers and the Turkish Government signed the Peace Treaty of Sèvres, whose Article 95 stated that, by application of the provisions of Article 22 of the League of Nations' Charter, the administration of Palestine would be entrusted to a Mandatory power selected by the High Contracting Parties, which would put into effect the Balfour Declaration. Article 95 also stated that "the Mandatory undertakes to appoint as soon as possible a special Commission to study and regulate" the questions and claims relating to the different religious communities and that its Chairman would be appointed by the Council of the League of Nations.[362] The same article stressed that "the religious interests concerned" should be considered in the determination of the Commission's composition.

It also mentioned the manifold duties of the Mandatory with regard to the Holy Places, such as the guarantee of free access and worship, and the preservation and protection of the Sanctuaries. Among other issues, the appointment of a Special Commission for the settlement of disputes was not only explicitly referred to but it was emphasized that it should "be put into operation with particular urgency."[363] However, Turkey never ratified the Peace Treaty of Sèvres of 1920, due to Ataturk's campaign against it. Nevertheless, the Turkish government accepted the Lausanne Treaty of 1923, whose provisions regarding the renunciation of its Arab territories broadly corresponded to Article 95 of the Treaty of Sèvres.

The terms of the British Mandate in Palestine were first framed in December 1920, fundamentally altered in August 1921, and further modified on the eve of its provisional approval by the Council of the League of Nations on July 24, 1922. The areas currently administered by the Kingdom of Jordan, the Palestinian Authority, (namely, West Bank and Gaza) and the State of Israel, corresponded to the region to be administrated by the Mandatory power.

The area on the eastern bank of the Jordan River was later separated from the rest of Palestine with the revision of Article 25 of the Terms of the Mandate, approved by the Council on September 16, 1922.[364] Subsequently, the Kingdom of Transjordan, in this day and age Jordan, was set up in this area. The decision to separate these areas had been proposed by Herbert Samuel, as a result of which Great Britain was relieved "from the cares and the risks of the direct government of a very extensive territory, with poor communications and backward conditions."[365]

The Mandate, as far as the League's Council was concerned, went into effect on September 29, 1923, after Turkey had signed the Lausanne Peace Treaty. So, the boundaries of Palestine had not yet been clearly determined on July 1, 1920, when a civil administration replaced the military one, which had been in force since British troops had occupied Palestine in 1917–1918. The new administration was responsible to the Foreign Office until February 1921, when the Colonial Office assumed jurisdiction over this mandate. Herbert Samuel officially took his position in 1920 as the first High Commissioner in Palestine, "to administer the country, not for the benefit of one section of the population only, but for all; not commissioned by the Zionists but in the name of the King."[366] Accordingly, he immediately announced his intention to form "a small Advisory Council,"[367] which would include "leading members of the Muslim, Christian and Jewish communities, to which all measures of importance would be submitted." The Advisory Council, which took into account the views of the religious communities representatives, was meant "to be a first step towards the establishment of self-governing institutions."[368]

In his Report to the Secretary of State for the Colonies, Samuel wrote an extensive and detailed account of the situation in the Mandatory area in the period 1920–1925. His report also referred to a declaration[369] made public by Colonial Secretary Winston Churchill on July 1, 1922. According to Hurewitz, this statement of policy on Palestine, also known as the Churchill White Paper, "survived, in its major aspects, until July 1937."[370] The official guidelines included in Samuel's Report confirmed the Churchill White Paper's policy vis-à-vis the various sections of the population, which "coupled with the maintenance of the fullest religious liberty in Palestine and with scrupulous regard for the rights of each community with reference to its Holy Places," was the basis for the development of "that spirit of co-operation upon which the future progress and prosperity of the Holy Land must largely depend."[371] Additionally, the Report stressed that Article 81 of the Draft Palestine Order-in-Council gave to "any religious community or considerable section of the population of Palestine" the "general right to appeal, through the High Commissioner and the Secretary of State, to the League of Nations." This right was so general as to cover "any matter on which"[372] the Government of Palestine would not properly fulfill as required by the terms of the mandate.

Samuel enacted the legislation which ensured that the area remained "one of the few countries in the world whose scenery and historic sites and buildings have remained unspoilt"[373] by the intrusion of outdoor advertisements, where a newly created Department of Antiquities "was active in revealing or preserving the precious relics of earlier epochs that have survived all over Palestine", while a Pro-Jerusalem Society "worked energetically to rescue the ancient city from the modern intrusions that had been thrust upon it." In this framework, he ordered the restoration of "the exquisite Muslim building of the eighth century which stands on the site of the Temples of Solomon and of Herod, and enshrines the rock which was their sacrificial altar — undoubtedly the most beautiful building in the Middle East." Samuel proudly recalled that he had also restored "the fine and fitting title which is its name in Arabic — the Dome of the Rock", generally misnamed until then as "the Mosque of Omar."[374] Since then, the Dome of the Rock has increased its symbolic importance for the Muslims, increasing the risk of religious confrontation with the Jewish claims to the same site.

Apparently Samuel's policy was inspired by the Terms of Mandate, which conferred upon the Mandatory Power the duty "of preserving existing rights[375] and of securing free access to the Holy Places, religious buildings and sites and the free exercise of worship,[376] while ensuring the requirements of public order and decorum" (Article 13). Moreover, Article 15 of the Mandate guaranteed "complete freedom of conscience and the free exercise of any form of worship."[377] This spirit of inter-religious freedom and peace inspired the development of Mandatory Palestine much more than a possible territorial compromise between the two main national-ethnic components of the Palestinian population.

At the beginning of the Mandate, Foreign Minister of Great Britain Lord Balfour issued a declaration on the specific issue of the Holy Places which stated: "The British Government never have had, have not now, and never can have any desire with regard to the Holy Places but that of administering historic justice between all the great communities concerned;" all the "ancient rights" that "any man", "community" or "nation" may claim "shall be carried on with decency and order in the future, and in a manner which will prevent any religious interest feeling that it has been unjustly treated by those who possess authority."[378]

In its Preamble's second paragraph, the Terms of the Mandate stressed the importance of the "religious rights" of non-Jewish communities resident in Palestine. Subsequently those "rights" became relevant in international law, the legal system which made the Mandate legally binding, although the specific content of those rights remained unclear. Articles 13, 14 and 15 of the Mandate dealt directly with the Holy Places and the interests of the religious communities. Article 13 of the Terms of Mandate conferred upon the Mandatory Power the duty "to preserve existing rights," a reference to the Status Quo in a narrow sense[379] and forced Great Britain "to secure free access to the Holy Places, religious buildings and sites and the free exercise of worship," a reference to the status quo in the broader sense.[380] Article 14 dealt with the sensitive issue of "the rights and claims in connection with the Holy Places and the rights and claims relating to the different religious communities in Palestine."[381] The reference to Articles 13 and 14 embodied in Article 28 of the Terms of Mandate is noteworthy.[382] Article 15 guaranteed "complete freedom of conscience and the free exercise of all forms of worship." The Palestine Order-in-Council of 1922 enacted by the British Mandatory Power and still currently in force in Israel, stated:

> All persons in Palestine shall enjoy full liberty of conscience and the free exercise of their forms of worship, subject only to the maintenance of public order and morals. Each religious community shall enjoy autonomy for the internal affairs of the community, subject to the provisions of any ordinance or order issued by the High Commissioner.[383]

The recognized Christian "religious communities" were listed in a schedule added in 1939 to the Palestine Order-in-Council:

> The Eastern (Orthodox), the Latin (Catholic), the Gregorian Armenian, the Armenian (Catholic), the Syrian (Catholic), the Chaldean (Uniate), the Greek (Catholic) Melkite, the Maronite, and the Syrian Orthodox.[384]

Several Christian communities in the territories currently administrated by Israel and the Palestinian Authority comprise the Catholic Church, namely, Latins and Uniates, Melkites, Maronites, Chaldeans, Syrian Catholics, and Armenian Catholics. "Each community belongs to an independent jurisdiction, but all depend, severally, upon the Sacred Congregation of the Oriental Churches in Rome."[385] According to Minerbi, "The Eastern churches, or Uniate" include the following different rites:

> (1) the Alexandrian rite, to which the Copts and Ethiopians belong; (2) the Antiochene, which includes the Maronites; (3) the Armenian, whose adherents returned to the Catholic Church in the eighteenth century; (4) the Byzantine, which includes the Melkites, or Greek Catholics; and (5) the Chaldean.[386]

In its annual Report for the year 1924 (hereinafter the 1924 Report), the British Government had informed the League of Nations' Council of the procedure adopted by the Mandatory to recognize the Maronite Religious Community. The 1924 Report referred to this community as having given "proof of having exercised jurisdiction in matters of personal status in the Ottoman regime", as a consequence becoming entitled, under the Palestine Order-in-Council, to continue to exercise "that jurisdiction over its members."[387]

In other words, the Mandatory by and large applied a criterion of continuity, as long as enough evidence was available from the Ottoman administration regarding the community's actual exercise of jurisdiction when recognition was concerned. Both the Jordanians and the Israelis, who ruled the Jerusalem area after the British, have ideally applied the same criteria in granting recognition to additional communities not originally included in the Mandatory list and in recognizing the internal rules of the community. According to the *Encyclopaedia Judaica*, this practice was applied to the Copts, Ethiopians, Anglicans and other Reformed Churches not mentioned in the 1939 British list. Jordan subsequently granted official status to the Church of England and the Evangelical Lutheran Church, while Israel recognized the Evangelical Episcopal Church in 1970. Normally, "a patriarch assisted by a synod" heads each community. "The clergy (sometimes with the assistance of lay assessors) constitute the ecclesiastical courts of first instance", while "the synods form ecclesiastical courts of appeal."[388]

Article 16 of the Terms of Mandate guaranteed the enterprise of "religious or eleemosynary bodies of all faiths in Palestine," while Article 23 dealt with the religious days of rest.[389] Finally, it should be noted that Article 21 provided for the enactment of a Law of Antiquities, known as the Antiquities Ordinance of 1929, since the Holy Places are "antiquities" in the sense of the law and are, in this regard, under the protection of the Department of Antiquities.[390] Therefore, the Mandate's provisions confirm the considerations developed in this work about the British global/trans-territorial attitude in Palestine which stresses the importance of the religious collective identity vis-à-vis the national one (following ethnic-linguistic criteria), with particular emphasis on the Holy Places and religious shrines.

It should be recalled that the first period of Ottoman rule was consistent with Roman tradition in granting formal recognition to new *Millets* in cases of groups that were anthropologically and sociologically endowed with specific ethnic-linguistic characteristics other than religious ones, comparable to a *natio* recognized in Roman law. Although British rulers proclaimed formal continuity of the Ottoman criteria by granting legal recognition to the various communities they, as well as Israeli rulers who followed them in taking control of the area, actually kept the practice adopted only in the last period of the Ottoman rule when under Western political–diplomatic pressure, legal recognition was given to groups of different religious or dogmatic denomination.

As British rulers consistently stressed that their presence in Palestine was for the benefit of the whole population, they impartially proceeded to protect shrines, *Waqf*s and religious sites of interest to vast masses of people outside Palestine making these places a value in themselves, regardless of to which local religious community they belonged. This consideration explains why the British strongly believed that a special regime universally approved through the Mandate of the League of Nations was needed to deal with these places since they claimed that only Great Britain as a Mandatory power could provide wise and firm guidance to its population.

3.3.2 The development of the Palestinian-Arab and the Jewish-Zionist national movements

An intriguing description of the political situation in the area during the early period of the Mandate may be found in the *Report of the Commission on the Palestine Disturbances of August, 1929*,[391] also known as the Shaw Commission's Report, named after its Chairman Sir Walter Shaw, in which the Commissioners underlined the lack of a specific national identity of the Arab component of the population. On the other hand, on December 13, 1920, leading Palestinian families such as the

Husseinis, convened the Third Palestinian Arab Congress in Haifa. The Congress clearly stressed for the first time the autonomous existence of the group of Palestinian Arabs and their unique circumstances and problems in Palestine thereby making two important decisions:

- To recognize the Arab Executive Committee as the legitimate representative of the Palestinian population before the British authorities;
- To ask Great Britain to establish an independent "national government responsible to a representative assembly, whose members would be chosen from the Arabic-speaking people — Muslims, Christians and Jews — who have been inhabiting Palestine until the outbreak of the war."[392]

Apart from unity among the Palestinian Arabs, to supersede any other loyalties, such as religion, region and clan being the centerpiece of this congress, a "narrower, territorially defined concept of a Palestinian state"[393] preoccupied the representatives attending the congress. The second of such congress was scheduled for May 1920 but was banned by the Mandate government because of rioting in the month of April the same year. The riots left 5 Jews and 4 Arabs dead, and 250 people (almost all of them Jews) gravely injured.

According to Pieraccini, this was the first occurrence in the history of Jerusalem and its Old City of attacks against Jews on the part of the Arab population.[394] Demonstrations against the Balfour Declaration coincided with the celebrations of the Jewish and Christian Orthodox Easters as well as the Islamic Nebi Musa procession, and were organized right before the San Remo Conference previously mentioned (where the Allies conferred Great Britain the Mandate on Palestine). The Nebi Musa procession was an occasion for a great national religious feast, which attracted Muslims from all over the country to Jerusalem, in particular from Nablus and Hebron. The procession ended at the mosque of the *Waqf* of Nebi Musa, where the alleged tomb of Moses is located.[395]

The purpose of the Third Congress of December 13, 1920 was "to make the world hear the voice of the Palestinians, to pay heed to their national demands, and to unite the various Palestinian associations and clubs."[396] Political and cultural organizations and the Muslim–Christian Association that emerged after World War I emphatically proclaimed the existence of a distinct Arab people in Palestine and of Palestine as a common homeland.[397] These organizations, whose members came from the more privileged sectors of the urban society, hammered out social demarcations, that is, a Palestinian profile that also ordinary workers and villagers began to adopt. According to Reiter, "the intercultural encounter between Arab society and the new yishuv, the pre-state Zionist Jewish community" contributed to lead "the two national movements, the Palestinian-Arabs and the Jewish-Zionists" to a clash. This took the form of "a struggle for sovereignty and dominion over the same land, for access to the Holy Places, and ultimately for the very character of the country as a whole and of Jerusalem in particular."[398]

Contrasting these two competing nationalistic groups claiming exclusive territorial title to the area under British administration were the specific provisions of the Terms of Mandate related to the different subject of the Holy Places. At the public meeting of the Council of the League of Nations on July 24, 1922, immediately after the provisional approval of the Terms of Mandate, British Foreign Minister Balfour explained that the Palestine Mandate consisted of two parts. According to Balfour, one part concerned "Palestine and its inhabitants," while the other part included provisions related to "the Holy Places, about which there would be further discussion."[399]

By stressing the importance of the Holy Places in particular, the British leadership had the specific purpose of persuading world opinion, indirectly represented at that time in the League of Nations, that it was more appropriate to define local communities along religious lines rather than national ones. The state/territorial criteria, which developed particularly during the nineteenth century in Europe's continental areas were relatively new paradigms of socio-political identification in the area, but Great Britain was eager to avoid any national development in Palestine and took great care in re-organizing the institutional and legal structure of the "religious communities," as defined in the Terms of the Mandate.[400]

In this respect, the organizational problems of the Greek Orthodox Patriarchate were among the first instances upon which the described policy could be enacted since "the Orthodox Church was in a deplorable state"[401] and so insolvent that the High Commissioner Samuel appointed a Commission of Inquiry "to restore the solvency of the Patriarchate". As a matter of fact, Samuel found that "most of the religious communities were disorganized"[402] to the point that he decided that even the Chief Rabbinate[403] ought to be restructured on the ecclesiastical, religious-oriented model of the Christian communities although the Ottomans, as well as any other Muslim rule, had never felt a need to define and identify the *umma*, as a proper Muslim community.

Therefore, this new organization as a religious community in Palestine was to a great extent a British invention; the creation the Supreme Muslim Council, was apparently meant to neutralize the Arab opposition to the Mandate.[404] In this respect, Reiter writes that "a non-Muslim government" now ruled the area "and the Muslims ceased to be the 'nation' [*umma*]" receiving, instead, "the status of a religious community — one of several." This new status implied a limitation to the application of the *shari'a*, whose courts' jurisdiction British authorities confined "exclusively to matters of personal status and *waqf* law."

Whereas in nineteenth century the Ottomans had introduced a policy of decentralization "by granting the district council and the local committees powers of their own" the British, by contrast, invested Hajj Amin al-Husayni, "the Mufti of Jerusalem, with supreme religious authority, designating him *al-Mufti al-Akbar*, 'chief Mufti', later, *ra'is al-'ulama*' ('Head of the *'ulama''*), and making him head of the Muslim community in Palestine,"[405] in this way "serving simultaneously as president of the Supreme Muslim Council and chairman of the General *Waqf* Committee."[406] It is noteworthy that, even though Mufti Hajj Amin came fourth in the 1921 election for this office, the British still appointed him to the position.

3.3.3 The 1929 disturbances and the Jewish–Muslim Status Quo

The Mandate's provisions and other relevant documents clearly illustrate the British attitude towards the Holy Places and the local religious communities in their handling of the Mandatory power on the subject. The Status Quo procedural principles, which initially exclusively applied to Christian Holy Places, were later extended by analogy to Jewish and Muslim sites and to the relationship among their respective communities.[407] British Foreign Minister Balfour explicitly clarified that "the term 'Holy Places' in Article 13 could not be regarded as synonymous with the three Christian Holy Places." The Commission appointed according to Article 14 of the Mandate had the task "to define the rights of worship in the three Christian Holy Places, as they would define the rights in any other Holy Place, religious building, or site in Palestine, whether Christian, Muslim, or Jewish."[408]

In his Memorandum titled *The Western or Wailing Wall in Jerusalem*, presented to the British Parliament in November 1928, British Secretary of State for the Colonies confirmed the Status Quo's purported progressive extension by stating, in relation to the terms of Article 13 of the Mandate for Palestine, that "the Palestine Government and His Majesty's Government" also felt "bound to maintain the *status quo*" in relation to this Holy Place.[409] A similar statement was included in the Shaw Commission's Report.[410]

The Western or Wailing Wall in Jerusalem Memorandum of November 1928 included a complaint made on September 23, 1928, Day of Atonement eve, by the Mutawali of the Abu Madian *Waqf* (property belonging to the religious Muslim endowment, in which the pavement and the whole area around the Western or Wailing Wall were vested), "that a dividing screen had been affixed to the pavement adjoining the Wall, and that other innovation had been made in the established practice."[411] The complaint was made through the *Waqf* representative to the Deputy District Commissioner of Jerusalem. The officer of the Palestine Government found these complaints to be substantive and decided to order "the removal of an appurtenance of Jewish worship," according to the Mandatory obligation "to preserve the *status quo*."

"On the following morning, worshippers present at the Wall themselves declined to remove it," and "some of the congregation" even "endeavoured to prevent" the removal, which eventually occurred, "without casualties of any but a light nature."[412] The British Government stated that "the responsible Jewish authorities" should have been aware of "the delicacy of the question of procedure at the Wall and the need for extreme discretion with regard to anything that might be regarded by watchful neighbours as a breach of the *status quo*." Lacking "any mutual agreement between themselves and the Muslim authorities regulating the conduct of services at the Wall," the Muslim authorities were allowed to take "exception to any innovations of practice," and the Palestine Government had the duty "to ensure that there is no infraction of the *status quo*."

Jewish representatives were aware of a similar complaint made by the Muslim authorities on the same day (Jewish Day of Atonement of 1925), when "the police had intervened to restore the *status quo*." Therefore, it should have been "clear to those concerned that the Palestine Government would regard it as their duty to take similar action in the event of any recurrence" of a complaint "against any departure from the status quo."

British authorities also responded to the objection "that the removal of the screen should have been postponed until the conclusion of the services and the Fast of the Day of Atonement" referring to "the practice to take immediate action where it is established that the status quo has been infringed." For example, they recalled that "in the Church of the Holy Sepulchre and other Holy Places, even in the most sacred services and upon the most holy days" the authorities had "from time immemorial" dealt "immediately and on the spot" with any "infraction of the *status quo*" in order to avoid "the risk of creating a precedent which would transform an infraction into an integral portion of the *status quo*."[413] The Memorandum of November 1928 recounted an incident where the authorities "had to remove seats and benches brought to the Wall." This event provides an example as to the procedure that was to be adopted for settling future similar disputes by British Mandatory authorities.

Realization of such procedure was initiated in May 1926, through a memorandum forwarded by the President of the Zionist Organization to the League of Nations through His Majesty's Government. In referring to this incident, both the Permanent Commission on the Mandates and the Council of the League concluded "that a solution of the difficulties could only be found by agreement." British authorities noted this conclusion and endorsed their comment "on the memorandum, which was that the dispute could not be settled except by common consent."[414]

British authorities regarded it to be both their intention and duty "to promote an arrangement eliminating the present obstacles to the free exercise of worship" at the Western Wall, "to maintain the established Jewish right of access to the pavement in front of the Wall for the purposes of their devotions and also their right to bring to the Wall those appurtenances that they were allowed to take to the Wall under the Turkish regime." However, they also stated that compelling "the Muslim owners of the pavement to accord any further privileges or rights to the Jewish community" would be "inconsistent with their duty under the Mandate."

These statements again illustrate the complex relationship between the general principles guaranteeing "freedom of worship" vis-à-vis the traditional arrangements, defined in this book as the Status Quo/Modus Vivendi, which risked appearing as discriminatory.[415]

The 1928 Memorandum warns that "the fact that public opinion in Palestine has definitely removed the matter from the purely religious orbit and has made of it a political or racial question" had narrowed "the possibility that such privileges or rights might be acquired by the Jews by mutual arrangement with the Moslem authorities."[416] The report sent on December 1930 by the Commission appointed by Great Britain, "with the approval of the Council of the League of Nations, to determine the rights and claims of Muslims and Jews in connection with the Western or Wailing Wall at Jerusalem," provides further evidence of British practice to extend the Status Quo procedural rules to Muslim and Jewish relationship.

"In view of the particular interest attaching to the *status quo* of the Christian Holy Places," the Commissioners decided to pay "prolonged visits especially to the Church of the Holy Sepulchre at Jerusalem and the Church of the Nativity at Bethlehem" where "well-qualified British officials and the officiating functionaries of the different Christian churches explained to the Commissioners the particular conditions of the *status quo*."[417]

In referring to the Latin expression "status quo," the Jews argued "that the use of such appurtenances as benches, a screen for separating men and women, an Ark with Scrolls of the Law, ritual lamps, a wash-basin, etc., was common." The existence of this custom, which "was also allowed by the authorities on the spot long before the Great War," had been authorized by "the Firmans of 1841, 1889 and 1893." Jewish authorities maintained that "this state of things should be held to constitute the *status quo* and the existing rights to which Art. 13 of the Mandate refers."[418]

3.4 Settlement of disputes on rights and claims in connection with the Holy Places

3.4.1 Immunity from ordinary jurisdiction according to the 1924 Palestine Holy Places Order-in-Council

According to Article 14 of the Terms of the Mandate, a commission should have dealt with the sensitive issue of "the rights and claims in connection with the Holy Places and the rights and claims relating to the different religious communities in Palestine."[419] Various statements by British officers, including the first High Commissioner in Palestine Herbert Samuel and Foreign Minister Balfour facilitate the interpretation of the Mandate's provisions.

Samuel, in a letter sent on October 12, 1920 to the Foreign Office, expressed his reluctance to appoint himself as chairman of the Commission on the Holy Places in view of the fact that any decision taken by such Commission might have created a conflict between the High Commissioner and sections of the population. Therefore, he favored the commission to be "in the nature of outside arbitration between local divergent claims."[420] Moreover, while urging that such commission be formed as soon as the Mandate was formally approved, he believed that it should be summoned only at long intervals. Minerbi stated that "Samuel elaborated his position one month later, in reply to questions from the Foreign Office," proposing "a commission of thirty-one members: eight Muslims recommended by the grand mufti; three Catholics recommended by the Vatican; three Greek Orthodox; two Armenians; eight Jews; and one each from the Coptic, Abyssinian, and Anglican Churches."

Samuel believed that the members of the Commission should not "have been actively engaged in controversies on the Holy Places," that they need not be "residents of Palestine," and that "four representatives of the administration"[421] should be included.

On July 22, 1922, while discussing the draft Mandate, the British delegate to the Council of the League of Nations, Lord Balfour, insisted "that the appointment of a permanent commission as a sort of executive power by the side of the Mandatory power must be avoided."[422] Instead, Balfour suggested that the commission meet whenever necessary. On December 28, 1922 Samuel responded to the Colonial Office in London, which had asked for his opinion about a proposal suggesting that ordinary Palestinian Courts should settle disputes regarding the Holy Places. After careful consideration, Samuel replied that "the question of the Holy Places cannot be satisfactorily dealt with by the Palestine Courts"[423] due to the "great difficulty" that would arise in adequately dealing with "such important issues" on a strictly legal basis, which would require the application of Ottoman Law.

Samuel had already encountered similar difficulties in relation to the questions of the *Coenaculum* (the location of the Last Supper) and the Wailing Wall, which "being of a nature deeply interesting to religious communities throughout the world should be dealt with by a higher authority than a local Court."[424] A claim raised by the Soviet Union concerning Christian property in Palestine presented him with an additional opportunity to re-state his views. On this occasion, he re-emphasized that cases involving intricate problems of history and international law, if handled by Palestine Courts, would seriously encumber their work and therefore ought to be decided by "jurists of international repute and standing."[425]

Pending the creation of the Holy Places Commission, Samuel proposed to enact an Order-in-Council which would permit the reference to "a special judicial procedure"[426] of "any question touching holy sites and religious buildings in Palestine." He made it clear that the expenditure of the proposed judicial body would not be paid for by the revenues of the Mandate, since such judicial service concerned "rather the whole Religious Community than the members or properties of the Community in Palestine."[427] This issue was again dealt with in the first annual report to the Council of the League, which was submitted by Great Britain in 1923 in accordance with Article 24 of the Mandate.[428] The British Report addressed one question regarding measures taken in connection with "the Holy Places and religious buildings or sites, including the responsibility of preserving existing rights, and of securing free access to the Holy Places, religious buildings and sites, and the free exercise of worship."

The British claimed to have assumed responsibility "as successor to the Turkish Government." Accordingly, "in all specific cases that have arisen" they claimed to have "strictly maintained the status quo" and to have "postponed the final determination of any disputed questions until the establishment of the Holy Places Commission, contemplated by Article 14 of the Mandate," whose functions included "the definition of the purely Muslim sacred shrines."[429] Samuel strongly advocated for the principle that disputes "in connection with the Holy Places or religious buildings or sites or the rights or claims relating to the different religious communities in Palestine" should not be referred to ordinary courts. He supported this principle until its formal adoption in the 1924 Order-in-Council. It is important to note that the same principle is still widely accepted in Israeli case law today.

On July 25, 1924, Great Britain as the Mandatory power adopted the Palestine Order-in-Council on the Holy Places and duly informed the Council of the League of Nations in its 1924 Report. The Order was meant to implement the principle embodied in the provisions of Article 14[430] and had the effect of withdrawing any case in connection with rights and claims in the Holy Places from the courts of Palestine. Additionally, the 1924 Report had to answer the question regarding the measures taken as well as their practical effects, "to place the country under such political, administrative and economic conditions as will safeguard the civil and religious rights of all the inhabitants of Palestine, irrespective of race and religion."[431]

To answer this question, Great Britain listed the main Ordinances adopted on Legal and Judicial matters, including "the Charitable Trusts Ordinance", and also referred to the Order-in-Council of July 1924, enacted to exclude the "matters within the purview of the proposed Holy Places Commission" from the jurisdiction of the Civil Courts.[432]

Accordingly, Great Britain gave a similar answer to the question related to the measures taken for "the assumption by the Mandatory of responsibility in connection with the Holy Places and religious buildings or sites, including the responsibility of preserving existing rights and of securing free access to the Holy Places, religious buildings and sites, and the free exercise of worship" in section "IX. *Holy Places*," included in the Appendix to the 1924 Report.[433]

3.4.2 The competent body to settle the Holy Places' disputes

The issue of how the 1924 Order-in-Council was to be construed in order to determine which body should have jurisdiction over the disputes is different from the preliminary one of the immunity from ordinary jurisdiction, discussed above in the previous section. Paragraph 3 of the Order-in-Council is interpreted in this study to mean that the task of the local authority, at that time Great Britain, was limited to a determination whether "any cause or matter comes within the terms of the preceding Article hereof."[434] In the essence, the power of the local authority should be limited to the decision as to whether any particular dispute should be referred to the ordinary courts and not the substance of the dispute under examination.

This interpretation also finds expression in the aforementioned British 1924 Report to the League of Nations Council, according to which the Holy Places Order-in-Council provided that actions regarding matters within the purview of the Commission on the Holy Places should not be heard or determined by any ordinary Civil Court. The High Commissioner had to decide, only in case of doubt, "*whether any action shall be withdrawn* from the Civil Courts."[435] However, Paragraph 3 of the Order-in-Council does not affect or limit the jurisdiction of the religious courts since the task of the British Mandatory Government is clearly limited to the preliminary procedural phase.

This interpretation can also be found in a letter dated June 5, 1924 sent by the British Colonial Office to the Foreign Office to which a draft of the proposed Order-in-Council was attached. The letter proposed the removal from the jurisdiction of the Palestine Courts of all cases related to the Holy Places, clarifying that the High Commissioner should only decide, under the instructions of the Secretary of State for the Colonies, "if any question were to arise as to whether the matter in dispute fell within this definition or not."[436] Accordingly, in every instance where the High Commissioner removed any cause or matter "from the jurisdiction of the Palestine Courts," such a "matter should be referred to the Council of the League of Nations, and proposals laid before that body for approval."[437]

Pending the formation of the Commission on the Holy Places contemplated in Article 14 of the Palestine Mandate, the British Colonial Secretary suggested that matters considered by the High Commissioner to fall within the competence of the Holy Places Commission, and not within the competence of ordinary civil courts, should be brought before a different special commission. According to the Colonial Secretary's proposal, this special commission was to be composed of the Chief Justice of Palestine and at least two British Judges of Palestine Courts. Furthermore, such a special commission would not sit as an ordinary Palestine Court, but as a special *ad hoc* commission "charged with the duty of enabling the Mandatory to carry out the provisions of Article 13 of the Mandate, subject to subsequent endorsement by the Commission referred to in Article 14."[438]

This study suggests a legal interpretation of the Order-in-Council provision compatible with the traditional global/trans-territorial approach that the British had supported in the area. As previously mentioned, British authorities were strongly against any move that could possibly favor the advancement of the state-national model of collective identity. In this respect, they opposed the appointment of a permanent commission as a sort of executive power alongside the Mandatory power, and suggested that the Commission meet only when necessary.

The quotations from British documents selected in this section confirm the global/trans-territorial approach which characterized the British administration, owing to the fact that the group-identity of reference for British policy and legislation in Palestine was borderless and not defined by local territorial boundaries, that is, people sharing common values and faith were enlisted into the same community regardless of any linguistic, ethnic or historical features connected to their place of residence.

3.4.3 The erroneous interpretation of the local government's authority according to the 1924 Paragraph 3 of the Order-in-Council

Although the text of the 1924 Order-in-Council appears to be quite clear, some authors[439] have interpreted Article 3 as authorizing the High Commissioner to make a decision on the substance of those causes or matters removed from the jurisdiction of the Palestine Courts. One of such authors, Walter Zander, corrected his misinterpretation expressed in a previous publication[440] and pointed out:

> The error is of importance because if the High Commissioner had been authorized by the Order to decide the disputes, this authority would have been transferred to the Israel Government.[441]

It is now possible to have a clearer understanding of this issue thanks to the readily available documentation, which has led Zander to quite radically change his point of view. He recognized that "the files of the Foreign Office contain a statement on this question which gives an irrefutable official interpretation of the Order." Zander referred to a statement that showed "which part of the arrangements was to be made known, and which was to be kept secret for the time being."[442]

On October 27, 1924, the Foreign Office had made reference to this misunderstanding when replying to the British Minister to the Holy See, Sir Odo Russell, who asked London for exact information on the interpretation of the Order in Council. The reply from the Foreign Office clearly stated that Article 3 of the Order did not empower the High Commissioner in Palestine to settle disputes connected with the Holy Places and religious questions, but merely entrusted the High Commissioner with the responsibility to decide whether or not a given case should be removed from the jurisdiction of the ordinary courts according to Article 2 of the Order, thus confirming the procedure indicated in the aforementioned Colonial Office's letter of June 5, 1924.

According to this interpretation, "if the High Commissioner decides that any case should be removed from the jurisdiction of the ordinary courts in Palestine, the matter will be referred to the Council of the League of Nations."[443] This explains why the question of implementing Mandate's Article 14 came up later, for example, in the occasion of the riots over the Western Wall in August 1929. On November 18, 1929,[444] according to Article 14, the British Government could only propose to appoint an *ad hoc* commission to settle the question of Jewish and Muslim rights and claims to the Western Wall to the Permanent Mandates Commission of the League of Nations. The British Government, in other words, did *not* have the power to set up such a body unilaterally.

However, the Permanent Mandates Commission rejected the British proposal on the grounds that Article 14 of the Mandate called for a special commission to deal with all the Holy Places as opposed to a specific one.[445] Despite this objection, during the debate in the Council of the League, the British delegate insisted that Great Britain was willing to proceed with the appointment of a special commission provided by Article 14 and to limit its duties, for the time being, to the problem of the Western Wall.[446]

Nevertheless, on January 14, 1930 the League Council decided that there should be no change in the interpretation and implementation of Article 14. In the essence, the League of Nations' body, pending the constitution of the commission provided for in the same article, was to continue to supervise directly, through its yearly reports, the Mandatory administration of the Holy Places.

On the other hand, the appointment of an *ad hoc* commission could be authorized only under Article 13,[447] a procedure adopted for the appointment of the "Wailing Wall Commission," as described in the Introduction of the Report of this Commission.[448]

Samuel assumed that the jurisdiction over the Holy Places could not be satisfactorily dealt with by the Palestine Courts, since such a function would be an additional one affecting interests outside the country and not within the juridical work in Palestine. Zander interpreted Samuel's words to mean that "the world-wide interest in the Christian Holy Places is relevant to the question of the jurisdiction over the Sanctuaries."[449] In Zander's view, this interest could be legally recognized in different ways, including proposals ranging from territorial internationalization of the Sanctuaries to the establishment of special tribunals since "self-imposed limitations of jurisdiction for the sake of a matter transcending the borders of a country" were a common feature of international law in the field of extraterritoriality and immunity.

Going by this interpretation, these principles of international law could be usefully applied, directly or by way of analogy, to the question of the jurisdiction over the Christian Holy Places, "in addition to the consideration of constitutional issues which hitherto have dominated the discussion."[450]

3.5 The proposals of a special regime for Jerusalem from 1937 to 1947

3.5.1 The Peel and Woodhead Commissions' partition plans

The rise to power of Adolf Hitler on January 30, 1933 along with his discriminatory policy of threats and violence against those labeled as non-Aryans and particularly Jews, produced effects in Palestine where in a three-year period the Jewish population grew from 18.9% to 27.7%.[451] Nationalistic ideology had simultaneously been developing in the Arab world, where demonstrations and strikes led Great Britain and France to promise the conclusion of treaties that recognized the independence of Syria and Egypt by March 1936. In the wake of these events, the Arab Higher Committee, formed on April 25, 1936 under the presidency of the Mufti of Jerusalem Hajj Amin al-Husayni, organized an uprising in Palestine. The Arab Muslim Mayor of Jerusalem Husayn al-Khalidi joined the Arab Higher Committee and politically endorsed the uprising, causing the Municipal Government composed of both Arabs and Jews to virtually stop his operations.

By 1936 the Arab and Jewish Palestinian national movements in competition considered control over the Holy Places of the city "as a prize for the victor in the struggle of Palestine."[452] According to former High Commissioner Herbert Samuel, the Italian and German Governments fostered the tension because they saw "in Palestine a sensitive spot which might easily be inflamed, to the injury of the whole British position, political and military, in the Middle East."[453] Against this background, in April 1936 the British Government established a Royal Commission on Palestine[454] which heard testimony from November 1936 to February 1937, both in Palestine and in London. Former Secretary of State for India William Robert Wellesley, better known as Earl Peel, headed the Palestine Royal Commission, which came to be known as the Peel Commission.

The Peel Commission's Royal Warrant, by Edward the Eighth, King of Great Britain, is dated 7 August 1936; George the Sixth, King of Great Britain, confirmed it on 17 December 1936. At that time, Samuel was still against the idea of partitioning Palestine according to state/territorial lines.

While "the ownership and control of their Holy Places, as now recognized, should be guaranteed in perpetuity to the Christian, Moslem and Jewish Faiths,"[455] Samuel suggested the establishment of self-governing institutions "not on the basis of the geographical constituencies to which we are accustomed, but on the basis of the Communities, such as had prevailed in the Turkish Empire [they were termed 'Millets']."[456]

However, the Peel Commission, in its Report to the Council of the League of Nations, proposed for the first time a territorial partition of Mandatory Palestine into two independent states, taking into account the historical reality of the development of the two nationalistic movements. The Commission concluded that Palestine should be partitioned into an Arab state and a Jewish state and that the separate special regime of the British Mandatory authority would apply only to the towns and districts in which the Holy Places are situated, including Jerusalem, Bethlehem, Lake Tiberias and Nazareth. In implicitly outlining the notion of a *corpus separatum* for the Jerusalem area, this arrangement was motivated by "the overriding necessity of keeping the sanctity of Jerusalem and Bethlehem inviolate and of ensuring free and safe access to them for all the world."[457] In fact the term *corpus separatum* "carries no special political or legal meaning. It indicates the existence of a separate body without indicating its juridical status."[458]

Despite the acceptance of the partition principle, Zander points out that the whole report of the Peel Commission carefully avoided to devote one single word to the role and presumed inability of the local populations to fulfill their planned tasks, in total disregard of Article 22 of the Covenant of the League of Nations which embodied the principles by which the creation of all mandates were founded and laid down for the sake of "peoples not yet able to stand by themselves under the strenuous conditions of the modern world" and that the purpose of the tutelage was "the well-being and development of such peoples."

Zander also stresses that the Covenant of the League of Nations "did not provide for the creation of mandates for the sake of religions, particularly if the adherents of the religion in question in their overwhelming majority lived outside the territory to be mandated." In the case of Palestine, the aim of a mandate was not to provide the local population with gradual development of self-governing institutions but, on the contrary, the local population had to renounce forever, for the sake of the Holy Places, its "fundamental and inalienable" title to self-government, a "sacred right," as Zander emphasizes, "one of the noblest aims of the Allies in the First World War" to be asserted "for all nations." Additionally, since the population in question had never given any indication that it would be unwilling to administer the Holy Places adequately by itself Zander concludes that "here was a conflict between the right to self-government and a religious interest of the world at large."[459]

It is noteworthy that the twenty-eight Articles of the Terms of the Mandate only mentioned the Holy Places, leaving out Jerusalem. In addition to the Peel Commission Report, various schemes proposed at the end of the League of Nations Mandate to deal with the special issue of the Holy Places included similar proposals for a different status of the city. Therefore, according to this rather new international concept, "the government of Jerusalem ought to be organized — not for the sake of the local inhabitants, but for that of the Holy Places."[460] In this light, the proposals suggested at that time "gave first priority to the territories involved and showed much less concern for the populations living in them."[461]

Contrary to this global/trans-territorial approach, in a memorandum[462] presented to the Royal Partition Commission, the Jewish Agency only recognized the need to place under the administration of the Mandatory Power, the Holy Places, mainly concentrated in the Old City of Jerusalem. Article 4 of the Terms of the Mandate had entrusted the Jewish Agency with the task of representing "the interests of the Jewish population in Palestine,"[463] always subject to the control of the Administration.

The (Peel) Royal Commission's Report was published on July 7, 1937 simultaneously with a statement of policy endorsing the Report published by the Secretary of State for the Colonies. The House of Commons, on July 2, 1937, approved a motion that the partition proposal be brought before the League of Nations "with a view to enabling His Majesty's Government, after adequate inquiry, to present to Parliament a definite scheme."[464]

In the Permanent Mandates' Commission, the British delegate Anthony Eden explained the proposal to retain a mandate over Jerusalem, which was later endorsed by both the Commission and the Council of the League.[465] Article 28 of the Terms of Mandate in Palestine clearly states:

> In the event of the termination of the mandate hereby conferred upon the Mandatory, the Council of the League of Nations shall make such arrangements as may be deemed necessary for safeguarding in perpetuity, under guarantee of the League, the rights secured by Articles 13 and 14.[466]

In the British Government's interpretation, the wish of the League of Nations was that the Holy Places concentrated in the three cities of Jerusalem, Bethlehem, and Nazareth, "should remain permanently under League supervision and control"[467] and "must always be a sacred trust," since this was the intention of the vast majority of states members of the League contemplating the establishment of Jewish and Arab states "in the Holy Land sacred to all three religions."[468]

After considerable delay, in March 1938, the British Government appointed the Woodhead Commission for Palestine Partition that endorsed the Peel Commission's suggestion for a Jerusalem enclave in the form of a permanent British Mandate, in so doing justifying a continued British presence in the area, under the pretext of protecting the Holy Places.

The boundaries of the Jerusalem Mandatory area were nearly identical in both plans, except that the Woodhead Commission's Report published in October 1938,[469] provided for a larger enclave than the one in the Peel Commission.

The 1938 Commission rejected the Jewish proposal that Mount Scopus and the western part of Jerusalem outside the walls be included in the Jewish state with the explanation that both the Muslim and Christian worlds would oppose the inclusion of any part of Jerusalem in a Jewish state and that the division of the city would impose serious although not insurmountable, administrative problems.

3.5.2 The 1939 White Paper, President Truman's policy and the termination of the British Mandate

On May 17, 1939, the British Government published a White Paper,[470] a policy statement on Palestine. Referring to the obligations embodied in Articles 2, 6 and 13 of the Mandate, the Paper stated that no dispute existed on the interpretation of the obligations arising out of Article 13, related to the protection of the Holy Places and religious buildings or sites as well as access to those places. On the other hand, the White Paper included a list of various major points of controversy between the parties. A bitter controversy, in particular, arose between the British and the Permanent Mandates Commission on the interpretation of two other Articles discussed in the White Paper. In the June 1939 session, with regard to Articles 2 and 6 of the Terms of the Mandate, the Commission criticized the British interpretation of the issues discussed in the Paper under the heading: "I. The Constitution", "II. Immigration" and "III. Land".

The Commission unanimously determined that the British Government's interpretation of the Mandate's obligations was "not in accordance with the interpretation which, in agreement with the Mandatory Power and the Council, the Commission had placed upon the Palestine mandate."[471] The Permanent Mandates Commission heavily criticized the restrictions on immigration in view of the organized Nazi persecution in Europe.

Because of the virtual suspension of the League of Nations operations, in September 1939, the League's Council was unable to review the Commission's advisory opinion.[472] As a result, the White Paper influenced the last period of the British Mandatory administration although the legality of its policy was questioned to the point that, when the matter came under discussion in the British Parliament, Winston Churchill labeled the 1939 White Paper's policy as "an act of repudiation (. . .) a plain breach of a solemn obligation."[473]

At the end of World War II, the Allied armies revealed to the world the horrible genocide that had been perpetrated by the Nazi regime, who had murdered 6 million people purely for Jewish affiliation or origin. On June 22, 1945 President Truman entrusted the mission of investigating the situation of the "Displaced Persons in Germany and Austria"[474] to the United States representative on the Intergovernmental Committee on Refugees, Earl G. Harrison.

The Harrison Report to Truman of August 1945 expressed the opinion "on a purely humanitarian basis with no reference to ideological or political considerations so far as Palestine is concerned" that Palestine was the most suitable resort for those refugees "who do not, for good reason, wish to return to their homes." Consequently, it urged that "some reasonable extension or modification of the British White Paper of 1939 ought to be possible without too serious repercussions." According to Hurewitz[475] the Harrison findings and recommendations, immediately endorsed by President Truman, contributed substantially to influence early post-war American public opinion in favor of Zionism.

The Harrison Report is also remarkable in reference to the collective identity of the Jews vis-à-vis the question of the Holy Places. The document stated that "the first and most basic need" of this category of refugees was the recognition of their actual status "as Jews," a definition of identity overlapping their national identity as Polish, German, Austrian or other state origin, whereas the general practice towards the refugees until then had generally followed national lines, with the declared goal to avoid separating "particular racial or religious groups from their nationality categories." Nevertheless, according to the Harrison Report, the Nazis had practiced a policy of racial and religious segregation for so long "that a group has been created which has special needs." Consequently, paradoxically, a refusal to recognize a separate identity for the Jews would have had the effect "of closing one's eyes to their former and more barbaric persecution, which has already made them a separate group with greater needs."[476]

On August 31, 1945, President Truman sent a copy of the Harrison Report to the British Prime Minister, Attlee. On October 19 of the same year, the British Prime Minister proposed the creation of a joint Anglo-American Committee in charge of investigating the issues related to the resettlement of Jewish refugees in Palestine and elsewhere, and to prepare a permanent solution for the Palestine problem to be submitted to the United Nations.

Recommendation Number 3 regarded it essential that "in order to dispose, once and for all, of the exclusive claims of Jews and Arabs to Palestine," the form of government to be established "shall, under international guarantees, fully protect and preserve the interests in the Holy Land of Christendom and of the Muslim and Jewish faiths" alike.[477] Finally, on July 10, 1946, an Anglo-American technical committee worked out the details of the aforementioned Anglo-American Committee's proposals.

In October 1945, immediately following the end of the war, British Prime Minister Attlee obtained from the United Nations the approval of his proposed creation of a joint Anglo-American Committee for the re-settlement of Jewish refugees in Palestine and elsewhere for a permanent solution to the Palestine problem. In its report submitted on April 22, 1946, this Committee suggested that the Mandate should continue, pending the execution of a trusteeship agreement under the United Nations,[478] which on July 25, 1946 resulted in the "the Morrison–Grady Plan," from the names of the chief British and American experts.

This Plan suggested the creation in Palestine of a cantonal state with autonomy for a Jewish and an Arab province. The plan also recommended that the two areas which embodied a separate Jerusalem enclave including "Jerusalem, Bethlehem and their immediate environs,"[479] would be under direct control of the British Central Government. A principal task of this government in the Jerusalem District should be full protection under international guarantees, of the interests of Christendom, Islam, and Judaism at the Holy Places, following the recommendation of the Anglo-American Committee.[480]

While the British Cabinet approved of the Morrison–Grady plan, both the Arab Higher Committee and the Jewish Agency rejected it,[481] each one for different reasons. The Jewish Agency's executive body met in Paris in early August and decided to propose a plan which provided for the partition of Palestine into a Jewish and an Arab state, with Jerusalem as part of the Arab state.[482] United States President Truman, assuming that the Morrison–Grady plan was unworkable, endorsed the Jewish Agency's plan on October 4, 1946.[483]

At this time, the British Government finally realized that the pretext of the preservation of the Holy Places was not sufficient anymore to keep control over any area included in the Palestinian Mandate. Hence, they similarly rejected the plan and, on February 18, 1947, decided to ask the United Nations to formulate a proposal for a resolution.[484] As the sections that follow will show, the various bodies set up to investigate and propose a solution have so far confirmed the idea that the Holy Places of Jerusalem should enjoy international legal protection.

3.5.3 The United Nations Special Committee on Palestine (UNSCOP)

On May 15, 1947, despite Arab opposition, the General Assembly set up an eleven-member committee known as the United Nations Special Committee on Palestine (UNSCOP). This body was appointed with a specific task, "(. . .) to give most careful consideration to the religious interests in Palestine of Islam, Judaism and Christianity."[485] Regarding the legal nature of the UNSCOP mission, Arangio-Ruiz analyzed "the setting up, with the consent of the United Kingdom of the Commission of the United Nations for Palestine and of the provisional government councils of the future States envisaged in the projects of partition of the same territory (. . .)."[486] He wrote that these were the first instances where the "governmental" activity of the United Nations received consent of the state or states exercising their jurisdiction on the area in question.

In fulfilling its mission, UNSCOP heard from several religious authorities of Jerusalem. One of them was the Custos of the Holy Land,[487] the head of the Franciscan Fraternity of the Custodia di Terra Santa under whose care are the Holy Places to which the Latin Catholics have rights. The Custos was concerned that a non-Christian government ruling Palestine might side with a Christian group, Orthodox or Armenian and have a rival claim in the complex balance of rights and interests regulated by the Status Quo, even more than that such a government might encroach upon the Holy Places.

As concerns the United States' position, Slonim has pointed out that the primary concern of this delegation during the General Assembly discussions at Lake Success was neither the partition scheme worked out by UNSCOP calling for the territorial internationalization of Jerusalem, nor "the institution of a territorial regime, as such,"[488] but rather to ensure "adequate safeguards for the holy places." On August 31, 1947, the Special Committee submitted two plans to the General Assembly:

- The majority plan recommended the partition of Palestine into three territorial units within one single economic union: one Jewish state, one Arab state and an international zone, defined as *corpus separatum*, composed of Jerusalem, Bethlehem and their rural suburbs to be under an international trusteeship system.
- The minority plan envisaged an independent federal state composed of a Jewish and an Arab province, with Jerusalem as the federal capital.

According to the majority plan a trusteeship agreement would designate the United Nations as the administering authority.[489] Part III, devoted to the "City of Jerusalem", included a proposal to place the city under international trusteeship. The "Justification" section of "Chapter VI — Recommendations (II)" of Part III included the following considerations:

1. Jerusalem is a Holy City for three faiths. Their shrines are side by side; some are sacred to two faiths. Hundreds of millions of Christians, Moslems and Jews throughout the world want peace, and especially religious peace, to reign in Jerusalem; they want the sacred character of its Holy Places to be preserved and access to them guaranteed to pilgrims from abroad.
2. The history of Jerusalem, during the Ottoman régime as under the Mandate, shows that religious peace has been maintained in the City because the Government was anxious and had the power to prevent controversies involving some religious interests from developing into bitter strife and disorder. The Government was not intimately involved in local politics, and could, when necessary, arbitrate conflicts.
3. Religious peace in Jerusalem is necessary for the maintenance of peace in the Arab and in the Jewish States. Disturbances in the Holy City would have far-reaching consequences, extending perhaps beyond the frontiers of Palestine.
4. The application of the provisions relating to the Holy Places, religious buildings and sites in the whole of Palestine would also be greatly facilitated by the setting up of an international authority in Jerusalem. The Governor of the City would be empowered to supervise the application of such provisions and to arbitrate conflicts in respect of the Holy Places, religious buildings and sites. The International Trusteeship System is proposed as the most suitable instrument for meeting the special problems presented by Jerusalem, for the reason that the Trusteeship Council, as a principal organ of the United Nations, affords a convenient and effective means of ensuring both the desired international supervision and the political, economic and social well-being of the population of Jerusalem.[490]

According to the majority plan's "Recommendations", the Governor of the City of Jerusalem appointed by the Trusteeship Council had to be "neither Arab nor Jew nor a citizen of the Palestine States nor, at the time of appointment, a resident of the City of Jerusalem." Moreover, the Governor had to determine whether the provisions of the constitution of the Arab and Jewish states in Palestine dealing with "the Holy Places, religious buildings and sites in any part of Palestine other than the City of Jerusalem," and the religious rights appertaining thereto, were properly applied and respected.

The protection of all such places, buildings and sites located in the city of Jerusalem was also to be the Governor's specific concern. In particular, he could make "decisions on the basis of existing rights in cases of disputes which may arise between the different communities in respect of such Holy Places, religious buildings and sites in any part of Palestine."[491] Moreover, the protection of such places would be entrusted to a special police force, whose members would be recruited outside Palestine, for that reason excluding local Arabs or Jews.

In accordance with this plan, the Governor appointed by the Trusteeship Council and aided by a legislative council, elected on the basis of universal and secret suffrage, was to administer the demilitarized and neutralized City; and in the Jerusalem area all people would enjoy freedom of access and worship. Additionally, the City residents could opt between retaining their Jerusalem citizenship and acquiring that of the Jewish or Arab state. In Arangio-Ruiz's opinion, the United Nations organ would have to exercise in the city operative, internal and external activities of state's nature, or "vicarious State activities."[492]

According to some statistics, Jerusalem had been comprised of a Jewish majority since 1860, and by 1947 its Jewish population numbered 100,000, as against a combined Moslem-Christian population of 65,000.[493] The minority plan, which envisaged an independent federal state, composed of a Jewish and an Arab province, with Jerusalem as the federal capital, would include the creation of a permanent international body to supervise and protect the Holy Places.

Both the majority and the minority plans embodied without any objection the principles of free access to the sanctuaries, freedom of worship and the preservation of the Holy Places, in accordance with all committees and commissions which have been dealing with the Holy Places. According to Zander,[494] these principles can, indeed, be considered essential for the continued existence and satisfactory functioning of the Holy Places.

The Jewish Agency's representative accepted the majority plan only on condition that "modern Jerusalem", that is the western part of the city outside the walls, be included in the Jewish state,[495] whereas the representative of the Arab Higher Committee rejected both UNSCOP plans on the ground that they failed to establish an independent Arab state in the whole Palestine.[496] The Arab representative added the observance of "human rights, fundamental freedoms and equality of all persons before the law as well as the protection of the legitimate rights and interests of all minorities" and "freedom of worship and access to the Holy Places" guaranteed to all[497] the principles guiding the future constitutional organization of this state.

A subcommittee recommended the majority plan to the Ad Hoc Committee, which made slight changes to the boundaries of the Arab and Jewish states. But, instead of the proposed international trusteeship agreement, the international zone was now to be placed under "a special international regime" related to the Trusteeship Council; and, under the name of "the City of Jerusalem," it was to be a *corpus separatum*, have a statute detailed and approved by the Trusteeship Council and a governor appointed by and responsible to the Trusteeship Council who would control freedom of entry and residence within the city for nationals of other states, under the direction of the Council.

In addition to the majority plan, a second report prepared by a Subcommittee composed of Iraq, Saudi Arabia and Syria, was submitted to the Ad Hoc Committee on November 19, 1947, whose recommendation was the formation of a unitary Palestinian state and a constituent assembly, which would draw a constitution guaranteeing the Holy Places' inviolability, maintenance, freedom of access and worship in accordance with the Status Quo of 1852.

3.5.4 The Partition Resolution's special regime for Jerusalem and the status of the General Consuls in the city

On November 29, 1947, the General Assembly finally adopted the "Partition Resolution" 181, II. UN General Assembly Resolution 181 (II) of 29 November 1947 was composed of the following four parts: Part I, "Future Constitution and Government of Palestine;" Part II, "Boundaries;" Part III, "City of Jerusalem;" Part IV, "Capitulations."[498]

The United Nations' body opted for the UNSCOP majority plan, adopted by the Ad Hoc Committee on November 25, 1947, and modified by a Swedish amendment meant to give permanency to the regime envisaged for the City of Jerusalem,[499] by allowing, ten years later, the inhabitants to re-examine the City's Statute through a referendum about possible modifications but no interruption, as provided for in the previous majority plan.

The results of the referendum, in any case, would be merely advisory; the will of the majority was not to bind to the United Nations' organs.[500] A "special international regime" for Jerusalem was to be set up, according to Article 1 of the Resolution, Part III, specifically devoted to Jerusalem. The envisaged "Administering Authority in discharging its administrative obligations shall":

> (b) (. . .) protect and to preserve the unique spiritual and religious interests located in the city of the three great monotheistic faiths throughout the world, Christian, Jewish and Moslem; to this end to ensure that order and peace, and especially religious peace reigns in Jerusalem.
> (c) (. . .) Promote the security, well-being and any constructive measures of development of the residents, having regard to the special circumstances and customs[501] of the various peoples and communities.

Although never implemented, both the General Assembly Resolution 181 and the Mandate entrusted to Great Britain by the League of Nations, found their inspiration in values which represented the views of a vast number of states at that time. The interested parties, in particular the parties involved in the Middle East peace process, never denied the existence and validity of such values and principles specifically related to the Holy Places and the recognized communities of Jerusalem. According to Zander, the Trusteeship Council incorporated "the generally accepted 'essentials' (free access, free exercise of worship and preservation of the Holy Places"), adding moreover freedom from taxation.[502]

Hirsch, Housen-Couriel and Lapidoth maintain that it was the sacred character of Jerusalem and its Holy Places[503] that inspire the idea, embodied in the 1947 General Assembly resolution, that the city should become a separate entity under the United Nations administration. As to the preservation of the *status quo* both in its broad and narrow sense, the same authors maintain that:

> In practice, Israel acts according to several principles:
> 1. Israel protects all the Holy Places against desecration and damage, and ensures free access and worship, subject to the safeguarding of public order. (. . .).
> 2. The courts have no jurisdiction to deal with disputes relating to rights at the Holy Places (such as questions of ownership and possession).[504] (. . .)
> 3. Although Israel has not undertaken by any express legislation to uphold the status quo, in practice the latter is normally preserved. The authorities ensure that there are no deviations from arrangements and accepted usages, subject, however, to changes that were introduced in order to enable Jews to reach and pray at their Holy Places. (. . .)
> 4. Administration of each Holy Place is entrusted to the religious community for which it is sacred.
> 5. The Holy Places enjoy certain fiscal privileges.[505]

On December 1, 1947, after the approval of the Partition Plan by the General Assembly, United Nations Secretary General Trygve Lie forwarded a copy of the resolution to the Trusteeship Council. Lie called attention to the Council's responsibility to elaborate a statute for the City of Jerusalem.

The following day, the Trusteeship Council appointed a Working Committee, whose members discussed the problems related to the City's Statute, particularly the composition of the legislative council, but no agreement was ever reached on whether this body should be composed of ethnic representatives (Arab, Jewish, or other) or religious ones (Muslim, Jewish or Christian). The Trusteeship Council was only able to come up with a complex compromise proposed by Benjamin Gerig, the Working Committee's United States elected Chairman.[506]

Part IV of the General Assembly Resolution 181, II, followed the suggestions of both UNSCOP plans also in relation to the Consuls' special status in Jerusalem. UNSCOP plans differed in many ways from the Terms of the British Mandate, whose Article 8 reads as follows:

> The privileges and immunities of foreigners, including the benefits of consular jurisdiction and protection as formerly enjoyed by Capitulation or usage in the Ottoman Empire, shall not be applicable in Palestine.
>
> Unless the Powers whose nationals enjoyed the aforementioned privileges and immunities on August 1st, 1914, shall have previously renounced the right to their re-establishment, or shall have agreed to their non-application for a specified period, these privileges and immunities shall, at the expiration of the mandate, be immediately re-established in their entirety or with such modifications as may have been agreed upon between the Powers concerned.[507]

Conversely, Resolution 181 requested that the "States whose nationals have in the past enjoyed in Palestine the privileges and immunities of foreigners, including the benefits of consular jurisdiction and protection, as formerly enjoyed by capitulation or usage in the Ottoman Empire," renounce any right pertaining to them. The aforementioned provision explicitly referred to the establishment of "the proposed Arab and Jewish states and the City of Jerusalem."

Therefore it made an indirect connection between the consuls' renunciation to their traditional privileges and the full implementation of the same resolution. On this issue, some authors have maintained that the status of Jerusalem would still be subject to the resolution of the United Nations General Assembly of 1947.[508] The Consular Corp in Jerusalem, composed of the General Consulates of 9 states plus the Holy See through an Apostolic Delegate, did not recognize the *de facto* situation that had been established in the city after the 1948 War. These countries, referring to the United Nations General Assembly Resolution of November 29, 1947, and contrary to diplomatic practice, have so far preferred to establish their embassies in cities (generally Tel Aviv) other than Jerusalem, which is the official capital of the State of Israel.

Moreover, their Consuls in Jerusalem have refused to request the traditional *exequatur* (permission to perform their functions in the city) to the host state, Israel or Jordan,[509] according to Consulate's location in the Jerusalem area. Spain, France, Greece, Italy, the United Kingdom, Sweden, Turkey and the Holy See have also decided to establish an additional office with an autonomous Secretariat in "East Jerusalem."

The protocol rules of the Consular Corp in Jerusalem which were established on December 8, 1947, days after the adoption of the aforementioned resolution of the General Assembly, were confirmed after the Armistice Agreements were signed on June 15, 1949, first modified on December 22, 1950, subsequently on December 8, 1960 and January 24, 1961. The regulations were reprinted in the Yearly Book of Consular Corp up to February 1977, and from then on they were only kept in the archives of the various consulates.[510]

4 | The Status Quo/Modus Vivendi of the Holy Places in the Arab–Israeli Conflict

4.1 The Jordanian–Israeli Armistice Agreement of April 3, 1949

4.1.1 The partition of Jerusalem between Israel and Jordan

After the adoption of the General Assembly Resolution of November 29, 1947, a civil war broke out in the Palestinian Mandate, which was particularly severe in the Jerusalem area. On May 14, 1948, when the British Mandate over Palestine officially drew to a close, representatives of the Jewish community in Palestine proclaimed the Declaration on the Establishment of the State of Israel.[511] Immediately after these events, the armed forces of Egypt, Jordan, Syria, Iraq and Lebanon (Saudi Arabia sent only token troops) joined the Palestinian Arabs in the fight against the *Yishuv*, the local Jewish community, now organized in the newly proclaimed State of Israel. Klein has pointed out that the Jordanian King Abdullah, in ordering the Arab Legion to conquer the Old City including its Jewish Quarter, on May 19, 1948, "acted against the military advice of John Glubb, British commander of his army, and of Kirkbride, the senior British representative in Jordan."[512]

On May 26 of the same year, the Security Council adopted a resolution ordering a four-week truce, which began on June 11. The resolution included one paragraph on the Jerusalem issue, which urged all concerned parties to be aware of the importance of "the protection of the Holy Places of the City of Jerusalem, including access to all shrines and sanctuaries for the purpose of worship by those who have an established right to visit and worship at them."[513] The request to add the clause on the access came from the Israeli representative.[514]

After the cease-fire, Jerusalem was divided along military lines between the two conflicting parties, and an exchange of Jewish and Arab populations in the two sections of the city followed national-ethnic affiliation. This division was later formalized in the Israeli–Jordanian Armistice of April 3, 1949, which remained in force until the Six Day War of 1967.

On July 25, 1948, the Israeli Provisional Government Cabinet decided to extend Israeli authority to the Western sector of Jerusalem by issuing the *Area of Jurisdiction and Powers Ordinance*.[515] This decree stated that the law in force in the State of Israel should be applied to any part of the former Palestinian Mandate that the Minister of

Defense may establish, by regulation, to be under the Israeli Army occupation. Israeli Defense Minister David Ben-Gurion enacted the proclamations a few days later, on August 2, 1948, retroactive to May 15. Proclamation # 1 stated that Israel Defense Force had the duty to maintain in the occupied [administered] area of Jerusalem "public safety and security and to preserve law and order," and Israeli law had to apply to this area, which included "most of the area of Jerusalem, part of its environs and western approaches as well as roads linking Jerusalem to the coastal plain."[516]

In accordance with Proclamation # 2, a "military commander"[517] was appointed for the occupied [administered] area of Jerusalem, who, on the same day, issued an Order, also retroactive to May 15, according to which (Section 2): "The Law of the State of Israel (. . .) shall apply in the occupied area."[518]

The General Assembly, for its part, adopted Resolution 194 (III) of December 11, 1948, where it:

> 7. *Resolves* that the Holy Places — including Nazareth — religious buildings and sites in Palestine should be protected and free access to them assured, in accordance with existing rights and historical practice; that arrangements to this end should be under effective United Nations supervision; that the United Nations Conciliation Commission, in presenting to the fourth regular session of the General Assembly its detailed proposals for a permanent international regime for the territory of Jerusalem, should include recommendations concerning the Holy Places in that territory; that with regard to the Holy Places in the rest of Palestine the Commission should call upon the political authorities of the areas concerned to give appropriate formal guarantees as to the protection of the Holy Places and access to them; and that these undertakings should be presented to the General Assembly for approval;
>
> 8. *Resolves* that, in view of its association with three world religions, the Jerusalem area, including the present municipality of Jerusalem plus the surrounding villages . . . should be accorded special and separate treatment from the rest of Palestine and should be placed under effective United Nations control (. . .)
>
> (. . .) *Instructs* the Conciliation Commission to present to the fourth regular session of the General Assembly detailed proposals for a permanent international regime for the Jerusalem area which will provide for the maximum local autonomy for distinctive groups consistent with the special international status of the Jerusalem area.[519]

Contrary to the "proposals for a permanent international regime for the territory of Jerusalem" proclaimed by Resolution 194, the Israel–Jordan Armistice Agreement of April 3, 1949 had frozen the *de facto* division of the city between the two countries, with sealed borders.[520] The Armistice's goal was to implement "effectively the terms of the truce imposed in Palestine by the Security Council Resolution of July 15, 1948."[521] The Agreement followed the lines of the truce that the two Jerusalem area's Lt. Colonels, Abdullah al-Tel (representing the Arab Legion and all other Arab forces) and Moshe Dayan (representing the Israeli Forces), had agreed upon on November 30, 1948.

Before the Armistice had entered into force, the new Israeli government had declared on January 30, 1949 that the western part of Jerusalem should no longer be considered as occupied territory. In accordance with the previously mentioned Israeli Government decisions, Minister of Defense David Ben-Gurion issued a proclamation which abolished the military government[522] and on February 14, 1949, Israel's Constitutional Assembly meeting in Jerusalem elected Chaim Weizmann as the first

President of the State. The seat of the Parliament was then transferred to Tel Aviv, until December 16, 1949.

While confirming the borders established by the truce with Israel on March 16, 1949, the Jordanian government replaced military rule with civil administration in the eastern section of the city.[523] According to Article VIII of the Armistice Agreement, a special committee, to be established by the parties, would examine the parties' plans and arrangements agreed upon, including matters on which an agreement in principle already existed, such as:

> Free movement of traffic on vital roads, including the Bethlehem and Latrun-Jerusalem roads; resumption of the normal functioning of the cultural and humanitarian institutions on Mount Scopus and free access thereto; free access to the Holy Places and cultural institutions and use of the cemetery on the Mount of Olives.[524]

In addition to Jerusalem, the Armistice Agreement partitioned the rest of the Mandatory territory along the lines of the cease-fire agreed upon by the two parties upon the suspension of hostilities. Jordan kept control of the West Bank of the Jordan River, including Bethlehem. Egypt, in accordance with a separate Armistice Agreement with Israel, continued to occupy the region of Gaza while the remaining areas of Palestine constituted the newborn State of Israel.

Two days after the United Nations General Assembly Resolution of December 9, 1949, calling again for 'territorial internationalization' of the Jerusalem area,[525] the Israeli Prime Minister announced to the Israeli Parliament that "Jerusalem is an inseparable part of the State of Israel and her eternal capital,"[526] and the Parliament approved this position. However, Ben-Gurion confirmed in the same speech that Israeli's undertaking to preserve the rights mentioned in the previous declaration "remains in force"[527] and his proposal to move the seat of the Knesset from Tel Aviv to Jerusalem was approved. Moreover, the Israeli Prime Minister made clear in his speech that "in all these arrangements there is, of course, nothing that alters in the slightest degree any of the existing rights in the Holy Places, which the Government of Israel will respect in full, or our consent to effective supervision of these Holy Places by the United Nations, as our delegation to the General Assembly declared."[528]

On December 15, 1949, the Prime Minister's Office was moved to Jerusalem and the Knesset held its first session in the city next day. Simultaneously, Ben-Gurion decided to transfer all the government offices to Jerusalem by January 1, 1950, with the exception of the Ministries of Defense and Police, and the Foreign Ministry.[529] Moreover, on January 23, 1950, the Knesset adopted a resolution whose preamble declared that "on the establishment of the State of Israel, Jerusalem once again became its capital."[530]

On January 4, 1950 the General Zionist and Herut Parties had proposed a Knesset legislation declaring Jerusalem the capital of Israel.[531] Ben-Gurion opposed this legislative act on the grounds that a law having prospective effect was unnecessary and might have deleterious consequences since King David had made Jerusalem the capital city.

Therefore, he succeeded in convincing the Knesset to adopt his resolution which proclaimed that Jerusalem had been the capital of Israel since time immemorial.[532] This decision, together with other administrative steps, placed West Jerusalem's status in Israel at a higher level than East Jerusalem's in Jordan, "although the center of Israeli economical, cultural and social life, the political parties, trade unions and main newspapers were all in Tel Aviv."[533]

4.1.2 Israeli position on the protection of the Holy Places

Although the Declaration on the Establishment of the State of Israel of May 14, 1948 does not mention Jerusalem, it states that Israel "will guarantee freedom of religion and conscience, of language, education and culture," and "will safeguard the Holy Places of all religions."[534] The Declaration is neither a constitution nor a statute but the Israeli Supreme Court refers to it in its interpretation or clarification of Israeli legislation.[535] Moreover, in two Basic Laws adopted in 1992, the Israeli Parliament has included a provision devoted to "Freedom of Occupation" and "Human Dignity and Liberty," respectively, thereby strengthening the legal position of the Declaration. Section 1, common to both Basic Laws, reads:

> Fundamental human rights in Israel are founded upon recognition of the value of the human being, the sanctity of human life, and the principle that all persons are free; these rights shall be upheld in the spirit of the principles set forth in the Declaration on the Establishment of the State of Israel.[536]

According to Bovis, the "ultraorthodox Jews,"[537] who viewed "the restoration of Israel as the proper work of the Messiah and human activity to that end as impious,"[538] declared their preference for the internationalization of Jerusalem rather than supporting the state proclaimed in Tel Aviv.

The view that Jerusalem was a universal religious symbol of identity was contested through a memorandum submitted to Foreign Minister Shertok on July 22, 1948 by Israeli liaison official to the United Nations, Leo Kohn, who urged Israel to propose "a new scheme for the partition of Jerusalem [with Jordan],"[539] and expressed fears that, with the proposed international regime, "a combination of anti-Jewish and anti-Zionist forces: the Anglican Bishop, the Papal Nuncio, Rabbi Dushinsky and Dr. Magnes" would govern Jerusalem, thus the city would be "consciously or subconsciously abandoned by many Jews in the Jewish State," since "the best of our people" would not accept living "under such a Vatican City."

The Israeli official instead suggested the renewal of the proposal made to the Woodhead Commission in 1938, according to which the New City of Jerusalem would be included in the Jewish state and connected to such state by a tenable and defensible corridor. Kohn advised that "the Old City plus some Arab Quarters outside the Walls, but minus the Jewish Quarter in the Old City, should go to the Arab state." He wrote that under such conditions "Jewish Jerusalem" would become the capital of the Jewish state, in so doing securing "that historical background which it badly needs both for itself and to impress the whole Jewish people and the world at large, as historical successor of the ancient Jewish state."

In a cable sent to the Israeli representative in Paris on July 30, 1948, Foreign Minister Shertok gave his interpretation of the proclamation of July 25, 1948 which extended the Provisional Government's authority and the application of Israeli law to the areas of Jerusalem under Israeli control. He believed that such measures would neither prejudice Israel's attitude towards the proposed international regime nor the future status of Jerusalem and that the exclusive goal was to regularize on a proper legal basis all financial transactions and administrative arrangements as well as the responsibility for maintenance of law and order.[540]

On May 5, 1949, during the deliberations concerning the admission of Israel to the United Nations, the Israeli representative to the United Nations *Ad Hoc* Political Committee, Abba Eban expressed the official views of the Government of Israel on the Jerusalem issues.[541] Eban began his speech by conveying his reservations about the procedure of the invitation. This procedure would force candidates to membership within the terms of Article 4 of the Charter to present their views on international problems in the course of discussing admission to membership. The Israeli representative claimed that this would create a new precedent for all future candidates.

Nevertheless, Eban did elaborate on the two main issues on the agenda: Jerusalem and the refugees. He stated that the Jews had kept Christian interests alive thereby avoiding the capture of Jerusalem by the combined Arab forces, which would have immediately and irrevocably incorporated Jerusalem within an Arab state and explicitly asserted Arab "complete sovereignty"[542] over the whole city, including its Holy Places. In so doing, Christian interests were accorded the possibility of receiving formal legal expression in Jerusalem. According to Eban, the sole motive for transferring personnel of non-political departments to Jerusalem had been to prevent Jerusalem from becoming the center of "rebellious and dissident elements" and that no legal effect resulted from such administrative and legal steps strictly dictated by necessity.

Hence, any statement claiming that the New City of Jerusalem had been proclaimed as part of the State of Israel was false and malicious. According to the Government of Israel, the juridical status of the city was to be determined by international consent, through an actual decision made by the United Nations General Assembly. Nevertheless, in Eban's opinion, the "international principle" ought to have been expressed more realistically, that is, the international regime should not apply to the entire city but to that part which contained the largest number of religious and historic shrines; alternatively, an international regime could have applied to the whole city of Jerusalem but its functions had to be restricted to dealing with the protection of the Holy Places and not with any purely secular aspects of government.

In line with this proposal, Eban pointed out that on April 23, 1949 Israeli President had already outlined Israel's "official policy". He said that the Government "pledged itself to ensure full security for religious institutions in the exercise of their functions; to grant the supervision of the Holy Places by those who hold them sacred; and to encourage and accept the fullest international safeguards and controls for their immunity and protection." He stated that, if the United Nations could secure such a "far-reaching commitment" from the Government of Transjordan and then establish in Jerusalem an international regime confining its jurisdiction to the Holy Places, then "the problem of Jerusalem could be successfully solved." He reiterated that the two main interests at stake were the universal interests in the Holy Places on the one hand and the welfare and national sentiments of the people of Jerusalem on the other.

He further added, that the United Nations would, in consequence, express the will of the "entire civilized world" by insisting that the Holy Places be protected and free access to them be assured for all religions as well as for all inhabitants of Jerusalem. The Government of Israel would, then, co-operate with any United Nations' international regime for Jerusalem which would exclusively be concerned with the control and protection of the Holy Places in Palestine, both within and outside of Jerusalem.

The Israeli President declared that the Israeli Government was ready to offer all religious authorities concerned the fullest safeguards and guarantees for the exercise of their functions, should they have come up in the negotiations then in progress with the Papal Envoy to Jerusalem, or with the Government of France. In his viewpoint, integration into the life of the state of the part of Jerusalem controlled by Israel filled the vacuum of authority created by the termination of the Mandate and the refusal of the United Nations to assume a direct administrative responsibility for the city. From the Israeli viewpoint, integration paralleled a similar process in the Arab area and was still compatible with the establishment of an international regime to govern the Holy Places. According to this claim, also indirectly supported by the Israeli Draft Resolution submitted to the General Assembly on November 25, 1949,[543] ongoing negotiations with Jordan would not affect the juridical status of Jerusalem to be defined by international consent.

The Conciliation Commission for Palestine was set up according to the provisions of the General Assembly Resolution 194 (III) of December 11, 1948 and submitted its Draft Instrument on Jerusalem on September 1, 1949.[544] On November 15 of the same year, the Israeli Delegation to the United Nations submitted to the General Assembly an analysis of the Palestine Conciliation Commission's Draft Instrument, under the title "Memorandum on the Future of Jerusalem."[545] In its preamble, the Israeli Memorandum stated that the United Nations possessed a special and widely recognized interest in Jerusalem and stressed the fact that Articles 15–20 of the Palestine Conciliation Commission's Draft Instrument, devoted to the Holy Places, religious buildings and sites located in the city, were completely self-sufficient and independent of any other provision of the Instrument and no administrative or judicial "intrusion" in the secular life of Jerusalem was necessary to exercise the United Nations' responsibility for the safeguarding of Holy Places, as the new Israeli proposals could show, including the Draft Resolution submitted by the Israeli delegation to the General Assembly a few days after the Memorandum, on November 25, 1949.[546]

Accordingly, a United Nations representative and not a Commissioner endowed with executive powers, was to supervise the responsibilities of the United Nations in that area, under the legal form of an international agreement. The Memorandum also stressed the fact that it was an Arab country, the Hashemite Kingdom of Jordan, that currently controlled "all places defined as Holy Places under the *status quo* and confirmed as such by an Ordinance[547] of the Mandatory Government," which included "the Holy Sepulchre, the Church of the Nativity, the Garden of Gethsemane, the Mount of Olives, the Grotto, the Shepherd's Fields, the Wailing Wall, Rachel's Tomb, the Haram el Sharif, and the Mosque of Al Aqsa." With regard to the places of religious interest under Israeli control, the Government of Israel expressed its intention to propose "agreements bringing them under direct United Nations supervision."

Only in the Old City could the Israeli Government accept that "religious interests predominate so irresistibly over modern political and secular realities as to justify an attempt at direct United Nations control" since the Old City "with its Holy Places, churches, synagogues, patriarchates and monasteries, with its historic streets such as the Via Dolorosa and the sites of the Stations of the Cross," was "saturated with sacred memories," indeed "a concentration of Holy Places and religious institutions and not an area of developed modern life," which did not possess the physical conditions for healthy prosperous developments. Hence, the Israeli Memorandum's suggestion of "its complete transformation into a center of devotion and pilgrimage" that would conform to its unique historic association.

The Memorandum stated that the international interest arising out of the existence of Holy Places and sites justified the United Nations' specific attention to the problems and future of this area, stressing that for "the first time in the history," a government in control of part of Jerusalem was willing to commit itself, by international agreement, to accept the principle of international supervision of Holy Places. The Memorandum remarked that this decision was motivated "out of reverent concern for the universal religious sentiment to which the General Assembly" had given "such moving expression," the moment this issue had been considered by the United Nations. The Old City's religious associations and the presence of Holy Places and religious buildings within the City had motivated such a proposal for "special treatment for Jerusalem".

These were the declared purposes of the Resolution adopted on November 29, 1947 and the political arrangements embodied therein "were merely elaborate means to achieve that end." Similarly, Resolution 194 (III) adopted on December 11, 1948, called for "separate treatment" and "effective United Nations control" of Jerusalem, specifically "with a view to its religious associations." Also, the Pope's Encyclical *In Multiplicibus Curis* stated that "a juridical status for Jerusalem should *assure the safety of the Holy Places and sites.*" This universally accepted purpose shared by the religious authorities' proposals sanctioned the United Nations to act in the area and the goal at which any particular political and administrative scheme proposed for Jerusalem should have aimed was assuring effective measures for the protection of Holy Places and religious rights.

The Israeli Memorandum cited the requests made on July 15, 1947 to the United Nations Special Committee on Palestine by the Custos of the Holy Land Brother Bonaventura, which focused on the international guarantee of religious immunities without suggesting any particular political status for the City.[548] The legal reasoning included in this Memorandum was expressed in a legal opinion conveyed a few days later, on November 4, 1949, to the British United Nations delegation by its Israeli counterpart, and provided an answer to the question: "What legal authority does the United Nations possess with respect to Jerusalem?"[549]

According to Slonim, the legal opinion was not intended to go against "the international community,"[550] but rather to enhance diplomatic support for Israel's "proposal for the institution of functional internationalization"[551] for the City's holy sites. This could be the reason why the Israeli document did not make any reference to the remarks made on March 19, 1948 by the United States Ambassador Warren Austin regarding the United Nations' inaction on May 15, 1948, which resulted in the loss of any "administrative and governmental responsibilities for Palestine."[552] According to the Israeli interpretation, the United Nations' interest was focused on the Holy Sites, but not on any secular territorial future.

The Israeli Government was "conscious of the universal associations of Jerusalem and of the reverence in which its shrines and sanctuaries are held by devout opinion throughout the world." As a result, the legal opinion proposed to conclude agreements with the United Nations "for the safety and immunity of Jerusalem's Holy Places" and to "embody international guarantees" in such agreements which would ensure "that sanctuaries be respected with local reverence and be continuously and unconditionally accessible not only to local inhabitants but also to Christians of the entire world."

The quotation above included in the Israeli legal opinion was taken from a letter sent to the United Nations Secretary General by the Director of the Catholic Near East Welfare Association in the United States, Msgr. Thomas G. McMahon. According to the same Israeli document, the ecclesiastical representative expressed "Catholic aspirations exclusively in terms of religious guarantees without mentioning any particular political status for Jerusalem as indispensable to the satisfaction of those needs."[553]

4.1.3 The Israeli Draft Resolution on Jerusalem submitted to the General Assembly on November 25, 1949

In order to clarify in what way the United Nations would protect this "special and widely recognized interest" in Jerusalem, on November 25, 1949, the Israeli delegation submitted the aforementioned Draft Resolution to the United Nations General Assembly[554] through its Foreign Minister Moshe Sharett. Sharett stated that "the Holy City was an object of interest to the entire civilized world", but such universal veneration should not overshadow the national interests of the peoples concerned. Interestingly enough, he also stated that the "contrast between national and international psychology in regard to Jerusalem was undeniable."[555] Sharett challenged the assumption that charging the churches and religious institutions centered on Jerusalem "with responsibility for permanently interfering with the normal course of secular life" and the "sovereign" full self-direction of Israel and its population was in their long-term interest, so as to satisfy their deep religious sentiments.

Sharett stated that his Government accepted "the sanctity of the religious associations" in Jerusalem and was ready to guarantee its full respect as well as freedom of worship, pilgrimage and safety of access to all Holy Places and shrines. Furthermore, the observance of religious customs and rites were among the fundamental principles of the Declaration on the Establishment of Israel.[556]

Prepared to undertake special responsibility for the safety and inviolability of the Holy Places, the Israeli Government accepted the supervisory authority of the United Nations. Indeed, the shrines of other religions in Jerusalem "held sacred by millions in countries near and far" imposed "obligations on its inhabitants and responsibility on their Government." This explained why the Israeli Government had accepted the principle of international concern with regard to the Holy Places. In Sharett's viewpoint, this principle was "expressed through the instrumentality of the United Nations" and the proposed creation of a "functional" international regime, concerning "the supervision of the Holy Places and the enforcement, through the appropriate authorities, of measures necessary for their protection and accessibility."

Moreover, Sharett stated that the Israeli Government could accept the idea "of supplementing the exercise of such functional authority by the United Nations throughout the area of Jerusalem with the complete internationalization of the Old City." This arrangement would become effective through an agreement solemnly concluded "by virtue of a special resolution of the General Assembly, between the United Nations and the Government of Israel, providing for the obligations of that Government and for the prerogatives of the United Nations in that regard." The agreement could be made without derogating "from the authority of the General Assembly, which remained supreme," on the assumption that "an obligation was more morally binding if contracted by virtue of an agreement freely entered into, rather than if formally imposed by a superior authority."

The "unique character of the Walled City should be kept in mind as a subject calling for special treatment," pending far-reaching reforms. As an example of such reforms, Sharett mentioned the possibility that the Arab inhabitants of the Walled City would willingly move "out of the congested quarters and settle in the free space outside the walls," induced by the offer of better housing facilities, with the result that "the Walled City could be converted into a site containing only Holy Places and religious foundations, consecrated to religious worship and pilgrimage by members of all faiths, under the aegis of the United Nations."

In the meantime, the Palestine Conciliation Commission had forwarded a draft instrument for a permanent international regime for the Jerusalem area,[557] to the Secretary General for submission to the General Assembly. Among other provisions, the plan prescribed a system of international courts to deal with questions involving the Holy Places and legal conflicts arising from the two zones of Jerusalem, occupied by Israel and Jordan. The United Nations Commissioner would be in charge of the protection of the Holy Places, both in Jerusalem and in the other areas belonging to the former Palestine's British Mandate.

On December 5, 1949, Israel's Prime Minister Ben-Gurion reiterated the Israeli commitment to the principles presented at the first Israeli Knesset convened in Tel Aviv, which had unanimously endorsed his declarations[558] and reemphasized the undertakings declared "before history and before the world" in the quoted Declaration on the Establishment of the State of Israel:

> (. . .) The State of Israel will guarantee freedom of religion, conscience, language, education and culture, will protect the Holy Places of all religions, and will be faithful to the principles of the Charter of the United Nations.

Accordingly, Israel undertook "to respect all existing rights regarding the Holy Places and religious buildings in Jerusalem," promising "freedom of worship and free access without discrimination to all the Holy Places and religious buildings under its control," recognizing "the right of pilgrims of all nations and religions to visit the Holy Places in the State, as well as freedom of movement to religious priests." Furthermore, Israel agreed that "there should be established on 'the part of the United Nations, adequate supervision of the Holy Places and of these existing rights in accordance with an agreement which should be reached between the United Nations and Israel.'"[559]

At the same time, the Israeli Prime Minister declared that the decision included in the General Assembly Resolution of November 29, 1947 to detach "Jewish Jerusalem" from the rest of the Jewish state, became "null and void" due to United Nations inaction. He repeated the statement quoted above, according to which it was "the first time in the history of this land that the State governing in Jerusalem has voluntarily accepted the principle of international supervision of the Holy Places in the city." According to Ben-Gurion, it was "no coincidence that this has been done by the very people which made Jerusalem a religious center for the world."

On February 20, 1950 the Israeli representative at the United Nations, Abba Eban, reaffirmed that "the sole abiding objective of the United Nations" in the destiny of Jerusalem was "the protection of the Holy Places and sites by the direct exercise of United Nations responsibility"[560] and that any particular statute or regime aimed at fulfilling that paramount end, for this reason, "is only a means," susceptible to change, "while the end remains inviolate." Accordingly, "the means envisaged in 1947 or 1948 for protecting the Holy Places may be replaced or adapted without the least betrayal of the end." As to the Israeli part of Jerusalem, "the fact that scarcely a brick or a house or a street" therein even existed eighty years earlier "makes it difficult to contend that the area is of such venerable significance that it must become an international trust."

Regarding the Holy Places, Eban affirmed that his Government was "prepared to explore with the [Trusteeship] Council and with other parties concerned any avenue which may lead to the effective fulfillment by the United Nations of its responsibility for the Holy Places" regardless of whether the United Nations preferred to see such an arrangement "embodied in statutory rather than in contractual terms."

In the latter event, the Israeli Government "would be prepared to consult on the form which might be given to a Statute for the Holy Places." Moreover, Abba Eban reaffirmed his government's readiness, "apart from arrangements for the Holy Places, to make binding declarations or agreements with the United Nations assuring religious freedom and full liberty for the pursuit of religious education and protection of religious institutions."[561] The Israeli Government later reconfirmed its position in a memorandum submitted to the United Nations Trusteeship Council on May 26, 1950.

4.1.4 The position of the United States on the partition of the city

On August 4, 1948, the United States Consul General in Jerusalem John D. MacDonald stressed the importance of making an effort "towards maintaining the *status quo*, pending the final political settlement,"[562] which included the possibility of dividing the city along the present cease-fire boundaries. Once more, the United States formally confirmed its approval of the 1947 Partition Resolution's proposal for Jerusalem. Nevertheless, according to United States Secretary of State Marshall, "any other arrangement satisfactory to both Jews and Arabs" would be acceptable to the United States' administration, "provided guarantees were given for access to and safety of holy places."[563]

On September 16, 1948, the United Nations Mediator Count Bernadotte, in the concluding section of his second progress report, recommended that the Jerusalem area be demilitarized and internationalized. Additionally, he suggested that the area be "placed under effective United Nations control with maximum feasible local autonomy for the Arab and Jewish communities, with full safeguards for the protection of the Holy Places and sites and free access to them, and for religious freedom."[564] This included the right of unimpeded access thereto. On October 16, 1948, the Head of the United States delegation Warren Austin sent an urgent cable to Washington through which he interpreted the Bernadotte proposal as excluding any "integral annexation" and as meaning "maximum local autonomy and some form of international guarantees of legitimate international religious interest."[565]

While the Soviet representative decided to participate in the ceremonies for the election of the first Israeli President of February 14, 1949,[566] the United States government, in a move similar to that of Great Britain and France, declined its attendance in the Israeli Parliament's opening ceremonies. This United States' decision was made upon consultation with the diplomats involved. It is noteworthy that the representative on the Palestine Conciliation Commission and the Consul in Jerusalem recommended attendance whereas the Ambassador to Israel opposed it.[567]

On April 5, 1949, United States Secretary of State Dean Acheson told Israeli Foreign Minister Sharett that the President preferred the December 11, 1948, General Assembly Resolution's proposal for Jerusalem which primarily recognized the international interest in the Holy Places but not in the inhabitants' day-to-day activities as stipulated in the November 29, 1947 Rresolution. Accordingly, "it should be possible to work out arrangements, perhaps under the trusteeship system, under which Israeli and Arab authorities could accept responsibilities in Jerusalem, but which recognize international interest and authority for the Holy Places."[568]

Some months later, on August 11, 1949, Truman delegated Acheson to formulate a reply to a letter Cardinal Francis Spellman had sent to the President on July 13, 1949. In his letter, Acheson again stressed what the General Assembly Resolution of December 11, 1948 had envisaged: that the area should be under "permanent international regime" and "integrated in so far as is consistent with its special international character with the people and institutions of the remainder of Palestine."[569] In his letter, Cardinal Spellman had stated that Jordan and Israel might refer to Article 2 Paragraph 7 of the Charter in order to avoid United Nations intervention. Acheson assured the Cardinal that the proposed type of international regime would only involve the distribution of governmental power among the three authorities concerned, that is, the two adjacent states and the United Nations authority and that it would be "a matter of precise definition of the location of respective governmental powers"[570] rather than "an application of the concept of sovereignty in the usual sense" for any state in the Jerusalem area, which the United States did not intend to recognize.

Taking into consideration the Israeli actions of the end of 1949 analyzed below, the State Department's Legal Adviser Leonard C. Meeker wrote a memorandum on the status of Jerusalem where he suggested that "the United States, as a Member of the United Nations, should not take any steps with respect to the functioning of American consular offices in Jerusalem which would recognize the sovereignty of any national State in that area."[571] Nevertheless, Meeker's memorandum stated that the United States should maintain in Jerusalem their consular offices "by agreement with the Israeli or Jordan Government, on a *de facto* basis and without exequaturs."[572]

By mid-January 1950, the State Department justified its refusal to the Israeli request that the United States embassy move to Jerusalem explaining that the Jerusalem question was still "*sub judice*" in the United Nations.[573]

4.2 Jordan's practice until 1967

4.2.1 Jordanian position on the administration of the divided city

On the Jordanian side, after entering the Old City on May 28, 1948, King Abdullah sent a cable to the Pope, assuring him that the Christian Sanctuaries would be protected.[574] An official reply came only on October 24, 1948, through the Encyclical *In Multiplicibus Curis*,[575] published by Pope Pius XII. According to Zander, the Encyclical incorporated "the universally accepted 'essentials' for the preservation and satisfactory functioning of the Sanctuaries,"[576] including the established customs and religious traditions:

> It will be equally appropriate to secure by international guarantees free access to the Holy Places, freedom of cult for the different Christian denominations and lastly the respect for the customs and religious traditions inherited from the past.[577]

With regard to the Jordanian administration of the eastern neighborhoods of Jerusalem, on September 20, 1948 the Arab League announced the establishment of an "Arab Government of All Palestine"[578] with headquarters in Gaza. The selected Prime Minister and Foreign Minister of the new Government was Ahmad Hilmi, formerly Military Governor of Arab-held Jerusalem, appointed by the Jordanian Government on July 1, 1948. On October 1, 1948 the "Palestine National Assembly"[579] met in Gaza and elected as its President Hajj Amin al-Husayni, the Mufti of Jerusalem. On the same day, some 5,000 notables, claiming to represent the Palestinian Arabs, organized a pro-Jordanian meeting in Amman, denouncing the Gaza Government, which King Abdullah refused to recognize. Abdullah also replaced Ahmad Hilmi with Abdallah al-Tall as Military Governor of Jerusalem.

On November 15, 1948, while visiting the Coptic convent, Abdullah was crowned by the Coptic bishop and proclaimed "King of Jerusalem."[580] A few days later, on December 1, the "Second Palestine Arab Conference," a mass meeting of Arab notables, was held in Jericho. The participants adopted a resolution[581] proclaiming Abdullah Bin Hussein King of Palestine and expressing the desire of the inhabitants of the West Bank to merge with the Hashemite Kingdom of Jordan, the new name for Transjordan since May 25, 1946. On December 7, 1948 the Jordanian Government declared its consent to the Jericho resolution.[582] PLO Chairman Yasser Arafat, during the Israeli–Palestinian peace negotiations secretly held in Oslo, probably kept in mind the precedent of this Jericho Conference when he insisted that Israel withdraw immediately not only from its redeployment in the Gaza Strip, but also from Jericho.[583]

Meanwhile, King Abdullah had made Sheikh Husam al-Din Jarallah, a former official of the Palestine Government, Mufti of Jerusalem in place of Hajj Amin al-Husayni. On December 13, 1949, after the approval of the Jordanian Parliament, King Abdullah issued a decree[584] to the effect that the Parliament would be dissolved as of January 1, 1950 and general elections would be held on April 11, 1950 on both banks of the Jordan River, including the portion of Jerusalem controlled by Jordan. Other decrees published on the same day amended the nationality law, which granted Jordanian citizenship to the residents of the West Bank, and the electoral law, which provided seats for the West Bank representatives[585] in the new Jordanian Parliament.

Seventy percent of all eligible voters participated in the general elections. Three days later, on April 24, 1950, the newly elected Parliament unanimously approved a resolution which formally declared the unification of the Kingdom under the Hashemite monarchy signed by King Abdullah on the same day.[586] The text of the resolution included a paragraph stating that Arab rights in Palestine shall be defended with all possible legal means and that the unity of the two countries shall in no way be related to "the final settlement of Palestine's just cause within the limits of national hopes, Arab cooperation and international justice".[587]

Ronzitti has qualified the Jordanian actions as "humanitarian intervention,"[588] expressing his opinion with some caution, given the complex definition of the legal status of the Palestinian territory after the end of the British Mandate and the fact that the members of the Security Council and the French government condemned the Jordanian intervention, whereas the United States accused the Arab states of invading

Palestine and committing aggression. At the same time, "The Soviet Union accused the Arab states of having attacked Israel with the connivance of the United Kingdom, seeing that the Transjordan troops were, in actual fact, under British command."[589] No state recognized Jordan's actions, except Pakistan and Great Britain, which three days later recognized its exercise of a *de facto* authority in the part of Jerusalem under its control, pending a final determination of the status of the city, therefore extending the Anglo-Jordan treaty of alliance to the West Bank, including Jerusalem, "unless or until the United Nations shall have established effective authority there."[590] A similar reservation applied to the British *de jure* recognition of the State of Israel.

In contrast, the Political Committee of the Arab League, on May 16, 1950 unanimously decided that the annexation of "Arab Palestine" by the Jordanian government violated the resolution of the League of April 12, 1950 which prohibited the annexation of any part of "Palestine." On this occasion, Egypt, Saudi Arabia, Syria and Lebanon voted for the expulsion of Jordan from the Arab League.[591] However, Iraq helped reach a compromise through mediation according to which Jordan declared that its administrative steps in the West Bank would not prejudice the final solution of the Palestinian question.[592]

4.2.2 Jordanian practice in the Holy Places

During its annual session in December 1950, the General Assembly voted on a Belgian draft resolution confirming the idea of a *corpus separatum* for Jerusalem. This vote (30 in favor, 18 against, 9 abstentions) failed to gain the two-thirds majority in the General Assembly which, according to the United Nations Charter, was necessary for the adoption of a resolution on an "important question," as the Jerusalem issue was classified.[593] During the debate, the Jordanian delegate assured that "[a]ll the faithful had free access to the Holy Places (. . .) and the churches and holy sites were protected,"[594] without explicitly clarifying whether his government's protection included synagogues and other Jewish Holy Places in Jordanian control.[595] Criticizing the Arab states campaigning for internationalization, the Jordanian delegate added: "It was because (. . .) Jordan wished to perpetuate the tradition of tolerance and understanding, of which it was so justly proud, that his government could not agree to the internationalization of Jerusalem."[596]

Unlike Israel, which became a member of the United Nations on May 11, 1949, only on December 14, 1955 did Jordan join the organization. In November 1949, the Jordanian representative, who had been invited to the Ad Hoc Political Committee, stated that any form of internationalization would serve no useful purpose, since the Holy Places under Jordanian control "were safe, and there was no need for a special regime."[597]

On January 5, 1951 King Abdullah appointed a "Guardian of the Haram Al-Sharif and Supreme Custodian of the Holy Places."[598] According to Zander, the meaning of the Guardian's title included the "Moslem, Christian and Jewish"[599] sanctuaries. His duty towards "all communities and the pilgrims of all nations" was to "safeguard with extreme diligence their rights, their beliefs, their cults and the places of their prayers," in the respect of public order "within the limits of the Status Quo." With this decision, the Jordanian King expressed his hope that "all the *firmans* of the sultans and the traditional rights, of which the patriarchs are the depositaries, will be checked and recorded 'ne varietur' in a special register for evidence to which one can refer in case of need."[600] During this period, "as far as the relationship between the Latin and the Orthodox Churches is concerned, no change took place under Jordanian rule, and the status quo in this respect was preserved."[601] The Christian Status Quo "was recognized by all the rulers of Palestine since the Turkish rule: Great Britain as a Mandatory power, Jordan and Israel."[602]

Contrary to its obligations toward Israel in accordance with the Armistice Agreement, Jordan did not allow Jews to visit the Holy Places in its territory, particularly the Har ha Bait/Haram al-Sharif and the Western Wall.[603] This was one of the few times in history when local authorities did not allow Jews to pray at the Wailing Wall:

> Even during the period of the Roman Emperor Hadrian, when Jews were not allowed to reside in Jerusalem, they were allowed on the feast of the Ninth of Av (Tisha b'Av) to pray at the Wailing Wall to commemorate the destruction of the Temple.[604]

Former Jordanian representative in the Mixed Armistice Commission, Ambassador Hazem Nuseibeh, who later became Minister of Foreign Affairs and Permanent Representative of the Hashemite Kingdom at the United Nations, maintained that Article VIII of the Armistice Agreement called for:

> (. . .) a Special Committee to direct its attention, among other matters, to free movement of traffic on vital roads, the return of the Arab citizens of West Jerusalem to their homes, the restoration of public services such as the water of Ras-ul Ein and electricity, in exchange for free access to the Holy Places and cultural institutions and use of the cemetery on the Mount of Olives. The Israelis (. . .) refused to permit the return of the Arab inhabitants to their homes or the re-opening of vital roads such as the Jerusalem-Bethlehem road or the restoration of the vital supplies of water and electricity to Arab Jerusalem. They preferred the seizure of Arab quarter and homes to visiting what they claim to be their holiest of holies, the Wailing Wall.[605]

The Jordanian authorities basically preserved the Christian Status Quo but reached no agreement with the Israelis vis-à-vis the Jewish Holy Places. On May 18, 1992 the Jordanian delegation's spokesperson at the Madrid peace negotiations Marwan Muasher, in explaining the Jordanian position, declared that Jewish-Israeli access to the Holy Places under Jordan's rule from 1948–1967 should be considered in light of the provisions of the Jordanian–Israeli Armistice Agreement, including further negotiation over access to Nazareth and other sites in Israel.

He justified the violation of the Armistice Agreement's provisions claiming that the Israeli side had made parallel violations of the same Agreement and claimed that the denial of access to the Western Wall was not motivated by religious discrimination but as "the result of the presence of the state of war between the Arab states and Israel."[606] More specifically Muasher, who later became first ambassador in Israel and Jordanian Foreign Minister, declared that:

> Jordan believes that as part of a settlement of the Arab–Israeli conflict, access to the Holy Sites in Jerusalem is a right that should be guaranteed to all, regardless of the political settlement that might be reached regarding Jerusalem.[607]

In this context, it is interesting to note that already in 1979 His Royal Highness (then Crown) Prince Hassan bin Talal, wrote:

> Jerusalem having been a city of "Holy Places" for the Jewish, Muslim and Christian religions existing together for some 13 centuries, a considerable body of customary rights, privileges and practices has accumulated in respect to access to, and worship at, the various Holy Places within and outside Jerusalem.[608]

4.3 Israeli practice in the Holy Places since 1967

4.3.1 Israeli jurisdiction over East Jerusalem

On June 5, 1967, the Israeli government attacked Egypt, which at that time was with Syria, part of the United Arab Republic. This followed the decision taken by the Egyptian President Nasser to blockade the Straits of Tiran and to move its forces into the Sinai. Israel immediately appealed to Jordan for mutual restraint but Jordan's response, on the same day, was its attack on Israeli territory, including the Jerusalem sector. As a result of its counter-attack, Israel captured and occupied the Sinai Peninsula, the Gaza Strip, the Golan Heights and the West Bank, which included the Jordanian-held part of Jerusalem.[609] Today, legal scholars are still divided in their opinions on the Six Day War of 1967; some consider the Israeli actions as an act of self-defense,[610] others as an act of aggression.[611]

According to Klein, "in accordance with accepted Israeli military thinking prior to the establishment of the state, Israel did not, in the 1960s, have military contingency plans for the conquest of the Old City of Jerusalem."[612] The decision to capture the Old City made by the Israeli Cabinet on the eve of the war was not an easy one to reach, for it had to take into account the international legal implications related to the administration of the Holy Places.

According to Ramon, after the capture of the Old City, two ministers, Moshe Haim Shapira and Zalman Aranne, considered the prospect of "internationalizing" it in order to avoid "international complications."[613] He maintains that the apprehensions expressed in 1967 by Prime Minister Levi Eshkol and others echoed the motivations of Theodore Herzl when he proposed the establishment of an international regime in Jerusalem.[614] Similarly, Chaim Weizmann stated in 1937: "I would not take the Old City [even] as a gift. There are too many complications and difficulties associated with it."[615]

From the Israeli legal perspective, since the end of the war several Israeli laws and ministerial decrees have determined the administrative situation of the new neighborhoods of Jerusalem within the enlarged borders of the city, where the state's law, jurisdiction and administration extended its application.[616] On June 27, 1967, the Knesset amended the Law and Administration Ordinance Law of 1967 through Amendment No. 11 which authorized the government to extend by order the application of "the law, jurisdiction and administration"[617] of Israel to any area that was formerly part of "Eretz Israel," corresponding to Mandatory Palestine.

On the same day, the Municipalities Ordinance of 1936, originally enacted under the British Mandate, was amended to allow the Minister of Interior to enlarge by proclamation the area of a particular municipality by including an area to which Israeli law, jurisdiction and administration had been extended.[618] The following day, on June

28, the government issued an order which applied Israeli law, jurisdiction, and administration to the municipal neighborhoods of Jerusalem that had been under Jordanian control prior to June 1967, as well as to other adjacent areas outside the municipal boundaries of the city.

On the same day, the Minister of Interior, by proclamation, enlarged the municipal area of the city of Jerusalem to include those neighborhoods and areas.[619] The new municipal area of Jerusalem widened to include municipal neighborhoods that had come under Israeli control following the Israel–Jordan cease-fire agreement of November 30, 1948; city boundaries now encompassed the area that had been under Jordanian control until June 1967, including areas outside the former municipal Israeli and Jordanian boundaries of the city. According to Benziman, the Knesset rushed the two amendments through on June 27, 1967, "actually abrogating Knesset norms by approving the amendment in all three readings in a single day."[620] As a possible reason for this special legislative process, Benziman cites as the Israeli government's fears of international reactions to a formal annexation of East Jerusalem. The term *annexation* in international law is used in several similar meanings although not identical:

1. "In the broad sense it refers to the acquisition of territory by a State by any means.
2. Addition of territory to a State as a result of an agreement transferring title, i.e., cession.
3. Acquisition of territory through unilateral appropriation by a conquering State."[621]

The Israeli government rejected a proposal by the then minister Menachem Begin to pass a special law formally declaring the city "reunified," without using the term "sovereignty" in the provisions. As a matter of fact, the word "Jerusalem" was not even mentioned in the proposed bill presented to the Knesset by Justice Minister Ya'akov Shimon Shapira. Benziman underlined that, in place of the word "Jerusalem," the government "chose thirteen obscure words and a nonsensical decree."[622]

In his official reply to a letter from United Nations Secretary General U Thant's General Assembly Resolution 2253 condemning Israeli measures on Jerusalem,[623] Israeli Foreign Minister Abba Eban maintained that Israeli actions in Jerusalem were merely administrative and not political, thereby ruling out the application of the term "annexation."[624] According to Eban, Israeli measures merely related "to the integration of Jerusalem in the administrative and municipal spheres, and [they] furnish a legal basis for the protection of the Holy Places in Jerusalem." The letter confirmed Israeli recognition of the "international interest in Jerusalem" derived "from the presence of the Holy Places" in the city, and maintained that "Israel does not doubt its own will and capacity to secure the respect of universal spiritual interests" and "has forthwith ensured that the Holy Places of Judaism, Christianity and Islam be administered under the responsibility of the religions which hold them sacred."

On July 14, 1967, the United States' representative Ambassador Goldberg explained his abstention on a new draft resolution introduced by Pakistan on the grounds that the draft's provisions wrongly implied that the Israeli measures constituted an "annexation of Jerusalem."[625] Shimon Agranot, President of the Israeli Supreme Court sitting as High Court of Justice, expressed a different interpretation of the Israeli measures:

The meaning of the said legislative amendment [referred to above], together with the Order issued thereunder is that, in addition to Israeli Defence Force administration, this constitutes, in the words of the Minister of Justice in the Knesset on the first reading of the Amendment, "an unequivocal act of sovereignty on the part of the State, so that Israeli law should apply to that area."[626]

In a decision given on October 13, 1970, two of the three members of the Israeli Supreme Court, sitting as High Court of Justice, stated that East Jerusalem unlike the West Bank, should not be considered "foreign territory" with respect to Israel.[627] Justice Kahan, in particular, denied the "need for any certificate from the Foreign Minister from any administrative authority to determine" the 'annexation' of "East Jerusalem" to the State of Israel, since by means of the two aforementioned enactments "this area constitutes part of the territory of Israel."[628]

The third member of the Court, Justice Cohn, objected to the arguments advanced by the respondents' attorney according to which "the application of Israeli law to a particular territory is equivalent to annexation of that territory to the State of Israel." Cohn maintained that *prima facie* nothing prevented "the application of Israeli law to occupied territories unaccompanied by any intention to annex those territories to the State."[629] Justice Cohn explained that "somewhat paradoxically" during the court's hearings both parties of the petition had never raised any argument, preliminary or otherwise, to challenge the assumption that East Jerusalem and the West Bank city of Hebron are situated in two different states. The two parties had created a sort of "united front" on the issue of the "annexation of East Jerusalem to the State of Israel, in such a way that it — but not Hebron — is now regarded as an inseparable part of the State of Israel".

If "East Jerusalem" is inside Israel and Hebron outside the country then these two places stand "to each other in a relationship of being 'abroad'", thus upholding the decision of the Military Tribunal which regarded East Jerusalem as being 'abroad' in relation to Hebron." In such a situation, Justice Cohn stated that the consequent decision "to annul the order *nisi* and dismiss the petition" did not profess "to make a judicial determination on a political issue" nor, Cohn added, did the Court decision necessarily concur "with the judicial determination of the Military Tribunal of the Hebron Region" on this point.

On the contrary, the decision was based on "the consent of the petitioners that East Jerusalem has been annexed to the State of Israel, while Hebron has not been annexed." Such consent was effective with respect to military proceedings and with regard to the petitioners, but "in every other case in which the question whether a particular place is situated 'abroad' should arise, the matter must be proved by a certificate signed by the Minister of Foreign Affairs or by the competent military administrative authority in the territories occupied by the Israeli Defence Force."[630]

4.3.2 The preservation of Status Quo in the Christian Holy Places

On the afternoon of June 7, 1967, immediately after the capture of the Old City by the Israeli army, Israeli Prime Minister Levi Eshkol met with the leaders of all Jerusalem religious communities, including the Chief Rabbis.[631] On this solemn occasion, he declared that he had requested that the Minister of Religious Affairs get in touch with the religious leaders in the Old City, in order to ascertain that they may "continue their religious and communal activities unhindered."[632] Following the

Prime Minister's request, the Minister of Religious Affairs Zerah Warhaftig issued instructions according to which:

> (...) arrangements at the Western Wall shall be determined by the Chief Rabbis of Israel, those in places sacred to Moslems by a council of Moslem ecclesiastics, and those in places sacred to Christians by a council of Christian religious dignitaries.[633]

These arrangements and the declarations which followed from both the Prime Minister and the Minister of Religious Affairs manifested Israel's desire to ensure religious freedom for the Christian communities and grant them considerable autonomy in administering their Holy Places. According to Ramon, Israel's decision that a council of Christian clerics would determine arrangements at the Christian holy sites, indicates that at this stage the Israeli government was not aware of the generation long internecine struggles among the Christian churches and communities over control of the Holy Places.[634] This situation was likely to prevent the cooperation essential to the joint administration of the holy sites and the establishment of the proposed joint council.

On the morning of the aforementioned declaration by the Israeli Prime Minister Eshkol, Israeli Defense Minister Moshe Dayan, accompanied by the Chief of Staff and other officers to the front side of the Western Wall and solemnly promised to the people of all faiths "full religious freedom and rights."[635]

Dayan declared that the Israeli army did not come to Jerusalem "to conquer the holy places of others nor to diminish by the slightest measure their religious rights, but to ensure the unity of the city, and to live in it with others, in harmony."[636] As for the Israeli legislation, on June 27, 1967, simultaneous to the passing of the law which applied Israeli law jurisdiction and administration to the eastern sector of enlarged Jerusalem, the Knesset passed the Protection of Holy Places Law:

1. The Holy Places shall be protected from desecration and any other violation and from anything likely to violate the freedom of access of the members of the different religions to the places sacred to them or their feelings with regard to those places.
2. a) Whosoever desecrates or otherwise violates a Holy Place shall be liable to imprisonment for a term of seven years.
   b) Whosoever does anything likely to violate the freedom of access of the members of the different religions to the places sacred to them or their feelings with regard to those places shall be liable to imprisonment for a term of five years.
3. This Law shall add to, and not derogate from, any other law.[637]
4. The Minister of Religious Affairs is charged with the implementation of this Law, and he may, after consultation with, or upon the proposal of, representatives of the religions concerned and with the consent of the Minister of Justice make regulations as to any matter relating to such implementation.
5. This Law shall come into force on the date of its adoption by the Knesset.[638]

On the day the Knesset adopted this law, Prime Minister Levi Eshkol gathered forty-one religious leaders, among them the two Chief Rabbis of Israel, the Greek Orthodox, Latin and Armenian Patriarchs and the Grand Mufti of Jerusalem and solemnly declared to them that the Holy Places in Jerusalem would be "open to all who wish to worship at them — members of all faiths, without discrimination."[639]

The three cardinal principles of the Israeli Government's policy, then, were preserving the Holy Places, ensuring their religious and universal character and guaranteeing free access. These principles were to be maintained and faithfully carried out through regular consultation with the heads of the communities, and with those designated by them for this purpose at the appropriate levels. Eshkol stated that in light of their common aims and interests, every proposal would be given full and sympathetic consideration. Moreover, it was the Israeli government's intention "to entrust the internal administration and arrangements of the Holy Places to religious leaders of the communities to which they respectively belong"; the task of carrying out all necessary procedures within this framework was given to the Minister of Religious Affairs.

The next day, Religious Affairs Minister Zerah Warhaftig announced that a temporary authority had been appointed pursuant to the Prime Minister's declaration and that detailed instructions for the faithful observance of the principles [had been] enshrined in the Declaration on the Establishment [of Israel, with regard to the Holy Places]."[640] He added that "within the next few days, I will set up responsible councils of the religious leaders in order to implement the legislation."[641] A comparison of the 1967 law to both the previous Eshkol's and Warhaftig's declarations of June 7, 1967 reveals an interesting difference: under the new law, it would be the Israeli Minister of Religious Affairs rather than the heads of the religious communities to decide the arrangements at their holy sites in consultation with representatives of the relevant religions or sects.

In principle, then, neither solution would contradict the Status Quo, provided there would be the consent of all interested parties. However, this Latin expression did not appear in the wording of either text.[642] To this very day, problems still linger over the "the question of who are the authorized representatives"[643] of the various religious communities due to the overlapping of the communities' interests over the same places of worship and the desire of some communities to avoid open cooperation with Israel. These problems have dissuaded the Ministry of Religious Affairs from promulgating regulations for the administration of the Christian holy places.

Immediately after Prime Minister Eshkol made his statement, Foreign Minister Eban addressed a letter to the Secretary-General of the United Nations in which he pointed out that the measures taken by the Israeli Government in 1967 to secure the protection of the Holy Places were "only a part of Israel's effort to ensure respect for universal interest in Jerusalem."[644] In the same letter Eban stated that the United Nations' discussions and documents show that "the international interest in Jerusalem has always been understood to derive from the presence of the Holy Places" and confirmed Israel's will and capacity "to secure the respect of universal spiritual interests."

It was for this reason that the Israeli Government had given formal assurance that the Holy Places of Judaism, Christianity and Islam would be "administered under the responsibility of the religions which hold them sacred" and "in a spirit of concern for historic and spiritual traditions"; the government had embarked on a constructive and detailed dialogue with "representatives of universal religious interests" with a view to reaching arrangements to maintain "the universal character of the Holy Places."

From 1967, Israeli authorities have generally declared their intention to respect the traditional principles that apply to the relationship between the Christian, Muslim and Jewish communities in their respective Holy Places and regarding the various rights acquired in particular by the Christian communities at their sacred sites, have decided to respect the Status Quo. Although the "specifics of the status quo were not enshrined in the declarations by Israeli leaders or in the Protection of Holy Places Law,"[645] as previously mentioned, "Israel in practice sought to uphold the status quo arrangements in accordance with the above quoted document written by the British Mandatory official L.G.A. Cust."[646]

This approach was further reflected in subsequent statements made on behalf of the State of Israel. For instance, on September 19, 1969, Foreign Minister Eban told the United Nations General Assembly that Israel did not claim exclusive or unilateral jurisdiction in the Holy Places of Christianity and Islam in Jerusalem and was willing to discuss this principle with those traditionally concerned and that a versatile range of creative solutions for a definition of the status of the Holy Places was available. According to Eban, these new possibilities would promote "Middle Eastern peace and ecumenical harmony."[647] In the meantime, the Israeli policy allowed the Muslim and Christian Holy Places to remain "under the responsibility of those who hold them sacred,"[648] a principle in practical effect since 1967.

On November 15, 1971, Ambassador Eban reaffirmed this position in his reply to Secretary-General U Thant who informed the Government of Israel of Security Council Resolution 298.[649] The Israeli representative denied that "an internationally accepted or valid status for Jerusalem"[650] had been set aside by any event that had occurred in the city since 1967 and that the concern expressed by the Security Council Resolution could only refer to "the effective status of the ethnic and religious communities."

Further, he gave his assurance that Israel was not undertaking or planning actions aimed at annulling the present heterogeneous character of the population and emphasized the central operative paragraph of the Security Council Resolution quoted above. It is noteworthy that the resolution called upon Israel "to rescind all previous measures and actions and to take no further steps in the occupied section of Jerusalem which may purport to change the status of the city, or which would prejudice the rights of the inhabitants and the interests of the international community, or a just and lasting peace."

Referring to his letter of July 10, 1967, Eban confirmed that Israel did not wish to "exercise unilateral jurisdiction or exclusive responsibility in the Holy Places of Christianity and Islam," and was willing, in consultation with the religious interests traditionally concerned, to give due expression to that principle. Therefore, the changes which had affected Jerusalem's life and destiny as a result of the measures adopted by Israel, did not rule out Israel's "willingness to work out arrangements with the world's religious bodies, Christian, Muslim and Jewish, which will ensure the universal religious character of the Holy Places." Eban concluded that for the first time a Government in Jerusalem had offered "special expression for universal interests" of the international community "in Jerusalem instead of asserting its exclusive jurisdiction over all of them."

This attitude has been confirmed several times in the Israeli diplomatic and legal practice relevant to the international law perspective. This includes the 1980 Basic Law: Jerusalem Capital of Israel; its Article 3 restated integrally the provisions included in Article 1 of the 1967 law which guarantees protection of the Holy Places.[651]

The declaration made in the Knesset on September 9, 1993 by the then Israeli Foreign Minister Shimon Peres a few days before the signing of the Oslo Agreement is an additional recent confirmation since he confirmed that Israel had always highlighted the religious importance and significance of Jerusalem to members of monotheistic faiths. The Israeli Foreign Minister pledged that Israel will continue to respect the unique value of the city and its sites for the spiritual and daily life of Jews, Muslims and Christians and quoted from the Prophet Isaiah: "For My house shall be called a house of prayer for all peoples."[652]

In so doing, Peres explicitly confirmed that Israel was committed to respect both freedom of worship and "the proper functioning of the various existing religious institutions which operate in the city," as well as to continue its policy vis-à-vis "the aspects relating to the existence of free religious life in the city," with the hope of broadening the dialogue at the time being conducted "with the institutions of the various religions." In line with this traditional policy, Israel would continue to "refrain from taking any step or action which might harm freedom of worship and freedom of access to the holy sites, or the feelings and sensibilities of members of the various communities."

Peres defined his declaration a "commitment" relating "both to residents of the city and to visitors, as well as to the holy sites in it" which would indeed allow Jews, Muslims and Christians of Jerusalem, "a city of many faces, religions and cultures," to harmoniously live together. In his viewpoint, each community in Jerusalem would be able to "preserve its cultural heritage, its unique character, and its social and religious institutions, including its own educational system" and therefore coexistence in Jerusalem needed to be thought of as "a matter of mutual respect between all residents and of the proper functioning of the relevant institutions and systems."

It should be noted that the Israeli attitude vis-à-vis the religious dimension of the Jerusalem question has never been formally contradicted. Quite the opposite, it has found indirect confirmation in various provisions of the Fundamental Agreement between Israel and the Holy See[653] and in Article IX of the Peace Treaty with Jordan.[654] Various Israeli governments have likewise never shown any clear or sharp deviation from this policy, although it has been periodically expressed with different terminology, and not always in the same extensive or detailed manner.

A recent example is the remark made to the Security Council on June 30, 1998 by the Israeli Ambassador to the United Nations Dore Gold, when he reaffirmed that Israel has "a special responsibility to preserve and protect Jerusalem as a city that is holy to each of the three great faiths in our region: Christianity, Islam, and Judaism."[655] Similarly, at the weekly cabinet meeting of March 14, 1999, Prime Minister Benyamin Netanyahu stated that the Government of Israel would continue to "ensure freedom of religion, worship and conscience in Jerusalem" as well as "the continuation of the status quo in the Holy Places of all religions[656] and freedom of access to them, while respecting freedom for all faiths."[657]

4.3.3 The new Modus Vivendi in the Muslim–Jewish Holy Places

Immediately after Israel took control of the area in 1967, the Chief Rabbi of the Israeli Army, Brigadier Shlomo Goren, and some of his followers entered the area of the Har ha Bait/Haram al-Sharif compound and conducted Jewish prayers. Israeli authorities immediately intervened "and the status quo in this respect was re-established."[658]

Minister of Defense Moshe Dayan left the compound under the control of the Muslim *Waqf* and allowed Muslims "to pray in the mosques there without restriction as in the past, under the Israeli regime."[659] On June 17, 1967,[660] Dayan informed the

Waqf leadership that the internal management of the Har ha Bait/Haram al-Sharif mosques and its large platform area would remain under the control of the *Waqf* and that it was up to Muslim leaders to determine its internal rules and regulations while Israel would be in charge of maintaining law and order as well as guarding the surrounding area.

Although the Report of the Commission of Investigation into the Events on the Temple Mount, finalized on October 8, 1990 and submitted on October 26, 1990, stated that "the Government of Israel has never modified the policy articulated by the late Prime Minister Levi Eshkol,"[661] while maintaining the religious Status Quo/Modus Vivendi, Israeli bulldozers razed 135 houses in the Mughrabi Quarter adjoining the Wailing Wall and adjacent to the Har ha Bait/Haram al-Sharif, offering alternative houses in compensation to the people living in those homes. Some of these buildings, comprising some houses and two small mosques, belonged to the Muslim *Waqf* while others were private property.[662] Additionally, all Israeli governments abolished the limitations and restrictions imposed on the Jews under the British Mandate and Jordanian rule; nevertheless, while they allowed them to visit the Har ha Bait/Haram al-Sharif that "absolutely prohibited Jews from praying there,"[663] and so, if Jews wished to pray in this controversial area, they would be directed to the Western Wall.

The then Mayor of Jerusalem Teddy Kollek, who was a firm advocate of the arrangements made for the Har ha Bait/Haram al-Sharif, would often explain to foreign diplomats who visited him in his office that "the holiest site in Judaism was to continue to be run by a Muslim religious authority — and furthermore, Jews were to be forbidden to pray there."[664] The fact that most Orthodox rabbis objected to any Jewish presence on the Har ha Bait/Haram al-Sharif apparently made it easier for Jews to accept this new Status Quo/Modus Vivendi. Since the start of the Jewish National Movement, some Muslims have been suspicious of the intentions of some Jewish groups, fearing that their aim was ultimately to regain control of the Har ha Bait/Haram al-Sharif, even if this should mean the destruction of Islamic Sanctuaries. Official Jewish, Zionist and Israeli spokesmen have on several occasions decisively denied such accusations despite the opposite opinion of a few Jewish writers, scholars and visionaries.[665]

It is clear why the complex and sensitive question of the right of the Jews to pray on the Har ha Bait/Haram al-Sharif has been the topic of political and diplomatic debate and the subject of several controversial decisions in Israeli courts. From the diplomatic perspective, it is worth recalling the heated debate in 1976 at the United Nations General Assembly on Arab protests at the Har ha Bait/Haram al-Sharif over the right of Jews to pray there, which simply underlined the deep religious attachment of Muslims, Jews and Christians to the Holy Places of Jerusalem.

The United States Ambassador Willian Scranton present at the debate, commented that "the ruling by a lower Israeli court (. . .) would have the effect of altering the status of Al Haram" by permitting Jews to pray on the Har ha Bait/Haram al-Sharif.[666] He stated that under Article 27 of the 1949 Geneva Convention on Law of War, Israel had the responsibility "to preserve religious practices as they were at the time the occupation began," a responsibility, he added, that "cannot be changed by the ruling of an Israeli court." Scranton expressed his government's deep relief in observing that "the Supreme Court of Israel has upheld the Israeli Government's position" not to allow such prayers there. The United States position seemed to imply that the Status Quo should continue to be upheld in view of international legal considerations, regardless of any reference to the status of the territory.

The changes in the relations between the Muslim and Jewish communities brought about by the new Status Quo/Modus Vivendi established by Israel in 1967 should be considered in light of the overall relationship between the specific principles of the Status Quo/Modus Vivendi and the universal principles of freedom of religion and worship.[667] The new arrangements applied to the ways of worship at the main Jewish and Muslim Holy Places, the Western Wall and the Har ha Bait/Haram al-Sharif do not necessarily contradict the general apparatus of the Status Quo/Modus Vivendi system of law.

Although Arab and Islamic authorities did object to the Israeli actions carried out in the Old City after 1967 and considered them an infringement of the Status Quo,[668] they for the most part did not explicitly challenge the legal value of the traditional principles embodied in the Status Quo established during the British Mandate. Moreover, the Jordanian *Waqf* authorities in charge of the Muslim Holy Places of Jerusalem since 1967 have indirectly given in to the aforementioned post-1967 Israeli actions and have also apparently accepted those actions through the Jordanian Government's endorsement of Article 9 in the Peace Treaty with Israel,[669] as they failed to insert any formal objection or reservation related to these arrangements.

In principle, the changes that occurred in Jerusalem as a result of the Six Day War which replaced Jordan as the responsible authority for the Holy Places in the Old City of Jerusalem and its immediate vicinity were not substantial changes in Israel's position with respect to the Holy Places. Nevertheless, according to Ramon,[670] Israeli Prime Minister Eshkol and Minister Warhaftig worded their declarations differently from their British and Jordanian predecessors. In December 1917, the British proclamation issued by General Allenby stated that the holy sites of the three religions would be held and maintained "according to the existing customs;"[671] in 1951, Jordan's King Abdallah declared that the guardian of the Holy Places would safeguard "their rights, their beliefs, their cults, and the places of the prayers (. . .) within the limit of the status quo order," while "the communities, the mosques and the churches will be assured in their respective rights";[672] whereas the statement made by Israeli Minister Warhaftig rested on the authority of Israel's Declaration of Independence."[673]

It is evident that the reason why Israeli authorities were much more cautious when referring to the Status Quo, lies in Israel's attempt to avoid suggesting that this legal regime might include the same restrictive and humiliating regulations applied to the Jewish Holy Places, particularly the Western Wall during the Mandate period, which they considered an obstacle to the full exercise of freedom of religion and conscience.[674] The Minister of Religious Affairs, in accordance with the Protection of the 1967 Holy Places Law previously mentioned, "set out the details of the implementation of this law in some of the Jewish holy places."[675] A special provision was added[676] to these Regulations to give statutory recognition to the new Status Quo at the Western Wall "(. . .) according to the *Halacha* — Jewish law:"[677]

> In order to protect the status quo in this Holy Place vis-à-vis attempts by Reform women to change it by praying in their own way, reading from the Torah and blowing the horn. It forbids any religious service at the Wall "not according to local custom, which may hurt the feelings of the worshippers toward the place". Vice-President of the Supreme Court M. Elon wrote in H.C.

Hoffman: "This regulation expresses the principle of upholding the *status quo*; 'local custom' and *status quo* are one and the same."[678]

Several Israeli declarations refer to the Jewish–Muslim relations in the Har ha Bait/Haram al-Sharif compound in various ways, further confirming that the Status Quo procedural norms apply today to the Holy Places of the three main recognized communities in Jerusalem. One good example is a late-night police operation to seal off a two-meter-high window that police suspected the *Waqf* — the Islamic trust endowment in charge of the Har ha Bait/Haram al-Sharif compound — had planned to open as a new entrance to the chambers underneath the Har ha Bait/Haram al-Sharif. Former Israeli Prime Minister Ehud Barak, stated: "We will not accept violations of the law. We will not accept a unilateral act and I praise the police and the ministry for public security for their swift and clear action on this matter."[679]

Barak defined the *Waqf* action as a violation of the Status Quo that "bars either side from introducing changes at the holy site," and stated that "it is important that we redress this situation and that we establish an atmosphere of dialogue and understanding and respect of the status quo (. . .) I think this is very important for the peace process."[680] The then Internal Security Minister Shlomo Ben Ami confirmed that "the intervention was necessary in order to prevent any change" to the delicate Status Quo/Modus Vivendi prevailing at the Har ha Bait/Haram al-Sharif.

Ever since the Netanyahu government opened the Hasmonean Tunnel which originates near the Western Wall and continues all the way to the Muslim Quarter of the Old City of Jerusalem, the *Waqf* has not allowed Israeli archeologists inside the compound to view the repair and reconstruction work underway. Jewish activists, particularly the group called "Faithful of the Temple Mount," have strongly objected to the transformation of the underground chamber into a mosque, which began in the early nineties and whose construction of a new floor was financially supported by Israeli Arabs.

The Jewish activists have planned to turn the large underground chamber into a synagogue. This would go against the long-standing rabbinical ban on visits by religious Jews to the open-air areas of the Har ha Bait/Haram al-Sharif. They have also claimed that these plans to turn the room into a synagogue was a decisive factor for Israeli Islamists' involvement in the transformation of the Solomon's Stables area. Named after Khalif Abd al Malak Ibn Marwan, the Muslims have termed this area as the Al Marwani vestry, which was allegedly destroyed by the Crusaders, who turned it into a stable.[681]

5 | The Legal Regime Applied to the Holy Places of Jerusalem

5.1 Legal–empirical criteria to define the Holy Places

This book illustrates that a selected number of sites within Jerusalem and in its immediate proximity are designated as *Holy Place* by the administrative practice of the local governments, which have applied to them a special legal regime. Furthermore, the interests of recognized communities entitled to raise claims over such places are protected by international law. However, contrasting opinions continue to exist even within the major religious denominations on the definition of *Holy Place*.[682] For example, Luther, in his *Appeal to the Christian Nobility of German Nationality*, denounced the "wrong illusion and misunderstanding of the Divine Laws" as misleading "simple-minded folk," who believed that "pilgrimages are valuable and good deeds" stressing instead that "repeated" pilgrimages are evil deeds: "God has not decreed them", and the money and work given away to such "devilish ghosts" should instead be spent on "the maintenance of one's family and for the poor."[683]

One of the documents issued by protestant religious organizations, the "*Déclaration du bureau de la fédération protestante de France*,"[684] states that: "There are no Holy Places for the Churches of the Reform."[685] Moreover, it adds that "Christian faith finds in the Bible a sufficient foundation, since this witness, in an undeniable way, [is] the historical reality of the coming of Christ."[686]

No formal list of Holy Places has been universally and permanently accepted by all parties involved or has been included in any statutory definition. The local authorities, as well as the parties of an international agreement, may virtually label *any* additional site that is the object of traditional worship as a Holy Place. Since this legal definition does not necessarily follow general and objective criteria, but it may depend on temporary global/transnational or state/territorial values, it is impossible to draw clear-cut conclusions on such an unstable subject, and any definition needs to be constantly redefined.

Alternative suggestions to solve this identification problem generate circuitous definitions, such as Article I, titled "Definitions," Section I, of Israel's Draft Resolution on Jerusalem, submitted to the General Assembly of the United Nations on November 25, 1949:

In this Agreement:

(a) The expression "The Holy Places" means those places, buildings and sites in Jerusalem which were recognized on 14 May 1948 as Holy Places and any other places, buildings or sites which may subsequently be considered as such by agreement between the parties. [687]

Within the Israeli law specific context, Shmuel Berkovitz points out the lack of a statutory definition of these terms: "definitions which have no meaning or, in certain laws, no reason whatsoever for why certain places, and these places only, are considered holy places."[688] Moreover, Berkovitz considers it particularly surprising the fact that "the most important Israeli law regarding the Holy Places, the Preservation of the Holy Places Law, 1967, does not include a definition of the term. It even adds a new, undefined term: 'sanctified place'."[689] According to this law, it is the Israeli Minister of Religious Affairs who is authorized to issue regulations for its implementation. This law also includes the definition of a site as a Holy Place, with all its legal ramifications.

Additionally, "in certain laws, the reader is referred to the definition in the Order-in-Council,[690] although this Mandatory statute makes no reference to this definition."[691] Therefore, the Israeli Supreme Court declared that to determine whether each site is a Holy Place or not, a "factual-religious"[692] test is needed. A 1942 letter to the Chief Secretary from Harold McMichael, the British High Commissioner in the Palestinian Mandate, did not include clear-cut objective criteria, and left the legal definition of the Holy Places open to different and controversial interpretations:

(. . .) The Order [in Council] was limited in its application to those places and buildings in Palestine to which an almost universal tradition accords the veneration of humanity because of their connection with historic events in the story of the three great religions forever associated with the name of this land.[693]

On June 30, 1949, the United Nations Conciliation Committee for Palestine proposed a broader and all-encompassing definition of those sites, without explaining the legal criteria adopted:

The Holy Places, sites and buildings consecrated by the veneration of the faithful; buildings used as places of worship, buildings used by religious congregations, by priest and by denominational associations; foundations established for pious and charitable ends; as well as the dependencies of these Holy Places, sites and buildings.[694]

On July 24, 1949, Shabtai Rosenne, the former Legal Advisor to the Israeli Ministry of Foreign Affairs, based his legal opinion on the subject: "The Problem of the Definition of the Terms 'Holy Places, Religious Buildings and Sites'.[695] After an extensive investigation of the British Mandatory legislative, administrative and judicial practice, Rosenne challenged the aforementioned suggestion by the United Nations Conciliation Commission in Palestine, and decided to limit the definition of the Holy Places to those sites regulated by the legal regime applied to them.

This issue has attracted vast international law literature aimed at grasping the intrinsic essence of this complicated and controversial topic. A significant example is Jan Willem Verzijl's *International Law in Historical Perspective*, in which a whole section is devoted to the "International Protection of Sacred Places":[696]

(...) the concurrence of different Christian denominations in the Church of the Holy Sepulchre in Jerusalem gave rise, at first to a continuous struggle between Roman-Catholics and others, and in the end to an extremely complicated system of partition of the building amongst them.[697]

Verzijl refers to "the special protection accorded by international law to such real property as the Holy Places of Jewry, Christianity and Islam in the Near East." He also extends such a special protection to "other religious places of pilgrimage," in addition to the recognized "Holy Places of Christianity" in Jerusalem and Bethlehem that "have always occupied a prominent place in this international protection," including specific sites in Nazareth. He also notes that other religious sites, such as Mecca and Medina, as well as other Islamic and Christian sanctuaries, "have formed the object of international concern and regulation (...) and have also been placed under international protection of some kind."[698]

This selected overview confirms the assumption that no universally recognized and objective hermeneutic criteria can properly define a *Holy Place*. Therefore, this study provides evidence that the *only* practical way to understand the meaning of the expression *Holy Places of Jerusalem* (capitalized), is through the legal–historical context of the normative system which applies to them, which is examined in the following section.

The criteria which define those sites as *Holy* are pragmatic-empirical and may change under mutable socio-political circumstances. As a result, this study demonstrates that a thorough investigation over the diplomatic, administrative and legal practice of the *pro-tempore* local authority can solve the problems concerning their identification, as well as the problems concerning their specific legal regime under different local governments.

5.2 The Status Quo in the Christian Holy Places

The first local authority in the area to decree the *Status Quo* in the Holy Places between the eighteenth and nineteenth century was the Ottoman Empire,[699] which imposed a truth among the Christian communities. As already illustrated, this act, which was imposed as an inter-Christian cease-fire, culminated in the crystallization of a new legal regime. To date, its rules regulated the interests of different recognized communities raising worship claims over the very same places.

This legal regime applied to the Holy Places of Jerusalem found its way into European diplomatic and international legal terminology during the reign of the Ottoman Empire. The expression *Status Quo* defined the inter-Christian complex balance of conflicting rights and interests vis-à-vis the main Christian sacred shrines in this particular area of the word. In this technical sense, the expressions *Holy Places* and *Status Quo* help define each other and assume a rather narrow meaning.

This could better explain the nexus between the Christian Holy Places and the Status Quo rules, which apply only to the conflicting claims in those selected shrines, and not to any other Christian sites in the Israeli–Palestinian areas, or anywhere else in the world. In fact, it is this complex web of conflicting claims that make the Christian Holy Places so renowned in the world media. Paradoxically, should those recognized communities that raise claims in Jerusalem ever settle their controversies over the Holy Places, these sites would no longer be defined as such, and there would be no more need for such a legal regime applied to them.

Originally, the Status Quo preserved a set of informal, partly codified arrangements. Over time, these arrangements developed through long-established practice as a legal regime. The complexity of the Status Quo is best understood within the same framework of this legal regime that regulates the relationship between the Christian communities.

In order to grasp the precise meaning of the expression *Holy Places of Jerusalem*, it is important to analyse the *types* of communities entitled to raise claims therein. This book shows that the interested communities could include on one hand the global religious Christian, Jewish and Muslim communities and on the other the Israeli or Palestinian national communities.

In fact, only some of the communities entitled to raise claims over the Holy Places are represented by entities that are formal subjects of this legal order. Within the rules of international law, *subject* as a formal legal concept refers to a factual group entity, such as a state government or a similar body, which exercises its power within a defined area of space.[700] In this sense, international law may be defined as an inter-state legal order, or law "*d'interpuissances,*"[701] and not as an inter-individual legal order, such as a national system of law. In other words, classic international law does *not* directly regulate relations among individuals.

The behavior of states and the creation of rules indirectly imply the material action of individuals, while formally referred as group entities. This feature of the international legal system explains the nature of the relationship between the territorial states, or other subjects of international law, and the members of the different recognized communities applying the Holy Places' legal regime. The recognized Jerusalem communities are legal *subjects* from the municipal law perspective, but *not* necessarily from the international law perspective. On the other hand, only international law subjects are entitled to directly exercise rights and perform duties within this legal order.

As discussed earlier, the inter-Christian administrative arrangement defined as the Status Quo dates back to the Ottoman *Millet* system, which recognized certain non-Islamic communities and gave them considerable autonomy.[702] The British Mandatory regime kept this arrangement alive to a large extent, and its framework is still applicable today under Israeli rule.[703] These communities respond to and are bound by rules dictated by separate and independent legal orders, as for example the Canon Law for the Latin Catholic community, with special courts tasked to enforce these rules.

The Status Quo in the Christian Holy Places was further confirmed in the important Memorandum on the Significance of Jerusalem for Christians of November 14, 1994 signed in Jerusalem by the Patriarchs and the Heads of Christian Communities, namely by the Greek Orthodox, Latin and Armenian Patriarchs, the Custos of the Holy Land, the Coptic, Syriac, Ethiopian Archbishops, the Anglican and Lutheran Bishops and the Greek Catholic, Maronite and Catholic Syriac Patriarchal Vicars, under the headline "Legitimate Demands of Christians for Jerusalem," which reads as follows:

> 11. (. . .) Those rights of property ownership, custody and worship which the different Churches have acquired throughout history should continue to be retained by the same communities. *These rights which are already protected in the same Status Quo of the Holy Places according to historical "firmans" and other documents should continue to be recognized and respected.*[704]

The purpose of this research has been to analyze the historical background of Jerusalem's Holy Places and the legal regime applied to them. Within these limits, the international legal implications of this political-historical analysis help interpret the relevant documents adopted in the Middle East Peace Process.

As revealed so far, since these international agreements have historically been surrounded by great political sensitivity, they generally include provisions which are bilateral in nature. Therefore, a comprehensive multilateral legal framework regulating the legal regime applied to the Holy Places is yet to emerge. This could explain why the provisions that more directly relate to the Israeli–Palestinian peace negotiations do not explicitly mention such a normative system. For example, Article V of the Declaration of Principles on Interim Self-Government Arrangements[705] does include *Jerusalem*[706] among the issues to be discussed during the permanent status negotiations, but neither mentions the Holy Places nor the Status Quo applied to them, while other three bilateral documents, listed below and issued within a relatively short period of time, deal with the issue of the Holy Places.

The provisions of these documents apparently confirm the emergence of a crystallized legal arrangement applied to the Holy Places, although no explicit reference to such a legal regime is mentioned in the text:

1 The letter sent by Israeli Foreign Minister Peres on October 11, 1993 to Norway's Foreign Minister Holst.[707]
2 Article B, Paragraph 3, of the Washington Declaration, signed by Israel and Jordan on July 25, 1994.
3 The third document, which has almost identical contents with the Washington Declaration, is Article IX of the Peace Treaty between Israel and Jordan signed on October 25, 1994, titled "Places of Historical and Religious Significance and Interfaith Relations."[708]

The provisions of two international documents, the first signed by Israel, the second signed by the PLO, mention the Status Quo as the legal regime applied to the Christian Holy Places of Jerusalem:

1 The first reference to the Status Quo is included in Article 4, Paragraph 1[709] of the Fundamental Agreement between Israel and the Holy See, signed on December 13, 1993.[710]
2 Except for this agreement, the only additional references to the Status Quo legal regime are included in Paragraph 8 (e) of the Preamble, as well as in the Article 4[711] of the Basic Agreement signed by the Holy See and the PLO on February 15, 2000.

The attitudes of the succeeding administrations in the area until 1967 reveal the complex web of interests and rights of the recognized communities over the Holy Places of Jerusalem. An investigation of self-imposed international obligations can determine which sets of rules are applicable, both within the municipal and the international systems of law.

5.3 Procedural and material norms of the Status Quo system of law

When discussing legal matters, two types of rules ought to be taken into account: material/substantial norms and procedural/instrumental norms. Material norms deal with rights and duties, whereas procedural norms deal with the way in which such rules are created. Within the complex legal context of the Status Quo, material norms regulate the division of space and time in the use and possession of the Holy Places; they define in detail which places belong to which communities as well as the specific conditions of ownership rights. On the other hand, Status Quo procedural norms define how the legal organization is regulated and the legal system's sources of law, that is, how material norms are created. Most scholars have failed to make a thorough analysis of these procedural norms in their studies, and have considered the material ones to be the Status Quo essence. A clear example of one such author is Emmett, whose main focus is on the inter-Christian Status Quo material norms:

> The (1852) *firman* [Ottoman Imperial Decree] granted the various religious communities shared rights in the holy places, demarcating which areas came under whose control and establishing time schedules for officiating in areas shared by more than one religious group.[712]

Likewise, England refers exclusively to the material norms regulating the contents of the Status Quo rights and duties, but explains why those norms may be considered *sui generis*:

> By its very nature, the dispute over the Holy Places lies outside the usual framework of settlement by means of law.
>
> (...) It is difficult, however, to define precisely what legal rights derive from the status quo. These 'rights' do not fit easily into the traditional categories of law, such as proprietary rights. The Supreme Court of Israel has touched upon the question where Justice Landau has said "we may perhaps regard the right of access to a Holy Place as a kind of easement (or servitudes) in the sense of the (Israeli) Land Law (of 1969).[713] Dr. Berkovitz, who dealt with the question in his doctoral thesis on the Holy Places, has suggested that the rights should be treated as *sui generis*.[714]

Hence, municipal law analogies, according to England, may lead to confusion with regard to rights of property, possession or use. Unfortunately, these terms cannot fully explain the type of relationship at stake because of the different legal context of the Status Quo rules. In the quotation mentioned above, England refers to Dr. Berkovitz, who also takes a similar stand on the subject:

> In a report dated December 1930, written by an international Commission appointed by the British Government to determine the rights of Jews and Muslims to the Western Wall,[715] the status quo was defined as a "deeply-rooted custom" or as ancient usage." These two legal terms are also familiar in Israeli law. One may categorize the rights included in the status quo arrangement as "easements" — a term also familiar in our law. I believe that these are proprietary rights *sui generis*.[716]

Therefore, a better understanding of the Status Quo/Modus Vivendi material norms is possible by taking into account their everyday symbolic, ritual, and religious context. From the legal theory point of view, these norms may only be correctly construed within their hermeneutic legal context, namely the Status Quo/Modus Vivendi legal order while considering the legal regime which establishing such material norms as *sui generis*.

Status Quo norms take into account both municipal and international law. Correspondingly, international law, the law of the recognized religious communities and the law of the local government, take into account the instrumental rules of the Status Quo. However, these legal orders apply the norms of the Status Quo as autonomous sources of law, *lex specialis*, which generally prevail over the general rules of those systems.

Neither the Jewish, Anglo-American nor the majority of civil law legal traditions have developed legal tools in order to systematically regulate the relationship between the communities' legal orders and the local governments, that regulate where the communities live.[717] In contrast, Italian legal theory has extensively dealt with these issues due to the presence of the Vatican City on Italian territory, and the consequent special arrangements required between the State of Italy and the Catholic Church.

The complex legal situation of the Status Quo may be explained through the theory of legal orders plurality, which presumes the relativity of legal values. In other words, different legal orders may evaluate the very same fact or behavior in ways and with effects radically different or even conflicting with each other. A renowned Italian legal scholar who developed this theory was Prof. Vezio Crisafulli, who also explained how every existing, sufficiently stable, and organized human group might have a legal order of its own.[718] A preliminary assumption of this theory is of course the legal nature of normative systems outside the state, a hypothesis that scholars from the Positivist School have been denying, asserting that "the law of the State is the only law having a positive character since it is the expression of sovereign command."[719]

On the other hand, according to the pluralist theory, there are two main conditions for a legal order to exist. The first condition is the consistent organization of its norms, that is, norms that do not contradict one another; the second condition is the actual applicability of such norms, in the sense that the rules of the legal order should be effective and not the mere result of creative but abstract thinking. The procedural aspects of the Status Quo/Modus Vivendi legal regime fulfill the exemplified conditions and confirm the hypothesis of the Status Quo/Modus Vivendi as an independent legal order, separate from other legal systems such as international or state law. Since the needed continuous and uninterrupted exercise of the existing rights in the Holy Places in order to claim the above-mentioned rights was quite difficult over the centuries, the material/substantial aspects of the Status Quo/Modus Vivendi legal regime have been constantly changing.

In contrast, the practice examined in this work illustrates stability and continuity with reference to the procedural/instrumental principles pertaining to the Status Quo legal regime in time of peace[720] from its early formation up to the present day. The three main procedural principles characterizing the Status Quo legal regime in time of peace may be listed as follows:[721]

1. The recognized communities must consent to any change in Status Quo, either in its procedural or material aspect.
2. A distinction among the different rights of access, possession and worship is

possible, since each corresponding right potentially belongs to a different recognized community.

3 Controversies over the Status Quo between the communities are currently immune from ordinary judicial jurisdiction.

5.4 The relationship between the Status Quo/Modus Vivendi and the principles of freedom of religion and worship

The Status Quo/Modus Vivendi legal regime should be interpreted in the wider context of the norms of general customs, addressed to all subjects of international law, which guarantees freedom of worship and religion as well as the principles described in this work as the broad cultural–religious status quo in Jerusalem.[722]

A progressive homogeneity has developed in the political-institutional systems of an increasingly wider number of European states, in particular after the fall of the Berlin Wall in 1989, developing correspondent manifestations of international practice. In the broader framework of human rights law, it is nowadays possible to ascertain the existence of general international norms protecting a number of civil and political freedoms.

Customary norms of universal scope have incorporated principles protecting freedom of religion and worship. The wide participation of states in establishing such principles reflects a similar behavior on the part of the United Nations in the field of human rights. Once the existence of such legal values is established, the need presents itself for a precise definition of the contents and scope of such principles, which allow various interpretations.

An important, although indirect, reference to the general principle of religious freedom in international law appears in Article 1 of the United Nations Charter, devoted to the goals of the organization. In Paragraph 3 the importance is stressed of achieving "international co-operation (. . .) in promoting and encouraging respect for human rights and for fundamental freedoms for all without distinction as to (. . .) religion."[723]

Such indirect reference to the principle of religious non-discrimination also appears, in almost identical terms, in Article 55 of the United Nations Charter. In Article 56 the observance of this international conventional obligation demands that all members of the United Nations respect religious freedom: "All Members pledge themselves to take joint and separate action in co-operation with the Organization for the achievement of the purposes set forth in Article 55."[724]

In addition to the obligation of cooperation in Article 56, the principle of religious freedom might have acquired the status of customary law. Such a conclusion takes into account the progressive attitude that states have manifested in adopting the provisions related to the issue at hand included in the main international acts of universal scope issued or stipulated in accordance with the Charter's provisions. In particular, among the acts without a direct binding effect, Article 18 of the Universal Declaration of the Human Rights[725] provides for the right of any individual to freedom of thought, conscience and religion.

According to Margiotta-Broglio, "the system of guarantee studied and planned in the framework of the United Nations Organization (. . .) focuses above all on religious freedom of the individual, without protecting sufficiently the rights of the religious groups as such."[726] The "European Convention for the Safeguard of the Human Rights and the Fundamental Freedoms," signed in Rome on November 4, 1950, was a move to fill such gap at least at a regional level.[727]

On December 16, 1966, the General Assembly reaffirmed those human rights principles, already included in the 1948 Declaration, in the text of two important United Nations treaties: the Convention on the Economical, Social and Cultural Rights and the Convention on the Civil and Political Rights. Both treaties were adopted after a long negotiations, during which states expressed and debated their positions concerning the declared human rights principles, and in so doing contributing to the progressive development of customary international law.

Paragraphs 1–3 of Article 18 of the International Covenant on Civil and Political Rights[728] is almost a literal reaffirmation of the expressions used in Article 18 of the Universal Declaration. This provision provides for a conventional obligation — of an essentially negative character — of abstention and non-interference in religious freedom. Its extensive interpretation implies a positive obligation to adopt the measures necessary to permit and guarantee the right of religious freedom allowing all state's residents to effectively exercise such a right.

The "Declaration on the Elimination of All Forms of Intolerance and Discrimination Based on Religion or Opinion," adopted by the General Assembly on November 25, 1981,[729] confirms this interpretation. Article 1 of the 1981 Declaration, which aims at respect of religious freedom, confirms the formula used in Article 18 mentioned above. Seven additional articles of the Declaration clarify this general principle. In particular, Article 6 includes the right "(a) To worship or assemble in connection with a religion or belief and to establish and maintain places for these purposes."[730]

It is fitting at this point to add that an Israeli Supreme Court decision made by Judge Cohn in 1967, one year after the conclusion of the Pact on Civil and Political Rights, also confirms the existence of the principle of religious freedom in customary international law:

> The principle of freedom of religion, that like other human rights proclaimed in the Universal Declaration of the Human Rights of 1948 and in the Pact on the Civil and Political Rights of 1966, represent today the heritage of all civilized countries, whether they are or not members of the Organization of the United Nations and whether they have ratified or not the 1966 Pact; such documents indeed have been written by legal experts from any area of the globe and have been approved by the General Assembly of the United Nations, with the participation of the overwhelming majority of the world States.[731]

An additional element providing evidence *opinio juris* to confirm the principle of religious freedom is the commitment undertaken in Article 1 of the Fundamental Agreement between the Holy See and the State of Israel of 1993. Although provided for in a bilateral agreement, this provision taken together with other similar international gestures suffice to establish a customary rule:

1. The State of Israel, recalling its Declaration of Independence, affirms its continuing commitment to uphold and observe the human right to freedom of religion and conscience, as set forth In the Universal Declaration of Human Rights and in other international instruments to which it is a party.

2. The Holy See, recalling the Declaration on Religious Freedom of the Second Vatican Ecumenical Council, 'Dignitatis Humanae', affirms the Catholic Church's commitment to uphold the human right to freedom of religion and conscience, as set forth in the Universal Declaration of Human Rights and in other international instruments to which it is a party. The Holy See wishes to affirm as well the Catholic Church's respect for other religions and their followers as solemnly stated by the Second Vatican Ecumenical Council in its Declaration on the Relation of the Church to Non-Christian Religions, 'Nostra Aetate.'[732]

The application of the general principles described above may follow special modalities. Taking into account the unique characteristics of the Jerusalem Holy Places, a conflict between the principle of religious freedom and the Status Quo/Modus Vivendi legal regime can be avoided. While the former is based on the universal principle of non-discrimination, the latter regime is, in contrast, discriminatory by definition:

Unlike the Preservation of the Holy Places Law [enacted by Israel in 1967], this arrangement [the Status Quo] is not egalitarian. It gives clear priority of rights over the Holy Places to the three large Christian denominations and mostly to the Greek-Orthodox community.[733]

For example, the Status Quo principles[734] imply that only the recognized bodies of selected communities have the possession and the right to worship in the Holy Places. This excludes communities or religious sects not recognized under the Status Quo/Modus Vivendi regime from freely exercising such rights. The application of the Status Quo/Modus Vivendi also excludes the recognized communities from the exercise of unlimited freedom of worship. According to the Muslim/Jewish Modus Vivendi, members of the Jewish community are allowed to visit the Har ha Bait/Haram al-Sharif Compound but are forbidden from collectively praying in the area.[735] From the point of view of universal human rights law this prohibition might be considered a violation of the principle of non-discrimination.

Should controversies arise on the interpretation of some of the Status Quo/Modus Vivendi principles, two conclusions could solve this apparent legal contradiction. Either the Status Quo/Modus Vivendi will prevail as a *lex specialis*[736] or the general principles of freedom of worship and non-discrimination will be the guiding criteria.

5.5 The broader cultural–religious status quo in Jerusalem

The main procedural rules regulating the Status Quo/Modus Vivendi in a narrow sense[737] should not be confused with a different sort of *acquis*, or common ground, accepted by all parties involved in the Holy Places and the cultural–religious dimension of the Jerusalem question. Various authors have described the latter with the expression *status quo*, in lower case, to distinguish it from the described Status Quo/Modus Vivendi legal regime, capitalized all through in this book. The expression status quo in the ordinary, not-capitalized, broad meaning of the term refers to the spiritual and eschatological dimension of the Jerusalem question, which stems from the universal religious interest in the fate of the city vis-à-vis the secular-national one.

Lapidoth confirms this distinction, clarifying that "in Israel in the religious context"[738] the expression status quo not only means the Status Quo in a narrow sense

— which she calls "the historical *status quo*"[739] — but also the status quo in a broad sense.

Additionally, the not-capitalized expression status quo is used in the context of relations between secular and religious Jews in Israel. The term in this context relates to "compromise arrangements on matters concerning the Jewish faith, such as respect for the precepts of Judaism in public places and in the army, safeguarding the rights of the religious establishment, and the application of religious law in marriage and divorce proceedings."[740]

Recent documents concerning Jerusalem issued by various interested parties, also confirm this interpretation. For example, the last part of Paragraph 2 of the Declaration by the European Council on the Middle East Peace Process, held in Florence on June 21–22, 1996 — known also as *the Florence Declaration* — implicitly aims at guaranteeing both the broad cultural–religious status quo in Jerusalem and the Status Quo/Modus Vivendi in a narrow sense:

> 2. The European Union encourages all parties likewise to re-engage themselves in the Peace Process, to respect and implement fully all the agreements already reached and to resume negotiations as soon as possible on the basis of the principles already accepted by all parties under the Madrid and Oslo frameworks. These cover all the issues on which the parties have agreed to negotiate, including Jerusalem, noting its importance for the parties and the international community, not least the need to respect the established rights of religious institutions.[741]

The broad cultural–religious status quo, in this respect, relates to all aspects and established principles, including freedom of worship, access and pilgrimage to the main places of worship within Jerusalem or in its immediate proximity of significant importance for Christians, Jews and Muslims. This meaning is to be distinguished from the Status Quo/Modus Vivendi in a narrow sense, despite the fact that the principle of non-interference limiting the power of the local governments is common to both sets of rules.[742] Therefore, in its broader meaning, the expression status quo, which applies to the cultural–religious dimension of the Jerusalem question, refers to the principles regulating the relationship between the recognized communities on one hand and the local government on the other, especially concerning their respective Holy Places.

The first High Commissioner in Palestine Herbert Samuel had already expressed a similar concept in 1925, while referring to the importance of archaeology in Jerusalem.[743] According to Berkovitz:

> (. . .) Eight principles are acceptable to all parties concerned and have never been disputed by anyone:
> 1. Protection of the Holy Places.
> 2. Respect for their dignity and sanctity.
> 3. Freedom of worship.
> 4. Freedom of access and exit.
> 5. Proper maintenance.
> 6. Exemption from taxation.
> 7. Observance of the "status quo" in its broad sense.
> 8. Precedence of the public interest in matters such as safety, health, and proper conduct, over the above principles.[744]

Thus, the broad cultural–religious status quo relates to all aspects and established principles embodied in the regulations enacted since the Ottoman Empire[745] vis-à-vis the various recognized communities present in the city.

Some authors also relate the broad religious status quo to the special status of general consulates located in Jerusalem,[746] although the possible relationship between the two is not officially and clearly defined:

> This was the situation which Israel (and Jordan) inherited in 1948; the fact that the UN resolution of November 29, 1947 called for international status for Jerusalem added a dimension to an international factor which, as noted, had existed beforehand.
>
> The various foreign consulates which had existed in Jerusalem before 1948 (with a British consulate now added to them) continued to function with no connection to the embassies of their respective countries in Tel Aviv and/or Amman. Both Israel and Jordan accepted this situation ex post facto, and Israel did not alter it after reuniting Jerusalem in 1967.
>
> For more than thirty years, then, a number of consulates (American, British, French, Belgian, Italian, Turkish and Spanish) operate without accreditation to any government; they and the authorities cooperate *de facto*; they receive all customs exemptions extended to full-fledged consulates, as well as other prerequisites. The tax and customs exemptions extended to the various churches remain in force; Israel has maintained the *status quo* throughout.
>
> (. . .) Israel extended the consular and ecclesiastical tax and customs reductions in force in the western sector to the eastern as well, thereby preserving to a greater or lesser degree, the *status quo* as observed by the Jordanian authorities.[747]

The extraordinary, if not unique, characteristic of the Holy Places of Jerusalem indirectly explains the above assumption, confirmed also by a series of acts adopted by UNESCO organs. The preamble of Resolution 15C/3.343, adopted by UNESCO General Conference, in view of the preservation of the cultural heritage of Jerusalem, begins by underlining the "exceptional importance of the cultural heritage in the Old City of Jerusalem, and in particular the Holy Places, not only for the states directly interested, but for the whole humanity, taking into account their artistic, historical and religious value."[748]

The "List of the natural and cultural world heritage" adopted in 1972 at the UNESCO Convention on the protection of World Heritage on September 10 and 11, 1981, included the Old City of Jerusalem and its walls. This inclusion was motivated by the unanimous recognition of "their unique importance in view of the universal values that in it are represented from the religious, historic, architectonic and artistic point of view."[749]

The Israeli Supreme Court has expressed a similar view in its decision titled "Nationalist Groups against the Ministry of Police" in which the area of the Har ha Bait/Haram al-Sharif of Jerusalem is defined as the most sacred area of Jerusalem for both Jews and Muslims. In Judge Witkon's words, "the situation is unique, probably without parallels in the history of this territory or in the whole world."[750] It is important to note that Israeli Attorney General has quoted Judge Witkon's words in the "Guidelines on the observation of the law on planning and building on the antiquities in the area of the Temple Mount."[751]

This study has broadly examined the practice of the various local governments administering the area vis-à-vis the special privileges, immunities, or exemptions granted to the recognized communities present in Jerusalem. These rights often extended beyond the standard of similar rights granted by most countries in the world in the context of freedom of religion and worship.

Since the more recent developments do not challenge the analysis above, it may be concluded that any authority exercising territorial jurisdiction on Jerusalem has the obligation to respect the various manifestations of religious freedom expressed in relation to the places in the city venerated as sacred.[752]

5.6 Hypothesis of an international local custom (objective regime) and the binding effects of the unilateral declarations

This book has considered how different governments and interested parties have applied and developed the principles applied to the cultural–religious status quo in Jerusalem which have been summarized in the previous section. However, it has *not* dealt with the various aspects of the local authorities' legitimacy in Jerusalem, because the aforementioned principles apply to the permanent status of the city, regardless of the handling of the question and the outcome of the negotiations.

In their respective administrative, legislative and diplomatic practice, particularly since 1947, the parties have generally used the expression *existing rights* to confirm a normative consistency. Such consistency in time of peace may represent the material element — *diuturnitas* — of an international custom based on the effective practice of the various governments in the area over the centuries.

The material sources of *custom* are numerous and include the following: diplomatic correspondence, policy statements, press releases, the opinions of official legal advisers, official manuals on legal questions, i.e. manuals of military law, executive decisions and practices, orders to naval forces etc., comments by governments on drafts produced by the International Law Commission, state legislation, international and national judicial decisions, recitals in treaties and other international instruments, a pattern of treaties in the same form, the practice of international organs, and resolutions relating to legal questions in the United Nations General Assembly.[753]

In order to ascertain the existence and/or the specific contents of customary norms — beside formal declarations of principle embodied in solemn documents — the interested parties, in particular the local governments must manifest the relevant practice with the legal belief, *opinio juris*, that such recurring conduct is legally binding:

> Some writers do not consider this psychological element to be a requirement for the formation of custom, but it is in fact a necessary ingredient. The sense of legal obligation, as opposed to motives of courtesy, fairness, or morality, is real enough, and the practice of states recognizes a distinction between obligation and usage. The essential problem is surely one of proof, and especially the incidence of the burden of proof . . . The choice of approach appears to depend upon the nature of the issues (that is, the state of the law may be a primary point in contention), and the discretion of the Court.[754]

Restrictions imposed on local governments limiting the full exercise of territorial jurisdiction to protect these principles may find their legal source in an international local custom, a sort of *objective regime* which binds all administrators of the territory in question:[755]

It is indeed perfectly conceivable a special custom producing norms for a limited number of States or even for two States only. The limit of a norm created by a special custom, as far as the sphere of its addressees is concerned, does not depend on the fact that some States only have taken part in the formation of the custom (. . .) but it is just an aspect of the norm's content. It is a customary norm created to regulate a limited number of relations: as a consequence, it is addressed to a limited number of subjects only.[756]

In the "Right of Passage in Indian Territory" case, the judges considered the possible formation of an international local custom. The *ad hoc* judge Chagla, designated by India to the panel of the International Court of Justice deciding this case, claimed that India merely "tolerated" the passage over its territory as a "*faveur et . . . complaisance.*"[757] Chagla wrote that Portugal did not prove the existence of an international obligation limiting Indian "sovereignty"[758] neither on the basis of a local custom, nor of a general custom, or of the general principles of international law.

The local customs, if recognized, would bind the local government. When there is a change in the local administration, the successor inherits its predecessor's obligations. Despite the apparent similarity, possible analogies with the so-called "servitudes" existing in private municipal law of various states should be considered with caution. The quoted *ad hoc* judge rejected any possible analogy, between an international right of passage and servitude of municipal law, as contrary to the very notion of "sovereignty."[759] According to Arangio-Ruiz, in the quoted "Right of Passage in Indian Territory" case:

> The essential question concerning the case was to find out if India was or was not obliged by customary or conventional international law to positive or negative behaviours that a State is obliged to when participating, with another international State-person, to a «*servitude de passage.*»[760]

Its is important to note that the International Court of Justice had earlier considered the abstract possibility of the formation of a local custom in the case of the "Rights of Nationals of the United States in Morocco," concerning the "Capitulations."[761] This term defines those typical bilateral agreements concluded during the Ottoman rule, which recognized certain privileges — such as fiscal exemptions or immunity from ordinary judicial jurisdiction — to Western residents. In its decision, the Court acknowledged the existence of the material element, the consistent relevant practice, of the alleged international custom. However a majority of the judges stated that the psychological element, the *opinio juris*, was not sufficiently proved to recognize the alleged binding character as evidence of the existence of customary norms in the consular practice of the United States. In fact, four of the eleven members of the Court issued a dissenting opinion which stated that the United States did produce enough evidence, consisting mainly of diplomatic correspondence, to ascertain the customary foundation of their claim. The four judges — Hackworth, Badawi, Levi Carneiro and Sir Benegal Rau — stated that custom is a recognized source of territorial jurisdiction.

Accordingly, the four dissenting judges rejected France's claim (the protecting power of Morocco at that time), which argued that its attitude in the subject matter should be considered as mere gracious tolerance. Thus, it is safe to conclude that the Court did not rule out the abstract possibility that the formation process of a particular customary norm began under the Ottoman rule.

In the case discussed above, the Court ruled that the United States did have the right to exercise consular jurisdiction over the French Zone of Morocco in all civil and criminal controversies between citizens and people *protected* by the United States. Further that such right stemmed from conventional, rather than customary law, that is to say, from the interpretation of provisions included in some treaties stipulated by the United States.

When considering the elements of custom, particularly the uniformity and consistency of the practice, Brownlie has stressed that a tribunal has considerable freedom of determination in many cases, since "Complete uniformity is not required, but substantial uniformity is."[762] It is important to recall in this context that Israeli law, following the common law tradition, distinguishes between international customary and conventional law. International customs are considered part of the domestic law and do not need a specific statute to transform the correspondent norms into Israeli municipal law, unless they conflict with an existing statute.[763] On the contrary, treaty-based norms have no legal effect unless they are incorporated in a statute within the Israeli legal order.

In the case of treaties containing both provisions reflecting existing customary law (declaratory treaty-law), and new prescriptions (constitutive treaty-law) "only the former would have internal effect"[764] in Israel. Israeli statutes must be so construed as to conform as much as possible to international customary obligations since there is a legal presumption that the Knesset, has no intention of derogating from them.[765]

When considering the principles described in the previous section, the analysis of the relevant practice leads to the conclusion that an *objective regime* characterizes the area in question. Such an international legal regime binds any local government, regardless of whether or not the government is a party of an international agreement on the same subject.

In addition to the discussed possibility of the formation of an international local custom, or an objective regime, the international obligations which protect these principles may find other legal sources of their binding nature. International law subjects may bind themselves to behave in a certain way by making solemn unilateral declarations either before other subjects directly interested, or before the rest of the states, i.e., *erga omnes*.

For a unilateral commitment to be recognized as binding, the International Court of Justice requires the fulfillment of three conditions,[766] which may be assumed in the unilateral declarations made by various authorities in control of the area in question:

1 The public nature of said declarations emanated by a competent organ.
2 The intention of creating legal obligations, on the other hand, may be deduced from the wording of such declarations, taking into account their political and diplomatic context.
3 Formal agreement on the subject could hardly be reached by the parties, due to the extreme complexity and sensitivity of the matter involving a great number of subjects of international law, as well as various communities whose interests are apparently protected by international law.

From an analysis of recent practice, it must be emphasized that the states raising claims over the Holy Places were at war with Israel or did not have diplomatic relations with this country. Israel signed a peace treaty with Egypt and Jordan only recently, in 1978 and 1994 respectively.

Moreover, it is worth recalling the principle of estoppel or preclusion. This principle is accepted in international law, with some reservations,[767] as Lord McNair attests:

> It is reasonable to expect that any legal system should possess a rule designed to prevent a person who makes or concurs in a statement upon which another person in privity with him relies to the extent of changing his position, from later asserting a different state of affairs.[768]

In conclusion, recent international practice confirms a general consistency of those broad and universally accepted principles in time of peace which regulate significant aspects of the Jerusalem question and bind any local authority in charge of the Jerusalem administration and especially of the walled city. This legal framework governing the international dimension of the Jerusalem question is therefore already settled and its analysis can serve to facilitate and perhaps accelerate the permanent status negotiations.

5.7 The partial suspension of the principles applied to the Holy Places in times of war

The local authority is responsible for public order, safety and decorum in the Holy Places and must not interfere in the internal matters of the recognized communities, the only entities authorized to manage the Holy Places. The analysis presented in this work shows that this principle has been applied only in time of peace.

From this perspective, it is apparent that the application of the previously mentioned inter-Christian Status Quo to the Jewish–Muslim relationship, initiated by the British Mandatory government, can be effective only as long as a relatively peaceful situation prevails. The full development of the extension of the inter-Christian Status Quo to the major Jewish–Muslim Holy Places has apparently been suspended by political instability created by the Arab–Israeli conflict, particularly as a result of certain Jordanian and, to a certain extent, Israeli actions.

However, the basic applicable procedural norms of this legal regime as well as of the broader cultural–religious status quo described above, have remained in force, showing their effectiveness over the years. The International Court of Justice has emphasized that the practice necessary to prove the formation of a custom did not have to be "in absolutely rigorous conformity" with the purported customary rule:

> In order to deduce the existence of customary rules, the Court deems it sufficient that the conduct of states should, in general, be consistent with such rules, and that instances of state conduct inconsistent with a given rule should generally have been treated as breaches of that rule, not as indications of the recognition of a new rule.[769]

Violent confrontations, in the form of all-out war, armed uprising or intensive and harmful terror attacks, have not barred the development of an international customary norm guaranteeing the principles applied to the Holy Places. The political–diplomatic situation has only temporarily prevented the full implementation of certain rules applied in the Holy Places.[770] Regardless of the temporary suspension of their application, these principles have remained unchanged and in force.

This is particularly significant for the Status Quo/Modus Vivendi procedural norms that have been developing over a long period of time, beginning — as far as the Christian Holy Places are concerned — from the Ottoman rule in the area. Any improvement of the political–diplomatic situation makes possible their full implementation.

The temporary and partial limitation of this long established legal regime in the Holy Places applies particularly to the first rule included in the list of Status Quo/Modus Vivendi principles presented in this book.[771] This rule requires the consent by the recognized communities for any change in the procedural or material principles of the Status Quo/Modus Vivendi. The political–diplomatic instability has limited the implementation of this Status Quo/Modus Vivendi rule even though it has kept their binding force.

In two instances in particular, namely during the 1948–1967 Jordanian rule over the Old City of Jerusalem[772] as well as the Israeli administration after the 1967 Six Day War,[773] changes have affected the Modus Vivendi in the Muslim/Jewish Holy Places without the explicit consent of the recognized communities. Jordanian behavior, in particular, may have gone far beyond the strictly limited responsibility over public order, safety and decorum in the Holy Places.

The Jordanian authorities never officially objected to the existence of an international obligation of the *pro-tempore* local authority to guarantee protection, religious freedom, including free access and worship, and the safeguard of the legal regime applying to the Holy Places of Jerusalem (the broader cultural–religious status quo).[774] It solemnly recognized those principles in the 1994 Jordanian–Israeli Peace Agreement provisions.[775]

The Jordanian claim that the situation of war and risks for public order allowed them to temporarily suspend the implementation of the obligation to guarantee freedom of access to the Holy Places of Jerusalem is subject to much dispute. When the Israelis could again access the Jewish Quarter in the Old City at the end of the 1967 War, they found out that "numerous synagogues, yeshivot (Jewish scholarly academies), and other religious buildings had been wantonly vandalized and destroyed."[776] These acts of vandalism are a clear violation of the Status Quo/Modus Vivendi legal regime, other basic cultural and religious principles governing the Holy Places of Jerusalem, as well as customary or conventional international obligations applicable in time of war.

In this respect, Israel has committed itself "on a *de facto* basis"[777] to act in accordance with "the humanitarian provisions"[778] of the Geneva Convention Relative to the Protection of Civilian Persons in Time of War.[779] Regardless of the question of the status of Jerusalem,[780] the official Israeli position is that "this convention does not apply *de jure* in the West Bank and the Gaza Strip." According to the Israeli position, "these areas are not 'occupied territory' in the meaning of the Convention, since sovereignty in these areas was never vested in Jordan and Egypt."[781]

The current diplomatic situation between Israel and Jordan, in the context of the Middle East peace process, has made it possible to put aside the issue of those Jordanian unjustified violations. It must be clear that the need to maintain public order cannot justify indiscriminate violations of international norms, such as the principles protecting human rights and religious freedom. The temporary suspension in time of war or other security emergencies of certain principles applied to the Holy Places must be limited and well defined in its scope, particularly concerning unimpeded freedom of access to them.

It is worth mentioning that in human rights law there is a distinction between *absolute* and *relative* human rights.[782] This distinction depends on whether international law, particularly human rights treaties, allows for the derogation of such human rights in case of public emergency. Only *relative* human rights can be derogated from under certain conditions, while *absolute* human rights are non derogable.

Article 4, Paragraph 1 of the International Covenant on Civil and Political Rights, adopted by General Assembly Resolution 2200A (XXI) of December 16, 1966 in force since March 23, 1976,[783] permits such derogation under the following limited conditions:

> 1. In time of public emergency which threatens the life of the nation and the existence of which is officially proclaimed, the States Parties to the present Covenant may take measures derogating from their obligations under the present Covenant to the extent strictly required by the exigencies of the situation, provided that such measures are not inconsistent with their other obligations under international law and do not involve discrimination solely on the ground of race, colour, sex, language, religion or social origin.

This possibility of derogation is limited only to certain specified human rights listed in the Covenant, while no derogation may be made under this provision from a number of *absolute* rights listed in Paragraph 2 of the same Article 4. Similarly, Article 15, Paragraph 1 of the European Convention on Human Rights and Fundamental Freedoms, signed in Rome on November 4, 1950,[784] includes an analogous possibility of derogation in case of war or officially declared public danger that threatens the life of the country:

> 1. TIn time of war or other public emergency threatening the life of the nation any High Contracting Party may take measures derogating from its obligations under this Convention to the extent strictly required by the exigencies of the situation, provided that such measures are not inconsistent with its other obligations under international law.

The careful wording of this provision clearly implies that such derogation should strictly remain within necessary limitations in order to face the emergency, without allowing any further derogation to other international law obligations. Like the International Covenant, the European Convention includes a provision in Article 15, Paragraph 2, which excludes the possibility of derogation from a number of human rights listed in the Convention.

Conclusions and Suggestions for Further Reserach

A: The Status Quo/Modus Vivendi and the Quartet's Road Map in the perspective of the state and global identity models

This study has attempted to clarify that under certain conditions the vested interests of the recognized communities in the Holy Places are protected by international principles. In times of peace, the different local authorities have been relatively consistent in their practice and attitude relating to the Holy Places in the area of Jerusalem, thereby justifying the adoption of the expression *status quo*. This consistency relates to two different aspects of the status quo, regulated by groups of norms, summarized in earlier chapters.

The first group includes a set of procedural principles applying to the aforementioned Status Quo/Modus Vivendi legal regime.[785] This work introduces an argument that describes the Status Quo/Modus Vivendi (in a narrow sense) as a consistent and effective legal regime whose legal nature is not dependent upon the changes of the different local rulers, or upon the applicability of the universal norms that guarantee religious freedom.

Additionally, an attempt has been made to afford an analysis of a problem that, so far, scholars have not fully examined in its wider implications and to emphasize the relationship and possible contradictions between the Status Quo/Modus Vivendi legal regime, exclusively applicable to the Holy Places of Jerusalem, and the universal principles of freedom of religion and worship, particularly the principle of non-discrimination.

As already stated, it is essential to distinguish the formal from the substantial aspects of the Status Quo/Modus Vivendi since the organization of this legal system is regulated by procedural norms whereas material norms regulate all the complex web of rights and claims concerning the Holy Places.

Most scholars have focused on the material rules, dividing space and time for the Holy Places' use and possession. It is noteworthy that this legal regime's material rules, which regulate the detailed rights and claims of the different communities, defining the contents of the Status Quo, have changed over the centuries. On the contrary, the legal system's instrumental or procedural norms have basically remained the same to the present day.

The second meaning of the expression status quo (non capitalized) refers to the *acquis* or common ground concerning the cultural–religious dimension of the

Jerusalem question and its Holy Places, a set of principles broadly accepted by all the parties involved, defined in this work as the status quo in the broader sense. These principles are summarized in a list, entitled "Basic Cultural and Religious Principles Governing the Holy Places of Jerusalem."[786]

The summarized principles are fully applicable only in time of peace whereas situations of war or other threats to public order, such as terrorism or general violent rioting, may prevent the implementation of some of its rules, but they have remained in force despite periods of temporary suspension.[787]

Furthermore, this research has presented a case study in particularly controversial areas, namely that of the practical application of objective regimes, of local customs, and of the legal effects of unilateral declarations in international law. New interpretations regarding the application of international norms to contemporary problems have been used to help clarify the different meanings of controversial terms such as *sovereignty* and *jurisdiction*.

The term *jurisdiction*, as distinguished in its territorial, functional and personal aspects, seems better suited than *sovereignty* to clarify the legal arrangements adopted in the Israeli–Palestinian agreements as well as setting the parameters for future settlement.

Limits to personal or functional jurisdiction are compatible with the exercise of territorial jurisdiction or territorial *sovereignty*. The Glossary to this work thoroughly defines the three different dimensions implied in the term *sovereignty*: *independence*, *title* and *authority* (or *jurisdiction*).[788] The latter concept is further defined according to its three aspects: functional, territorial and personal *jurisdiction*.

This case study of Jerusalem and its Holy Places significantly shows how international practice is often more complex than any abstract model can show. It includes a wide range of options in shaping the relationship between the human groups and their territory.

Regardless of this flexible and dynamic reality, Western political élites have tried to use and manipulate Jerusalem and the Holy Places located therein as symbols of their respective socio-political models of identity. Modern media and intellectual debate focus their attention only on two dimensions of the Jerusalem question, corresponding to two ways which define the collective interests at stake.

Jerusalem and its Holy Places have become the symbolic frontier, charged with emotional meanings, for the competition between the two following parallel approaches and opposite ways of considering territory, in its real or immaterial dimension:

1 The *state/territorial model*, which regards territory in its tangible, material dimension as the physical geographical boundary of the polity where the group resides and develops its collective memory;
2 The *global/trans-territorial model*, which emphasizes the virtual, metaphorical significance of territorial space. Here, the criteria used to define the community stress common personal features, which are borderless, in the geographical sense, by definition: race, values, ideologies or faith.

The conclusions reached through this methodology represent the leitmotif of the research, emerging in different ways throughout the text. In particular, its epistemological perspective highlights a dichotomist Western approach that offers a hermeneutic key for the interpretation of the documents under examination and helps understand in a new light the complex subject of Holy Places and the whole of the Arab–Israeli conflict.

While the analysis and interpretation of the diplomatic and legal documents on this specific issue greatly differs from the works of other scholars, it is hoped that the multidisciplinary approach[789] coupled with the adoption of innovative models, may shed a new light on complicated and contentious issues and highlight the potential practical results.

An example of the desired results of this study's methodology is the clarification of the controversial issue of immunity from ordinary jurisdiction according to the 1924 British Holy Places Order in Council. This conclusion can be reached by analyzing the issue through a combination of diplomatic history and legal hermeneutics, used to explain British interests in stressing a global/trans-territorial approach on the issue of the adjudication of the Status Quo's disputes.

This assumption inescapably rules out a different interpretation of the relevant applicable provisions since a state/territorial-oriented approach that ascribed the competence to settle the substance of such disputes to the local ruler, would forcefully clash with some perceived British interests at that time.

The limited scope of this research allows for the development of certain aspects of the contrast between the state/territorial and the global/trans-territorial models of collective identity. If the epistemological assumptions are correct, these two models help re-interpret the whole modern Western history and historiography in a different perspective.

Considering another example, the "Performance-Based Roadmap to a Permanent Two-state Solution to the Israeli–Palestinian Conflict,"[790] released by the United States Department on April 30, 2003 and approved by both the State of Israel and the PLO, could be interpreted in light of the dichotomist model suggested in this research.

The Roadmap provides specific provisions relating to Jerusalem and specifies a timeline and the steps the two parties must undertake to reach a settlement under the auspices of the Quartet: the United States, the European Union, the United Nations, and Russia.

Accordingly, the parties are to "reach final and comprehensive permanent status agreement that ends the Israel-Palestinian conflict in 2005" and "a negotiated resolution on the status of Jerusalem that takes into account the political and religious concerns of both sides, and protects the religious interests of Jews, Christians, and Muslims worldwide."

Such provisions afford a two-fold dimension of the Jerusalem question, which includes its Holy Places and the whole city, and corresponds to the two previously described ways of defining the collective interests at stake. The parties involved in the conflict rally themselves behind the banner of Jerusalem and use it as a pretext to stage a verbal or physical attack against their opposing side.

In fact the communities mentioned in the Road Map provision define two corresponding models of collective identity. In the first part of the quoted Roadmap provision, the first model relates to the "political and religious concerns of" Israel and the PLO, respectively representing the Israeli and the Palestinian national identities in their separate territories.

Following this state/territorial-oriented model, only the official authorities of the two local groups, which desire mutual acceptance within the territory of their respective ethnic national states, should be the ultimate claimants of rights and claims in the Holy Places and Jerusalem.

The symbolic value of these places for the competing Israeli and Arab, later Palestinian, national movements is strongly related to the development of their respective collective identities which, particularly since the 1930s, were influenced by the state/territorial model. According to Avraham Yehoshua:

> National or ethnic-national groups preceded the formation of states; but the state has been a powerful instrument for the crystallization of nations for unifying national identities;[791]

The second part of the quoted Roadmap provision refers to the protection of "the religious interests of" millions of people worldwide identified as "Jews, Christians, and Muslims".

According to this global/trans-territorial definition of collective identity, the religious communities share their faith and interests with the faithful who reside outside Jerusalem or the Israeli–Palestinian areas. Following this view, only the religious communities' representatives, who consider the city and its Holy Places as a focus for worship and spiritual devotion, are entitled to exercise rights in and raise claims to the Holy Places.

B: Suggestions for further research

B.1. The competition between the two identity models and the cycles of Western history

Samuel Huntington has emphasized the importance of the debate about identity in his book *The Clash of Civilizations and the Remaking of World Order*:

> Peoples and nations are attempting to answer the most basic question humans can face: Who are we? And they are answering that question in the traditional way human beings have answered it, by reference to the things that mean most to them. People define themselves in terms of ancestry, religion, language, history, values, customs, and institutions. They identify with cultural groups: tribes, ethnic groups, religious communities, nations, and, at the broadest level, civilizations. People use politics not just to advance their interests but also to define their identity. We know who we are only when we know who we are not and often only when we know whom we are against.[792] (. . .) People define their identity by what they are not.[793]

The inherent competition between state/territorial and global/trans-territorial models of collective identity has shaped the reality and the perception of Western institutions and political organizations. These models characterize socio-political needs on one hand and administrative structures on the other, in a continuous osmotic relationship of cause-effect.

The development of collective identity along state/territorial lines finds its basis in the organization of governmental power according to institutional frameworks touching upon the European-born concept of territorial *sovereignty*.[794]

On the contrary, trans-territorial models of global-oriented group identification such as universal religious affiliation have the strong support of some scholars, such as Huntington:

> Of all the objective elements which define civilizations, (. . .) the most important usually is religion (. . .). To a very large degree, the major civilizations in human history have been closely identified with the world's great religions; and people who share ethnicity and language but differ in religion may slaughter each other as happened in Lebanon, the former Yugoslavia and the Subcontinent.[795]
>
> (. . .) In the modern world, religion is a central, perhaps the central, force that motivates and mobilizes people.[796]

One may subject the homogeneous character of Lebanon, the Indian subcontinent and especially the former Yugoslavia to dispute. In any case, even if in Huntington's opinion the extent to which global-oriented models of identities, "cultures of civilizations," resemble or differ from one another may vary considerably, real and significant lines are never as sharp as the state geographical boundaries which mark such collective identities:

> Civilizations have no clear-cut boundaries and no precise beginning and endings. People can and do refine their identities and, as a result, the composition and shapes of civilizations change over time. The cultures of peoples interact and overlap.

Both state/territorial and global/trans-territorial models represent the source of political–philosophical justifications in legitimating Western political elites and affecting different academic fields in social and political sciences. This study develops the idea that these two contrasting principles have forged political institutions following an apparent dichotomist cyclical process[797] and have alternatively influenced different periods in history like waves in an ocean tormented by conflicting winds.

Thus, around the middle of the seventeenth century, international relations have developed the egalitarian structure based on the national-oriented state. The 1648 Peace of Westphalia, which includes the two Treaties of Münster and Osnabrück and marked the end of the Thirty Years' War, is considered as the foundation of modern international law.[798] This date is purely symbolic since no announcement was ever made on that glorious morning in 1648, that international law was born.

The structure of international relations and a corresponding set of norms have been the fruit of a slow and discontinued evolution since the path of these developments has varied in relation to the different norms. Many customary norms and just as many rules regulating the law of treaties, reprisals, or diplomatic and consular relations, started developing their *usus* long before the seventeenth century.

What really changed in the Westphalia period was the socio-political context in which the *communis opinio*, that is, the predominant thinking, evaluated them. The lack of a central authority above the states along with the idea of equality among independent states, regardless of their dimension or the sovereign's religious belief, developed during this period.

This state/territorial-oriented approach was the result of a long evolution that replaced the Middle Age global-oriented concept based on feudal relations and on the recognition of the institutional preeminence of the two classical authorities, the Pope and the Emperor, the two "suns" of Dante Alighieri's *De Monarchia*.[799]

However, such change did not suddenly replace all previous norms. Whereas all customary norms evolve from a continuous and imperceptible movement, the norms characterizing Westphalia's structure started developing over the years within a different structure, which was basically hostile to them.

The new norms had to temporarily adapt their meaning within the Middle Age old structure, as long as it continued to prevail. As the new norms increased in number, they contributed to the erosion of the old framework, leading to a general change in the system of the new Westphalia's characters which became prevalent on both the socio-political and normative front, that is, two faces of one reality.[800]

From this moment on, the whole set of rules inspired by the old vertical structure seemed to be in clear contradiction to the new system and underwent a process of slow erosion, leading to the gradual change of its contents almost in entirety. An example is the complex feudal relations that remained in force in Germany, the heart of the Holy Roman Empire, until the beginning of the nineteenth century.

Given the customary basis of the international legal system, this parallel evolution of both norms and general structure can neither stop nor reach 100 percent of its substantial consistency, while formal consistency exists by definition. There always are some recalcitrant elements, either relics of a previous structure or anticipation of a future order.[801]

In the twentieth century, state-oriented and global-oriented Western political elites competed with one another, each trying to impose its *Weltanschauung* and model of collective identity as the most legitimate and suitable one to interpret world politics:

> In 1917, as a result of the Russian Revolution, the conflict of nation states was supplemented by the conflict of ideologies, first among fascism, communism, and liberal democracy and then between the latter two. In the Cold War these ideologies were embodied in the two superpowers, each of which defined its identity by its ideology and neither of which was a nation state in the traditional European sense.[802]

From the foregoing it can be deduced that, during the Cold War, which set up transnational boundaries between the Communist and the capitalist blocs following trans-territorial ideological criteria, global-oriented models of identity prevailed once again.

In contrast, the period following the fall of the Berlin Wall characterized the resurgence of academic, journalistic and popular debate about national identity, according to the territorial criteria, typical of the continental European nation-state.

This way of interpreting conflicts between newborn political homogeneous territorial-ethnic entities of Europe, by emphasizing their national dimension, has influenced the territorial two-national interpretation of the Israeli–PLO negotiations, which secretly started in Oslo culminating in the Declaration of Principles in 1993.[803]

Despite this trend, recent events, following the terrorist attacks on September 11, 2001 in the United States, have marked a new wave of trans-territorial discourse on a global basis, where transnational terrorists challenge traditional state frontiers and replace old-fashioned conflicts by marking territorial boundaries with a newly created global Islamic-Western civilization divide.

One of the main problems in political and social science research is the position of the observer in relation to his/her social and political environment or background. Keeping this epistemological consideration in mind, this research gives the reader an insight into both theoretical issues and their political implications.

After several years of study, the results of this research were arrived at after consultation with a plethora of religious and political authorities from conflicting backgrounds: Arab, Israeli, Christian, Jewish, Muslim, European and American.

They all extensively discussed the main assumptions regarding the study with me, and this fieldwork experience has contributed to my growing awareness about both the sensitivity of the issue and the risks involved in taking sides with one over the other of the interested parties. Despite the vastness of the research, this effort has also helped me avoid the danger of an ivory-tower intellectual investigation, perhaps attractive from an abstract point of view, but devoid of significant connection with the real world.

Given the fact that this research has attracted the attention of several decision-makers, some of whom were contacted in the process, its conclusions may lead to further investigation and developments, in consideration of their possible practical ramifications for future negotiations on the Holy Places of Jerusalem.

If the basic principles of this work are widely accepted, the entire religious dimension of the Jerusalem question may be perceived as having already found a reasonable solution, at least in the framework of some very broad principles.

Whatever the outcome of the ongoing permanent status negotiations, if the assumption that certain principles of international law are already applicable to the Holy Places is accepted, these will be binding on *any entity* administering Jerusalem and, in particular, the walled city. Once accepted and a concession is made to the effect that a settled legal framework governs the religious dimension of the Jerusalem question, the present and future negotiations on the issues of territorial jurisdiction and political administration may be facilitated and perhaps accelerated.

In fact, an acceptable solution may already be in place. This conclusion applies in particular to Israel and the PLO which, according to the Declaration of Principles signed in Washington DC on September 13, 1993, are the parties that are to negotiate the issue of Jerusalem and its Holy Places in talks regarding the final status. Additionally, it may apply to all other parties interested in the Holy Places.

B.2 Legal implications of the three alternative definitions of sovereignty

Given the potentially misleading effects of the term *sovereignty*, expounding on the distinction between its different meanings may help clarify the debate about the complex negotiations on Jerusalem. Negotiators may consider the possibility of drawing special arrangements among themselves, each of whom may exercise governmental powers in areas under the territorial jurisdiction of others.

A typical example that may assist this process is Saint Peter's Square in Rome, where the Holy See has the title under international law, while Italy exercises a set of governmental powers. Drawing from this, each of the two parties to the negotiations on Jerusalem may establish part of their capital *abroad* or, more precisely, in an area under the other party's territorial jurisdiction. The example of exercising governmental powers abroad is an expression of the utility of recognizing the distinctions between the *three main meanings of sovereignty as independence, authority,* or *title*, clarified in the Glossary (see Appendix IV) below.[804]

It cannot be stressed enough how these distinctions may apply to Jerusalem and its Holy Places, where the parties can feel free to distinguish discussions regarding the actual exercise of *authority* in the city apart from the *title* applied to it.

For example, capital cities may be established in the territorial jurisdiction of the other party, with each retaining personal jurisdiction over its citizens residing outside their own territory. In negotiating their rights in Jerusalem, Israel and the PLO do not need to ascertain in advance to whom the city presently belongs.

An example of the need to challenge the all-encompassing term *sovereignty* in the context of Jerusalem and its Holy Places is the unofficial European Union document defined as a "non-paper". This text, "acknowledged by the parties as being a relatively fair description of the outcome of the negotiations on the permanent status issues in Taba,"[805] was prepared by the European Union Special Representative to the Middle East Process, Ambassador Moratinos, and his team, after consultation with the Israeli and Palestinian sides present at the negotiations in January 2001. The negotiators have tried to develop an alternative concept to *sovereignty* that would relate to the Old City and its surroundings, with the Israeli side putting forward several alternative models for discussion.

Setting up a mechanism for close coordination and cooperation in the area or a special police force regime are just two examples of the ideas discussed at Taba. During the Taba talks the Israeli side expressed interest and raised its concern regarding the area conceptualized as the Holy (or Historic) Basin, which includes the Jewish Cemetery on the Mount of Olives, the City of David and Kidron Valley.

An alternative idea informally suggested by the Israeli side was the creation of a special regime or some form of internationalization for the entire Holy Basin or a joint regime with special cooperation and coordination; whereas the Palestinian side, although willing to take into account Israeli interests and concerns, claimed *sovereignty* over these places. According to the Glossary (Appendix IV) proposed in this book,[806] *sovereignty* could be replaced in this context by a clearer term *title*, whose holder is not necessarily the same subject of international law exercising authority over the area in question.

Both parties accepted the principle of respective control over each side's holy sites, including religious control and management. The parties have also considered practical arrangements regarding evacuations, building and public order in the area of the Har ha Bait/Haram al-Sharif compound for an agreed period, such as three years.

It was suggested that during this period the compound should be "under international sovereignty" of the five permanent members of the Security Council of the United Nations, plus Morocco, or other Islamic presence, whereby the Palestinians would be the "Guardian/Custodians."[807] The quoted Moratinos report states that at the end of this period, either the parties agree on a new solution or agree to extend the existing arrangement.

C: Israeli–Palestinian meetings behind closed doors on Jerusalem and its Holy Places

As a practical proposal for future research on the complex subjects of the Holy Places' Status Quo/Modus Vivendi, I have suggested that a series of meetings be organized by a third-party, whom both Palestinians and Israelis see as unbiased, among scholars and specialists. Of course, asking a third party to be involved in this matter would substantiate the serious interest and desire of both parties in establishing a lasting peace in the region and a satisfactory outcome regarding the Holy Places.

The suggested meetings should aim at clarifying several issues on which the parties may find an agreement in principle, even before the conclusion of the official negotiations between them.

The possibility of inviting, on an advisory basis, religious experts or authorities to such meetings should be considered. Their participation could serve to represent a concession towards a global-religious approach. In contrast, a purely state/territorial-oriented approach would have given exclusive responsibility for permanent status decisions to Palestinian and Israeli representatives.

The same logic applies to the type of body in charge of settling the Status Quo/Modus Vivendi disputes between the recognized communities. The larger the international participation, the better the global/trans-territorial perspective described in this work would be satisfied. On the contrary, a solution favoring ordinary judicial jurisdiction could signal a prevalence of the national states over global interests.

Specifically, once a definition of the Status Quo/Modus Vivendi legal regime in the Holy Places of Jerusalem in view of the Israeli–Palestinian negotiations is agreed upon, the following three policy options to settle potential disputes between the recognized religious communities on the interpretation and the implementation of the Status Quo/Modus Vivendi principles may be adopted:

- Ordinary judicial jurisdiction (state/territorial model);
- Political settlement (state model with global influences);
- A special body in charge of such disputes, namely a body that is recognized by the concerned parties as being able to take decisions independently from the interests of the parties, while at the same time taking them into due account (global/transnational model).

In 2006, *Mediterranean Perspectives*, a cultural association I have the honor of chairing, has developed the Project titled "The Holy Places of Jerusalem in the Middle East Agreement," sponsored by the Representation in Italy of the European Commission, the Foreign Ministry of Italy, the Municipality of Rome, the Province of Rome, the Lazio Region, the Institute for International Legal Studies (ISGI) at the Council for National Research (CNR) and the Italian Centre of Studies for International Conciliation (CISCI).

Mediterranean Perspectives has organized a series of seminars behind closed doors in Rome, with the goal of facilitating cooperative development of dialogue between Israeli and Palestinian experts, with the contribution of a Scientific Committee made up of other experts and diplomats, regarding Jerusalem and its Holy Places in and around the city.

The Association has also held several meetings with Israeli and Palestinian experts during a number of visits to Jerusalem over the period 2006–2008. Listed below are the past Israeli–Palestinian seminars held behind closed doors in Rome on December 17–18, 2006 (*Casina del Cardinal Bessarione*), March 12–13, June 28–29 and December 16–17, 2007 and December 3, 2008 (*Villa Piccolomini*).

Future seminars will examine the complex issue of the three different meanings of *sovereignty* (independence, title and jurisdiction) applied to the two scenarios currently proposed for the territorial and political settlement in Jerusalem: one relating to a special regime for the Old City to be separate from the Israeli and Palestinian States (global/transnational model), the other concerning exclusively the Holy Places area (state/territorial model).

In this context, Israeli and Palestinian participants to these seminars behind closed doors have already taken part in the drafting of two documents on Jerusalem and its Holy Places. The first document, titled "The Holy Places of Jerusalem: Guidelines for a Future Arrangement," under the joint supervision of Dr. Nazmi Al Jubeh and Att. Gilead Sher, outlines the shared principles on the management of the Holy Places, in the framework of a Special Regime to be applied to the Old City of Jerusalem. The second document, titled "Jerusalem: Cultural and Religious Shared Guidelines," is focused on the shared principles to be applied in the event of a territorial division of the city between the two national actors.

Additionally, in future seminars *Mediterranean Perspectives* intends to discuss the three policy options on the settlement of disputes regarding the Status Quo in the Holy Places of Jerusalem in the perspective mentioned above.

In order to produce positive results, the Israeli–Palestinian meetings are kept informal, confidential and based on a legal/practical-oriented approach rather than a purely political or religious one. Both Israeli and Palestinian participants have requested that the project should continue and its final conclusions should be presented to the local political and religious community leaders.

Annexes

Annex I

The Palestine (Holy Places) Order in Council, 1924[808]

AT THE COURT AT BUCKINGHAM PALACE;
The 25th day of July, 1924.
PRESENT:
THE KING'S MOST EXCELLENT MAJESTY IN COUNCIL.

WHEREAS by the Palestine Order in Council, 1922, it is (among other things) provided that the Civil Courts in Palestine shall exercise jurisdiction in all matters and over all persons in Palestine:

AND WHEREAS it is expedient that certain matters shall not be cognisable by the said Courts:

AND WHEREAS by treaty, capitulation, grant, usage, sufferance and other lawful means His Majesty has power and jurisdiction within Palestine:

NOW, THEREFORE, His Majesty, by virtue and in exercise of the powers in this behalf by the Foreign Jurisdiction Act, 1890, or otherwise, in His Majesty vested, is pleased, by and with the advise of His Privy Council, to order, and it is hereby ordered, as follows: –

1. This order may be cited as "The Palestine (Holy Places) Order in Council, 1924."
2. Notwithstanding anything to the contrary in the Palestine Order-in-Council 1922, or in any Ordinance or Law in Palestine, no cause or matter in connection with the Holy Places or religious buildings or sites or the rights or claims relating to the different religious communities in Palestine shall be heard or determined by any Court in Palestine.

    Provided that nothing herein contained shall affect or limit the exercise by the Religious Courts of the jurisdiction conferred upon them by, or pursuant to, the said Palestine Order in Council.
3. If any question arises whether any cause or matter comes within the terms of the preceding Article hereof, such question shall, pending the constitution of a Commission charged with jurisdiction over the matters set out in the said Article, be referred to the High Commissioner, who shall decide the question

after making due enquiry into the matter in accordance with such instructions as he may receive from one of His Majesty's Principal Secretaries of State.

The decision of the High Commissioner shall be final and binding on all parties

4 His Majesty, His Heirs and Successors in Council, may at any time revoke, alter or amend this Order.

AND the Right Honourable James Henry Thomas, one of His Majesty's Principal Secretaries of State, is to give the necessary directions herein accordingly.

Annex II

Provisions included in international documents adopted in the context of the Middle East Peace Process mentioning the Holy Places of Jerusalem

(in chronological order)

II. a. Letter sent on 11 October 1993 by Israeli Foreign Minister Peres to Norway's Foreign Minister Holst

Dear Minister Holst,

I wish to confirm that the palestinian institutions of East Jerusalem and the interests and well being of the palestinians of East Jerusalem are of great importance and will be preserved.

Therefore, all the palestinian institutions of East Jerusalem, including the economic, social, educational and cultural, and the holy Christian and Moslem places, are performing an essential task for the palestinian population.

Needless to say, we will not hamper their activity; on the contrary, the fulfillment of this important mission is to be encouraged.

Sincerely,
Shimon Peres

II. b. Fundamental Agreement between Israel and the Holy See, signed on 13 December 1993

Article 4 § 1.
The State of Israel affirms its continuing commitment to maintain and respect the "Status quo" in the Christian Holy Places to which it applies and the respective rights of the Christian communities thereunder. The Holy See affirms the Catholic Church's continuing commitment to respect the aforementioned "Status quo" and the said rights.

II. c. Section 3 of the Washington Declaration, signed by Israel and Jordan on 25 July 1994

Israel respects the present special role of the Hashemite Kingdom of Jordan in Muslim holy shrines in Jerusalem. When negotiations on the permanent status will take place, Israel will give high priority to the Jordanian historic role in these shrines.

In addition, the two sides have agreed to act together to promote interfaith relations among to three monotheistic religions. (. . .)

II. d. Article IX of the Peace Treaty between Israel and Jordan, signed on 25 October 1994, titled "Places of Historical and Religious Significance and Interfaith Relations"

1 Each Party will provide freedom of access to places of religious and historical significance.
2 In this regard, in accordance with the Washington Declaration, Israel respects the present special role of the Hashemite Kingdom of Jordan in Muslim holy shrines in Jerusalem. When negotiations on the permanent status will take place, Israel will give high priority to the Jordanian historic role in these shrines.
3 The Parties will act together to promote interfaith relations among the three monotheistic religions, with the aim of working towards religious understanding, moral commitment, freedom of religious worship, and tolerance and peace.

II. e. Basic Agreement between the Holy See and the Palestine Liberation Organization, concluded on 15 February 2000

Preamble, Paragraph 8 (e).
Calling, therefore, for a special statute for Jerusalem, internationally guaranteed, which should safeguard the following: a. Freedom of religion and conscience for all b. The equality before the law of the three monotheistic religions and their institutions and followers in the City; c. The proper identity and sacred character of the City and its universally significant, religious and cultural heritage; d. The Holy Places, the freedom of access to them and of worship in them. e. The Regime of the "Status Quo" in those Holy Places where it applies;
Article 4.
The regime of the "Status Quo" will be maintained and observed in those Christian Holy Places where it applies.

Annex III

Principles governing the cultural and religious status quo in Jerusalem

The following list of principles is the result of an analysis of the documents that the parties involved in the Middle East Peace negotiations and the UN issued in regards to the religious and cultural dimension of Jerusalem.

The selected principles apply today, as a sort of broad cultural and religious status quo, to the relationship between the territorial authority, on one hand, and the communities living in Jerusalem on the other.

This author assumes that the parties that have a recognized interest in the Holy Places consider most of the cardinal points quoted below as internationally binding, whose full respect may help preserve a future peaceful and dynamic coexistence between the different collective identities represented in the city. The author has discussed a draft copy of this Statement of Policy at several conferences on Jerusalem (some held behind closed doors) with Palestinian and Israeli participants on an individual basis.

Among them, the conference held in El Escorial (Madrid), Spain, on 5–9 August, 1996 at the Complutense University, the International Colloquium held in Toledo, Spain, on 17–18 March 1998, organized jointly by the Arab Study Society and the Jerusalem Institute for Israel Studies and the International Conference held in Bellagio, Italy, on 13–17 July 1998, organized by the Rockefeller Foundation, with academicians and diplomats from Israel, Egypt, Morocco, Saudi Arabia, the Palestinian Authority, and the Kingdom of Jordan.

Different versions of the Statement of Policy have been published by and reprinted in various journals, among them, the Palestinian weekly, *The Jerusalem Times* (8 November 1996), the *Bulletin of the Christian Information Center* (No. 393, November-December 1966), a newsletter reporting about the major Christian recognized communities present in Jerusalem, *La Nuova Frontiera. International Human Rights and Security Review* (Year IV, n.12, Spring 1998) *Hiwarat* (n. 5, February 1999), monthly newsletter of *Arabroma. Website of the Rome Group for Arab Culture* [www.arabroma.com], and *Nonviolence*, an Internet site linked to the Latin Patriarchate of Jerusalem [www.lpj.org/Nonviolence].

a. Preamble: special objectives of the authorities administering the city

The government/s or administering authority/ies (hereinafter, "the Government") in discharging administrative obligations in Jerusalem shall pursue the following special objectives:

(a) To protect and to preserve the unique religious and cultural interests of Christians, Jews and Moslems related to the city; to this end, to ensure that order and peace, and especially religious peace, reign in Jerusalem;

(b) To foster co-operation among all the inhabitants of the city in their own interests, as well as to encourage and support the peaceful development of the relations between the Arab and Jewish peoples throughout the area under British Palestinian Mandate until 14 May, 1948; to promote the security, well-being and any constructive measures of development of the residents, having regard to the special circumstances and customs of the various peoples and communities.

b. Principles applying to the Holy Places, religious buildings and sites

1. Existing rights in respect of the Holy Places and of religious buildings or sites shall not be denied or impaired.

2. Insofar as the Holy Places are concerned, the liberty of access and visits to the city and the Holy Places therein shall be guaranteed, in conformity with existing rights, to the residents of Jerusalem as well as to all other persons, without distinction of nationality, subject to requirements of national security, public order and decorum.

Similarly, freedom of worship shall be guaranteed in conformity with existing rights, subject to the maintenance of public order and decorum.

3. Holy Places and religious buildings or sites shall be preserved. No act shall be permitted which may in any way impair their recognized sacred character. If at any

time, it appears to the Government that any particular Holy Place, religious building or site is in need of urgent repair, the Government may call upon the community or communities concerned to carry out such repair. The Government may carry it out itself at the expense of the community or communities concerned if no action is taken within a reasonable time.

4. No taxation shall be levied in respect of any Holy Place, religious building or site that was exempt from taxation on May 14, 1948, date of the termination of the League of Nations Mandate in Palestine.

No change in the incidence of such taxation shall be made which would either discriminate between the owners or occupiers of Holy Places, religious buildings or sites, or would place such owners or occupiers in a position less favourable in relation to general incidence of taxation than existed on May 14, 1948.

c. Religious and cultural rights of the local communities

1. The personal status and family law of the various communities and their religious interests, including endowments, shall be respected.

2. The Government shall ensure adequate primary and secondary education for the Arab and Jewish community, respectively, in its own language and its cultural traditions.

The right of each community to maintain its own schools for the education of its own members in its own language, while conforming to such educational requirements of a general nature as the Government may impose, shall not be denied or impaired. Foreign educational establishments shall continue their activity on the basis of their existing rights.

d. Religious and cultural rights applying to all visitors and residents

1. Freedom of conscience and the free exercise of all forms of worship subject only to the maintenance of public order and decorum shall be ensured to all.

2. No discrimination of any kind shall be made between the inhabitants on the ground of race, religion, language or sex.

3. All persons shall be entitled to an equal protection of the law.

4. Except as may be required for the maintenance of public order and good government, no measure shall be taken to obstruct or interfere with the activities of religious or charitable bodies of all faiths or to discriminate against any representative or member of these bodies on the ground of his religion or nationality.

5. No restriction shall be imposed on the free use of any language in private intercourse, in commerce, in religion, in the Press or in publications of any kind, or at public meetings.

Annex IV

Glossary of key terms related to sovereignty and status quo

a. Different meanings of the term *sovereignty*

1 **Independence.** This is an essential prerequisite for States to be subjects of international law. The State has no other authority over itself in relation to persons, things and legal relationships within its territory. A State is considered as independent of other external legal orders or systems of law, and any external interference must be justified by a specific norm of international law.
2 **Title** (in Latin, *titulus*). This is the source of authority of any particular State to a portion of territory. Legal titles correspond to the vestitive facts, in the sense that the law recognizes these facts as creating a right from which the State's authority flows.
3 (Full) **Authority.** It encompasses all possible rights, duties, powers, liberties, and immunities that a State may exercise within the limits of customary international law. It is also defined as governmental *control, jurisdiction,* or (State) *power.* Authority, in this sense, must be distinguished from its exercise, manifestation or actual display.

In relation to **authority** the term **jurisdiction** defines the content's limits or scope of the *powers* attributed to the State vis-à-vis a defined area of the globe and a category of people. The authority exercised by States may be limited according to the criteria of a) **functional,** b) **territorial,** and c) **personal jurisdiction.** A brief description of these three criteria follows:

- **Functional jurisdiction** refers to the wide range of powers (*ratione materiae*) that a State's authority implies. One may draw additional distinctions between **legislative, executive, or judicial jurisdiction**, depending on the organization of the particular State's constitutional system.
- **Territorial jurisdiction** refers to the spatial (*ratione loci*) dimension or scope of authority in international law.
- **Personal jurisdiction** refers to the (categories of) people (*ratione personarum*) — whether citizens or not — under the State's authority.

b. Different meanings of the expression *status quo* in Jerusalem

1 **The Status Quo (capitalized) in the Holy Places between the recognized communities.**

The Latin expression, when, refers to the temporary legal regime to manage and suspend disputes on respective rights and interests with regard to several important sacred sites in the Jerusalem area (including Bethlehem), crystallized since Ottoman rule (1517–1917). This rather coherent, sufficiently organized, set of norms is a special, *sui generis* system of law, related to the relationship between the recognized communities.

2 **The cultural/religious status quo (not capitalized) between the recognized religious communities and the territorial authorities.**

This expression broadly defines the cultural and religious aspects of the city, including the relations between the recognized religious communities and the territorial authorities.

3 **The political/territorial status quo (not capitalized) between the Israelis and the Palestinians.**

The political balance of powers *in situ* between the Israeli and the Arab sides since 1967, pending a final solution that the relevant parties will negotiate.

Notes

1 On the British Mandate's provisions related to the recognized religious communities see *infra*, section 3.3.1; see also Paolo Pieraccini, *Jerusalem, Holy Places and Religious Communities in International Politics* [Italian] (Bologna: Edizioni Dehoniane, 1997), and bibliography cited therein.
2 On the Har Ha Bait/Haram Al Sharif see *infra*, sections 1.3, 4.2.2, 4.3.3, 5.4, 5.5 and B.2.
3 Walter Zander, *Israel and the Holy Places of Christendom* (Worcester: The Trinity Press, 1971), p. 98.
4 Shmuel Berkovitz, *The Temple Mount and the Western Wall in Israeli Law* (Jerusalem: The Jerusalem Institute for Israel Studies, 2001), p. 9.
5 See Zander, *Israel*, p. 99. On Jewish plans to rebuild the destroyed Temple in Jerusalem and to renew the sacrificial services in the ancient way see also *infra*, sections 3.1.1 and 4.3.3.
6 See Berkovitz, *The Temple Mount*, p. 11; the Koranic verses are in Sura 17, Verse 1. Berkovitz, translates the Arabic *Haram al-Sharif* as "the Exhalted Holy Place." See also my article "Alternative Definitions of Sovereignty. Drawing on the European and Mediterranean Legal Heritage: an Analysis of Coexisting of National and Religious Identities in Jerusalem" in Stefania Bazzoni and May Chartouni-Doubarry (eds.), *Politics and Economics in the Search for Stability in the Mediterranean Region* (Monte Carlo: Institut d'études politiques méditerranéennes (IEPM), 2001), p. 104.
7 Berkovitz, *The Temple Mount*, p. 10, n. 4.
8 Berkovitz.
9 For the different meanings of the polysemous expression *status quo* in Jerusalem, distinguishing its capitalized and not capitalized forms see *infra*, section 5.5; see also the Glossary of key terms *infra*, Annex IV. Raymond Cohen similarly capitalizes "the term Status Quo" in his *Saving the Holy Sepulchre. How Rival Christians Came Together to Rescue Their Holiest Shrine* (New York: Oxford University Press, 2008), p. 8.
10 This issue has been analyzed in several studies and publications, including my work, "Problematic Issues Related to the Borders of the State of Israel" [Italian] (Master's dissertation, University "La Sapienza," Rome, 1990) and my article, "Jerusalem and its Holy Places" [Italian], *La Comunità Internazionale*, Vol. 49, No. 2 (1994): pp. 243–273. On the state/territorial and global/transnational identity models see my article: "Nation, religion and collective identity between Europe and the Mediterranean", in Eva Pfoestl (ed.), *The Creation of a Zone of Peace and Stability Surrounding the European Union* [Italian] (Roma: Istituto di Studi Politici S. Pio V, 2007), pp. 301–448.
11 SCOR, 22nd year, Resolutions and Decisions, pp. 8–9.
12 See, among the more recent scholarly articles on the subject: Abu Odeh et al., *UN Security Council Resolution 242: the Building Block of Peacemaking* (Washington D.C.: Washington Institute for Near East Policy, 1993); Ruth Lapidoth," Security Council Resolution 242

at Twenty five," *Israel Law Review*, Vol. 26 (1992): pp. 295–318.
13 See, among others, Yehuda Blum, "From Camp David to Oslo," *Israel Law Review*, Vol. 28, Nos. 2–3 (1994): p. 216.
14 Letter sent by Jimmy Carter, President of the United States, to Egyptian President Sadat on 22 September 1978; letter sent by Sadat to Carter on 17 September 1978; letter sent by Israeli Prime Minister Begin to Carter on 17 September 1978.
15 Reproduced in PASSIA, *Documents on Jerusalem* (Jerusalem: Palestinian Academic Society for the Study of International Affairs, 1996), p. 148; Ruth Lapidoth and Moshe Hirsch (eds.), *The Jerusalem Question and Its Resolution: Selected Documents* (Dordrecht: Martinus Nijhoff, 1994), p. 299. On the hypothesis of an international local custom or objective regime protecting such traditional principles applied to the Holy Places see *infra*, section 5.6.
16 The text of the letter of invitation, sent by the United States and the Soviet Union to Israel, Syria, Jordan (including the representatives of the Palestinians resident in West Bank and Gaza), and Lebanon on 18 October 1991, is reproduced in Ruth Lapidoth and Moshe Hirsch (eds.), *The Arab–Israeli Conflict and its Resolution: Selected Documents* (Dordrecht: Martinus Nijhoff Publishers, 1992), pp. 384–386.
17 Reproduced in PASSIA, *Documents*, p. 185.
18 *Passia Diary 2003* (Jerusalem: Palestinian Academic Society for the Study of the International Affairs, 2003), pp. 260–261.
19 See Menachem Klein, *Jerusalem. The Contested City* (New York: New York University Press; The Jerusalem Institute for Israel Studies, 2001), pp. 137–138.
20 UN Doc. A/48/486 — S/26560 (Annex), 11 October 1993; reproduced in *International Legal Material*, Vol. 32 (Washington, D.C.: American Society of International Law, 1993): pp. 1525–1544.
21 *Declaration of Principles on Interim Self-Government Arrangements*, 13 September 1993 (Jerusalem: Israeli Ministry of Foreign Affairs, 1993), p. 23 (emphasis added).
22 "The Status of Jerusalem, March 1999," available on the Israeli Foreign Ministry website: www.mfa.gov.il/mfa.
23 *Declaration of Principles*, p. 35 (emphasis added).
24 *Israeli–Palestinian Interim Agreement on the West Bank and the Gaza Strip* (Jerusalem: Israeli Ministry of Foreign Affairs, 1995).
25 See Ruth Lapidoth, "Jerusalem and the Peace Process," *Israel Law Review*, Vol. 28, Nos. 2–3 (1994): p. 422; this article is reproduced also in the Internet site of the Foreign Ministry of Israel: www.mfa.gov.il/mfa ; Ruth Lapidoth, "Jerusalem — Some Jurisprudential Aspects," *Catholic University Law Review*, Vol. 45 (1996): p. 677.
26 The proposed boundaries were shown on a map, included in Annex B to the resolution. On the resolution see *infra*, section 3.5.4.
27 Article V of the Armistice Agreement established these boundaries, delineated on maps included in Annex 1 to the Agreement: see *infra*, section 4.1. See also the map in Martin Gilbert, *Jerusalem: Illustrated History Atlas* (New York: Macmillan, 1977): p. 101; and Dan Bahat, *Carta's Historical Atlas of Jerusalem* (Jerusalem: Carta, 1993): p. 77.
28 Martin Gilbert, *The Arab–Israeli Conflict: Its History in Maps*, 5th ed. (London: Weidenfeld and Nicolson, 1992): p. 123; Bahat, *Historical Atlas*, p. 81.
29 See map in Ruth Lapidoth and Moshe Hirsch, *Jerusalem — Political and Legal Aspects* (Jerusalem: Jerusalem Center for Israel Studies, 1994) [Hebrew].
30 See Lapidoth, "Jerusalem and the Peace Process," p. 422; Lapidoth, "Jerusalem — Some Jurisprudential Aspects," p. 677.
31 Lapidoth, "Jerusalem and the Peace Process," p. 422.
32 Lapidoth, "Jerusalem and the Peace Process," p. 424. Lapidoth, "Jerusalem — Some Jurisprudential Aspects," p. 678. In this context, see also the proposal included in Cecilia Albin, Moshe Amirav and Hanna Siniora, *Jerusalem: An Undivided City as Dual Capital*,

(Jerusalem: Israeli–Palestinian Peace Research Project, Working Paper Series, No. 16, Harry Truman Research Institute for the Advancement of Peace and the Arab Study Society, Winter 1991/1992.)

33 Lapidoth, "Jerusalem," p. 424.
34 Yehuda Blum, "From Camp David", p. 218, n. 20.
35 *Ibid.*
36 See *ibid.*
37 Klein, *Jerusalem*, p. 176.
38 Sami F. Musallam, *The Struggle for Jerusalem: A Program of Action for Peace* (Jerusalem: Palestinian Academic Society for the Study of International Affairs, 1996), p. 109.
39 Yehuda Blum, "From Camp David," p. 218, n. 20. On the appointment of the two Muftis and the controversy and competition between the PLO and Jordan on this issue see also *infra*, section 1.3.
40 Musallam, p. 110.
41 See Musallam, p. 110.
42 Yehuda Blum, "From Camp David," p. 218, n. 20. See also Klein, *Jerusalem*, p. 176.
43 Klein, *Jerusalem*, p. 176.
44 *Law Implementing the Agreement on the Gaza Strip and the Jericho Area (Restriction on Activities)*, 1994, translation in English reproduced in the website of the Foreign Ministry of Israel, www.mfa.gov.il/mfa. See also Lapidoth, "Jerusalem and the Peace Process," p. 428; Blum, "From Camp David," p. 218, n. 20.
45 *Law Implementing, op. cit.*
46 See Lapidoth, "Jerusalem and the Peace Process," p. 428. For the Cairo Agreement see U.N. Doc. A/49/180 — S/1994/727 (Annex), of 20 June 1994.
47 Security Council, 3900th Meeting (AM and PM), SC/6541, 30 June 1998.
48 *Ibid.*
49 Menachem Klein, *Jerusalem*, p. 156.
50 Sami F. Musallam, *The Struggle for Jerusalem: A Program of Action for Peace* (Jerusalem: Palestinian Academic Society for the Study of International Affairs, 1996), p. 37; the author refers also (*ibid.*, n. 37) to "similar fears for the Oslo talks, and consequently for the DoP," expressed in an interview in al-Aayat (a daily Arabic newspaper published in London), 13 September 1994, p. 7, with Mahmoud Abbas (Abu Mazen), "the architect of the Oslo talks" (Musallam, *ibid.*) See also Menachem Klein, *Jerusalem. The Contested City* (New York: New York University Press; The Jerusalem Institute for Israel Studies, 2001), p. 150.
51 Musallam, p. 37.
52 See Musallam, *ibid.*
53 Klein, *Jerusalem*, p. 151
54 Musallam, p. 39.
55 Quoted from Musallam, *ibid.*
56 Quoted from Musallam, *ibid.*
57 *Jerusalem*, p. 150.
58 For the text, see the website of the Israeli Foreign Ministry: www.mfa.gov.il/mfa, in which the document is referred to as "published in *Jerusalem Post*, on June 7, 1994." See also Musallam, pp. 39–40 and *infra*, Annex II a.
59 Musallam, p. 38; the same author adds that Holst delivered the letter to "Mahmoud Abbas (Abu Mazen), the architect of the Oslo talks and the DoP" (*ibid.*, p 39.)
60 Klein, *Jerusalem*, p. 150.
61 For the full text of the Peres Letter see *infra*, Annex II a. For a reference to this letter also *infra*, section 5.2.
62 For the Cairo Agreement see *infra*, the previous section.
63 Musallam, p. 21.

64 See Musallam, *ibid*. On 23 May 1994, the Israeli daily, Haaretz published a Hebrew translation of this speech.
65 Musallam, p. 23.
66 Musallam, *ibid*.
67 Klein, *Jerusalem*, p. 155.
68 Musallam, p. 27. For excerpts of the agreement signed between Caliph Omar and Patriarch Sophronius in 638 see Walter Zander, *Israel and the Holy Places of Christendom* (Worcester, Great Britan: The Trinity Press, 1971), p. 99. For reference to Omar's declaration in the Husayn–McMahon exchanges of letters see *infra*, section 3.1.2. On the Caliph Omar Ibn Khattab see also *infra*, section 3.2.1 and 3.3.1.
69 See also Klein, *Jerusalem*, p. 151. A similar reference to "East Jerusalem" was included in the U.S. letter of assurances to the Palestinians, issued on 18 October 1991. For the text see Madhi F. Abdul Hadi (ed.), *Documents on Palestine, Vol. II: From the Negotiations in Madrid to the Post-Hebron Agreement Period* (Jerusalem: Palestinian Academic Society for the Study of International Affairs, 1997), p. 8.
70 Available at: www.mfa.gov.il/mfa.
71 "The Status of Jerusalem," *ibid*.
72 Lapidoth, "Jerusalem," p. 430. See also *infra*, section 1.3, on possible conflicts with article 9 of the Peace Treaty between Israel and Jordan.
73 Klein, *Jerusalem*, p. 152.
74 Klein, *Jerusalem*, p. 151.
75 Lapidoth, "Jerusalem," pp. 428, 430.
76 Joel Singer, "Aspects of Foreign Relations under the Israeli–Palestinian Agreements on Interim Self-Government Arrangements for the West bank and Gaza," *Israel Law Review*, Vol. 28, Nos. 2–3 (1994): text preceding n. 47.
77 Moshe Hirsch, "The Future Negotiations over Jerusalem, Strategic Factors and Game Theory," *Catholic University Law Review*, 45 (1996): p. 715.
78 Moshe Hirsch, *ibid*.
79 Vienna Convention on the Law of Treaties (23 May 1969). For the text see, among other sources, Paul Reuter, *Introduction to the Law of Treaties* (London: Kegan Paul, 1995), pp. 260–261. On Article 31 of the Vienna Convention see also *infra*, section 1.4.2.
80 Lapidoth, "Jerusalem," p. 429.
81 See Lapidoth, "Jerusalem," *ibid*. On the binding effects of unilateral declarations see also *infra*, section 5.6.
82 For the text see PASSIA, *Documents on Jerusalem* (Jerusalem: Palestinian Academic Society for the Study of International Affairs, 1996), pp. 121–122.
83 For the text of the Peace Treaty see *Peace between the State of Israel and the Hashemite Kingdom of Jordan* (Jerusalem: Ministry of Foreign Affairs, 1994), pp. 7–36.
84 *Peace, ibid*. On Jordan's practice regarding access to the Holy Places until 1967 see *infra*, section 4.2.2.
85 Ruth Lapidoth, "Jerusalem and the Peace Process," *Israel Law Review*, Vol. 28, Nos. 2–3 (1994): p. 431.
86 Sami F. Musallam, *The Struggle for Jerusalem: A Program of Action for Peace* (Jerusalem: Palestinian Academic Society for the Study of International Affairs, 1996), p. 76.
87 Musallam, *ibid*.
88 See *supra*, section 1.2 for the Peres letter and *infra*, section 1.4.1 and 1.4.2 for the Fundamental Agreement and the Basic Agreement respectively. See also *infra*, section 4.3.2.
89 Antonio F. Perez, "Sovereignty, Freedom and Civil Society: Toward a New Jerusalem," *Catholic University Law Review*, Vol. 45 (1996): p. 857 (italics in the original text.). On the new Modus Vivendi in the Muslim–Jewish Holy Places see also *infra*, section 4.3.3.
90 See *infra*, Chapter 3; see also *infra* section 4.3.3; for a list of the inter-Christian Status Quo

procedural norms see *infra*, section 5.3.

91 See Ruth Lapidoth, "Jerusalem — Some Jurisprudential Aspects," *Catholic University Law Review* 45 (1996): p. 663; a similar comment appears in Ruth Lapidoth, "Jerusalem and the Peace Process," *Israel Law Review*, Vol. 28, 2–3 (1994): p. 404; see also Moshe Hirsch, Deborah Housen-Couriel and Ruth Lapidoth (eds.), *Whither Jerusalem? Proposals and Positions Concerning the Future of Jerusalem* (The Hague: Martinus Nijhoff), 1995, p. 158; Shmuel Berkovitz, "The Legal Status of the Holy Places in Israel," [Hebrew] (Ph.D. dissertation, The Hebrew University of Jerusalem, Jerusalem, 1978) pp. 35–45; *Id.*, *The Temple Mount and the Western Wall in Israeli Law* (Jerusalem: The Jerusalem Institute for Israel Studies, 2001), pp. 13, 83; L.G.A. Cust, *The Status Quo in the Holy Places. With an Annex on the Status Quo in the Church of the Nativity, Bethlehem* (London: His Majesty's Stationery Office, 1930), pp. 1, 12, 43–48; Alisa Rubin Peled, "The Crystallization of an Israeli Policy Towards Muslim and Christian Holy Places, 1948–1955," *The Muslim World*, Vol. 84, Nos. 1–2 (1994): p. 99.

92 Cust, p. 12. On the Cust memorandum see also Cohen, *Saving the Holy Sepulchre*, p. 23.

93 On the Nazareth controversy see Joseph Algazy, "Gov't will ask Muslims to evacuate Nazareth site," www.haaretz.com, February 23, 2000; *id.*, "Muslims refuse Nazareth eviction," www.haaretz.com, 24 February, 2000.

94 Menahem Klein, "The Islamic Holy Places as a Political Bargaining Card (1993–1995)," *Catholic University Law Review*, 45 (1996): p. 748.

95 Klein, "The Islamic," *ibid.*

96 Klein, "The Islamic," p. 748. See also Klein, *Jerusalem*, p. 164.

97 Klein, "The Islamic," p. 750.

98 See Lapidoth, "Jerusalem," p. 431, see also Musallam, pp. 96–97.

99 Quoted from Musallam, pp. 93–95.

100 On the new Status Quo/Modus Vivendi in the Holy Places of Jerusalem after 1967 see *infra*, section 4.3.3.

101 See Lapidoth, "Jerusalem," p. 431. On the Israeli–Palestinian negotiations on the permanent status see *supra*, sections 1.1.

102 Lapidoth, "Jerusalem," p. 431.

103 See Lapidoth, "Jerusalem," *ibid.*

104 See *supra*, section 1.2.

105 See Article 30(IV) and (5) of the Vienna Convention on the Law of Treaties, (23 May 1969). For the text see, among other sources, Paul Reuter, *Introduction to the Law of Treaties* (London: Kegan Paul, 1995), pp. 260–261.

106 See Lapidoth, "Jerusalem," p. 432.

107 See Lapidoth, "Jerusalem," p. 432, n. 114. On the Israeli–Egyptian Peace Treaty see *supra*, section 1.1.1.

108 Klein, *Jerusalem*, p. 166.

109 See *supra*, section 1.2. On the appointment of the two Muftis and the controversy and competition between the PLO and Jordan see also *supra*, section 1.1.3.

110 Ifrah Zilberman, "Palestinian Customary Law in the Jerusalem Area," *Catholic University Law Review*, Vol. 45 (1996): 809.

111 Zilberman, *ibid.*

112 Klein, *Jerusalem*, p. 176; see also Musallam, pp. 105–109.

113 Musallam, *ibid.*, p. 77.

114 Musallam, *op.cit*, p. 76. See also *supra*, section 1.2.

115 Musallam, *ibid.* See also Klein, *Jerusalem*, p. 167.

116 Quoted from Shlomo Slonim, *Jerusalem in America's Foreign Policy* (The Hague: Kluwer Law International, 1998), pp. 315–316.

117 Quoted from Slonim, *Jerusalem*, *ibid.*

118 *Jerusalem Post*, 23 July 1994.

119 Quoted from Menachem Klein, "The Islamic," pp. 747–748.
120 Klein, "The Islamic," p. 749; see Adnan Abu Odeh, "Religious Inclusion, Political Inclusion: Jerusalem as an Undivided Capital," *Catholic University Law Review*, Vol. 45 (1996): 687, second footnote.
121 Adnan Abu Odeh, "Two Capitals in an Undivided Jerusalem," *Foreign Affairs*, Vol. 71, No. 2 (1992): pp. 183, 185.
122 Odeh, "Religious Inclusion," p. 693.
123 Quoted from Musallam, p. 81.
124 Quoted from Klein, "The Islamic," p. 761.
125 Klein, "The Islamic," p. 750.
126 Arafat's speech in the presence of a delegation from the industrial and commercial association, quoted from Musallam, p. 88.
127 www.haaretz.com, 27 July 1994.
128 Quoted by Musallam, p. 113.
129 Quoted from Musallam, p. 115.
130 On the general features of the Status Quo see *infra*, sections 5.2 and 5.3.
131 For the text of these as well as other relevant provisions of the Agreement see *infra*, Annex II b. For the full text of the Agreement see, among other sources, *International Legal Material*, Vol. 33 (Washington, D.C.: American Society of International Law, 1994): p. 153; Eugene J. Fisher and Leon Klenicki (eds.), *A Challenge Long Delayed. The Diplomatic Exchange Between, the Holy See and the State of Israel* (New York: Anti-Defamation League, 1996), pp. 49–53. See also *infra*, section 5.4, for an analysis of the Agreement's provisions related to religious freedom.
132 Rabbi David Rosen, "The Negotiations on the Permanent Bilateral Commission between the Holy See and the State of Israel, and Their Fundamental Agreement Signed on December 30, 1993," in Fisher and Klenicki, p. 20.
133 Shmuel Hadas, "Diplomatic Relations between the Holy See and the State of Israel," in Fisher and Klenicki, p. 26.
134 "New Ambassador to the Holy See," *L'Osservatore Romano* (Weekly Edition in English), 12 October 1994, p. 22; reproduced in Fisher and Klenicki, p. 55. See also the Pope's reply in the same article, "New Ambassador to the Holy See", p. 21; reproduced in Fisher and Klenicki, p. 54.
135 The quotation from the interview (published in *Parade* magazine) is reproduced by David Rosen, *The Impact of the Papal Visit to Israel* (Jerusalem: Israel Information Center, 2000), p. 21.
136 Dr. Eugene J. Fisher, "Readings on the Vatican/Israel Accord," in Fisher and Klenicki, p. 47.
137 John T. Pawlikowski, OSM, "The Vatican–Israeli Accords: Their Implications for Catholic Faith and Teaching," in Fisher and Klenicki, p. 11.
138 Pawlikowski, *ibid.*
139 Pawlikowski, p. 12.
140 Pawlikowski, p. 13.
141 Quoted form Zander, *Israel*, p. 17. The following quotations of the documents are from the same source.
142 Quoted form Zander, *Israel*, p. 18 (see also the bibliography cited there). On the different but related idea of "God's sovereignty" and *res divinis juris* see *supra*, section 1.3 and *infra*, section 2.1.3.
143 Pawlikowski, p. 16.
144 Shmuel Hadas, "Diplomatic Relations," p. 30.
145 See *supra*, section 1.1.
146 See, among others, Rosen, "The Negotiations," pp. 20–21; Hadas, "Diplomatic Relations," p. 31; Sergio I. Minerbi, *The Visit of the Pope to the Holy Land* (Jerusalem: Israel

Information Center, 2000), pp. 5, 11.
147 See Hadas, "Diplomatic Relations," p. 21.
148 Minerbi, *The Visit*, p. 11.
149 Quoted from Minerbi, *The Visit*, *ibid.*
150 Rosen, "The Negotiations," pp. 20–21. See also Ambassador Hadas' address, "New Ambassador to the Holy See," reproduced in Fisher and Klenicki, p. 55.
151 Hadas, "Diplomatic Relations," p. 31.
152 "New Ambassador to the Holy See," reproduced in Fisher and Klenicki, p. 54.
153 Rosen, "The Negotiations," p. 22.
154 Article 11, Par. 1, of the Fundamental Agreement.
155 Article 11, Par. 2, of the Fundamental Agreement.
156 Rosen, "The Negotiations," p. 21.
157 See *infra*, section 5.5.
158 Emphasis added.
159 See *infra*, section 5.3.
160 See also Charalambos K. Papastathis, "A New Status for Jerusalem? An Eastern Orthodox Viewpoint," *Catholic University Law Review*, Vol. 45 (1996): p. 729.
161 For the text of the relevant provisions of the Basic Agreement see *infra*, Annex II e.
162 Vienna Convention on the Law of Treaties (23 May 1969). For the text see, among other sources, Paul Reuter, *Introduction to the Law of Treaties* (London: Kegan Paul, 1995), pp. 260–261. On Article 31 of the Vienna Convention see also *supra*, section 1.2.
163 Eduardo Vitta, "The Conflict of Personal Laws," *Israel Law Review*, Vol. 5, No. 2 (1970): p. 170.
164 For an overview on the treatment of the Jewish *natio* under Roman Empire see, among others, Alfredo Mordechai Rabello, "Sui rapporti fra Diocleziano e gli ebrei", *Rassegna mensile di Israel* (January–February–March 1979), pp. 43–78, and bibliography there quoted. On the *praetor peregrinus qui inter peregrinos* and *inter cives et peregrinos jus dicit* see *infra*, section 2.2.2.
165 "Roman judges will be competent for cases between Romans, Gothic judges for Gothics. A single justice, however, will result from the combined application of the different jurisdictions" (my translation). Quotation from a letter of Mr. Bayard to Mr. Straus, Department of State, Washington, 20 April 1887, quoted from *Foreign Relations of the United States*, 1887, p. 1094; the following quotations, if not stated otherwise are all from the same document. See also *FRUS* 1887, Exhibit F, "Legal opinion of Edwin Pears, barrister at law, on the naturalization treaty," Constantinople, January 21,1887, p. 1111. Cassiodorus' Roman name was Flavius Magnus Aurelius (490–583). Theodoricus (454–526) was the king of the Ostrogothic people, a population living in Germany at the end of the Roman Empire.
166 Walter Zander, "Jurisdiction and Holiness: Reflections on the Coptic-Ethiopian Case," *Israel Law Review*, Vol. 17, No. 3 (1982): p. 270. See also *ibid.*, for the information about the legal concept of *res divini juris* in Antiquity. On this subject and on the right of *asylia* in the comparison to the Holy Places of Jerusalem see also my article "Alternative Definitions of Sovereignty. Drawing on the European and Mediterranean Legal Heritage: an Analysis of Coexisting of National and Religious Identities in Jerusalem," in Stefania Bazzoni and May Chartouni-Doubarry (eds.), *Politics and Economics in the search for Stability in the Mediterranean Region* (Monte Carlo, *Institut des Etudes Politiques Méditerranéennes* (2001): pp. 11–12. On the principle of immunity from ordinary local jurisdiction see also *infra*, section 5.6, and *infra*, sections 2.3.3 and 3.4. On the concept of *res divini juris* see also *infra*, section 3.1.1.
167 John Gerard Ruggie, "Territoriality and beyond: Problematizing modernity in international relations," *International Organizations*, Vol. 47, No. 1 (1993): p. 149.
168 Ruggie, *ibid.*, p. 150 (Italics in the original text); see also Kalevi Jaakko Holsti, *International*

Politics: A Framework for Analysis (New Jersey: Prentice-Hall, 1967), p. 84 and the entry "Sovereignty" in the 'Lexicon of Terms' in Moshe Hirsch, Deborah Housen-Couriel and Ruth Lapidoth (eds.), *Whither Jerusalem? Proposals and Positions Concerning the Future of Jerusalem* (The Hague: Martinus Nijhoff, 1995), p. 163.
169 See Eduardo Vitta, "The Conflict", p. 170.
170 Vitta, *ibid.*, p. 172.
171 John Gerard Ruggie, "Territoriality and beyond: Problematizing modernity in international relations," *International Organizations*, Vol. 47, No. 1 (1993): p. 179.
172 See "Reparation for Injuries" *ICJ Reports* (1949) p. 179; see also Ian Brownlie, *Principles of Public International Law* 5th edn. (New York: Oxford University Press, 1998), p. 57. On the subjects of international law see also *infra*, sections 2.1.3 and 5.2.
173 Ruth Lapidoth, "Redefining Authority: The Past, Present and Future of Sovereignty," *Harvard International Review*, Vol. 17, No. 3 (1995): p. 8. See also *infra*, section 2.1.2.
174 Georg Schwarzemberger and Edward Duncan Brown. *A Manual of International Law*. (Milton: Professional Books, 1976), pp. 73–74. See also Sir Robert Yewdall Jennings and Sir Arthur Watts (eds.) *Oppenheim's International Law*, Vol. 1, *Peace* (Garlow: Longman, 1992) p. 384; Helmut Steinberger, "Sovereignty," entry in Rudolf Bernhardt (ed.), *Encyclopedia of Public International Law*, Vol. 10, *States; Responsibility of States; International Law and Municipal Law* (Amsterdam: Elzevire Science, 1997), p. 399.
175 See, among others, Brownlie, *ibid.*, p. 76, p. 292; "Palmas Arbitral Award" reproduced in Sir Robert Yewdall Jennings, *The Acquisition of Territory in International Law* (Manchester: Manchester University Press), 1963, p. 91 ("Palmas Arbitral Award" — Arbitral Award Rendered In Conformity with the Special Agreement Concluded on January 23, 1925, between the United States of America and the Netherlands Relating to the Arbitration of Differences Respecting Sovereignty over the Island of Palmas [or Miangas]," April 4, 1928); Yoram Dinstein, "*Par in Parem non Habet Imperium*," *Israel Law Review*, Vol. 1, No. 3 (1966): p. 413. Charles Rousseau, *Droit International Public, Tome II, Les sujets de Droit* (Paris: Dalloz, 1974), p. 60, has clearly drawn the distinction between *independence* and *authority*.
176 Judge Dionisio Anzilotti, in his Individual Opinion of September 5, 1931, given in the "Austro-German Customs Union case," *PCIJ*, Series A/B, no. 41 (1931): p. 57; see also Elihu Lauterpacht, "Sovereignty: myth or reality?" *International Affairs*, Vol. 73, No. 1, (1997): p. 140.
177 See Gaetano Arangio-Ruiz, "*Le domaine réservé. L'organisation international et le rapport entre droit internationale et droit interne (Cours général de droit international public)*", Vol. 225, *Recueil des Cours de l'Académie de droit international de La Haye* 1990/VI (Dordrecht: Martinus Nijhoff Publishers, 1993 [French]), p. 445, no. 848. According to Dinstein ("*Par in Parem non Habet Imperium*," p. 413), the term *imperium* "clearly appears to connote power in the sense of authority, control or even dominion."
178 See also the Glossary *infra*, Annex IV.
179 "Palmas Arbitral Award," reproduced in Jennings *The Acquisition*, p. 88 and p. 90.
180 "Right of Passage in Indian Territory" *ICJ Reports* (1957), pp. 175–176; the decision adopted in 1812 quoted by Justice Chagla was taken by Justice Marshall, Chief of the United States' Supreme Court.
181 See James Leslie Brierly, *The Law of Nations* (Oxford: Clarendon Press, 1955), p. 150. See also Huber in the "Palmas Arbitral Award," reproduced in Jennings, *The Acquisition*, p. 91. On *territorial sovereignty* in general as well as on different theories about the international legal qualification of the territory see in particular Rolando Quadri, *Public International Law* [Italian] (Napoli: Liguori 1968), p. 628 ff; Mario Giuliano, "*State, Territory and Territorial Sovereignty* [Italian]", *Comunicazioni e studi*, 6 (1955): p. 23. Santi Romano, *Principles of General Constitutional Law* [Italian] (Milano: Giuffré Editore, 1955), p. 257 et seq. suggested the Italian expression "*potestà territoriale*."

182 "Palmas Arbitral Award," reproduced in Jennings, *The Acquisition*, p. 91. For a definition of *title* to territory, see Jennings, *The Acquisition*, p. 4.
183 See also *supra*, section 2.1.1.
184 See Gaetano Arangio-Ruiz, "*Le domaine réservé. L'organisation internationale et le rapport entre droit international et droit interne (Cours général de droit international public)*," Vol. 225, *Recueil des Cours de l'Académie de Droit International de la Hague, 1990–VI*. (Dordrecht: Martinus Nijhoff Publishers, 1993 [French]), p. 476.
185 Charles Rousseau, *Droit International Public, Tome II, Les sujets de Droit* (Paris: Dalloz, 1974), p. 60. See also, among others, Joseph A. Camilleri and Jim Falk, *The End of Sovereignty? The Politics of a Shrinking and Fragmenting World* (Aldershot: E. Elgar, 1992), pp. 141–142; Sergio Marchisio, *Le basi militari nel diritto internazionale* (Milano: Giuffré Editore, 1984), pp. 11–15 and 149 ff. On the subjects of international law see also *supra*, section 2.1.2 and *infra*, section 5.2.
186 "S.S. Lotus", *P.C.I.J.*, Series A, No 10 (1927) p. 19; see also Ruth Lapidoth, "Redefining Authority: The Past, Present and Future of Sovereignty," *Harvard International Review*, 17, 3 (1995) p. 10. On the limits of judicial jurisdiction in criminal matters see, among others, Paolo Benvenuti, "*Sui limiti internazionali alla giurisdizione penale*," *Rivista di diritto internazionale*, 2 (1974).
187 On the debate about the term *sovereignty* see, among others, Ian Brownlie, *Principles of Public International Law* (Oxford: Clarendon Press; New York: Oxford University Press, 1998, 5th ed.), p. 106; Louis Henkin, "*International Law: Politics, Values and Functions. General Course on Public International Law*, Recueil des Cours de l'Académie de Droit International de la Hague, 1989–IV. (Dordrecht and Boston: Martinus Nijhoff Publishers, 1989), pp. 24–25; Jean Maritain, "The Concept of Sovereignty," in Wladyslaw. J. Stankiewicz (ed.), *In Defence of Sovereignty* (New York/London/Toronto, 1969), pp. 61–64. On the European model of territorial sovereignty, with particular reference to Jerusalem and Holy Places therein see my article: "Nation, religion and collective identity between Europe and the Mediterranean", in Eva Pfoestl (ed.), *The Creation of a Zone of Peace and Stability Surrounding the European Union* [Italian] (Roma: Istituto di Studi Politici S. Pio V, 2007), pp. 301–448, particularly 316–327 and 386–391.
188 Eduardo Vitta, "The Conflict of Personal Laws," *Israel Law Review*, Vol. 5, No. 2 (1970): p. 170. On the *Millet* system see *infra*, section 5.2.
189 Judge Henry Eli Baker, "Judiciary and Legislation (Religious Legal and Judicial System)," in Israel Pocket Library, *Religious Life and Communities* (Jerusalem: Keter, 1974), p. 102.
190 *Ibid.*
191 Vitta, "The Conflict," p. 175.
192 Letter of Rev. Mr. Dwight to Mr. King, Bible House, Constantinople, 9 October 1886, quoted from *FRUS* 1887, p. 1080.
193 Walter Zander, *Israel and the Holy Places of Christendom* (Worcester: The Trinity Press, 1971), p. 38.
194 *Foreign Relations of the United States*, 1887, Exhibit F, p. 1110. On the Capitulations see also *supra*, section 1.7.
195 *Ibid.*, p. 1112.
196 *Ibid.*, p. 1110.
197 See Eduardo Vitta, "The Conflict of Personal Laws" [Italian], *Israel Law Review*, Vol. 5, No. 2, (1970): p. 174.
198 See Lassa Francis Lawrence Oppenheim and Hersch Lauterpacht, *International Law. A Treatise*, (London, New York: Longmans, Green, 1967, Vol. I), pp. 682–683. As an example, see the case of Great Britain, regulated upon the basis of the Foreign Jurisdiction Act, 1890. On the Consul's special status in Jerusalem under the Capitulations' regime see *infra*, section 3.5.4.
199 See *supra*, section 2.1.

200 *FRUS* 1887, Exhibit F, p. 1111.
201 *Ibid.*, p. 1112. On the combination of territorial and personal jurisdiction used during the Roman Empire see *supra*, sections 2.1.1, 2.2.1.
202 See, on this account, the Adolf Berger, entry "*Ius Gentium*" in Adolf Berger, *Encyclopedic Dictionary of Roman Law*, Vol. 43, pt. 2 (Philadelphia: American Philosophical Society, 1953) pp. 528–529. See also Mariano Scarlata Fazio, "Praetor" entry in Antonio Azara and Ernesto Eula (eds.), *Novissimo Digesto Italiano* (Torino: Unione tipografico-editrice torinese, 1953) p. 550; Vitta "The Conflict" p. 171.
203 Article 6 of the Treaty of Amity and Commerce. For the text in English, see Jacob Coleman Hurewitz (ed.), *Diplomacy in the Near and Middle East. A Documentary Record: 1914–1956*, Vol. 1 (Princeton, N.J.: Van Nostrand, 1956), p. 10.
204 See Hurewitz, *ibid.* On the principle of immunity from ordinary local jurisdiction see *supra*, section 2.1.1 and *infra*, sections 2.3.3, 3.4 and 5.6.
205 See Sergio Izhak Minerbi, *The Vatican and Zionism: Conflict in the Holy Land, 1895–1925* (New York: Oxford University Press, 1990), p. 24.
206 See Saul Paul Colbi, *Christianity in the Holy Land, Past and Present* (Tel Aviv: Am Hassefer, 1969), p. 70.
207 See Hurewitz, *Diplomacy*, Vol. 1, p. 10.
208 Walter Zander, *Israel and the Holy Places of Christendom* (Worcester: The Trinity Press, 1971), p. 46.
209 Zander, *ibid.* See *infra*, section 2.3.2 and Zander, *Israel*, p. 24. On the related "liturgical honors" the priests had to give to the French representatives see Minerbi, *The Vatican*, p. 25.
210 Translation in English from *FRUS*, 1887, Exhibit A, p. 1101.
211 Provision quoted from a letter of Mr. King to Mr. Bayard, Legation of the United States, Constantinople, October 19, 1886, *FRUS* 1887, p. 1079.
212 *Ibid.*
213 *Ibid.*, p. 1080.
214 On the Paris and Berlin treaties see *infra*, section 2.3.2.
215 Letter of Mr. Bayard to Mr. Straus of April 20, 1887, p. 1100.
216 *Ibid.*
217 Quoted from Zander, *Israel*, p. 24.
218 Quoted from Walter Zander, *Israel*, p. 24. See also the example of the treaty stipulated between Louis XIV and the Sultan placing the Maronite community of Lebanon under French protection in Hurewitz, *Diplomacy*, Vol. 1, *op. cit* p. 24.
219 See Colbi, *op. cit* p. 68.
220 See Hurewitz, *Diplomacy*, Vol. 1, pp. 50, 56–58; see also Zander, p. 45–46.
221 Quoted from Zander, *Israel*, p. 25.
222 Quoted from Zander, *ibid.*
223 Minerbi, *The Vatican*, p. 24.
224 See Minerbi, *ibid.*
225 Minerbi, *ibid*
226 See Article LXII of the Berlin Treaty quoted *infra*, section 2.3.2.
227 Minerbi, *The Vatican, ibid.*
228 On the European powers' intervention in 1841 against Mohammed Ali see also *infra*, section 2.3.3.
229 Quotation from Walter Zander, *Israel and the Holy Places of Christendom* (Worcester: The Trinity Press, 1971), p. 49.
230 Zander, *Israel, ibid.*
231 Zander, *Israel, ibid.*
232 A *firman*, in Turkish, is an order or edict of the Ottoman sultan.
233 For a detailed account of the conflict on the Holy Places in diplomatic history see Paolo

Pieraccini, *Gerusalemme, Luoghi Santi e comunitá regiose nella politica internazionale* [Italian] (Bologna: Edizioni Dehoniane, 1997) and bibliography quoted therein.
234 See Zander, *Israel*, pp. 44–48.
235 See H. Eugene Bovis, *The Jerusalem Question, 1917–1968*. (Stanford: Hoover Institution Press, 1971), p. 2. See also Zander, *Israel*, p. 54.
236 Walter Zander, "On the Settlement of Disputes about the Christian Holy Places," *Israel Law Review*, Vol. 8 (1973): p. 333.
237 Zander, *Israel*, p. 180 (translation of the 1852 *firman* into English). For a translation into French see Bernardin Collin, *Le Problème Juridique des Lieux Saints* [French] (Le Caire: Centre d'Etudes Orientales, 1956), pp. 157–158.
238 Quotation from Zander, *Israel*, p. 178.
239 Quotation from Zander, *Israel*, pp. 178–179.
240 See Chad F. Emmett, "The Status Quo Solution for Jerusalem," *Journal of Palestine Studies*, XXVI, 2 (1997): p. 19.
241 For the text of the Paris Treaty (Ratification exchanged in Paris on April 27, 1856), stipulated by the Ottoman Empire, Austria, France, Great Britain, Prussia, Russia and Sardinia see Jacob Coleman Hurewitz, *Diplomacy in the Near and Middle East. A Documentary Record: 1914–1956* (ed.), Vol. 1 (Princeton: Van Nostrand, 1956), pp. 153–156.
242 For an English translation of the 1856 *firman* (generally labeled by Westerners a Hatti Humayun, Imperial rescript), see Hurewitz, *Diplomacy*, Vol. 1, pp. 149–153. For a French translation see George Young, *Corps de Droit Ottoman. Recueil des Codes, Lois, Règlements, Ordonnances et Actes les plus importants du Droit Intérieur, et d'Études sur le Droit Coutumier de l'Empire Ottoman* (Oxford: The Clarendon Press, 1905, Vol. 2), pp. 3–9.
243 See an indirect reference also in Arts. 13, 14 and 28 of the Terms of Mandate quoted *infra*, section 2.3.
244 Walter Zander, "On the Settlement of Disputes about the Christian Holy Places," *Israel Law Review*, Vol. 8 (1973): p. 333. For an extensive analysis of the Treaty provisions see Zander, *ibid.*, pp. 333–335.
245 Hurewitz, *Diplomacy*, Vol. 1, p. 191.
246 Article LXII obliged the parties to let "the monks of Mount Athos, of whatever country they may be natives" to keep "their former possessions and advantages," continuing to "enjoy, without any exception, complete equality of rights and prerogatives."
247 Zander, "On the Settlement," p. 337.
248 Zander, *ibid.*, p. 351, no. 49.
249 See *infra*, section 3.4.
250 Sergio Izhak Minerbi, *The Vatican and Zionism: Conflict in the Holy Land, 1895–1925* (New York: Oxford University Press, 1990), p. 4.
251 L.G.A. Cust, *The Status Quo in the Holy Places. With an Annex on the Status Quo in the Church of the Nativity, Bethlehem* (London: His Majesty's Stationery Office, 1930), pp. 9, 11.
252 See, among others, Minerbi, *The Vatican*, p. 4.
253 On this contradiction see also *infra*, section 5.4.
254 Article XXII of the Preliminary Treaty of San Stefano of 3 March 1878. Quotation from Zander, "On the Settlement," p. 333. For a critical comparison of the relevant provisions of the two treaties (San Stefano and Berlin) see Zander, *ibid.*, pp. 332–336. For a translation of the proceedings of the quoted Berlin's Conference related to this issue see also *Foreign Relations of the United States*, 1887, exhibit D, p. 1107.
255 *FRUS, ibid.*, p. 1106.
256 Zander, "On the Settlement," *ibid.* The following quotations in this section of the thesis are all taken from the same article, respectively from pages 334, 334, 335, 335 and 336.
257 On the origin of the French Ambassadors' precedence in the Ottoman Empire see *supra*,

section 2.2.2.
258 Zander, "On the Settlement," pp. 336–337.
259 Manuel Hassassian, "Historical Dynamics Shaping Palestinian National Identity," *Palestine–Israel Journal of Politics, Economics and Culture*, Vol. 8, No. 4, 2001 and Vol. 9, No. 1, 2002, p. 51. On Israeli–Palestinian and Jewish–Muslim national/religious identity see also the other articles published in the same Vol.s of the Journal, devoted to "National Identity." On the same issue see also Gershon Baskin and Zakaria al Qaq, *Creating a Culture of Peace* (Jerusalem: IPCRI – Israel/Palestine Center for Research and Information, 1999).
260 *Ibid.*
261 See *supra*, section 2.1.2, 2.1.3.
262 Walter Zander, *Israel and the Holy Places of Christendom* (Worcester: The Trinity Press, 1971), p. 26.
263 Quoted from Zander, *Israel*, p. 28.
264 *Ibid.* p. 27.
265 *Ibid.*
266 *Ibid.* On possible Napoleon's "steps towards a restoration of the Jews to Palestine" see *ibid.*, p. 28. On Jewish plans to rebuild the destroyed Temple in Jerusalem and to renew the sacrificial services in the ancient way see also *supra*, section 1.3.1 and *infra*, sections 3.1.1 and 4.3.3.
267 On the European powers' intervention in 1841 against Mohammed Ali see also *supra*, section 2.3.1. On France's approval of Ali's conquest of Syria see Zander, *Israel*, p. 49.
268 Nadav Safran, *Egypt in Search of Political Community, an analysis of the intellectual and political evolution of Egypt, 1804–1952* (Cambridge, MA: Harvard University Press, 1961), pp. 31–33. On the role of the "Arab Christian intellectuals" in introducing "Western perception of nation and nationalism" see also Hassassian, "Historical Dynamics," p. 51.
269 Hassassian, "Historical Dynamics," p. 52.
270 *Ibid.*
271 *Report of the Commission appointed by His Majesty's Government in the United Kingdom in the United Kingdom of Great Britain and Northern Ireland, with the approval of the Council of the League of Nations, to determine the rights and claims of Moslems and Jews in connection with the Western or Wailing Wall at Jerusalem, December, 1930* (London: His Majesty's Stationery Office, 1931); p. 12. For a translation into English of the document, titled "Letter from Mohammed Shari to the Governor of Jerusalem about a decree issued by Ibrahim Pasha concerning the Wailing Wall, 1840," see Annex VI of the Report, p. 67; the letter is reprinted also in PASSIA, *Documents on Jerusalem* (Jerusalem: Palestinian Academic Society for the Study of International Affairs, 1996), p. 143.
272 Henry O. Dwight, "Memorandum in regard to the schools of the American missionaries in Turkey. A. Their history." Constantinople, November 23, 1886, in *Foreign Relations of the United States*, 1887, p. 1085.
273 Henry O. Dwight, "Memorandum in regard to the schools of the American missionaries in Turkey. B. The right of the American missionaries in these schools," Constantinople, November 23, 1886, in *ibid.*
274 Dwight, *ibid.*; for the quoted Capitulations see *supra*, section 2.2.2. On the principle of immunity from ordinary local jurisdiction see *supra*, section 2.1.1 and *infra*, sections 3.4 and 5.6.
275 Dwight, *ibid.*, p. 1087.
276 For a description of the rising of Arab nationalism (including the role of Christian institutions) see also *Palestine [Peel] Partition Commission Report*, 1937, particularly Chapter II, "The War and the Mandate. 1. The Arab Revolt;" see also Muhammad Y. Muslih, *The Origins of Palestinian Nationalism* (New York: Columbia University Press, 1988) p. 53. On this issue in general, as well as other developments of Palestinian nationalism, see

Baruch Kimmerling, "The formation of Palestinian collective identities: The Ottoman and mandatory periods," *Middle Eastern Studies*, Vol. XXXVI, 2, 2000.
277 Muslih, *ibid.*
278 Letter by Mr. Said (the Ottoman government) to Mr. King (Chargé d'affaires, the United States), Sublime Porte, Department of Foreign Affairs, March 22, 1887, *FRUS* 1887, p. 1092.
279 See Jacob Coleman Hurewitz, *Diplomacy in the Near and Middle East. A Documentary Record. 1914–1956*, Vol. 2 (Princeton: Van Nostrand, 1956), p. 268.
280 Eduardo Vitta, "The Conflict of Personal Laws," *Israel Law Review*, Vol. 5, No. 2 (1970): p. 174. Kemal Ataturk was the Turkish military officer leader of the secular revolution in Turkey.
281 On this model see *supra*, sections 2.1.2.
282 See Vitta, "The Conflict," p. 177.
283 Vitta, *ibid.*
284 Award of the Arbitral Tribunal between Eritrea and Yemen (1998) Phase I: Chapter IV — Historic Title And Other Historical Considerations, Par. 131. I wish to thank Shabtai Rosenne, former legal adviser of the Israeli Foreign Ministry, for having kindly suggested to me to examine this relevant decision of the Permanent Arbitral Court.
285 *Ibid.*, Phase I: Chapter III — Some Particular Features of This Case, Par. 96.
286 *Ibid.*, Par. 98.
287 *Ibid.*, Par. 99.
288 *Ibid.*, Par. 126.
289 *Ibid.*
290 *Ibid.*, Phase II, Par. 94.
291 *Ibid.* Phase II, Par. 93.
292 *Report of the Commission appointed by His Majesty's Government in the United Kingdom of Great Britain and Northern Ireland, with the approval of the Council of the League of Nations, to determine the rights and claims of Muslims and Jews in connection with the Western or Wailing Wall at Jerusalem, December, 1930* (London: His Majesty's Stationery Office, 1931) p. 12; (hereinafter *The Rights and Claims*), p. 12.
293 *The rights and claims*, Jewish Exhibit no. 32, pp. 67–69. For a reference to the 1889 Firman see also *infra*, section 3.3.3.
294 See, among others, Daniela Fabrizio, *The Question of the Holy Places and the Situation in Palestine 1914–1922* [Italian] (Milano: Franco Angeli, 2000), p. 103, n. 35.
295 Letter from Messrs. Ascher and Weinberg to Mr. Wallace, Constantinople, June 6, 1882, quoted from *Foreign Relations of the United States*, 1882, p. 517.
296 Letter quoted above, *ibid.*, p. 518.
297 Quotation from Sergio Yitzhak Minerbi, *The Vatican and Zionism: Conflict in the Holy Land, 1895–1925* (New York: Oxford University Press, 1990), p. 95. On this Herzl's idea see also *infra*, section 4.3.1.
298 Quotation from Minerbi, *The Vatican, ibid.*
299 Marvin Lowenthal (ed.), *The Diaries of Theodor Herzl* (New York: The Dial Press, 1956), p. 127 (diary entry of May 7, 1896). On the restoration by the first British Mandate's High Commissioner of the Arabic name "the Dome of the Rock", instead of "the Mosque of Omar" see *infra*, section 3.3.1.
300 *Ibid.*
301 Quotation from Minerbi, *The Vatican*, p. 97.
302 Quotation from Minerbi, *ibid.*
303 *Ibid.*
304 Quotation from Minerbi, *The Vatican*, p. 98, who translates the Latin expression as "a holy matter outside the nations' jurisdiction" (*ibid.*); for the concept of *res divini juris* see *supra*, section 2.1.1.

305 Minerbi, *The Vatican*, p. 102. On this issue see also *infra*, sections 2.3.3, 3.1.1, 4.3.3 and 1.4.
306 Herbert Samuel, *Memoires* (London: The Cresset Press, 1945), p. 141. The citations of Samuel's words in this section are taken from the same book, respectively pp. 140, 141, *ibid.*, 139, *ibid.*, 143, 144, *ibid.*
307 Quoted from Minerbi, *The Vatican*, p. 12.
308 Quoted from Minerbi, *ibid.*
309 "French Ambassador in Petrograd to Russian Foreign Minister," March 1/14, 1915, quoted from Jacob Coleman Hurewitz, *Diplomacy in the Near and Middle East. A Documentary Record: 1914–1956*, Vol. 2 (Princeton: Van Nostrand, 1956) p. 8.
310 "Russian Assistant Minister of Foreign Affairs to Russian Foreign Minister," March 2/15, 1915, quoted from Hurewitz, *ibid.*, p. 9.
311 "Russian Foreign Minister to Russian Ambassador in Paris," March 3/16 1915, quoted from Hurewitz, *ibid.*
312 See Hurewitz, *ibid.*, p. 13.
313 Quoted from Ruth Lapidoth and Moshe Hirsch (eds.), *The Arab–Israeli Conflict and its Resolution: Selected Documents* (Dordrecht: Martinus Nijhoff Publishers, 1992), p. 8.
314 Quoted from Lapidoth and Hirsch, *ibid.*, pp. 9–10. For Yasser Arafat's recent reference to Omar's declaration see *supra*, section 1.2. On the Caliph Omar Ibn Khattab see also *infra*, section 3.2.1 and 3.3.1.
315 Quoted from Lapidoth and Hirsch, *ibid.*, pp. 11–12.
316 See Hurewitz, *Diplomacy*, Vol. 2, p. 18.
317 Sergio Yitzhak Minerbi, *The Vatican and Zionism: Conflict in the Holy Land, 1895–1925*. New York: Oxford University Press, 1990, p. 15.
318 See Minerbi, *ibid.*, p. 13.
319 Quoted from Minerbi, *The Vatican*, p. 13. On the restoration by the first British Mandate's High Commisioner of the Arabic name "the Dome of the Rock", instead of "the Mosque of Omar" see *infra*, section 3.3.1.
320 Quoted from Walter Zander, "On the Settlement of Disputes about the Christian Holy Places," *Israel Law Review*, Vol. 8, No. 3 (1973): p. 338.
321 Quoted from Zander, *ibid.*, p. 339.
322 Quoted from Zander, *ibid.*
323 Quoted from Zander, *ibid.*
324 See Hurewitz, *Diplomacy*, Vol. 2, p. 19; see also Moshe Hirsch, Deborah Housen-Couriel, and Ruth Lapidoth (eds.), *Whither Jerusalem? Proposals and Positions Concerning the Future of Jerusalem* (The Hague: Martinus Nijhoff Publishers, 1995), p. 25.
325 See Minerbi, *The Vatican*, p. 204, n. 58.
326 Quoted from Minerbi, *The Vatican, ibid.*
327 On the Palestinian Authority and the Israeli–Palestinian Middle East Peace Agreements see *supra*, sections 1.1. and 1.2.
328 Quoted from Jacob Coleman Hurewitz, *Diplomacy in the Near and Middle East. A Documentary Record: 1914–1956*, Vol. 2 (Princeton: Van Nostrand, 1956) p. 26.
329 Quoted from Hurewitz, *ibid.*
330 See John Norton Moore (ed.), *The Arab–Israeli Conflict. Vol. III: Documents* (Princeton, New Jersey: Princeton University Press, 1974), p. 30, where the letter is reproduced from M.P.A. Hankey, Secretary of the British War Cabinet, containing a Proposed Draft of the Balfour Declaration (October 6, 1917).
331 See *Report of the Commission appointed by His Majesty's Government in the United Kingdom of Great Britain and Northern Ireland, with the approval of the Council of the League of Nations, to determine the rights and claims of Moslems and Jews in connection with the Western or Wailing Wall at Jerusalem, December, 1930* (London: His Majesty's Stationery Office, 1931), p. 14. On the Jewish Agency's tasks see also *infra*, section 3.5.1.

332 Quoted from Moore, *The Arab–Israeli Conflict* (Vol.III), p. 108.
333 See "Memorandum by the Chief of the Division of Near Eastern Affairs (Murray)," Washington, September 22, 1936, in *Foreign Relations of the United States*, 1936, Vol. III (the Near East and Africa), p. 451.
334 Moore, *The Arab–Israeli Conflict* (Vol. III), *ibid.*
335 *Report of the High Commissioner on the Administration of Palestine, 1920–1925* (London: His Majesty's Stationery Office, 1925), p. 25.
336 See *ibid.*
337 For a description of the territorial-national approach see *supra*, section 2.1.2.
338 Bernard Lewis, *The Multiple Identities of the Middle East* (London: Phoenix, 1998), p. 15–16.
339 The Message's quotations are taken from Jacob Coleman Hurewitz, *Diplomacy in the Near and Middle East. A Documentary Record: 1914–1956*, Vol. 2 (Princeton: Van Nostrand, 1956), p. 29.
340 Sergio Yitzhak Minerbi, *The Vatican and Zionism: Conflict in the Holy Land, 1895–1925* (New York: Oxford University Press, 1990), p. 18.
341 Proclamation read from the steps of David's Tower, ("The Citadel"), inside Jaffa Gate, quoted in the *Report of the Commission appointed by His Majesty's Government in the United Kingdom of Great Britain and Northern Ireland, with the approval of the Council of the League of Nations, to determine the rights and claims of Moslems and Jews in connection with the Western or Wailing Wall at Jerusalem*, December, 1930. London: His Majesty's Stationery Office, 1931, p. 18.
342 Paolo Pieraccini, *Jerusalem, the Holy Places and the Religious Communities in International Politics* [Italian], (Bologna: Edizioni Dehoniane, 1997, p. 204 (the translation into English is mine); see also Amedeo Giannini, *L'ultima fase della questione orientale (1913–1932)* (Milano: ISPI, 1933), pp. 288–292. On the Caliph Omar Ibn Khattab see *supra*, sections 1.2 and 3.1.2 and *infra*, section 3.3.1.
343 Quoted from Hurewitz, *Diplomacy* (Vol. 2), p. 30.
344 Lapidoth and Hirsch, *The Arab–Israeli Conflict*, p. 22.
345 Quoted from Hurewitz, *Diplomacy* (Vol. 2), p. 40.
346 Quoted from Hurewitz, *ibid.*, pp. 43–44.
347 Quoted from Hurewitz, *ibid.*, p. 46. For statements by the "Zionist Representatives and the technical experts in Zionism" see *Foreign Relations of the United States*, 1919 (Paris Peace Conference, Vol. IV), pp. 161–170.
348 Quoted from Minerbi, *The Vatican*, p. 28.
349 Quoted from Minerbi, *ibid.*
350 The document bears no a date but is commented upon in the files of the Foreign Office on March 1, 1919; quoted from Walter Zander, "On the Settlement of Disputes about the Christian Holy Places," *Israel Law Review*, Vol. 8, 3 (1973): p. 340.
351 Quoted from Zander, *ibid.*, p. 341.
352 See "Summary record of a secret meeting of the Supreme Council at Paris to consider the Sykes–Picot Agreement," March 20, 1919, quoted from Jacob Coleman Hurewitz (ed.), *Diplomacy in the Near and Middle East. A Documentary Record. 1914–1956*, Vol. 2 (Princeton: Van Nostrand, 1956), p. 57. According to PASSIA, *Documents on Jerusalem* (Jerusalem: Palestinian Academic Society for the Study of International Affairs, 1996), p. 293, the commission's findings "were kept secret for three years and not published until 1947."
353 The quotations from the report are taken from Hurewitz, *Diplomacy*, Vol. 2, pp. 70–71.
354 See also *infra*, sections 3.3.1. and 4.1.
355 For the Terms of the Mandate, which came into effect on September 29, 1923, see *League of Nations Official Journal*, August, 1922, pp. 1007–1012; see also *Report to the General Assembly of the United Nations Special Committee on Palestine*, Vol. II, *Annexes, Annex and*

Maps 18–22, U. N. Doc. A/364 Add.1 (9 Sept. 1947); see *Terms of League of Nations Mandates*, UN Doc. A/70 (Oct. 1946), pp. 2–7; John Norton Moore (ed.), *The Arab–Israeli Conflict. Vol. III: Documents* (Princeton, New Jersey: Princeton University Press, 1974), pp. 891–901; Ruth Lapidoth and Moshe Hirsch (eds.), *The Arab–Israeli Conflict and Its Resolution: Selected Documents* (The Hague: Martinus Nijhoff Publishers, 1992), p. 25.

356 Quoted from Minerbi, *The Vatican*, p. 37.
357 Herbert Samuel, *Memoires* (London: The Cresset Press, 1945), p. 153.
358 Samuel, *ibid.*, pp. 153–154.
359 Walter Zander, *Israel and the Holy Places of Christendom*, (Worcester: The Trinity Press, 1971), p. 1.
360 Zander, *ibid.*
361 Yitzhak Reiter, *Islamic Endowments in Jerusalem Under British Mandate* (London: Portland, 1996), p. 35; the *shari'a* is the Muslim law.
362 Quoted from Jacob Coleman Hurewitz (ed.), *Diplomacy in the Near and Middle East. A Documentary Record: 1914–1956*, Vol. 2 (Princeton, N.J.: Van Nostrand, 1956), p. 84. For the negotiations leading to the drafting of both the Sèvres and the parallel Mandate articles see H. Eugene Bovis, *The Jerusalem Question, 1917–1968* (Stanford, California: Hoover Institution Press, 1971), pp. 8–14.
363 Walter Zander, "On the Settlement of Disputes about the Christian Holy Places," *Israel Law Review*, Vol. 8, No. 3 (1973): p. 347.
364 Quoted from Bovis, *op. cit.* p. 26.
365 Herbert Samuel, *Memoires* (London: The Cresset Press, 1945), p. 161.
366 Samuel, *Memoires*, p. 168.
367 Samuel, *Memoires*, p. 157.
368 *Ibid.*
369 See the quoted part of the Report (Section on Public Security), p. 5. The text of the Churchill's declaration is reproduced in the *Report of the [Shaw] Commission on the Palestine Disturbances of August, 1929*, (London: H.M Stationary Office, 1930). On the Shaw Commission see *infra*, the following section.
370 Hurewitz, *Diplomacy*, Vol. 2, p. 103.
371 Quoted from Hurewitz, *Diplomacy*, Vol. 2, p. 106.
372 Quoted from Hurewitz, *ibid.*
373 Samuel, *Memoires*, p. 164.
374 *Ibid.* On the Caliph Omar Ibn Khattab see also *supra*, section 1.2 and *infra*, sections 3.1.2 and 3.2.1.
375 This can be a reference to the Status Quo in the narrow sense. See *infra*, sections 5.2 and 5.3, on this type of status quo. On this provision's interpretation see the *Report of the [Shaw] Commission on the Palestine Disturbances of August, 1929*, London: His Majesty's Stationery Office, 1930, p. 27. On the Shaw Commission see *infra*, the following section.
376 This can be a reference to the broader cultural–religious status quo in Jerusalem. See *infra*, section 5.5, on this type of status quo.
377 See *supra*, preceding footnote.
378 *The Times*, 25 July 1922.
379 See *infra*, sections 5.2 and 5.3, on this type of status quo. On the interpretation suggested here see the *Report of the [Shaw] Commission on the Palestine Disturbances of August, 1929*, p. 27; excerpts reproduced *infra*, Annex IV. On the Shaw Commission see *infra*, the following section.
380 See *infra*, section 5.5, on this type of status quo.
381 See also Par. 2 of the aforementioned Article 95, of the Treaty of Sèvres, signed by Turkey on 10 August 1920; on the commission to be appointed according to Article 14 of the Mandate see also *infra*, sections 3.3.3. and section 3.4.1.
382 For the text of the Article see *infra*, Annex II. See also *infra*, section 3.5.1.

383 *The Palestine Order in Council, 1922*, reproduced in Robert Harry Drayton (ed.), *Laws of Palestine*, 3 (London : Waterlow, 1934), 2587, Section 83.
384 *Encyclopaedia Judaica*, Vol. 9: "Is-Jer" (Jerusalem: *Encyclopaedia Judaica*, 1971), p. 909.
385 *Encyclopaedia Judaica*, ibid., p. 912.
386 Minerbi, *The Vatican*, p. 5.
387 *Report by his Britannic Majesty's Government on the Administration under Mandate of Palestine and Transjordan for the year 1924* (London: Government of Palestine, 1925), p. 20.
388 *Ibid.*
389 For the text of the Article see *infra*, Annex I.
390 *Report of the Commission appointed by His Majesty's Government in the United Kingdom of Great Britain and Northern Ireland, with the approval of the Council of the League of Nations, to determine the rights and claims of Moslems and Jews in connection with the Western or Wailing Wall at Jerusalem, December (*London: His Majesty's Stationery Office, 1931); p. 14. For the text of the Mandate's Article see *infra*, Annex I.
391 *Report of the [Shaw] Commission on the Palestine Disturbances of August, 1929* (London: His Majesty's Stationery Office, 1930), p. 6 (Presented by the Secretary of State for the Colonies to Parliament by Command of His Majesty, March, 1930). For selected excerpts of the Report see *infra*, Annex IV. On the Shaw Commission see also *infra*, the following section.
392 Muhammad Y. Muslih, *The Origins of Palestinian Nationalism* (New York: Columbia University Press, 1988), p. 208.
393 Muslih, p. 209.
394 See Paolo Pieraccini, *Jerusalem, the Holy Places and the Religious Communities in International Politics* [Italian] (Bologna: Edizioni Dehoniane, 1997), p. 308.
395 See Pieraccini, *Jerusalem*, p. 318.
396 Muslih, p. 201.
397 On the Congress of the Islamic-Christian Committees held in Jerusalem at the beginning of 1919 and its outcome see, among others, Pieraccini, *Jerusalem*, pp. 305–306.
398 Yitzhak Reiter, *Islamic Endowments in Jerusalem Under British Mandate* (London: Portland, 1996), p. xii.
399 Quoted from Sergio Izhak Minerbi, *The Vatican and Zionism: Conflict in the Holy Land, 1895–1925* (New York: Oxford University Press, 1990), p. 77.
400 On the Mandate's provisions related to the recognized religious communities see *supra*, section 3.3.1.
401 Herbert Samuel, *Memoires* (London: The Cresset Press, 1945), p. 167. See also reference in Annex III ("The Religious Communities"): *Report of the High Commissioner on the Administration of Palestine, 1920–1925* (London: His Majesty's Stationery Office, 1925).
402 Minerbi, *The Vatican*, p. 51.
403 See reference in *Report of the High Commissioner on the Administration of Palestine, 1920–1925*, (London: His Majesty's Stationery Office, 1925), excerpts reproduced *infra*, Annex III: "The Religious Communities;" see also Pieraccini, *Jerusalem*, p. 324, who refers also to the legal personality recognized to the various communities by the *Religious Communities (Organization) Ordinance*, enacted in 1926 (see also Pieraccini, *ibid.*, p. 326).
404 See Pieraccini, *ibid.*, p. 312. See also Samuel, *Memoires*, p. 167.
405 Reiter, *Islamic*, pp. x-xi; see also, on the establishment of the Supreme Moslem Sharia Council, Pieraccini, *Jerusalem*, pp. 311–312.
406 Reiter, *Islamic*, p. 24.
407 See *supra*, section 1.3.1 and *infra*, section 4.3.3.
408 Balfour to de Saint-Aulaire (French Ambassador in London), August 5, 1922; quoted from Minerbi, *The Vatican*, p. 79; on the commission appointed according to Article 14 of the Mandate see also *supra*, section 3.3.1 and *infra*, section 3.4.1.

409 *The Western or Wailing Wall in Jerusalem*, Memorandum by the Secretary of State for the Colonies to the British Parliament (London: His Majesty's Stationery Office), 19 November 1928, p. 3.
410 See the *Report of the [Shaw] Commission on the Palestine Disturbances of August, 1929* (London: H.M Stationary Office 1930), (Presented by the Secretary of State for the Colonies to Parliament by Command of His Majesty March, 1930), pp. 27–28. For selected excerpts see *infra*, Annex IV. On the Shaw Commission see also *supra*, the previous section.
411 *The Western or Wailing Wall in Jerusalem*, p. 2.
412 *Ibid.*, p. 4.
413 *Ibid.*, p. 5.
414 *Ibid.*, p. 4.
415 On this issue see *infra*, section 5.4.
416 *Ibid.*, p. 6.
417 *Report of the Commission appointed by His Majesty's Government in the United Kingdom of Great Britain and Northern Ireland, with the approval of the Council of the League of Nations, to determine the rights and claims of Moslems and Jews in connection with the Western or Wailing Wall at Jerusalem, December, 1930.* London: His Majesty's Stationery Office, 1931, p. 7; see *infra*, Annex V.
418 *The rights and claims, ibid.*, p. 17; see *infra*, Annex V. For a reference to the 1889 Firman see *supra*, section 3.1.1.
419 For the full text of the Terms of the Mandate's Article see *infra*, Annex I; on the commission to be appointed according to Article 14 of the Mandate see also *supra*, sections 3.3.1 and 3.3.3. On the principle of immunity from ordinary local jurisdiction see *supra*, sections 2.1.1 and 2.3.3 and *infra*, section 5.6.
420 Samuel to Foreign Office, October 12, 1920; quoted from Sergio Izhak Minerbi, *The Vatican and Zionism: Conflict in the Holy Land, 1895–1925* (New York: Oxford University Press, 1990), p. 48.
421 Cable from Samuel to Foreign Office, n. 367, November 12, 1920; quoted from Minerbi, *ibid.*, who quotes Foreign Office to Samuel, October 19, 1920.
422 Quoted from H. Eugene Bovis, *The Jerusalem Question, 1917–1968* (Stanford: Hoover Institution Press, 1971), p. 13.
423 Quoted from Walter Zander, "On the Settlement of Disputes about the Christian Holy Places," *Israel Law Review*, Vol. 8, No. 3 (1973): pp. 353–354.
424 *Ibid.*
425 Quoted from Zander, "On the Settlement," p. 359.
426 *Ibid.*
427 *Ibid.*
428 For the full text of the Terms of this Mandate's Article see *infra*, Annex I.
429 *Report by His Britannic Majesty's Government on the Palestine Administration for 1923 to the Council of the League of Nations* (London: Government of Palestine, 1925), p. 19.
430 *Palestine (Holy places) Order in Council, 1924*. The text may be found in *Official Gazette of the Government of Palestine*, No. 123 (Jerusalem: Government of Palestine, 15 September 1924), p. 814. Reproduced also *infra*, Annex II.
431 *Appendices to the Report by His Britannic Majesty's Government on the Palestine Administration for the year 1924 to the Council of the League of Nations* (London: Government of Palestine, 1925), p. 4.
432 *Appendices, ibid.*
433 *Ibid.*, p. 11.
434 *Palestine (Holy places) Order in Council, 1924*, *op. cit.* Reproduced also *infra*, Annex II.
435 *Report by His Britannic Majesty's Government on the Administration under Mandate of Palestine and Transjordan for the year 1924* (London: Government of Palestine, 1925), p.

20 (italics added).
436 Quoted from Zander, "On the Settlement," p. 360.
437 *Ibid.*
438 *Ibid.*
439 Jacob Stoyanovski, *The Mandate for Palestine; a contribution to the theory and practice of international mandates* (London: Longmans, Green, 1928), p.302; Bernardin Collin, *Les Lieux Saints* (Paris: Éditions Internationales, 1948) [French], p. 152; Bernardin Collin, *Le Problème Juridique des Lieux-Saints* (Paris: Centre d'Etudes Orientales, 1956), p. 98, n. 5; Walter Zander, *Israel and the Holy Places of Christendom* (Worcester: The Trinity Press, 1971), p. 70; H. Eugene Bovis, *The Jerusalem Question, 1917–1968* (Stanford: Hoover Institution Press, 1971), p. 17; Ruth Lapidoth, and Ora Ahimeir (eds.), *Freedom of Religion in Jerusalem* (Jerusalem: Jerusalem Institute for Israel Studies, 1999), p. 13; Daniela Fabrizio, *La questione dei Luoghi Santi e l'assetto della Palestina. 1914–1922* [Italian] (Milano: Franco Angeli, 2000) p. 223, Shmuel Berkovitz, *The Temple Mount and the Western Wall in Israeli Law* (Jerusalem: The Jerusalem Institute for Israel Studies, 2001) p. 77. See also Chapter 3 section 6 of the 1947 Report of the United Nations Special Committee on Palestine (UNSCOP), *GAOR*, Vol. 1 (1947) (UN Doc. A/364), analyzed *infra*, sections 3.5.3. and 3.5.4.
440 Walter Zander, "On the Settlement of Disputes about the Christian Holy Places," *Israel Law Review*, Vol. 8, No. 3 (1973): pp. 362–363. See also Edward Every, "The Cust Memorandum and the Status Quo in the Holy Places," *Christian News from Israel*, Vol. 23, No. 4 (12), 1973, pp. 229–234. The latter author, without taking an explicit position on the issue, correctly quotes the relevant British Mandatory provision (*ibid.*, p. 231).
441 Zander, "On the Settlement", p. 362, n. 74. On this issue see also *supra* section 1.1. Recent works also include the same error; see, for example, Paolo Pieraccini, *Gerusalemme, Luoghi Santi e comunità religiose nella politica Internazionale (Jerusalem, Holy Places and religious communities in international politics)* (Bologna: Edizioni Dehoniane, 1997), p. 246.
442 Zander, "On the Settlement," pp. 362–363.
443 Quoted from Zander, *ibid.*, p. 363.
444 See Bovis, p. 17, n. 34.
445 See Bovis, *ibid.*, n. 35.
446 See Bovis, *ibid.*, n. 36.
447 Bovis, p. 17, footnote.
448 *Report of the Commission appointed by His Majesty's Government in the United Kingdom of Great Britain and Northern Ireland, with the approval of the Council of the League of Nations, to determine the rights and claims of Moslems and Jews in connection with the Western or Wailing Wall at Jerusalem, December, 1930* (London: His Majesty's Stationery Office, 1931), p. 3; for excerpts of the Report see *infra*, Annex VI
449 Zander, "On the Settlement," pp. 365–366.
450 *Ibid.*
451 See Eugene Bovis, *The Jerusalem Question, 1917–1968* (Stanford: Hoover Institution Press, 1971), pp. 21–22.
452 Bovis, *ibid.*, 21.
453 Herbert Samuel, *Memoires* (London: The Cresset Press, 1945), p. 283.
454 *Palestine [Peel] Partition Commission Report* (London: His Majesty's Stationery Office, 1937); for excerpts of the document see *infra*, Annex VII.
455 Herbert Samuel, *Memoires*, p. 284.
456 *Ibid.*
457 *Palestine [Peel] Partition Commission Report* (London: His Majesty's Stationery Office, 1937), chap. XXII.
458 Moshe Hirsch, Deborah Housen-Couriel and Ruth Lapidoth (eds.), *Whither Jerusalem? Proposals and Positions Concerning the Future of Jerusalem* (The Hague: Martinus Nijhoff

Publishers, 1995), p. 158.
459 Walter Zander, *Israel and the Holy Places of Christendom* (Worcester: The Trinity Press, 1971), p. 73.
460 Zander, *ibid.*, p. 72.
461 *Ibid.*
462 See *Palestine [Peel] Partition Commission Report* (London: His Majesty's Stationery Office, 1937), p. 73; see also Shlomo Slonim, *Jerusalem in America's Foreign Policy* (The Hague: Kluwer Law International, 1998), p. 8.
463 On the Jewish Agency's tasks see also *supra*, section 3.1.3.
464 Quoted from Bovis, p. 24.
465 See Bovis, *ibid.*, pp. 25–26.
466 For the text of the Article see *infra*, Annex II. See also *supra*, section 3.3.1.
467 Quoted from Bovis, p. 25.
468 *Ibid.*
469 *Palestine Partition [Woodhead] Commission Report*, Presented by the Secretary of State for the Colonies to Parliament by Command of His Majesty (London: His Majesty's Stationery Office, 1938).
470 Reprinted in Jacob Coleman Hurewitz, *Diplomacy in the Near and Middle East. A Documentary Record: 1914–1956*, Vol. 2 (Princeton: Van Nostrand, 1956), p. 218.
471 Quoted from Hurewitz, *ibid.*, p. 219.
472 See Hurewitz, *ibid.*
473 Quoted from Herbert Samuel, *Memoires* (London: The Cresset Press, 1945), p. 286.
474 Reprinted in Hurewitz, *ibid.*, p. 249.
475 See Hurewitz, *ibid.*
476 Hurewitz, *ibid.*, quoting the aforementioned Preliminary Report to President Truman.
477 Reprinted in Hurewitz, *ibid.*, pp. 264–266.
478 Quoted from Eugene Bovis, *The Jerusalem Question, 1917–1968* (Stanford: Hoover Institution Press, 1971), p. 38.
479 See *FRUS 1946*, p. 656. For excerpts of the plan see also *New York Times*, 26 July 1946; and Bovis, p. 39.
480 See *FRUS 1946*, p. 656; see also Shlomo Slonim, *Jerusalem in America's Foreign Policy* (The Hague: Kluwer Law International, 1998), p. 9, n. 3; Moshe Hirsch, Deborah Housen-Couriel and Ruth Lapidoth (eds.), *Whither Jerusalem? Proposals and Positions Concerning the Future of Jerusalem* (The Hague: Martinus Nijhoff, 1995), p. 33.
481 See Bovis, p. 40.
482 *New York Times*, 24 October 1946.
483 *New York Times*, 5 October 1946.
484 *Report of the United Nations Special Committee on Palestine (UNSCOP), GAOR*, Vol. 1, (1947) (UN Doc. A/364), p. 27.
485 *Report of the United Nations Special Committee on Palestine (UNSCOP), GAOR*, Vol. 1, (1947) (UN Doc. A/364) p. 36 (hereinafter *UNSCOP Report*) See also the extracts of the *Report of the First Committee on a Special Committee on Palestine* reprinted in *FRUS 1947*, pp. 1083–86. For a review of earlier plans see UNSCOP Report, Vol. 1 (chap. 4, titled: "The Main Proposals Propounded [Hitherto] for the Solution of the Palestine Question"), pp. 39–48.
486 Gaetano Arangio-Ruiz, "*Le domaine réservé. L'organisation international et le rapport entre droit international et droit interne (Cours général de droit international public)*" [French], Vol. 225, *Recueil des Cours*. (Dordrecht: Martinus Nijhoff Publishers, 1990-VI) p. 375 (the translation into English is mine).
487 UN Doc. A/364/Add. 2, in *UNSCOP Report*, pp. 135–138 and A/364/Add. 3, *ibid.*, pp.13–19.
488 Shlomo Slonim, *Jerusalem in America's Foreign Policy* (The Hague: Kluwer Law

International, 1998), p. 11. See Telegram sent by Mr. Austin, the U.S. Representative at the United Nations, to the Secretary of State concerning the internationalization of Jerusalem, 11 November 1947, *FRUS*, 1947, Vol. V (1971), pp. 1249–1251; excerpts reproduced in Ruth Lapidoth and Moshe Hirsch (eds.), *The Jerusalem Question and Its Resolution: Selected Documents* (Dordrecht: Martinus Nijhoff), 1994, p. 5.
489 See *UNSCOP Report, op. cit.*
490 UNSCOP Report, *op. cit* pp. 57–58 (majority), p. 63 (minority). For extracts see Lapidoth and Hirsch, *The Jerusalem Question*, p. 2.
491 Quoted from Lapidoth and Hirsch, *ibid.*, p. 3.
492 Arangio-Ruiz, *Le domain réservé*, p. 404.
493 See Susan Hatti Rolef (ed.), *Political Dictionary of the State of Israel* (New York-London: 1987), p. 164; Joëlle Le Morzellec, *La Question de Jérusalem devant l'Organisation des Nations Unies* (Bruxelles: Bruylant 1979), p. 53. For the 1946 census, see Pfaff, "Jerusalem, Keystone of an Arab–Israeli Settlement," in John Norton Moore (ed.), *The Arab–Israeli Conflict* (Princeton, New Jersey: Princeton University Press 1977), p. 262; for the period from 1800 to 1967, see Eugene Bovis, *The Jerusalem Question, 1917–1968* (Stanford: Hoover Institution Press, 1971), p. 128.
494 Walter Zander, *Israel and the Holy Places of Christendom* (Worcester: The Trinity Press, 1971), p. 75. See also *infra*, the following section.
495 *GAOR* (II), *Ad Hoc Committee on the Palestinian Question*, 4th Meeting.
496 *GAOR* (II), *Ad Hoc Committee on the Palestinian Question*, 3rd Meeting.
497 "Statement to the Ad Hoc Committee on the Palestinian Question by the representative of the Arab Higher Committee, 29 September 1947," *GAOR* (II), Ad Hoc Committee on the Palestine Question, 1947, pp. 5–11; excerpts reproduced in Lapidoth and Hirsch, *The Jerusalem Question*, pp. 13–14.
498 The text of the Partition Resolution 181 (II), Nov. 29, 1947, is reprinted in *FRUS 1948*, pp. 1709–30.
499 United Nations, *Official Records of the Second Session of the General Assembly, Ad Hoc Committee on the Palestinian Question*, 26th Meeting.
500 See on this subject Menachem Klein, *Jerusalem. The Contested City* (New York: New York University Press; The Jerusalem Institute for Israel Studies, 2001), p. 43.
501. Par.s 1–4 of Chapter 1 and Par.s 1–7 of Chapter 2 of Part III of the Resolution refer to the specific contents of these "special circumstances and customs."
502 Walter Zander, *Israel and the Holy Places of Christendom* (Worcester: The Trinity Press, 1971), p. 76. For an attempt to list these principles see infra, Annex X to this thesis, titled "Basic Cultural and Religious Principles Governing the Holy Places of Jerusalem." On Zander's generally accepted 'essentials' see also *supra*, the previous section and *infra*, section 4.2.1.
503 See Moshe Hirsch, Deborah Housen-Couriel, Ruth Lapidoth (eds.), *Whither Jerusalem? Proposals and Positions Concerning the Future of Jerusalem* (The Hague: Martinus Nijhoff, 1995), p.158.
504 On the specific question as to which body should have jurisdiction over the said disputes see *supra*, section 3.4.
505 Hirsch, Housen-Couriel, Lapidoth (eds.), *ibid.*, p.159.
506 TCOR (II), 2nd Part, 29th and 30th Meetings.
507 For excerpts of the Terms of the Mandate see *infra*, Annex I.
508 See United Nations (ed.), *The Status of Jerusalem* (New York: 1979), prepared for the Committee on the Exercise of the Inalienable Rights of the Palestinian People; William T. Malllison and Sally V. Mallison, *The Palestine Problem in International Law and World Order* (London: Longman, 1986), pp. 197–201; *id.*, "The Jerusalem Problem in Public International Law: Juridical Status and a Start Towards Solution," in Hans Koechler (ed.), *The Legal Aspects of the Palestine Problem with Special Regard to the Question of Jerusalem*

(Wien: Braumuller, 1981), p. 107; Antonio Cassese, "Legal Considerations on the International Status of Jerusalem," in Koechler, *ibid.*, pp. 149 and 151.

For a critical discussion of this idea see my article "Jerusalem and the Holy Places" [Italian], *La Comunitá Internazionale*, Vol. 2 (1994), pp. 243–273. See also, on the general question of the legal effects of recommendations (in particular of the Declarations of principles) of the General Assembly, Gaetano Arangio-Ruiz, *of the General Assembly of the United Nations and the Declarations of Principles of Friendly Relations with an Annex on the Concept of International Law and the Theory of International Organization*, Vol. 137, *Recueil des Cours de Académie de Droit International de la Hague, 1972-III*. Dordrecht: Martinus Nijhoff Publishers, 1993 pp. 434 ff.

509 See, among others, Ruth Lapidoth, "Jerusalem and the Peace Process," *Israel Law Review*, Vol. 28, Nos. 2–3 (1994): p. 415.
510 On the exercise of personal jurisdiction of the consuls over their fellow-subjects under the Capitulations' regime see *supra*, section 2.2.2.
511 *Laws of the State of Israel, Authorized Translation*, Vol. 1, 5708–1948, p. 3. On the Declaration see also *infra*, sections 4.1.2. and 4.3.2.
512 Menachem Klein, *Jerusalem. The Contested City* (New York: New York University Press; The Jerusalem Institute for Israel Studies, 2001), p. 45.
513 Resolution S/801, reproduced in *UNYB 1948*, p. 427.
514 See Shlomo Slonim, *Jerusalem in America's Foreign Policy* (The Hague, The Netherlands: Kluwer Law International, 1998), p. 92.
515 Mahdi Abdul (ed.) *Documents on Palestine*, Vol. 2, 1948–1973 (Jerusalem, Palestinian Academic Society for the Study of International Affairs (PASSIA), 2007), p. 72.
516 Proclamation No. 1 of the Israel Defense Forces in Jerusalem, translated from Hebrew in Meron Medzini (ed.), *Israel's Foreign Relations, Vol. 1: Selected Documents, 1947–1974* (Jerusalem: Ministry for Foreign Affairs, 1976), pp. 219–220. See also Ruth Lapidoth and Moshe Hirsch (eds.), *The Jerusalem Question and its Resolution: Selected Documents* (Dordrecht, The Netherlands: Martinus Nijhoff, 1994), p. 27; Slonim, *Jerusalem*, p. 111.
517 Proclamation No. 2 of the Israel Defense Forces in Jerusalem, translated from Hebrew in Lapidoth and Hirsch, *The Jerusalem Question*, p. 28. See also Medzini, *ibid.*
518 Order No. 1 of the Military Commander in the Occupied Area of Jerusalem, translated from Hebrew in Lapidoth and Hirsch, *The Jerusalem Question*, p. 29.
519 G.A. Res. 194 (III), in *GAOR* (III), Part 1, Resolutions, 1948, p. 21; reproduced in Lapidoth and Hirsch, *The Jerusalem Question*, p. 30–32.
520 Israel signed armistice agreements with Egypt (*Israel-Egypt*, UN Doc., S/1264/Rev.), Lebanon (*Israel-Lebanon*, UN Doc. S/1296/Rev.), Jordan (*Israel–Jordan*, UN Doc. S/1302/Rev.) and Syria (*Israel–Syria*, UN Doc. S/1353/Rev.) respectively on 24 February, 23 March, 3 April and 20 July 1949.
521 Preamble to the Cease-Fire Agreement; text reprinted in Lapidoth and Hirsch, *The Jerusalem Question*, p. 35, n. 1. See also Bovis, p. 69, n. 35.
522 Quoted from Bovis, p. 69, n. 34. English translation in Medzini, Vol. 1, p. 222.
523 General Administration of Palestine Law No. 17, enacted 14 March 1949 and published in the Official Gazette on 16 March1949, quoted from Bovis, p. 69, n. 36.
524 Article VIII, No. 2 of the Israel–Jordan Armistice Agreement of 3 April 1949.
525 GA Res. 303 (IV), 9 December 1949.
526 For an English translation, see Medzini, p. 226; Lapidoth and Hirsch, *The Jerusalem Question*, pp. 81–83.
527 Quoted from Lapidoth and Hirsch, *ibid.*
528 *Ibid*; on the declarations of the Israeli delegation to the General Assembly see *infra*, the following sections.
529 See Moshe Hirsch, Deborah Housen-Couriel and Ruth Lapidoth (eds.), *Whither Jerusalem: Proposals and Positions Concerning the future of Jerusalem* (The Hague: Martinus

Nijhoff, 1995), p. 5, n. 14 and 15; see also *FRUS 1949*, pp. 1542, 1551, quoted from Slonim, *Jerusalem*, p. 146.

530 For an English translation, see Lapidoth and Hirsch, *The Jerusalem Question*, p. 105; see also Gabriel Padon, "The Divided City: 1948–1967," in Msgr. John M. Oesterreicher and Anne Sinai (eds.), *Jerusalem*, (New York: John Day, 1974), p. 74, and Shlomo Slonim, "The United States and the Status of Jerusalem. 1947–1948," *Israel Law Review*, Vol. 19 (1984): p. 197.

531 Quoted from Bovis, p. 150, n. 52.

532 Quoted from Bovis, p. 82; See also Slonim, *Jerusalem*, p. 147, n. 55.

533 Menachem Klein, *Jerusalem: The Contested City* for the Jerusalem Institute for Israel Studies (New York: New York University Press), 2001, p. 53.

534 *Laws of the State of Israel, Authorized Translation*, Vol. 1, 5708–1948, p. 3. On the Declaration see *supra*, the previous section and *infra* sections 4.1.3 and 4.3.2.

535 See Ruth Lapidoth, and Ora Ahimeir (eds.), *Freedom of Religion in Jerusalem* (Jerusalem: Jerusalem Institute for Israel Studies, 1999), p. 7.

536 For the text of the Declaration see Meron Medzini (ed.), , *Israel's Foreign Relations, Vol. 1: Selected Documents, 1947–1974* (Jerusalem: Ministry for Foreign Affairs, 1976), p. 1, see also reference in Lapidoth, and Ahimeir, *Freedom of Religion*, p. 34, n. 17.

537 H. Eugene Bovis, *The Jerusalem Question, 1917–1968* (Stanford, California: Hoover Institution Press, 1971), p. 61.

538 *Ibid.*

539 Mahdi Abdul (ed.) *Documents on Palestine*, Vol. 2, 1948–1973 (Jerusalem, Palestinian Academic Society for the Study of International Affairs (PASSIA), 2007), p. 72.

540 For the text of the cable see *Israeli Documents*, Vol. 1 (1948), pp. 434–445; reproduced in Slonim, *Jerusalem*, pp. 109–110; On the Israeli Provisional Government Cabinet decision of July 25, 1948 see *supra*, the preceding section.

541 *GAOR* (III), 2nd Part, *Ad Hoc Political Committee*, 45th Mtg., 5 May 1949, pp. 233–234. For excerpts, see Lapidoth and Hirsch, *The Jerusalem Question*, p. 43; Slonim, *Jerusalem*, p. 128.

542 *GAOR, ibid.* All the following quotations from the document are taken from the same source.

543 For the text see *infra*, Annex VIII; on this Draft Resolution see *infra*, sections 4.1.3 and 5.1.

544 UN Doc. A/973, summarized in *UNYB 1948–1949*, p. 199; see also Shlomo Slonim, *Jerusalem in America's Foreign Policy* (The Hague, The Netherlands: Kluwer Law International, 1998), pp. 126–127. On General Assembly Resolution 194 (III) see *supra*, section 4.1.1

545 For the text see Ruth Lapidoth and Moshe Hirsch (eds.), *The Jerusalem Question and its Resolution: Selected Documents* (Dordrecht, The Netherlands: Martinus Nijhoff, 1994), pp. 49–73. All the following quotations from the document are taken from this source.

546 For the text see *infra*, Annex VIII; on this Draft Resolution see also *infra*, in this section.

547 It is not clear to which Ordinance the Israeli Memorandum refers. The 1924 (Holy Places) Order-in-Council mentioned *supra*, section 3.4 (for the text, see *infra*, Annex II), for instance, does not include a list of Holy Places, nor does it refer indirectly to any such list. Reference, probably, was here to the aforementioned British confidential Memorandum by L.G.A. Cust, *The Status quo in the Holy Places*. Jerusalem: Government of Palestine, 1930 (Reprinted Jerusalem: Ariel Publishing House, 1980).

548 On the Custos' comments at the UNSCOP see also *supra*, section 3.5.3.

549 Quoted from Slonim, *Jerusalem*, pp. 131–132.

550 Slonim, *Jerusalem*, p. 135.

551 *Ibid.*

552 *SCOR*, 271st Mtg., 19 Mar. 1948, pp. 157–168; see also Slonim, *Jerusalem*, p. 135.

553 For the full text of this letter, see Lapidoth and Hirsch, *The Jerusalem Question*, p. 72.
554 For the text of the Draft Resolution see *infra*, Annex VIII. on this Draft Resolution see also *supra*, section 4.1.2 and *infra*, section 5.1.
555 For this text see Lapidoth and Hirsch (eds.), *The Jerusalem Question*, p. 74. All the following quotations from the document are taken from the same source. See also Bovis, *ibid*.
556 On the the Declaration on the Establishment of the State of Israel see *supra*, sections 4.1.1 and 4.1.2 and *infra*, section 4.3.2.
557 See *GAOR* (IV), Ad Hoc Political Committee, Annex, Vol. I, UN Doc. A/973 and A/973/Add. 1.
558 For the text of the statement, see Meron Medzini (ed.), *Israel's Foreign Relations*, Vol. 1, *Selected Documents, 1947–1974* (Jerusalem: Ministry for Foreign Affairs, 1976), p. 223. All the following quotations from the document are taken from the same source.
559 The quotation within Ben-Gurion's statement refers to a previous declaration of the Israeli delegation at the United Nations.
560 Quoted from Medzini, Vol. 1, pp. 227–236. All the following quotations from the document are taken from the same source. See also Slonim, *Jerusalem*, p. 155, n. 80.
561 Medzini, Vol. 1, pp. 227–236. See also Slonim, *Jerusalem*, p. 155, n. 80.
562 See *FRUS 1948*, p. 1278; see also Slonim, *Jerusalem*, p. 114.
563 US Secretary of State Marshall's message to Ben-Gurion and Sharett, 1 September 1948, *FRUS 1948*, 1368; see also Slonim, *ibid.*, p. 115.
564 "Progress Report of the United Nations Mediator in Palestine, "*GAOR* (III), Supp. No. 11, (UN Doc. A/684), pp. 17 ff. Extracts of the report are reprinted in PASSIA, *Documents on Jerusalem, op. cit* pp. 231–232; Slonim, *Jerusalem*, pp. 115–116. For the first set of proposals suggested by the UN Mediator, see "Text of Suggestions Presented by Count Bernadotte, at Rhodes, to the Two Parties on June 28, 1948, "*SCOR*, 3rd Yr., Supp. July 1948, pp. 18–21. The suggestions themselves are reproduced in *FRUS 1948*, pp. 1152–1154 and also in *Israeli Documents*, Vol. 1 (1948), pp. 230–234. For a summary, see *UNYB, 1948*, p. 432.
565 *FRUS 1948*, p. 1485; see also Slonim, *Jerusalem*, p. 115.
566 See Bovis, p. 92.
567 See Slonim, *Jerusalem*, p. 122.
568 *FRUS 1949*, p. 891; see also Slonim, *ibid.*, p. 123.
569 *FRUS 1948*, pp. 1293–1294; see also Slonim, *ibid.*, pp. 125–126 (see *ibid.* also for excerpts of the Cardinal's letter).
570 *FRUS ibid.*; see also Slonim, *ibid.*
571 *FRUS 1950*, pp. 686–689; see also Slonim, *Jerusalem*, p. 148.
572 See *FRUS 1950*, pp. 686–689; see also Slonim, *ibid.*
573 See *FRUS 1950*, p. 706, n. 3; see also Slonim, *ibid.*
574 See Walter Zander, *Israel and the Holy Places of Christendom* (Worcester, Great Britain: The Trinity Press, 1971), p. 76.
575 Original Latin text in *Oriente Moderno* 28 (October–December 1948): pp. 172–174. Translated text in *New York Times*, 24 October 1948.
576 Zander, *Israel*, p. 78. On Zander's generally accepted 'essentials' see also *supra*, sections 3.5.3 and 3.5.4.
577 This quotation from the Pope's Encyclical is reprinted in Zander, *ibid.*
578 See H. Eugene Bovis, *The Jerusalem Question, 1917–1968* (Stanford, California: Hoover Institution Press, 1971), p. 64.
579 See Bovis, *ibid.*
580 Bovis, *ibid.*
581 Resolution, n. 1; see *The New York Times*, 2 December 1948; Bovis, *ibid.*; Marjorie Millace Whiteman (ed.), *Digest of International Law*, Vol.2 (Washington, D.C.: U.S. Department

of State, 1963), pp. 1163–4; Lapidoth and Hirsch, *The Jerusalem Question*, p. 145.
582 See Lapidoth and Hirsch, *The Jerusalem Question*, p. 145. Bovis, p. 64, however, mentions the date of 13 December.
583 Menachem Klein, *Jerusalem. The Contested City* (New York: New York University Press; The Jerusalem Institute for Israel Studies, 2001), p. 168.
584 See *The New York Times*, 14 December 1948. See also Klein, *Jerusalem*, p. 51.
585 See Bovis, p. 81.
586 See Bovis, p. 88; see also Shlomo Slonim, *Jerusalem in America's Foreign Policy* (The Hague, The Netherlands: Kluwer Law International, 1998), p. 160. For a legal analysis of the Jordanian actions see, among others, my article "Jerusalem and the Holy Places" [Italian], *La Comunità Internazionale*, Vol. 2 (1994): pp. 254–255.
587 See Whiteman, *Digest*, pp. 1165–1166; Lapidoth and Hirsch, *The Jerusalem Question*, p. 147.
588 Natalino Ronzitti, *Rescuing nationals abroad through military coercion and intervention on grounds of humanity* (Dordrecht: M. Nijhoff Publishers, 1985), pp. 92–95.
589 Ronzitti, *ibid.*, p. 95. On Jordan's legitimacy to represent the interests of the West Bank population (including that of Jerusalem), see Yoram Dinstein, "Autonomy," in Yoram Dinstein (ed.), *Models of Autonomy* (New Brunswick: Transaction Books, 1981), pp. 291, 300.
590 See Whiteman, *Digest*, p. 1168; Lapidoth and Hirsch, *The Jerusalem Question*, p. 149; see also Bovis, p. 88.
591 See Whiteman, *Digest*, pp. 1166–1167.
592 See Whiteman, *Digest*, ibid.
593 See Slonim, *Jerusalem*, p. 169.
594 Quoted from Slonim, *Jerusalem*, p. 164.
595 See Slonim, *Jerusalem*, *ibid.*, n. 7.
596 Quoted from Slonim, *ibid.*
597 Quoted from Walter Zander, *Israel and the Holy Places of Christendom* (Worcester, Great Britan: The Trinity Press, 1971), p. 80.
598 Quoted from Zander, p. 87.
599 *Ibid.*
600 Quoted from Zander, *ibid.*
601 Zander, p. 89.
602 Shmuel Berkovitz, *The Temple Mount and the Western Wall in Israeli Law* (Jerusalem: The Jerusalem Institute for Israel Studies, 2001), p.83
603 See, among others, Berkovitz, *The Temple Mount*, p. 13.
604 Eugene H. Bovis, *The Jerusalem Question, 1917–1968* (Stanford, California: Hoover Institution Press, 1971), p. 119. On the acts of vandalism against Jewish Holy Places under Jordanian administration in Jerusalem see *infra*, section 5.7. On the Har Ha Bait/Haram Al Sharif see *supra*, section 1.3.1 and *infra*, sections 4.3.3, 5.4, 5.5 and B.2.
605 Hazem Zaki Nuseibeh, *Palestine and the United Nations* (London: Quartet Books Limited, 1981), p. 88.
606 Quoted from *Defending the Faith: The Hashemites and Jerusalem*, n. 13, Amman, 1994, pp. 79–80.
607 Quoted from *Defending the Faith, ibid*. On the provision guaranteeing "freedom of access to places of religious and historical significance" in the Jordanian–Israeli Peace Treaty see *supra*, section 1.3.
608 Prince Hassan bin Talal, *A Study on Jerusalem* (London: Longman, 1979). Significantly, Prince Hassan's sentence was also quoted in the above mentioned Jordanian book *Defending the Faith* (ibid., p.81)
609 See Shlomo Slonim, *Jerusalem in America's Foreign Policy* (The Hague, The Netherlands: Kluwer Law International, 1998), pp. 191–192; Allan Gerson, "Trustee-Occupant: The

Legal Status of Israel's Presence in the West Bank," *Harvard International Law Journal*, Vol.14 (1973): pp. 8, 14–16.

610 See, for example: Julius Stone, *The Middle East under Cease-Fire* (Sydney: The Bridge, 1967), pp. 6 ff.; Quincy Wright, "Legal Aspects of the Middle East Situation," *Law and Contemporary Problems*, Vol. 33, No. 1 (1968): p. 27; Nathan Feinberg, *The Arab-Israel Conflict in International Law: A Critical Analysis of the Colloquium of Arab Jurists in Algiers*, (Jerusalem: Magnes Press, 1970), pp. 114–115; Stephen Schwebel, "What Weight to Conquest?" *American Journal of International Law*, Vol. 64 (1970): p. 346; Gerson, pp. 14–22; Yoram Dinstein, *War, Aggression and Self-Defence*, 2nd ed. (Cambridge: Cambridge University Press, 1994); Edward Miller, "Self-Defence, International Law, and the Six Day War," *Israel Law Review*, Vol. 20 (1985); Yehuda Blum, "The Missing Reversioner: Reflections on the Status of Judea and Samaria," *Israel Law Review*, Vol. 3 (1968): pp. 287–314.

611 See, for example: Henry Cattan, *Jerusalem*, (New York: Croom Helm, 1981), pp. 104, 107; Id., *Palestine and International Law*, 2nd ed. (London: Longman, 1976), pp. 112–121; Id., *The Palestine Question*, (London: Croom Helm, 1988), pp. 324–326.

612 Klein, Menachem Klein, *Jerusalem: The Contested City* (New York: New York University Press, 2001), p. 53.

613 Amnon Ramon, "Freedom of Religion and the Status of Christians in Jerusalem 1967–1997," in Ruth Lapidoth and Ora Ahimeir (eds.), *Freedom of Religion in Jerusalem* (Jerusalem: The Jerusalem Institute for Israel Studies, 1999), p. 82.

614 See *supra*, section 3.1.1.

615 Quoted from Amos Elon, *Jerusalem, City of Mirrors* (London: Weidenfeld and Nicolson, 1989), pp. 239–240; see also Ramon, p. 82.

616 For the debate among scholars on the legal status of the territories administered by Israel, including Jerusalem see Moshe Hirsch, Deborah Housen-Couriel and Ruth Lapidoth (eds.), *Whither Jerusalem: Proposals and Positions Concerning the future of Jerusalem* (The Hague, The Netherlands: Martinus Nijhoff, 1995), pp. 15–24. For an analysis of the debate see, among others, my "Problematic Issues Related to the Borders of the State of Israel" [Italian] (Master's dissertation, University "La Sapienza," Rome, 1990, unpublished); see in particular the section on Jerusalem, (pp. 191–290) and the included bibliography. See also my article "Jerusalem and the Holy Places" [Italian], *La Comunità Internazionale*, Vol. 2 (1994), pp. 247–262.

617 English translations in Meron Medzini (ed.), *Israel's Foreign Relations, Vol. 1: Selected Documents, 1947–1974* (Jerusalem: Ministry for Foreign Affairs, 1976), p. 245, and Ruth Lapidoth and Moshe Hirsch (eds.), *The Jerusalem Question and Its Resolution: Selected Documents* (Dordrecht, The Netherlands: Martinus Nijhoff, 1994), p. 167. The full text of the law reads as follows:
Law and Administration Ordinance (Amendment No. 11) Law, 5727–1967, 27 June 1967.
Addition of section 11B.
1. In the Law and Administration Ordinance, 5708–1948, the following section shall be inserted after section 11A:
"Application of law.
11B. The law, jurisdiction and administration of the state shall extend to any area of Erez Israel designated by the Government by order."
Commencement.
2. This law shall come into force on the date of its adoption by the Knesset.

618 English translation in Medzini, pp. 245–26; and Lapidoth and Hirsch, *The Jerusalem Question*, p. 167. See also Shmuel Berkovitz, *The Temple Mount and the Western Wall in Israeli Law* (Jerusalem: The Jerusalem Institute for Israel Studies, 2001), p. 15, n. 10. The full text of the law reads as follows:

Municipalities Ordinance (Amendment No. 6) Law, 5727–1967, 27 June 1967.
Addition of section 8a. a. In the Municipalities Ordinance, the following section shall be inserted after section 8:
"Enlargement of area of jurisdiction in certain cases.
8A. (a) The Minister may, at his discretion and without an inquiry under section 8 being made, enlarge, by proclamation, the area of a particular municipality by the inclusion of an area designated by order under section 11B of the Law and Administration Ordinance, 5708–1948.
8A. (b) Where the Minister has enlarged the area of a municipality as aforesaid, he may, by order, appoint additional councilors from among the inhabitants of the newly-included area. A councilor appointed as aforesaid shall hold office so long as the council holds office: Provided that the Minister may, by order, appoint another person in his stead."
2. This law shall come into force on the date of its adoption by the Knesset.

619 *Jerusalem (Enlargement of Municipal Area) Proclamation, 5727–1967*; for the English translation see Lapidoth and Hirsch (eds.), *The Jerusalem Question*, p. xxiv.
620 Uzi Benziman, "Calling Jerusalem By Its Name," www.haaretz.com, 9 July 2000.
621 Hirsch, Housen-Courel and Lapidoth (eds.), *Whither Jerusalem?*, p. 145.
622 Benziman, *op. cit.*
623 G.A. Res. 2253 (ES-V), 4 July 1967. The text of the resolution is reproduced in Medzini, pp. 247–248. On the U.N. reaction to the Israeli actions on Jerusalem, see Slonim, *Jerusalem*, pp. 193 ff.; Shepard Jones, "The Status of Jerusalem: Some National and International Aspects," in John W. Halderman (ed.), *The Middle East crisis: test of international law* (Dobbs Ferry: Oceana Publications, 1969), pp. 169–182; Joëlle Le Morzellec, *La Question de Jerusalem devant l'Organisation des Nations Unies*, (Brussels: Établissements Émile Bruylant, 1979), part 3; and Julius Stone, *No Peace-No War in the Middle East*, (Sidney: Maitland Publications for the International Law Association (Australian Branch), 1969), pp. 17–24.
624 *GAOR* (ES-V), 4 July 1967, 1 (UN Doc. A76753 or S78052). See also Lapidoth and Hirsch, *The Jerusalem Question*, pp. 171–173 (the quotation is at p. 173); Slonim, *Jerusalem*, pp. 194–195. The letter dated July 10,1967, is also reproduced in Medzini, pp. 248–251; and in *New York Times*, 12 July 1967. The following quotations from the letter are taken from the same source. On Israeli policy in East Jerusalem since 1967 see also my article "Alternative Definitions of Sovereignty: an Analysis of Coexisting National and Religious Identities in Jerusalem" in Stefania Bazzoni and May Chartouni-Doubarry (eds.), *Politics and Economics in the Search for Stability in the Mediterranean Region*. Monte Carlo: *Institut des études politiques méditerranéennes* (IEPM), 2001, pp. 121–123, where the complex intertwining of personal and territorial jurisdiction between different subjects of international law sharing powers in Jerusalem is analyzed; Ian S. Lustick, "Has Israel Annexed East Jerusalem", *Middle East Policy*, V, 1, 1997, pp. 38–39.
625 *GAOR* (ES-V), Plenary, 1554th Mtg., 14 July 1967, pp. 9–11; see also Slonim, *Jerusalem*, pp. 196–197, particularly n. 20.
626 *Ben Dov vs. Minister of Religious Affairs*, 1968 (1) P.D. p. 440; for a summary in English see Lapidoth and Hirsch, *Jerusalem Question*, pp. 487–488.
627 *Ruidi and Maches v. Military Court of Hebron*, H.C. 283/69, 1970 (2) P.D. p. 419; for a summary in English see Lapidoth and Hirsch, *The Jerusalem Question*, pp. 502–506.
628 Lapidoth and Hirsch, *ibid.*, p. 505.
629 Quoted from *Ruidi and Maches v. Military Court of Hebron, ibid*; English translation in Lapidoth and Hirsch, *The Jerusalem Question*, p. 505.
630 *Ibid.*
631 See Meron Medzini (ed.), *Israel's Foreign Relations, Vol. 1: Selected Documents, 1947–1974* (Jerusalem: Ministry for Foreign Affairs, 1976), p. 243.
632 Walter Zander, *Israel and the Holy Places of Christendom* (Worcester, Great Britain: The

Trinity Press, 1971), p. 101; see also Medzini, *ibid.*

633 Quoted from Zander, *ibid.*; see also Medzini, *Israel's Foreign Relations, Vol. 1*, p. 244; Amnon Ramon, "Freedom of Religion and the Status of Christians in Jerusalem 1967–1997," in Ruth Lapidoth and Ora Ahimeir, (eds.), *Freedom of Religion in Jerusalem* (Jerusalem: The Jerusalem Institute for Israel Studies, 1999), p. 84. Ramon adds that Yaacov Herzog (then Director-General of the Prime Minister's office) formulated the quoted declaration.

634 See Ramon, p. 85. See also *supra*, sections 2.3.1 and 2.3.2, on the conflicts between the Christian communities over the Status Quo.

635 Ramon, p. 83; see also Zander, p. 98. See also *infra*, section 4.3.3.

636 Quoted from Ramon, *ibid.*

637 This provision subsequently caused legal complications that arose from the question of how far the new law overrode earlier legislation, particularly in relation to the British Palestine (Holy Places) Order-in-Council of 1924 mentioned *supra*, section 3.4. See also Ramon, p. 87.

638 *Protection of the Holy Places Law, 5272–1967*, 27 June 1967, quoted from Lapidoth and Hirsch, *The Jerusalem Question*, p. 169.

639 Address of June 7, 1967, published in Medzini, *Israel's Foreign Relations, Vol. I*, pp. 244–245; the following quotations of the speech are taken from the same source. See also Lapidoth and Hirsch, *The Jerusalem Question*, pp. 163–164; Zander, p. 103.

640 Quotation from Ramon, p. 84; see also Zander, *Israel*, p. 102. On the the Declaration on the Establishment of the State of Israel see *supra*, sections 4.1.1, 4.1.2, and 4.1.3.

641 Ramon, 87.

642 For a definition of the Status Quo procedural principles see *infra*, section 5.3.

643 Ramon, *ibid.*

644 Ramon, *ibid.* The letter is also mentioned *supra*, in the previous section; the following quotations of the speech are taken from the same source.

645 Ramon, p. 90.

646 Ramon, *ibid.* On Cust's Memorandum see also *supra*, section 1.3.1.

647 Quoted from Medzini, p. 260.

648 Quoted from Medzini, *ibid.*

649 Security Council Resolution 298 (1971), adopted on 25 September 1971.

650 "Letter from Foreign Minister Eban to Secretary-General U Thant on Jerusalem, 15 November", document no. 20 in Meron Medzini (ed.), *Israel's Foreign Relations, Selected Documents*, Vol. 1–2: 1947–1974 (Jerusalem: Ministry for Foreign Affairs), also available at: www.mfa.gov.il/mfa.

651 *Basic Law-Jerusalem*, Knesset Resolution, 30 July 1980; for the text see Lapidoth and Hirsch (eds.), *The Arab–Israeli Conflict and Its Resolution: Selected Documents* (Dordrecht: Martinus Nijhoff Publishers, 1992), p. 322.

652 Statement in the Knesset by the then Israeli Foreign Minister Peres on Jerusalem, 9 September 1993, document no. 106 in Medzini, Vols. 13–14: 1992–1994, also available at: www.mfa.gov.il/mfa.

653 See, among them, Article 4, Par. 1 of the Fundamental Agreement quoted *supra*, section 1.4.1.

654 See *supra*, section 1.3.1.

655 See "Remarks by Israel Ambassador Dore Gold to the UN Security Council on the Subject of Jerusalem; June 30, 1988," available at: www.mfa.gov.il/mfa.

656 These expressions seem to refer to the Status Quo/Modus Vivendi in a narrow sense; see *supra*, section 1.3.1 and *infra*, sections 5.2 and 5.3.

657 See "Cabinet Communiqué of March 14 1999, document no. 150 in Medzini, Vol. 17, 1998–1999, available at: www.mfa.gov.il/mfa. These expressions seem to refer to the Status Quo in a broader sense; see *infra*, section 5.5.

658 Walter Zander, *Israel and the Holy Places of Christendom* (Worcester: The Trinity Press, 1971), p. 99. On the Har Ha Bait/Haram Al Sharif see *supra*, sections 1.3.1 and 4.2.2 and *infra*, sections 5.4, 5.5 and B.2.
659 Shmuel Berkovitz, *The Temple Mount and the Western Wall in Israeli Law* (Jerusalem: The Jerusalem Institute for Israel Studies, 2001), p. 13. See also *supra*, section 4.3.2.
660 Nadav Shagrai, "Absurdity scales the heights of the Temple Mount," www.haaretz.com, 16 August 1999.
661 Translation from Hebrew in Ruth Lapidoth and Moshe Hirsch (eds.), *The Jerusalem Question and Its Resolution: Selected Documents* (Dordrecht, The Netherlands: Martinus Nijhoff, 1994), pp. 455–470 (citation, p. 467). See reference to Prime Minister Levi Eshkol's speeches *supra*, in the previous section.
662 See the Report (including appendices) of the U.N. Secretary-General concerning the situation in Jerusalem, submitted to the General Assembly in accordance with General Assembly Resolution 2254 (ES-V), September 12, 1967, Annex I. Documents submitted to the personal representative of the Secretary-General by Arab personalities: B. Memorandum concerning the measures taken by Israel with respect to the city of Jerusalem, submitted by Mr. Rauhi El-Khatib on August 26 1967," *GAOR* (ES-V), 1967, 1 (UN Doc. A/6793 or S/8146), reprinted in Lapidoth and Hirsch, *The Jerusalem Question*, p. 204.
663 Berkovitz, *The Temple Mount*, p. 13.
664 Quoted from Shagrai, *ibid*. For a critical review of Israeli law and jurisprudence on the subject see Shmuel Berkovitz, "The Holy Places in Jerusalem: Legal Aspects (Part I)," *Justice*, Vol. 11, (December 1996): pp. 4–14; "(Part II)," *Justice*, Vol. 12, (March 1997): pp. 17–21.
665 See, among others, Zander, *Israel*, 2. On the first incidents in the area after the beginning of Israeli rule see *Jerusalem Post*, August 18 and October 22, 1969. For reference to the Mandate period see *supra*, section 3.3.3. On Jewish plans to rebuild the destroyed Temple in Jerusalem and to renew the sacrificial services in the ancient way see also *supra*, sections 1.3.1 and 3.1.1.
666 Quoted from Shlomo Slonim, *Jerusalem in America's Foreign Policy* (The Hague, The Netherlands: Kluwer Law International, 1998), p. 221, n. 76. The following quotations from the US Ambassador's speech are taken from the same source.
667 On this issue see *infra*, section 5.4.
668 See, among other documents, the "Resolution adopted by the Higher *Waqf* Council and the Committee for Muslim Affairs, 14 August 1967", in PASSIA, *Documents on Jerusalem*, Jerusalem: Palestinian Academic Society for the Study of the International Affairs, 1996, p. 13.
669 On the terms of this treaty's article see *supra*, section 1.3.
670 Amnon Ramon, "Freedom of Religion and the Status of Christians in Jerusalem 1967–1997," in Ruth Lapidoth and Ora Ahimeir, (eds.), *Freedom of Religion in Jerusalem* (Jerusalem: The Jerusalem Institute for Israel Studies, 1999), pp. 84–85.
671 Quoted from Ramon, *ibid*. See also *supra*, section 3.2.1.
672 Quoted from Ramon, *ibid*.
673 Quoted from Ramon, *ibid*.
674 On this issue see also *infra*, section 5.7.
675 Lapidoth and Ahimeir, *Freedom of Religion*, p. 11, who quotes the Regulations on the Protection of Places Holy for Jews of 16.7.1981, 5741–1981, *Kovets Ha-Takanot* (collection of regulations) 4252, 5471 (1980–1981), p. 1212, amended in 1990 — *Kovets Ha-Takanot*, 5237, 5750 (1989–1990), p. 190.
676 See footnote above.
677 Berkovitz, *The Temple Mount*, p. 86.
678 Berkovitz, *The Temple Mount*, *ibid*.

679 www.haaretz.com, "Sealing Temple Mount window brings no protests. Late-night operation by police raises eyebrows, but no rocks", August 11, 1999. See *infra*, section 3.3.3, on the new Jewish–Muslim Status Quo established by Israel after 1967.
680 Ben Lynfield, "Temple Mount window resealed peacefully", *Jerusalem Post*, 11 August 1999, www.jpost.com.
681 See www.haaretz.com, "Sealing Temple Mount", *op. cit.*
682 See, among others, Sergio Izhak Minerbi, *The Vatican and Zionism: Conflict in the Holy Land, 1895–1925* (New York: Oxford University Press, 1990), p. 201, note 1.
683 Quotations from Walter Zander, *Israel and the Holy Places of Christendom* (Worcester: The Trinity Press, 1971), p. 21.
684 For the text of this document, issued in August 1967, see Bernardin Collin, *Pour une Solution au Problème des Lieux Saints* (Paris : G. P. Maisonneuve et Larose, 1974), p. 141.
685 *Ibid.*, my translation.
686 *Ibid.*
687 *GAOR* (IV), *Ad Hoc Political Committee*, Annex, Vol. 1, UN Doc. A/AC.31/L.42. See also H. Eugene Bovis, *The Jerusalem Question, 1917–1968* (Stanford, California: Hoover Institution Press, 1971), p. 75. For the full text of the draft resolution, see *infra*, Annex VIII; on this Draft Resolution see also *supra*, section 4.1.3.
688 Shmuel Berkovitz, "The Legal Status of the Holy Places in Israel" [Hebrew] (Ph.D. dissertation, The Hebrew University of Jerusalem, Jerusalem, 1978): p. 39.
689 Shmuel Berkovitz, *The Temple Mount and the Western Wall in Israeli Law* (Jerusalem: The Jerusalem Institute for Israel Studies, 2001), pp. 19–20. For an analysis of the 1967 law see *supra*, section 4.3.
690 This reference is to the Palestine (Holy Places) Order in Council of 1924 analysed *supra*, section 3.4. For the text of the Order see *infra*, Annex II.
691 Berkovitz, "The Legal Status," p. 39. See also Alisa Rubin Peled, "The Crystallization of an Israeli Policy towards Muslim and Christian Holy Places, 1948–1955," *The Muslim World*, Vol. 84, Nos. 1–2, (1994): p. 98.
692 Moshe Hirsch, Deborah Housen-Couriel, and Ruth Lapidoth (eds.), *Whither Jerusalem? Proposals and Positions Concerning the Future of Jerusalem* (The Hague: Martinus Nijhoff, 1995), p. 157.
693 Quoted in Ytzhak Reiter, Marlene Eordegian and Marwan Abu Khalaf, "Between Divine and Human: The Complexity of Holy Places in Jerusalem," in Moshe Ma'oz and Sari Nusseibeh (eds.) *Jerusalem: Points of Friction and Beyond* (The Hague: Kluwer Law International, 2000), p. 108.
694 "United Nations Conciliation Commission for Palestine: Definition of Holy Places, Religious Buildings and Sites" (June 30, 1949), quoted in Peled, "The Crystallization," p. 98.
695 Quoted from Peled, *ibid.*
696 Jan Hendrik Willem Verzijl, *International Law in Historical Perspective. Vol. 3: State Territory.* (Leyden, The Netherlands: A. W. Sijthoff, 1970), pp. 490–494: In this book, the Chapter entitled "Other Exceptional Territorial Situations" includes the section on "International Protection of Sacred Places."
697 Verzijl, *ibid.*, p. 490.
698 Verzijl, *ibid.*, p. 494.
699 See *supra*, section 2.3.
700 On the subjects of international law see also *supra*, sections 2.1.2 and 2.1.3.
701 Gaetano Arangio-Ruiz, "*Le domaine réservé. L'organisation internationale et le rapport entre droit international et droit interne (Cours général de droit international public)*" [French], Vol. 225, *Recueil des Cours de l'Académie de Droit International de la Hague 1990–VI* (Dordrecht: Martinus Nijhoff Publishers, 1993), p. 450. See also *supra*, section 2.1.2.
702 See Izhak Englard, *Religious Law in the Israel Legal System* (Jerusalem: Harry Sacher

Institute for Legislative Research and Comparative Law, the Hebrew University of Jerusalem, 1975), p. 13. On the application of personal jurisdiction in the *Millet* system see *supra*, section 2.2.1.

703 For the recognized Christian "religious communities" listed in a schedule added in 1939 to the British Palestine Order-in-Council see *supra*, section 3.3.1.

704 Emphasis in italics from the original text; Reproduced in my *Negotiating Jerusalem: Preconditions for Drawing Scenarios Based on Territorial Compromises* (Jerusalem: Palestinian Academic Society for the Study of the International Affairs), 2002, p. 112.

705 U.N.Doc. A/48/486-S/26560 (Annex), 11 October 1993; reproduced in *International Legal Material* 32 (1993): 1525–1544. On the Declaration see *supra*, section 1.1. Par. B of the "Agreed Minutes to the DoP" and Article XVII (titled "Jurisdiction") of the Israeli–Palestinian Interim Agreement on the West Bank and the Gaza Strip, signed in Washington, D.C. on September 28, 1995, titled "Specific Understanding and Agreements," also refer to *Jerusalem*. On both provisions see *supra*, section 1.1.

706 On the meaning of the word "Jerusalem" in the Middle East peace agreements and the municipal boundaries of the city see *supra*, section 1.1.

707 For the text of the letter see *infra*, Annex IX and the website of the Israeli Foreign Ministry: www.mfa.gov.il/mfa, where the document is merely referred to "as published in *Jerusalem Post*, on June 7, 1994." See *supra*, section 1.2 for an analysis.

708 For the text see *infra*, Annex IX; for an analysis of both documents signed by Israel and Jordan see *supra*, section 1.3.

709 For the text of these as well as other relevant provisions of the Fundamental Agreement see *infra*, Annex IX; for an analysis see *supra*, section 1.4.1. See *infra*, section 5.3, for a survey of the Status Quo legal regime.

710 For the text of these as well as other relevant provisions of the Fundamental Agreement see *infra*, Annex IX. For a comparison between the Agreement and the Basic Agreement between the Holy See and the PLO see *supra*, section 1.4.

711 For the text of these as well as other relevant provisions of the Basic Agreement see *infra*, Annex IX; for an analysis see *supra*, section 1.4.2.

712 Chad F. Emmett, "The Status Quo Solution for Jerusalem," *Journal of Palestine Studies*, Vol. 26, No. 2, (1997): p. 19.

713 Englard, *Religious Law*, in his footnotes quotes the Israeli Supreme Court decision: *The Orthodox Coptic Metropolitan Patriarchate v. The Government of Israel*, (1979) 33 P.D. (I) 225, p. 238.

714 Itzhak Englard, "The Legal Status of the Holy Places," in Ora Ahimeir (ed.), *Jerusalem — Aspects of Law*, Discussion Paper No. 3 (Jerusalem: The Jerusalem Institute for Israel Studies, 1983), pp. iv–v. On the relevance of "spiritual matters" of religious bodies (such as the Catholic Church of the Holy See) in international law to ascertain whether an act is legitimate or not see Arangio-Ruiz, *L'Etat dans le sens du Droit des Gens et la Notion du Droit international* (Bologna: Cooperativa Libraria Universitaria,1975), p. 39.

715 On this Report see *infra*, section 3.4.1. and Annex VI.

716 Berkovitz, *The Temple Mount*, p.84; for a detailed discussion of the legal essence of the rights in the Holy Places see Berkovitz, "The Legal Status," pp. 551–589.

717 Englard, *Religious Law*, pp. IV-V.

718 Vezio Crisafulli, *Lessons of Constitutional Law, I. Introduction to the Italian Constitutional Law* [Italian], 2nd Ed. (Padova: CEDAM, 1970), pp. 1–7, 15–16.

719 Englard, *Religious Law*, p. 14; among the scholars of the Positivist school see Roberto Ago, *Legal Science and International Law* [talian], (Milano: Giuffré, 1950), pp. 32 *et seq*; for a critique of this view see, among others, Santi Romano, *The Legal Order* [Italian] (Pisa: Mariotti, 1917), spec. Ch. II, "*Plurality of Legal Orders and their relations*", pp. 94 *et seq.*

720 For the partial suspension of the Status Quo/Modus Vivendi legal regime in time of war see *infra*, section 5.7.

721 The list of the Status Quo procedural norms suggested in this section was confirmed by "The Holy Places in Jerusalem Old City. Guidelines for a Future Arrangement," a Document developed, under the supervision of Nazmi Al-Ju'beh and Gilead Sher, at the Israeli–Palestinian Seminars, which *Mediterranean Perspectives*, the cultural association I have the honor to chair, organized in Rome from 2006 until 2008.
722 On the broad cultural–religious status quo in Jerusalem see *infra*, section 5.5.
723 For the text of the United Nations' Charter see the United Nations' Internet site, URL: http://www.un.org/aboutun/charter/index.html.
724 For the text of the United Nations' Charter see *ibid*.
725 The Declaration was adopted on December 10, 1948 by the General Assembly without any vote against and with only eight abstentions.
726 Francesco Margiotta-Broglio,*The International Protection of Religious Freedom in the European Convention of the Human Rights)* [Italian] (Milano: Giuffré Editore, 1967), p. 78 (the translation into English is mine.)
727 See Margiotta-Broglio, *ibid*.
728 International Covenant on Civil and Political Rights, U.N. Doc. A/6316 (1966), 999 U.N.T.S. 171, *entered into force* Mar. 23, 1976; also availble at the Office of the High Commissioner's for Human Rights' website:http://www.unhchr.ch/ html/menu3/b/a_ccpr.htm.
729 *Declaration on the Elimination of All Forms of Intolerance and of Discrimination Based on Religion or Belief 1981*, UN Resolution A/RES/36/55. Reproduced in the United Nations' website: URL: http//www.un.org./Depts/dhl/resguide/resins.htm. See also Principle VII the Final Act of the Helsinki's Conference on Security and Cooperation in Europe, reprinted in *International Legal Materials*, Vol. 14 (Washington, D.C.: American Society of International Law, 1975), pp. 1292, 1295.
730 *International Covenant on Civil And Political Rights*, URL: www.hrweb.org/legal/cpr.html.
731 Eyal Benvenisti, "The Influence of International Human Rights Law on the Israeli Legal System: Present and Future," *Israel Law Review*, Vol. 28, No. 1 (1994): p. 141, n. 23, translating into English from Hebrew a passage from Israeli High Court of Justice 205/67 *The American-European Beth-El Mission v. Minister of Public Welfare et al.* 21 (ii) P.D. p. 325.
732 For the text of these as well as other relevant provisions of the Agreement see *infra*, Annex IX. For the full text of the Agreement see, among other sources, *International Legal Material*, Vol. 33 (Washington, D.C.: American Society of International Law, 1994): p. 153; Eugene J. Fisher and Leon Klenicki (eds.), *A Challenge Long Delayed. The Diplomatic Exchange Between, the Holy See and the State of Israel* (New York: Anti-Defamation League, 1996), pp. 49–53. For a comparison between the Agreement and the Basic Agreement between the Holy See and the PLO see *supra*, section 1.4.
733 Shmuel Berkovitz, *The Temple Mount and the Western Wall in Israeli Law* (Jerusalem: The Jerusalem Institute for Israel Studies, 2001) p. 85. See also *infra*, section 2.3.2 on this contradiction.
734 See, by inplication, Status Quo principle no. 1 in the list *supra*, section 5.3.
735 On the Har Ha Bait/Haram Al Sharif see *supra*, sections 1.3.1, 4.2.2 and 4.3.3 and *infra*, sections 5.5 and B.2.
736 See *supra*, section 5.3.
737 For a list of Status Quo legal regime's procedural principles see *supra*, section 5.3.
738 Ruth Lapidoth, "Freedom of Religion and Conscience in Israel," in Ruth Lapidoth and Ora Ahimeir (eds.), *Freedom of Religion in Jerusalem*. Jerusalem: Jerusalem Institute for Israel Studies, 1999, p. 36, n. 36; the following quotations from Prof. Lapidoth's articles are taken from the same article. On the meaning and the content of this cultural–religious status quo in Jerusalem see, among others, Chamman P. Shelach, "Freedom of Religion and Conscience in a Heterogeneous City," in Lapidoth and Ahimeir, *Freedom of Religion*,

pp. 47–60; this article was first published in Ora Ahimeir (ed.), *Jerusalem — Aspects of Law*, Discussion Paper No. 3 (Jerusalem: The Jerusalem Institute for Israel Studies, 1983), pp XIII-XVIII.

739 Ruth Lapidoth, "Freedom of Religion", *ibid.*
740 Ruth Lapidoth, "Freedom of Religion", *ibid.*
741 *Declaration by the European Council on the Middle East Peace Process* held in Florence on 21–22 June 1996; for the text see the URL: http://www.europarl.europa.eu/summits/fir1_en.htm#mideast
742 For the principle of non-interference see *infra*, Annex X, principle 8 of the list of the Basic Cultural and Religious Principles Governing the Holy Places of Jerusalem. This list was also confirmed by a Document, "The Holy Places in Jerusalem Old City. Guidelines for a Future Arrangement," developed, under the supervision of Nazmi Al-Ju'beh and Gilead Sher, at the Israeli–Palestinian Seminars, which *Mediterranean Perspectives*, the cultural association I have the honor to chair, organized in Rome from 2006 until 2008.
743 *Report of the High Commissioner on the Administration of Palestine, 1920–1925*, (London: His Majesty's Stationery Office, 1925), pp. 14–15 [in the section titled "Antiquities" of his Report to the Secretary of State for the Colonies]. For excerpts of the document see *infra*, Annex III.
744 Shmuel Berkovitz, "Proposals for the Political Status of the Holy Places within the Context of a Peace Treaty," in Ora Ahimeir (ed.) p. xi.
745 See for example the Ottoman Firman issued on February 18, 1856, referred to *infra*, section 2.3.1.
746 On the protocol of the Jerusalem Consuls and the reference to the privileges of the General Consuls in UN General Assembly resolution 181 (II) of November 29, 1947 see *infra*, section 3.5.4.
747 Shlomo Avineri, "The Status of Jerusalem in the International Arena," in Ora Ahimeir, Ed.) p. XXIX. On the United Nations resolution of November 29, 1947 see *infra*, section 3.5.4.
748 Resolution No.15C/3.343, Unesco, Resolutions, 50th General Conference in Ruth Lapidoth and Moshe Hirsch (eds.), *The Jerusalem Question and its Resolution. Selected Documents* (Dordrecht: Martinus Nijhoff Publishers, 1994), p. 235.
749 Report of the 1st extraordinary Session of the UNESCO World Heritage Committee, Paris, 10 and 11 September 1981, Section IV, Par. 9, CC — 81/CONF. 008/2 Rev., Paris, September 30, 1981; for the text see the URL: http://whc.unesco.org/archive/repext81.htm.
750 Israeli Court of Justice, Judge Watkin in H.C 222/68: *Nationalist Circles* vs. *Minister of Police* (14. P.D. (2), 141 at 168) quoted from Lapidoth and Hirsch, *The Jerusalem Question*, p. 471.
751 *Attorney General Guidelines* (1988), reproduced in Lapidoth and Hirsch, *The Jerusalem Question*, p. 471.
752 See *infra*, sections 5.6 and 5.7 for the hypothesis of an international local custom or objective regime protecting the principles applied to the Jerusalem cultural–religious status quo in time of peace and the binding effects of the unilateral declarations about the Holy Places.
753 Ian Brownlie, *Principles of Public International Law*, 5th Ed. (New York: Oxford University Press, 1998), p. 5. See also Luigi Ferrari-Bravo, *Evidence in International Trial Procedures* [Italian] (Napoli: Jovene, 1958) pp. 64 et seq; Malcolm N. Shaw, *International Law* (Cambridge: Cambridge University Press, 2003), pp. 77–80.
754 Brownlie, *Principles*, p. 7.
755 On this hypothesis see also my article "Israel's position on Jerusalem and international norms for the Holy Places," a *Jerusalem letter* (Jerusalem: the Jerusalem Center for Public Affairs), no. 342, September 15, 1996.
756 Gaetano Morelli, *Concepts of International Law* [Italian] (Padova: Cedam, 1967), p. 31 (the

translation into English is mine).
757 "Right of Passage in Indian Territory," *ICJ Reports*, 1957, p. 178.
758. "Right of Passage," *ibid.*
759. "Right of Passage," *ibid.*
760 Gaetano Arangio-Ruiz, «*Le domaine réservé. L'organisation internationale et le rapport entre droit international et droit interne (Cours général de droit international public)*», [French], Vol. 225, *Recueil des Cours de l'Académie de droit international de La Haye* 1990/VI (Dordrecht: Martinus Nijhoff Publishers, 1993 p. 261 (the translation into English is mine.)
761 "Rights of Nationals of the United States in Morocco," *I.C.J. Reports* 1952, p. 200 s. On the Capitulations see *infra*, section 2.2.2. On the principle of immunity from ordinary local jurisdiction see also *infra*, sections 2.1.1, 2.3.3 and 3.4.
762 Brownlie, *Principles*, p. 5. On the need of a higher standard of proof required in ascertaining local, regional or special custom, see Shaw, p. 87.
763 See, among others, Eyal Benvenisti, "The Influence of International Human Rights Law on the Israeli Legal System: Present and Future," *Israel Law Review*, Vol. 28, No. 1 (1995): p. 138.
764 Eyal Benvenisti, *ibid.*
765 See Eyal Benvenisti, *ibid.*
766 See the cases "Eastern Greenland", *P.C.I.J.*, Series A/B, No. 53, 1933, p. 53; "Nuclear Tests", 1974, *I.C.J. Reports*, p. 472; "Military and Paramilitary Activities in and against Nicaragua (Nicaragua v. USA)," *ibid.*, 1986, pp. 130–132; *Case Concerning the Frontier Dispute (Burkina Faso/Mali)*, 1986, *ibid.*, pp. 573–574, in particular on the last condition. On the possible binding effects of the "Peres Letter" as a unilateral declaration see *supra*, section 1.2.
767 See Sir Robert Yewdall Jennings, *The Acquisition of Territory in International Law* (Manchester: Manchester University Press, 1963), p. 41.
768 Arnold Duncan McNair, *The Law of Treaties* (Oxford: Clarendon Press, 1961), p. 485.
769 *Nicaragua v. USA* (The Case Concerning the Military and Paramilitary Activities in and against Nicaragua) *ICJ Reports*, 1986, p. 98.
770 Judge Ferrari Bravo in his Declaration on the Advisory Opinion of July 8, 1996 by the International Court of Justice on the "Legality of the Use by a State of Nuclear Weapons in Armed Conflict" has expressed a similar idea in relation to the theory of deterrence, which had temporarily prevented the full development of an international customary norm prohibiting nuclear weapons. For the text of Ferrari Bravo's Declaration appended to the Advisory Opinion see the International Court Website:http://www.icj-cij.org/docket/files/95/7507.pdf For the text of the opinion in English see: http://www.icj-cij.org/docket/files/95/7495.pdf
771 For a list of procedural principles included in the Status Quo legal regime see *supra*, section 5.3.
772 For an analysis of Jordanian attitudes and practices vis-à-vis the Holy Places under their control from 1948 to 1967 see *infra*, section 4.2.2.
773 For an analysis of the new Status Quo/Modus Vivendi imposed by Israel in the Muslim–Jewish Holy Places after the 1967 War see *infra*, section 4.3.3.
774 For an overview of Jordanian practice on the Holy Places in Jerusalem under its administration from 1948 to 1967 see *infra*, section 4.2.2.
775 On the Jordanian–Israeli Peace Agreement see *supra*, section 1.3.
776 Slonim, *Jerusalem*, p. 164, n. 7.
777 Joel Singer, "Aspects of Foreign Relations under the Israeli–Palestinian Agreements on Interim Self-Government Arrangements for the West Bank and Gaza," *Israel Law Review*, Vol. 28, No. 20 (1994): p. 274. When he wrote this article, Mr. Joel Singer was the Legal Adviser at the Israeli Ministry of Foreign Affairs.
778 *Ibid.*, p. 274, No. 20.

779 For the text of the Convention see *The Geneva Conventions of August 12, 1949*, ICRC Publications (International Committee of the Red Cross), Geneva (without a date), 153–158. For the Additional Protocols of June 8, 1977 see *Protocols Additional to the Geneva Conventions of August 12, 1949*, ICRC Publications (International Committee of the Red Cross), Geneva (without a date).

780 On this issue see *infra*, section 4.3.1.

781 Singer, p. 274, n. 20.

782 See, among others, Andrea Saccucci, *Profili di tutela dei diritti umani tra Nazioni Unite e Consiglio d'Europa* [Italian] (Padova: CEDAM, 2002), pp. 7–8.

783 International Covenant on Civil and Political Rights, U.N. Doc. A/6316 (1966), 999 U.N.T.S. 171, *entered into force* Mar. 23, 1976; also available at the Office of the High Commissioner's for Human Rights' website: http://www.unhchr.ch/html/menu3/b/a_ccpr.htm.

784 Convention for the Protection of Human Rights and Fundamental Freedoms, signed by the members of the Council of Europe in Rome, on November 4, 1950 213 U.N.T.S. 222.signed by the members of the Council of Europe in Rome, on November 4, 1950; available at see the website: http://www.pfc.org.uk/legal/echrtext.htm.

785 For this list see *supra*, section 5.3; for the Status Quo/Modus Vivendi legal regime see *supra*, sections 1.3.1, 4.3.3 and Chapter 5.

786 On status quo in the broader sense see *supra*, section 5.5; for the list of "Basic Cultural and Religious Principles Governing the Holy Places of Jerusalem" see *infra*, Annex III.

787 On the partial suspension of the Status Quo legal regime in time of war see *supra*, section 5.7.

788 For the Glossary see *infra*, Annex IV.

789 I developed this idea in a lecture that I gave on March 21, 2001 at the Hebrew University of Jerusalem, Faculty of Humanities, entitled "The Need of a Multidisciplinary Approach to Study the Holy Places of Jerusalem."

790 For the text of the Roadmap, see:
http://www.un.org/media/main/roadmap122002.html,
http://www.un.org/News/dh/mideast/roadmap122002.pdf or
http://usembassy-israel.org.il/publish/press/2003/may/050101.html.
For the Israeli endorsement of the Quartet's plan see the Press Release related to the Government meeting at the PM's office in Jerusalem about the Prime Minister's statement on the Roadmap of 25/05/2003, available at: http://www.pmo.gov.il/PMOEng

791 Avraham B. Yehoshua (interviewed by Bictor Cygielman), "Separating Religion from National Identity," *Palestine–Israel Journal of Politics, Economics and Culture*, Vol. 8, No. 4 (2001) and Vol. 9, No. 1 (2002) (Special issue on "National Identity"): p. 100.

792 Samuel P. Huntington, *The Clash of Civilizations and the Remaking of World Order* (London, Sidney: Simon and Schuster, 1998), p. 21.

793 Huntington, *The Clash*, p. 67.

794 See *supra*, section 2.1. on this subject.

795 Huntington, *The Clash*, p. 42.

796 Huntington, *The Clash*, p. 66.

797 On June 4, 2001 I developed this idea a lecture that I gave at the Department of Italian Literature of the Hebrew University of Jerusalem, Faculty of Humanities. The title of the lecture was "Vico, Rome, Jerusalem, the Intifada and the Yin-Yang cycles," during a seminar in honour of the Italian philosopher Gianbattista Vico.

798 See, among others, Luigi Ferrari Bravo, *Lessons of International Law* [Italian] (Napoli: Editoriale Scientifica, 2002, IV Ed.), pp. 26–27. See also Huntington, *The Clash*, p. 52. On the legal–historical background of the term *sovereignty* see *supra*, 2.1.2.

799 See Ferrari Bravo, *Lessons*, p. 28. On the personal criteria for organizing political authority in the Middle Ages see *supra*, 2.1.1.

800 See Ferrari Bravo, *ibid.*
801 See Ferrari Bravo, *Lessons*, p. 29.
802 Huntington, *The Clash*, p. 52. On the limits of the European state model see *supra*, 2.1.3.
803 See *supra*, section 1.1, on the Declaration of Principles (DoP).
804 For the Glossary of key terms see *infra*, Annex IV.
805 Akiva Eldar, "EU description of the outcome of permanent status talks at Taba," www.haaretz.com, 28 February 2002.
806 For the Glossary of key terms see *infra*, Annex IV.
807 Eldar, "EU description," *ibid.* On the Har Ha Bait/Haram Al Sharif see *supra*, sections 1.3, 4.2.2, 4.3.3, 5.4, and 5.5.
808 The Palestine (Holy Places) Order in Council 1924 *Official Gazette of the Government of Palestine* No. 123 (Jerusalem: Government of Palestine, 1924) p. 814; reprinted in Enrico Molinaro, *Negotiating Jerusalem: Preconditions for Drawing Scenarios Based on Territorial Compromises* (Jerusalem: Palestinian Academic Society for the Study of the International Affairs, 2002), p. 93.

References

1. Books
2. Journals
3. Unpublished material
4. Official documentation (in chronological order)
5. United Nations documentation (in chronological order)
6. International jurisprudence (in chronological order)
7. Other documents
8. Electronic sources
9. Newspaper articles

1 Books

Adelson, Roger. *Mark Sykes, Portrait of an Amateur.* London: Cape, 1975.

Albin, Cecilia; Amirav, Moshe; & Siniora, Hanna. *Jerusalem: An Undivided City as Dual Capital,* Israeli–Palestinian Peace Research Project: Working Paper Series no. 16. Jerusalem: Harry S. Truman Research Institute for the Advancement of Peace & the Arab Study Society, Winter 1991/1992.

Ago, Roberto. *Scienza Giuridica e diritto internazionale.* Milano: Giuffré, 1950 [Italian].

Arangio-Ruiz, Gaetano. "*Le domaine réservé. L'organisation internationale et le rapport entre droit international et droit interne (Cours général de droit international public),*" Vol. 225, *Recueil des Cours de l'Académie de Droit International de la Hague, 1990–VI.* Dordrecht: Martinus Nijhoff Publishers, 1993 [French], pp. 9484.

Arangio-Ruiz, Gaetano. *L'Etat dans le sens du Droit des Gens et la Notion du Droit international* (Bologna: Cooperativa Libraria Universitaria, 1975 [French].

Arangio-Ruiz, Gaetano. *The Normative Role of the General Assembly of the United Nations and the Declarations of Principles of Friendly Relations with an Appendix on the Concept of International Law and the Theory of International Organization,* Vol. 137, *Recueil des Cours de l'Académie de Droit International de la Hague, 1972–III.* Dordrecht: Martinus Nijhoff Publishers, 1993 [French], pp. 419–742.

Ahimeir, Ora. (ed.). *Jerusalem — Aspects of Law* (Discussion Paper no. 3). Jerusalem: The Jerusalem Institute for Israel Studies, 1983.

Azara, Antonio & Eula, Ernesto (eds.). *Novissimo Digesto Italiano.* Torino: Unione tipografico-editrice torinese, 1953 [Italian].

Bahat, Dan. *Carta's Historical Atlas of Jerusalem.* Jerusalem: Carta, 1983.

Baskin, Gershon & al Qaq, Zakaria. *Creating a Culture of Peace.* Jerusalem: IPCRI – Israel/Palestine Center for Research and Information, 1999.

Bazzoni, Stefania & Chartouni-Doubarry, May (eds.). *Politics and Economics in the Search for*

Stability in the Mediterranean Region. Monte Carlo: *Institut des Études politiques méditerranéennes* (IEPM), 2001

Berkovitz, Shmuel. *The Temple Mount and the Western Wall in Israeli Law*. Jerusalem: The Jerusalem Institute for Israel Studies, 2001.

Bernhardt, Rudolf (ed.). *Encyclopedia of Public International Law*, Vol. 10, *States; Responsibility of States; International Law and Municipal Law*. Amsterdam: Elzevire Science, 1997.

Berger, Adolf. *Encyclopedic Dictionary of Roman Law*. Philadelphia: American Philosophical Society, 1953.

Brownlie, Ian. *Principles of Public International Law*, 5th ed. New York: Oxford University Press, 1998.

Bovis, H. Eugene. *The Jerusalem Question, 1917–1968*. Stanford, California: Hoover Institution Press, 1971.

Brierly, James Leslie. *The Law of Nations*. Oxford: Clarendon Press, 1955.

Camilleri, Joseph A. & Falk, Jim. *The End of Sovereignty? The Politics of a Shrinking and Fragmenting World*. Aldershot: E. Elgar, 1992.

Cattan, Henry. *Palestine and International Law*, 2nd ed. London: Longman, 1976.

Cattan, Henry. *Jerusalem*. New York: Croom Helm, 1981.

Cattan, Henry. *The Palestine Question*. London: Croom Helm, 1988.

Cohen, Raymond. *Saving the Holy Sepulchre. How Rival Christians Came Together to Rescue Their Holiest Shrine*. New York: Oxford University Press, 2008.

Colbi, Saul Paul. *Christianity in the Holy Land, Past and Present*. Tel Aviv: Am Hassefer, 1969.

Collin, Bernardin. *Les Lieux Saints*. Paris: Editions Internationales, 1948 [French].

Collin, Bernardin. *Le Problème Juridique des Lieux Saints*. Le Caire: Centre d'Etudes Orientales, 1956 [French].

Dinstein, Yoram (ed.). *Models of Autonomy*. New Brunswick: Transaction Books, 1981.

Dinstein, Yoram. *War, Aggression and Self-Defense*, 2nd ed. Cambridge: Cambridge University Press, 1994.

Elon, Amos. *Jerusalem, City of Mirrors*. London: Weidenfeld and Nicolson, 1989.

Encyclopaedia Judaica. Jerusalem: Encyclopaedia Judaica, 1971.

Englard, Izhak. *Religious Law in the Israel Legal System*, Jerusalem: Harry Sacher Institute for Legislative Research and Comparative Law, the Hebrew University of Jerusalem, 1975

Fabrizio, Daniela. *La questione dei Luoghi Santi e l'assetto della Palestina. 1914–1922*. Milano: Franco Angeli, 2000 [Italian]

Feinberg, Nathan. *The Arab–Israel Conflict in International Law: A Critical Analysis of the Colloquium of Arab Jurists in Algiers*. Jerusalem: Magnes Press, 1970.

Ferrari Bravo, Luigi. *La prova nel processo internazionale*. Napoli: Editoriale Scientifica, 1958 [Italian].

Ferrari Bravo, Luigi. *Lezioni di diritto internazionale*. Napoli: Editoriale Scientifica, 2002, IV ed. [Italian].

Fisher, Eugene J.; & Klenicki, Leon (eds.). *A Challenge Long Delayed: The Diplomatic Exchange Between the Holy See and the State of Israel*. New York: Anti-Defamation League, 1996.

Giannini, Amedeo. *L'ultima fase della questione orientale (1913–1932)*. Milano: ISPI, 1933 [Italian].

Gilbert, Martin. *Jerusalem: Illustrated History Atlas*. New York: Macmillan, 1977.

Gilbert, Martin. *The Arab–Israeli Conflict: Its History in Maps*, 5th ed. London: Weidenfeld and Nicolson, 1992.

Hadi, Madhi F. Abdul (ed.). *Documents on Palestine*, Vol. 2, *From the Negotiations in Madrid to the Post-Hebron Agreement Period*. Jerusalem: Palestinian Academic Society for the Study of International Affairs, 1997.

Halderman, John W. (ed.). *The Middle East crisis: test of international law*. Dobbs Ferry: Oceana Publications, 1969.

Henkin, Louis. *International Law: Politics, Values and Functions. General Course on Public*

International Law, Recueil des Cours de l'Académie de Droit International de la Hague, 1989–*IV*. Dordrecht: Martinus Nijhoff Publishers, 1989.

Hirsch, Moshe; Housen-Couriel, Deborah; & Lapidoth, Ruth (eds.). *Whither Jerusalem? Proposals and Positions Concerning the Future of Jerusalem*. The Hague: Martinus Nijhoff, 1995.

Holsti, Kalevi Jaakko. *International Politics: A Framework for Analysis*. New Jersey: Prentice-Hall, 1967.

Howard, Harry Nicholas. *The King–Crane Commission*. Beirut: Khayat, 1963.

Huntington, Samuel P. *The Clash of Civilizations and the Remaking of World Order*. London, Sidney: Simon & Schuster, 1998.

Hurewitz, Jacob Coleman (ed.). *Diplomacy in the Near and Middle East. A Documentary Record: 1914–1956*, vols. 1 & 2. Princeton: Van Nostrand, 1956.

Koechler, Hans (ed.). *The Legal Aspects of the Palestine Problem with Special Regard to the Question of Jerusalem*. Wien: Braumueller, 1981.

Israel Pocket Library, *Religious Life & Communities*. Jerusalem: Keter, 1974.

Jennings, Sir Robert Yewdall. *The Acquisition of Territory in International Law*. Manchester: Manchester University Press, 1963.

Klein, Menachem. *Jerusalem: The Contested City*. New York: New York University Press, 2001.

Lapidoth, Ruth. & Hirsch, Moshe (eds.). *The Arab–Israel Conflict and its Resolution: Selected Documents*. Dordrecht: Martinus Nijhoff Publishers, 1992.

Lapidoth, Ruth. & Ahimeir, Ora (eds.). *Freedom of Religion in Jerusalem*. Jerusalem: Jerusalem Institute for Israel Studies, 1999.

Lapidoth, Ruth. & Hirsch, Moshe. *Jerusalem — Political and Legal Aspects*. Jerusalem: Jerusalem Center for Israel Studies, 1994 [Hebrew].

Lapidoth, Ruth. & Hirsch, Moshe (eds.). *The Jerusalem Question and Its Resolution: Selected Documents*. Dordrecht: Martinus Nijhoff, 1994.

Le Morzellec, Joëlle. *La Question de Jerusalem devant l'Organisation des Nations Unies*. Bruxelles: Bruylant, 1979 [French].

Lewis, Bernard. *The Multiple Identities of the Middle East*. London: Phoenix, 1998.

Lowenthal, Marvin (ed.). *The Diaries of Theodor Herzl*. New York: The Dial Press, 1956.

McNair, Arnold Duncan. *The Law of Treaties*. Oxford: Clarendon Press, 1961.

William T. Malllison & Sally V. Mallison. *The Palestine Problem in International Law and World Order*. 1986.

Ma'oz, Moshe & Nusseibeh, Sari (eds.). *Jerusalem: Points of Friction and Beyond*. The Hague: Kluwer Law International, 2000.

Marchisio, Sergio. *Le basi militari nel diritto internazionale*. Milano: Giuffré Editore, 1984 [Italian].

Margiotta-Broglio, Francesco. *La protezione internazionale della libertá religiosa nella convenzione europea dei diritti dell'uomo*. Milano: Giuffré Editore, 1967. [Italian].

Medzini, Meron (ed.). *Israel's Foreign Relations, Volume One: Selected Documents, 1947–1974*. Jerusalem: Ministry for Foreign Affairs, 1976.

Medzini, Meron (ed.). *Israel's Foreign Relations, Selected Documents*. Vol. 1–18, Jerusalem: Ministry for Foreign Affairs, available at: www.mfa.gov.il/mfa .

Minerbi, Sergio Yitzhak. *The Vatican and Zionism: Conflict in the Holy Land, 1895–1925*. New York: Oxford University Press, 1990.

Minerbi, Sergio, I. *The Visit of the Pope to the Holy Land*. Jerusalem: Israel Information Center, 2000.

Molinaro, Enrico. *Negotiating Jerusalem: Preconditions for Drawing Scenarios Based on Territorial Compromises*. Jerusalem: Palestinian Academic Society for the Study of the International Affairs, 2002.

Moore, John Norton (ed.). *The Arab–Israeli Conflict. Volume III: Documents*. Princeton, New Jersey: Princeton University Press, 1974.

Morelli, Gaetano. *Nozioni di diritto internazionale*. Padova: Cedam, 1967 [Italian].
Musallam, Sami F. *The Struggle for Jerusalem: A Program of Action for Peace*. Jerusalem: Palestinian Academic Society for the Study of International Affairs, 1996.
Muslih, Muhammad Y. *The Origins of Palestinian Nationalism*. New York: Columbia University Press, 1988.
Oppenheim, Lassa Francis Lawrence; & Lauterpacht, Hersch. *International Law. A Treatise*, Vol. 1. London: Longmans, 1967.
Oesterreicher, Msgr. John M. & Sinai, Anne (eds.). *Jerusalem*. New York: John Day, 1974.
Passia Diary 2003. Jerusalem: Palestinian Academic Society for the Study of International Affairs, 2003.
Pieraccini, Paolo. *Gerusalemme, Luoghi Santi e comunità religiose nella politica internazionale*. Bologna: Edizioni Dehoniane, 1997 [Italian].
Pfoestl, Eva (ed.). *La creazione di una zona di pace e stabilità attorno all'Unione Europea*. Roma: Istituto di Studi Politici S. Pio V, 2007 [Italian].
Quadri, Rolando. *Diritto internazionale pubblico*. Napoli: Liguori, 1968 [Italian].
Reiter, Yitzhak. *Islamic Endowments in Jerusalem under British Mandate*. London: Portland, 1996.
Reuter, Paul. *Introduction to the Law of Treaties*. London: Kegan Paul, 1995.
Romano, Santi. *L'ordinamento giuridico*. Pisa: 1918 [2nd ed., Firenze: 1962] [Italian].
Romano, Santi. *Principi di diritto costituzionale generale*. Milano: Giuffré Editore, 1945 [Italian].
Rolef, Susan Hatti (ed.). *Political Dictionary of the State of Israel*. New York-London: 1987.
Ronzitti, Natalino. *Rescuing nationals abroad through military coercion and intervention on grounds of humanity*. Dordrecht: M. Nijhoff Publishers, 1985.
Rosen, Rabbi David. *The Impact of the Papal Visit to Israel*. Jerusalem: Israel Information Center, 2000.
Rousseau, Charles. *Droit International Public, Tome II, Les sujets de Droit*. Paris: Dalloz, 1974.
Saccucci, Andrea. *Profili di tutela dei diritti umani tra Nazioni Unite e Consiglio d'Europa*. Padova: CEDAM, 2002 [Italian].
Safran, Nadav. *Egypt in search of political community: an analysis of the intellectual and political evolution of Egypt, 1804–1952*. Cambridge, MA: Harvard University Press, 1961.
Samuel, Herbert. *Memoires*. London: The Cresset Press, 1945.
Schwarzemberger, Georg & Brown, Edward Duncan. *A Manual of International Law*. Milton: Professional Books, 1976.
Shaw, Malcolm N. *International Law*. Cambridge: Cambridge University Press, 2003.
Slonim, Shlomo. *Jerusalem in America's Foreign Policy*. The Hague: Kluwer Law International, 1998.
Stankiewicz, Wladyslaw, J. (ed.). *In Defence of Sovereignty*. New York/London/Toronto, 1969.
Stone, Julius. *The Middle East under Cease-Fire: notes on the legal position before the Security Council in October, 1967*. Sydney: The Bridge, 1967.
Stone, Julius. *No Peace-No War in the Middle East*. Sydney: Maitland Publications for the International Law Association (Australian Branch), 1969.
Stoyanovski, Jacob. *The Mandate for Palestine*: a contribution to the theory and practice of international mandates. London: Longmans, Green, 1928.
Talal, Hassan bin, Prince. *A Study on Jerusalem*. London: Longman, 1979.
Temperley, Harold William Vazielle. *A History of the Peace Conference of Paris*, Vol. 6. London: H. Frowde, 1924.
United Nations (ed.). *The Status of Jerusalem* (prepared for the Committee on the Exercise of the Inalienable Rights of the Palestinian People). New York: 1979.
Verzijl, Jan Hendrik Willem. *International Law in Historical Perspective, Volume 3, State Territory*. Leyden: A. W. Sijthoff, 1970.
Whiteman, Marjorie Millace (ed.). *Digest of International Law*, Vol. 2. Washington, D.C.: U.S. Department of State, 1963.

Young, George. *Corps de Droit Ottoman. Recueil des Codes, Lois, Règlements, Ordonnances et Actes les plus importants du Droit Intérieur, et d'études sur le Droit Coutumier de l'Empire Ottoman*, Vol. 2. Oxford: The Clarendon Press, 1905.

Zander, Walter. *Israel and the Holy Places of Christendom*. Worcester: The Trinity Press, 1971

2 Journals

Abu Odeh, Adnan. "Two Capitals in an Undivided Jerusalem," *Foreign Affairs*, Vol. 71, No. 2, 1992, pp. 183–188.

Abu Odeh, Adnan. "Religious Inclusion, Political Inclusion: Jerusalem as an Undivided Capital," *Catholic University Law Review*, Vol. 45, 1996, pp. 687–694.

Benvenisti, Eyal. "The Influence of International Human Rights Law on the Israeli Legal System: Present and Future," *Israel Law Review*, Vol. 28, No. 1, YEAR, pp. 136–153.

Benvenuti, Paolo. "*Sui limiti internazionali alla giurisdizione penale,*" *Rivista di diritto internazionale*, Vol. 2, 1974, pp. 238–249.

Blum, Yehuda. "The Missing Reversioner: Reflections on the Status of Judea and Samaria," *Israel Law Review*, Vol. 3, 1968, pp. 287–314.

Blum, Yehuda. "From Camp David to Oslo," *Israel Law Review*, Vol. 28, Nos. 2–3, 1994, pp. 211–231.

Dinstein, Yoram. "*Par in Parem non Habet Imperium,*" *Israel Law Review*, Vol. 1, No. 3, 1966, pp. 407–420.

Emmett, Chad F. "The Status Quo Solution for Jerusalem," *Journal of Palestine Studies*, Vol. 26, No. 2, 1997, pp. 16–28.

Every, Edward. "The Cust Memorandum & the Status Quo in the Holy Places," *Christian News from Israel*, Vol. 23, No. 4(12), 1973, pp. 229–234.

Gerson, Allan. "Trustee-Occupant: The Legal Status of Israel's Presence in the West Bank," *Harvard International Law Journal*, Vol. 14, 1973, pp. 1–49.

Giuliano, Mario. "Lo Stato, il territorio e la sovranità territoriale," *Comunicazioni e studi*, Vol. 6, 1955, pp. 21–54.

Manuel, Hassassian. "Historical Dynamics Shaping Palestinian National Identity," *Palestine–Israel Journal of Politics, Economics and Culture*, Vol. 8, No. 4, 2001 & Vol. 9, No. 1, 2002, pp. 50–60.

Hirsch, Moshe. "The Future Negotiations over Jerusalem, Strategic Factors and Game Theory," *Catholic University Law Review*, Vol. 45, 1996, pp. 699–722.

Kimmerling, Baruch. "The formation of Palestinian collective identities: The Ottoman and Mandatory periods," *Middle Eastern Studies*, Vol. XXXVI, 2, 2000 pp. 48–81.

Klein, Menachem. "The Islamic Holy Places as a Political Bargaining Card (1993–1995)," *Catholic University Law Review*, Vol. 45, 1996, pp. 745–763.

Lapidoth, Ruth. "Security Council Resolution 242 at Twenty five," *Israel Law Review*, Vol. 26, 1992, pp. 295–318

Lapidoth, Ruth. "Jerusalem and the Peace Process," *Israel Law Review*, Vol. 28, Nos. 2–3, 1994, pp. 402–434.

Lapidoth, Ruth. "Jerusalem — Some Jurisprudential Aspects," *Catholic University Law Review*, Vol. 45, 1996, pp. 661–686.

Lapidoth, Ruth. "Redefining Authority: The Past, Present and Future of Sovereignty," *Harvard International Review*, Vol. 17, No. 3, 1995, pp. 8–11.

Lauterpacht, Elihu. "Sovereignty: myth or reality?" *International Affairs*, Vol. 73, No. 1, 1997, pp. 137–150.

Lustick, Ian S. "Has Israel Annexed East Jerusalem," *Middle East Policy*, Vol. V, No. 1, 1997, pp. 34–45.

Miller, Edward. "Self-Defence, International Law, and the Six Day War," *Israel Law Review*, Vol. 20, 1985, pp. 49–73.

Molinaro, Enrico. "Gerusalemme e i Luoghi Santi)," *La Comunitá Internazionale*, Vol. 2, 1994, pp. 254–255 [Italian].

Molinaro, Enrico. "Israel's position on Jerusalem and international norms for the Holy Places", a *Jerusalem letter* (Jerusalem: the Jerusalem Center for Public Affairs), n. 342, 15 September 1996.

Papastathis, Charalambos K. "A New Status for Jerusalem? An Eastern Orthodox Viewpoint," *Catholic University Law Review*, Vol. 45, 1996, pp. 723–731.

Peled, Alisa Rubin. "The Crystallization of an Israeli Policy Towards Muslim and Christian Holy Places, 1948–1955," *The Muslim World*, Vol. 84, Nos. 1–2, 1994, pp. 95–126.

Perez, Antonio F. "Sovereignty, Freedom and civil Society: Toward a New Jerusalem," *Catholic University Law Review*, Vol. 45, 1996, pp. 661–685.

Rabello, Alfredo Mordechai. "Sui rapporti fra Diocleziano e gli ebrei," *Rassegna mensile di Israel*, January–February–March 1979, pp. 43–78.

Ruggie, John Gerard. "Territoriality and Beyond: Problematizing Modernity in International Relations," *International Organizations*, Vol. 47, No. 1, 1993, pp. 139–174.

Schwebel, Stephen. "What Weight to Conquest?" *American Journal of International Law*, Vol. 64, 1970, pp. 345–347.

Singer, Joel. "Aspects of Foreign Relations under the Israeli–Palestinian Agreements on Interim Self-Government Arrangements for the West Bank and Gaza," *Israel Law Review*, Vol. 28, Nos. 2–3 1994, pp. 268–296.

Slonim, Shlomo. "The United States and the Status of Jerusalem, 1947–1948," *Israel Law Review*, Vol. 19, 1984, pp. 179–252.

Vitta, Eduardo. "The Conflict of Personal Laws," *Israel Law Review*, Vol. 5, No. 2, 1970, pp. 170–351.

Wright, Quincy. "Legal Aspects of the Middle East Situation," *Law and Contemporary Problems*, Vol. 33, No. 1, 1968, pp. 5–31.

Zander, Walter "Jurisdiction and Holiness: Reflections on the Coptic-Ethiopian Case" *Israel Law Review*, Vol. 17, No. 3, 1982, pp. 245–273.

Zander, Walter. "On the Settlement of Disputes about the Christian Holy Places," *Israel Law Review*, Vol. 8, No. 3, 1973, pp. 331–366.

Zilberman, Ifrah. "Palestinian Customary Law in the Jerusalem Area," *Catholic University Law Review*, Vol. 45, 1996, pp. 795–811.

Avraham B. Yehoshua (interviewed by Bictor Cygielman), "Separating Religion from National Identity," *Palestine–Israel Journal of Politics, Economics and Culture*, Vol. 8, No. 4 (2001) & Vol. 9, No. 1 (2002) (Special issue on "National Identity"): pp. 94–101.

3 Unpublished material

Berkovitz, Shmuel. "The Legal Status of the Holy Places in Israel," Ph.D. diss., Hebrew University of Jerusalem, 1978 [Hebrew].

Molinaro, Enrico. "*La problematica dei confini dello Stato di Israele,*" Tesi di Laurea (equivalent to a Master's Thesis), University of Rome "La Sapienza," 1990 [Italian].

4 Official documentation (in chronological order)

The Palestine (Holy Places) Order in Council, 1924. *Official Gazette of the Government of Palestine* no. 123 (Jerusalem: Government of Palestine, 1924) p. 814.

Report by His Britannic Majesty's Government on the Palestine Administration for 1923 to the Council of the League of Nations. London: Government of Palestine, 1925 (Colonial no. 9).

Appendices to the Report by His Britannic Majesty's Government on the Palestine Administration for the year 1924 to the Council of the League of Nations. London: Government of Palestine, 1925 (Colonial no. 20).

Report by His Britannic Majesty's Government on the Administration under Mandate of Palestine and Transjordan for the year 1924. London: Government of Palestine, 1925 (Colonial no. 9).

Report of the High Commissioner on the Administration of Palestine, 1920–1925. London: His Majesty's Stationery Office, 1925.

The Western or Wailing Wall in Jerusalem. Memorandum by the Secretary of State for the Colonies, London: His Majesty's Stationery Office, 19 November 1928 (Cmd. 3229)

Report of the [Shaw] Commission on the Palestine Disturbances of August, 1929. Presented by the Secretary of State for the Colonies to Parliament by Command of His Majesty, March 1930, London: H.M. Stationery Office, 1930 (Cmd.3530).

Report of the Commission appointed by His Majesty's Government in the United Kingdom of Great Britain and Northern Ireland, with the approval of the Council of the League of Nations, to determine the rights and claims of Moslems and Jews in connection with the Western or Wailing Wall at Jerusalem, December, 1930. London: His Majesty's Stationery Office, 1931.

Cust, L.G.A. *The Status quo in the Holy Places. (With an Annex on the Status Quo in the Church of the Nativity, Bethlehem).* Jerusalem: Government of Palestine, 1930, Reprinted Jerusalem: Ariel Publishing House, 1980.

The Laws of Palestine in Force on the 31st day of December, 1933. Prepared under the Authority of the revised edition of the laws ordinance, 1934 by Robert Harry Drayton, London: Waterlow, 1934.

Palestine [Peel] Partition Commission Report. London: His Majesty's Stationery Office, 1937 (Cmd. 5479) (Reprinted 1946).

Palestine Partition [Woodhead] Commission Report. Present by the Secretary of State for the colonies to Parliament by Command of His Majesty, London: His Majesty's Stationery Office, 1938 (Cmd. 5854).

League of Nations Official Journal. Geneva : League of Nations. LNOJ1 (E), 2nd year, 1921 20th Year, 1939. 21st Year, No. 1–3, 1940.

United States Department of State, "Anglo-American Committee of Inquiry: Report to the United States Government and His Majesty's Government in the United Kingdom" (Washington, 1946), *Dept. of State Publication on Palestine and Related Problems*, 20 April 1946, No. 2536.

Israeli Documents. Vol. 1, 1948.

(The) Geneva Conventions of 12 August 1949, ICRC Publications (International Committee of the Red Cross), Geneva (n.d.).

Protocols Additional to the Geneva Conventions of 12 August 1949, ICRC Publications (International Committee of the Red Cross), Geneva (without a date).

International Covenant on Civil and Political Rights, 1977, URL: www.hrweb.org/legal/cpr.html.

Declaration of Principles on Interim Self-Government Arrangements, 13 September 1993. Jerusalem: Israeli Ministry of Foreign Affairs, 1993.

Peace between the State of Israel and the Hashemite Kingdom of Jordan. Jerusalem: Ministry of Foreign Affairs, 1994.

International Legal Materials, Vol. 14. Washington, D.C.: American Society of International Law, 1975

International Legal Materials, Vol. 32. Washington, D.C.: American Society of International Law, 1993.

International Legal Materials, Vol. 33. Washington, D.C.: American Society of International Law, 1994.

Letter sent by Israeli Foreign Minister Peres on 11 October 1993 to Norway's Foreign Minister Holst, available at: www.mfa.gov.il/mfa .

Law Implementing the Agreement on the Gaza Strip and the Jericho Area (Restriction on Activities), 1994, S.H. no. 1497, 85. [English Translation] available at: www.mfa.gov.il/mfa.

PASSIA. *Documents on Jerusalem.* Jerusalem: Palestinian Academic Society for the Study of the International Affairs, 1996.

Papers Relating to the Foreign Relations of the United States (FRUS), Washington: Government Printing Office, 1961–2000.
Declaration on the Middle East Peace Process by the European Council held in Florence on 21–22 June 1996 URL: http://www.europarl.europa.eu/summits/fir1_en.
"The Status of Jerusalem," Israel Ministry of Foreign Affairs, March 1999 available at: www.mfa.gov.il/mfa.
Performance-Based Roadmap to a Permanent Two-State Solution to the Israeli–Palestinian Conflict, 30 April 2003. URL: http://www.un.org/media/main/roadmap122002.html, http://www.un.org/News/dh/mideast/roadmap122002.pdf or http://usembassy-israel.org.il/publish/press/2003/may/050101.html (the Israeli endorsement of the Roadmap is available at: http://www.pmo.gov.il/PMOEng).
Laws of the State of Israel, Authorized Translation.

5 United Nations documentation (in chronological order)

Charter of the United Nations, 1945. URL: http://www.un.org/aboutun/charter/index.html.
Report of the United Nations Special Committee on Palestine (UNSCOP), GAOR, Vol. 1, 1947, (UN Doc. A/364).
Terms of League of Nations Mandates, October 1946 (UN Doc. A/70).
Report to the General Assembly of the United Nations Special Committee on Palestine, Vol. 2, Annexes, Appendix and Maps 18–22, 9 September 1947 (UN Doc. A/364 Add. 1).
Report of the 1st extraordinary Session of the UNESCO World Heritage Committee, Paris, 10 and 11 September 1981, Section IV, paragraph 9, CC – 81/CONF. 008/2 Rev., Paris, 30 September 1981, URL: http://whc.unesco.org/archive/repext81.htm.
Declaration on the Elimination of All Forms of Intolerance and of Discrimination Based on Religion or Belief 1981, UN Resolution A/RES/36/55. Reproduced in the United Nations' website: URL: http://www.un.org./Depts/dhl/resguide/resins.htm.
General Assembly, *Official Records*.
Security Council, *Official Records*.

6 International jurispruducence (in chronological order)

"S.S 'Lotus,'" *PCIJ*, Series A, No 10, 1927.
"Palmas Arbitral Award" — Arbitral Award Rendered In Conformity with the Special Agreement Concluded on 23 January 1925, between the United States of America and the Netherlands Relating to the Arbitration of Differences Respecting Sovereignty over the Island of Palmas [or Miangas]," 4 April 1928.
"Eastern Greenland," *PCIJ*, Series A/B, No.53, 1933.
"Austro-German Customs Union case," *PCIJ*, Series A/B, no. 41, 1931.
"Reparation for Injuries," *ICJ Reports*, 1949.
"Rights of Nationals of the United States in Morocco," *ICJ Reports* 1952.
"Right of Passage in Indian Territory," *ICJ Reports*, 1957.
"Nuclear Test," *ICJ Reports*, 1974.
"Military and Paramilitary Activities in and against Nicaragua (Nicaragua v. USA)," *ICJ Reports*, 1986.
"Case Concerning the Frontier Dispute (Burkina Faso/Mali)," *ICJ Reports*, 1986.
Award of the Arbitral Tribunal in the matter of an Arbitration pursuant to an Agreement dated 3 October 1996 between Eritrea and Yemen, First Stage — (Territorial Sovereignty and Scope of the Dispute), 9 October 1998. Reproduced in Permanent Court of Arbitration website: http://pca-cpa.org/.

7 Newspaper articles

Algazy, Joseph. "Gov't will ask Muslims to evacuate Nazareth site," *Haaretz* (English Edition), 23 February 2000.

Benziman, Uzi. "Calling Jerusalem By Its Name," *Haaretz* (English Edition), 9 July 2000.

Shagrai, Nadav. "Absurdity scales the heights of the Temple Mount," *Haaretz* (English Edition), 16 August 1999.

Index

Abbas, Mahmoud, 7
Abdeen, Sheik Abdul Kader, 9–10
Abdul Hamid, 46
Abdullah I Bin Hussein, King of Jordan, 81, 91, 92, 93, 103
Abu Ala (Ahmed Qureia), 6, 7
Abu Madian *Waqf*, 65
Abu Mazen (Mahmoud Abbas), 7
Abu Odeh, Adnan, 17
Acheson, Dean, 91
Adam, 19
Adana, 50
Agranot, Shimon, 96–7
Ahimeir, Ora, 4
Al-Ahram, 17
Al Quds, 1
Aleppo, 50
Alexandretta, 50
Alexandria, 42
Alexandrian rite, 61
Ali, Mohammed, 36, 42–3, 45
Allenby, E.H.H., 54, 55, 103
American University of Beirut, 43
Anglicans, 62
annexation, meanings, 96
Antiochenes, 61
Antiquities Ordinance (1929), 62
Anzilotti, Dionisio, 28
Appeal to the Christian Nobility of German Nationality (Luther), 105
al-Aqsa (extreme mosque), 2
al-Aqsa Mosque, 2, 9, 86
Arab Executive Committee, 63
Arab Higher Committee, 71, 75, 78
Arab League, 6, 15, 92, 93
Arab Legion, 81, 82
Arab nationalism, 42, 43, 45, 46, 62–4, 71
Arab Study Society, 136
Arab–Israeli conflict *see* Six-Day War (1967)
Arab–Israeli War (1948), 81
Arab-Syrian Congress (1913), 43–4
Arabic textbooks, 43
Arabroma, 136
Arabs
   Hogarth's message (1918), 54
   Husayn–McMahon correspondence, 49–50

   state/territorial perspective, 2
   see also Palestinians
Arafat, Yasser
   appointment of Imam of al-Aqsa Mosque, 9
   Cairo Agreement, 12
   God's sovereignty, 18
   Islamic Holy Places, 18
   Johannesburg speech (1994), 11–12
   leader of Fateh, 6
   Oslo Agreements, 12, 92
   Palestinian jurisdiction in Jerusalem, 12, 18
   Peres's letter (1993), 11, 12, 13
   signing of Interim Agreement (1995), 8
Arangio-Ruiz, Gaetano, 76, 77, 118
Aranne, Zalman, 95
Arches of the Holy Mary, 37
Armenian (Catholic) Christian community, 61
Armistice Agreement (1949), 8, 80, 81, 82–3, 94
asylia, 26
Ataturk, Kemal, 59, 152*n*
Attlee, Clement, 75
Austin, Warren, 87, 90
Austria-Hungary
   appointment of Resident of the Catholics, 36
   Berlin Treaty (1878), 41
   Frederick William's memorandum, 36
   nationalities, 53
   tripartite alliance (1841), 36
authority
   defined, 138
   and sovereignty, 27–8, 31, 129, 138
   state jurisdiction, 28, 29–31

Babylonians, 1
Badawi, A.H., 118
Baker, Henry Eli, 31
Balfour, Arthur James, 52, 60, 63–4, 65, 67
Balfour Declaration, 52, 53–4, 56, 59, 63
Barak, Ehud, 104
Barrow, Sir Edmund, 48
Basilica of the Nativity *see* Church of the Nativity, Bethlehem
Begin, Menachem, 5, 96
Beirut, 43, 50
Belgium
   Jerusalem consulate, 116

Belgium *(continued)*
  UN draft resolution (1950), 93
Belgrade, Treaty of Peace of, 35
Bellagio International Conference (1998), 136
Ben Ami, Shlomo, 104
Ben-Gurion, David, 82, 83, 89
Benedict XV, Pope, 57
Benziman, Uzi, 96
Berkovitz, Shmuel, 106, 110, 115
Berlin, Congress of (1878), 35, 39, 40–1, 44
Berlin, Treaty of (1878), 14, 34, 35, 39–40, 41
Berlin Wall, fall of (1989), 112, 128
Bernadotte, Count Folke, 90
Bethlehem
  Armistice Agreement (1949), 83
  Frederick William's memorandum, 36
  Herzl's proposal, 47
  Holy Places, 4, 14, 36, 37, 72, 73, 107
  international administration proposal (1916), 51
  Morrison–Grady Plan (1946), 75
  Peel Commission (1937), 72
  Sykes–Picot Agreement, 50
  Treaty of Amity and Commerce (1535), 33–4
  UNSCOP, 76
  see also Church of the Nativity, Bethlehem; Grotto of the Milk, Bethlehem; Rachel's Tomb, Bethlehem; Shepherd's Field, Bethlehem
Bismarck, Otto von, 39, 41
Blum, Yehuda, 9
Bodin, Jean, 27
Bonaventura, Brother, 87
Bovis, Eugene, 4, 36, 84
Britain
  Anglo-American Committee, 75
  Anglo-Jordan treaty alliance, 93
  Balfour Declaration, 52, 53–4, 56, 59, 63
  Berlin Congress (1878), 35, 41
  Berlin Treaty (1878), 35, 41
  Constantinople Agreement, 49
  "Declaration to the Seven", 55–6
  Egyptian independence (1936), 71
  extraterritorial status in China, 47
  Frederick William's memorandum, 36
  Husayn–McMahon correspondence, 49–50
  international administration proposal (1916), 51–2
  International and Inter-religious Commission for Holy Places, 58
  Israeli Parliament opening ceremony, 90
  Jerusalem consulate, 80, 116
  Jews in Ottoman Empire, 32
  Jordanian actions (1948), 93
  Memorandum (1919), 56–7
  Morrison–Grady Plan (1946), 75–6
  Palestine as "Jewish National Home", 52, 53, 54
  Paris Peace Conference (1919), 54–7
  Peel Commission (1937), 71–2, 73
  protection of Holy Sites, 52, 54–7
  Sokolow's request (1917), 52
  Sykes–Picot Agreement, 51–2
  tripartite alliance (1841), 36
  White Paper (1939), 74
  Woodhead Commission (1938), 73, 84
British Colonial Office, 59, 67, 69, 70
British Foreign Office, 59, 67, 69, 70
British Mandate
  Advisory Council, 59
  Annual Report (1923), 68
  Annual Report (1924), 68, 69
  Antiquities Ordinance (1929), 62
  closure (1948), 81
  granted at San Remo Conference (1920), 57
  Holy Places, 54, 59, 60, 61, 62, 63–5, 67–71, 72–3
  impartiality element, 58
  Jerusalem city limits, 8
  national movements, 62–4
  Palestine (Holy Places) Order-in-Council (1924), 60, 61, 67–71, 125, 133–4
  recognition of Zionist Organization, 52
  reluctance to intervene, 58
  restoration in Jerusalem, 60
  Status Quo, 14, 40, 54, 58, 61, 64–6, 108, 125
  terms of, 52, 54, 56, 57, 58–62, 63–4, 65, 67, 72–3, 74, 80
Brownlie, Ian, 119
Bulletin of the Christian Information Center, 136
al-Buraq, 2
al-Bustani, Butros, 43
Byzantine period, 26
Byzantines, 61

Cairo Agreement (1994), 10, 11, 12
Camamat, 34
Cambon, Paul, 50, 51, 52, 54
Camp David Accords (1978), 5, 6
Capitulations, Ottoman Empire, 32–5, 36, 43, 80, 118
Carneiro, Levi, 118
Carter Jr., James E., 5
Cassiodorus, 25, 146*n*
Catholic Church
  attitude towards Jewish people, 19, 20
  Church of the Holy Sepulchre, 107
  concern for Catholic minorities, 20, 21
  freedom of religion and conscience, 114
  German pressure, 50
  Holy Places, 21–2, 41, 58
  Nostra Aetate declaration, 19
  religious guarantees, 88
  respect for Status Quo, 21
  special Vatican arrangements with Italy, 111
  Vatican II, 19
  see also Holy See
Catholic community
  Frederick William's memorandum, 36
  Holy See's concern for, 20, 21
  see also Armenian (Catholic) Christian community; Greek Catholic community; Latin Catholic community; Syrian (Catholic) Christian community
Cave of Machpela, 14
Chagla, M.C., 28, 118

Chaldean (Uniate) Christian community, 61
Charitable Trusts Ordinance, 68
China
   British extraterritorial status, 47
   territorial–political status quo in Jerusalem, 10
Christian community
   British Mandate policy, 58–62
   global/transnational perspective, 2
   non-recognition of Holy Places, 105
   in Ottoman Empire, 31, 32, 34–5, 36–9, 40, 110
   PLO–Holy See Basic Agreement (2000), 13, 22–4, 109, 135
   significance of Holy Land, 19–20
   see also Catholic Church; Catholic community; Copts; Eastern Orthodox community; Greek Orthodox community; Holy Places, Christian; Status Quo
Christian–Jewish relations, 1, 19
   Israeli–Holy See Fundamental Agreement (1993), 13, 18–22, 23, 101, 109, 113–14, 134
Christian–Muslim relations, Nazareth Basilica, 14
Christopher, Warren, 8, 17
Church of England, 62
Church of the Nativity, Bethlehem
   Jewish lack of claim, 1
   Status Quo, 14, 66, 86
Churchill, Winston, 59–60, 74
citizenship, 29, 53, 56
City of David, 130
civilizations, 126, 127
The Clash of Civilizations and the Remaking of World Order (Huntington), 126
Clinton, Bill, 8
Coenaculum, 67
Cohn, Justice, 97, 113
Cold War, 128
Constantinople Agreement, 49
Copts, 61, 62, 92
Crimean War, 37, 44
Crisafulli, Vezio, 111
Crusaders, 20, 42, 104
Cust, L.G.A., 14, 100
customary norms, 117–20, 127
Custos of the Holy Land, 76, 87

D'Agostino, Colonel, 55
Dante Alighieri, 127
David, King, 83
Dayan, Moshe, 82, 98, 101–2
de Bunsen, Sir Maurice, 48–9
De Monarchia (Dante), 127
de Newlinsky, Philip Michael, 47
Déclaration du bureau de la fédération protestante de France, 105
Declaration of Principles (DoP) (1993), 128
   compatibility with Jordan–Israel Treaty, 15
   exchange of letters, 10–11, 12–13
   Holy Places not mentioned, 109
   Jerusalem references, 7–8, 12, 109, 129
   "Oslo channel", 6–7
   signing, 7, 10, 20

   Status Quo not mentioned, 109
   territorial–political status quo in Jerusalem, 9
   see also permanent status negotiations
"Declaration to the Seven", 55–6
Deir al Sultan, 14
Diepape, Colonel, 55
Disraeli, Benjamin, 48
divine law, Roman Empire, 25–6
Dome of the Rock (Mosque of Omar), 2, 15, 51, 54, 60
Dushinsky, Rabbi, 84

Eastern Orthodox community
   German pressure, 50
   Jordanian rule, 94
   Palestine Order-in-Council schedule, 61
   privileges in the Holy Places, 41
   right of protection, 35
   Russian interests, 51
   Sykes–Picot Agreement, 51
Eban, Abba, 85, 89, 90, 96, 99, 100
Eden, Anthony, 73
Edward VIII, King, 72
Egypt
   Arab nationalism, 45
   Arab–Israeli War (1948), 81
   Armistice Agreement with Israel, 83
   Camp David Accords (1978), 5, 6
   control of Gaza, 2
   expulsion of Jordan from Arab League, 93
   foreign religious bodies, 43
   independence (1936), 71
   Interim Agreement witness, 8
   Islamic Holy Places, 18
   Napoleon's expedition, 2, 42, 45
   Six-Day War (1967), 95
Egyptian–Israeli Peace Treaty (1979), 16, 120
El Escorial (Madrid) Conference (1996), 136
Elon, M., 103
Emmett, Chad F., 110
Encyclopaedia of International Law, 45
Encyclopaedia Judaica, 62
Englard, Izhak, 110
Eritrea, 44
Eshkol, Levi, 95, 97, 98, 99, 102, 103
Ethiopians, 61, 62
ethnos, 25
European Convention on Human Rights (1950), 113, 122
European Union
   Florence Declaration (1996), 115
   Interim Agreement witness, 8
   Quartet Road Map, 125
   Taba summit (2001), 130
Evangelical Episcopal Church, 62
Evangelical Lutheran Church, 62
exterritoriality, 33, 36, 47
extraterritoriality, 47, 48, 71

"Faithful of the Temple Mount", 104
Fateh, 6
Faysal of Hedjaz, Emir, 55

firmans, Ottoman Empire, 36–9, 40, 46, 66, 93, 110, 149*n*
First World War *see* World War I
Florence, 34
Florence Declaration (1996), 115
Foreign Relations of the United States (FRUS), 4
France
   Berlin Congress (1878), 35, 40–1
   Berlin Treaty (1878), 35, 39, 40, 41
   Capitulations of 1604, 34
   Capitulations of 1740, 34, 35, 43
   Constantinople Agreement, 49
   Frederick William's memorandum, 36
   Husayn–McMahon correspondence, 50
   independence of Holy Places, 54
   intention to annex Syria (1915), 49
   Israeli Parliament opening ceremony, 90
   Jerusalem consulate, 80, 116
   Jordanian actions (1948), 92
   missionaries in Lebanon, 43
   and Ottoman Empire, 33–4, 35, 40
   protection of Latin Catholic community, 35, 41
   rights of US nationals in Morocco, 118–19
   Sokolow's request (1917), 52
   Sykes–Picot Agreement, 51–2
   Syria as part of France, 50
   Syrian independence, 71
   territorial–political status quo in Jerusalem, 10
   Treaty of Amity and Commerce (1535), 33–4
Francis I, King of France, 33
Franciscan Fraternity, 76
Franks, 26
Frederick William IV, King of Prussia, 36
FRUS (Foreign Relations of the United States), 4
functional jurisdiction, 28, 29, 124, 138

Gasparri, Cardinal, 57
Gaza
   application of Geneva Conventions, 121
   Arab Government of All Palestine, 92
   British Mandate, 59
   Cairo Agreement (1994), 10
   control by Egypt, 6, 83
   Declaration of Principles (DoP), 7, 8
   Madrid Peace Conference (1991), 6
   permanent status negotiations, 6, 7
   Six-Day War (1967), 95
Gaza/Jericho Agreement Implementation Law, 10
General Zionist Party, 83
Geneva Conventions (1949), 102, 121
Genoa, 34
George VI, King, 72
Gerig, Benjamin, 80
Germany
   ambitions in the Middle East, 50
   Berlin Treaty (1878), 41
   British concerns over Palestine, 50
   customs in Middle Ages, 26
   feudal relations, 128
   fostering of tensions in Palestine, 71
Gethsemane, 14, 86
global/transnational perspective

   Berlin Treaty (1878), 41
   British attitude in Palestine, 51, 62, 69, 73, 125
   cycles of Western history, 126–8
   definition of Holy Places, 105
   influence on local governments, 4
   Jerusalem, 2, 58, 124, 126, 131
   Middle Ages, 127
   National Home for the Jewish People, 53
   and national-state identity, 42
   Ottoman Empire, 35
   Quartet Road Map, 126
   Status Quo talks, 131
   support from scholars, 126–7
   Western political elites, 32
   see also state/territorial perspective
Glubb, John, 81
Golan Heights, 95
Gold, Dore, 101
Goldberg, Arthur, 96
Golgotha, 37
Goren, Shlomo, 101
Gothics, 25
Great Britain *see* Britain
Greece, Jerusalem Consul, 80
Greece, ancient, 25, 26
Greek Catholic community, 61
Greek Orthodox community
   Frederick William's memorandum, 36
   organizational problems, 64
   priority of rights over the Holy Places, 114
Gregorian (Armenian) Christian community, 61
Grey, Sir Edward, 48, 50, 51
Grotto of the Milk, Bethlehem, 14, 37, 86

Hackworth, G.H., 118
Hadas, Shmuel, 19, 20
Hadjir el Moughtesil, 37
Hadrian, Roman Emperor, 94
Hafiz Ahmed Pasha, 36
Halacha, 103
Hamas activists, 21
Har Ha Bait/Haram Al Sharif
   discussion on practical arrangements, 130
   Guardian appointed by Jordan, 93
   Israeli policies (post-1967), 101–2, 104
   Israeli–Palestinian disputes, 1
   Jewish prayers forbidden, 102, 114
   Jewish prayers (June 1967), 101
   Jordanian exclusion of Jews, 94
   Palestinian preventive security service, 9
   significance to Jews, 1–2, 116
   significance to Muslims, 2, 116
   Status Quo, 13–18, 86, 101–2, 103, 104
   Waqf control, 13, 101–2, 104
   Washington Declaration (1994), 13
Harrison, Earl G., 74
Harrison Report (1945), 74–5
Hasmonean Tunnel, 104
Hassan bin Talal, HRH Prince, 95
Hebron, 14, 63, 97
Hellenistic civilization, 25, 26
Herod, King, 1
Herut Party, 83

Herzl, Theodore, 47–8, 95
Hibbat Ziyyon, 46
Hilmi, Ahmad, 92
Hirsch, Moshe, 12, 79
Hirschfeld, Yair, 6
Hitler, Adolf, 71
Hiwarat, 136
Hobbes, Thomas, 27
Hoffman, H.C., 103–4
Hogarth, D.G., 54
Holst, Johann Jorgen, 6, 10, 11, 13, 109, 134
Holy Basin, 130
Holy Land
  emergence of expression, 19
  King–Crane Commission, 57
  PLO–Holy See Basic Agreement (2000), 23
  Samuel's Report, 60
  significance to Christians, 19–20
Holy Places
  Arab Report (1947), 78
  Ben-Gurion's speech (1949), 83
  Bernadotte's Report (1948), 90
  Berlin Treaty (1878), 14, 39–40, 41
  Bethlehem, 4, 14, 36, 37, 72, 73, 107
  British guarantees to protect, 52, 54–7
  British Mandate period, 54, 59, 60, 61, 62, 63–5, 67–71, 72–3
  British Memorandum (1919), 56–7
  British proposal to internationalize, 47, 51–2
  British White Paper (1939), 74
  competition among local communities, 1
  competition between nationalist movements, 71
  Custos of the Holy Land, 76
  Cust's Memorandum, 14
  De Bunsen committee proposals, 49
  Declaration of Principles (DoP) (1993), 109
  defined, 105–7
  first mention in a treaty, 34
  First Temple, 1
  global/trans-territorial perspective, 2
  Grey's suggestion, 48
  Harrison Report (1945), 74–5
  inter-faith controversies, 1
  Israeli definition, 105–6
  Israeli Draft Resolution (1949), 86, 88–9, 105–6
  Israeli practice, 79, 84–9, 96, 97–104, 105–6, 121
  Jewish–Christian relations, 1
  Jordanian practice, 93–5, 121
  King–Crane Commission, 57
  lack of formal list, 105
  League of Nations supervision, 56, 63–4, 69, 71, 73, 137
  Morrison–Grady Plan (1946), 75–6
  Nazareth, 36, 72, 73, 82, 107
  Palestine Conciliation Commission, 82, 86, 89, 106
  Palestine (Holy Places) Order-in-Council (1924), 60, 61, 67–71, 125, 133–4, 162*n*
  Paris Peace Conference (1919), 54–7
  Peel Commission (1937), 72
  Peres's letter (1993), 11, 12, 23
  PLO–Holy See Basic Agreement (2000), 22–3
  Sadat's letter to Carter (1978), 5–6
  Samuel's policies, 49, 60, 67–8, 71, 72
  Second Temple, 1
  state/territorial perspective, 2, 41, 42, 58, 105
  Taba summit (2001), 130
  in times of war, 120–2, 124
  Treaty of Amity and Commerce (1535), 33–4
  UN General Assembly Resolution 194(III) (1948), 82, 91
  UN "Partition Resolution" 181 (1947), 79
  UN Security Council Resolution (1948), 81
  UNSCOP, 77, 78
  US position, 90–1
  veneration through generations, 1
  Weizmann–Faysal agreement (1919), 55
  Woodhead Commission (1938), 73
  Zionist Memorandum (1919), 56
  see also Dome of the Rock; Har Ha Bait/Haram Al Sharif; Holy Sepulchre; Western Wall
Holy Places, Christian
  Berlin Congress (1878), 40–1
  Berlin Treaty (1878), 14, 39–40, 41
  Capitulations, 32, 34, 35
  Catholic Church, 21–2, 41, 58
  Eastern Orthodox community, 41
  Frederick William's memorandum, 36
  Greek Orthodox community, 114
  Herzl's proposal, 47–8
  Israeli practice, 97–101
  Israeli–Holy See Fundamental Agreement (1993), 13, 18–22, 23, 101, 109, 134
  Israeli–Jordanian Peace Treaty (1994), 16
  Jordanian position, 91
  Latin Catholic community, 76
  non-recognition, 105
  "Oslo channel", 17
  Ottoman Empire, 32, 34, 35, 36–45, 93, 107, 108, 110, 121
  Peres's letter (1993), 11, 12, 23
  PLO position, 17
  PLO–Holy See Basic Agreement (2000), 22–3, 24, 109, 135
  Russian concerns, 49
  Status Quo, 14, 22–3, 24, 36–45, 64, 94, 97–101, 107–9
  Treaty of Paris (1856), 37, 39
  see also Church of the Nativity, Bethlehem; Deir al Sultan; Grotto of the Milk, Bethlehem; Holy Sepulchre; Sanctuary of the Ascension; Shepherd's Field, Bethlehem; Tomb of the Virgin
Holy Places, Islamic
  British Proclamation (1917), 55
  Hussein's interview, 18
  Hussein's speech, 17
  Israeli practice (post-1967), 99, 100, 101–4
  Israeli recognition of Jordanian role, 13, 14–15, 16
  Israeli–Jordanian Peace Treaty (1994), 13, 14–15, 16, 17, 18, 24, 109, 135
  Jordan's role, 13, 14–15, 16, 17, 18, 24
  Ottoman Empire, 42

Holy Places, Islamic *(continued)*
  Peres's letter (1993), 11, 12, 23
  PLO–Holy See Basic Agreement (2000), 23
  Status Quo, 14, 23, 64–5, 66, 101–4
  in times of war, 120
  Washington Declaration (1994), 13, 16, 18, 24, 109, 134–5
  wider Arab concern, 18
  see also al-Aqsa Mosque; Dome of the Rock; Har Ha Bait/Haram Al Sharif; Mecca; Medina
Holy Places, Jewish
  Israeli practice, 99, 101–4
  Jordanian exclusion of Jews, 94
  Jordanian violations, 121
  Ottoman Empire, 42
  Peres's letter (1993), 12
  PLO–Holy See Basic Agreement (2000), 23
  Status Quo, 14, 23, 64–6, 101–4
  in times of war, 120
  see also Har Ha Bait/Haram Al Sharif; Rachel's Tomb, Bethlehem; Tombs of the Patriarchs; Western Wall
Holy See
  Basic Agreement with PLO (2000), 13, 22–4, 109, 135
  concern for Catholic community, 20, 21
  Fundamental Agreement with Israel (1993), 13, 18–22, 23, 101, 109, 113–14, 134
  Jerusalem Consul, 80
  and Ottoman Empire, 35
  Saint Peter's Square, Rome, 129
Holy Sepulchre
  British Proclamation (1917), 55
  Capitulations of 1740, 34
  firman (1852), 37
  inter-Christian disputes, 1
  Jewish lack of claim, 1
  Netherlands-Turkish treaty (1680), 35
  Status Quo, 14, 65, 66, 86
  struggle between Roman-Catholics and others, 107
Housen-Couriel, Deborah, 79
Huber, Max, 28–9
human rights, 112–14, 121–2
  Israeli position, 84
  Israeli–Holy See Fundamental Agreement (1993), 21
  UNSCOP plans, 78
Huntington, Samuel, 126–7
Hurewitz, Jacob Coleman, 4, 55–6, 59–60, 74
Husam al-Din Jarallah, 92
Husayn, Sharif, 49–50, 54
al-Husayni, Hajj Amin, 64, 71, 92
Hussein, King of Jordan, 15, 16, 17–18
Husseini family, 63

Ibrahim Pasha, 42, 43, 45
Ibrahimi Mosque, 14
identity models *see* global/transnational perspective; state/territorial perspective
In Multiplicibus Curis, 87, 91

independence
  defined, 28, 138
  and sovereignty, 27–8, 31, 129, 138
India, 118
Indian subcontinent, religious conflict, 127
influence on local governments, 4
Interim Agreement (1995), 7–8
International Colloquium (1998), 136
International Court of Justice, 27, 28, 30, 118, 119, 120
International Human Rights and Security Review, 136
international law
  birth of, 127
  concept of annexation, 96
  concept of independence, 28, 138
  concept of sovereignty, 27, 28, 130
  customary norms, 112, 113, 118, 128, 138
  defined, 108
  doctrine of exterritoriality, 33, 47
  exercise of authority within the territory of a state, 27, 28, 29–30, 130
  extraterritoriality and immunity, 71
  Holy Places, 105, 106–7, 108, 129
  human rights, 122
  Islamic system, 44
  Israeli practice, 100
  Peace Treaty provisions, 16
  principle of estoppel or preclusion, 120
  relations among individuals, 108
  religious rights, 60, 112, 113
  Status Quo norms, 111
  subject as a formal legal concept, 108
  territorial sovereignty, 44, 138
International Law in Historical Perspective (Verzijl), 106–7
Iraq
  Arab–Israeli War (1948), 81
  expulsion of Jordan from Arab League, 93
  foreign religious bodies, 43
  Palestine report (1947), 78
Isaiah, 101
Islam
  conversion of French subjects, 34
  as a political community, 45
  religion of Ottoman Empire, 31–2, 44
  system of international law, 44
  see also Holy Places, Islamic; *Umma*
Islamic Endowments, 16
Islamic *Waqf see Waqf*
Israel
  Camp David Accords (1978), 5, 6
  Christian communities, 61
  Christian Holy Places, 97–101
  control of administered territories, 6
  Declaration of Independence, 81, 84, 103, 113
  decree on Jerusalem (1948), 81–2
  Draft Resolution to UN (1949), 86, 88–9, 105–6
  expulsion of Hamas activists, 21
  Fundamental Agreement with Holy See (1993), 13, 18–22, 23, 101, 109, 113–14, 134

Gaza/Jericho Agreement Implementation Law, 10
Holy Places, 79, 84–9, 96, 97–104, 105–6, 121
Holy Places definition, 105–6
international customary obligations, 119
Islamic Holy Places, 13, 14–15, 16, 99, 100, 101–4
Jerusalem policies, 81–2, 83, 84–90, 95–101, 121
Law and Administration Ordinance Law (1967), 95, 165*n*
Memorandum to UN (1949), 86–7
Municipalities Ordinance (1967), 95, 166*n*
Palestine (Holy Places) Order-in-Council (1924), 61, 68
Parliament opening ceremony (1949), 90–1
personal law, 44
Quartet Road Map, 125
recognition of religious communities, 61–2
Rome seminars, 131–2
Status Quo, 97–104, 108
Taba summit (2001), 130
territorial–political status quo in Jerusalem, 10, 12
UN membership, 85, 93
War of Independence (1948), 81
see also Six-Day War (1967)
Israel Radio, 11
Israeli Foreign Ministry, 7, 12
Israeli Supreme Court, 84, 97, 102, 106, 110, 113, 116
Israeli–Egyptian Peace Treaty (1979), 16, 120
Israeli–Jordanian Peace Treaty (1994), 13–18, 22, 23, 24, 101, 103, 109, 120, 121, 135
Israeli–Jordanian relations
  Armistice Agreement (1949), 8, 80, 81, 82–3, 94
  Washington declaration (1994), 13, 16, 18, 23, 24, 109, 134–5
Israeli–Palestinian relations
  closed door meetings, 130–2
  disputes over Har Ha Bait/Haram Al Sharif, 1
  Madrid Peace Conference (1991), 5, 6, 12, 30
  post-Madrid bilateral meetings, 6
Israeli–PLO relations
  Cairo Agreement (1994), 10, 11, 12
  exchange of letters (1993), 10–13
  Interim Agreement, 7–8
  Oslo "channel", 6–7, 16–17
  see also Declaration of Principles (DoP) (1993); permanent status negotiations
Italian legal theory, 111
Italy
  Berlin Treaty (1878), 41
  fostering of tensions in Palestine, 71
  Jerusalem consulate, 80, 116
  Saint Peter's Square, 129
  Sokolow's request (1917), 52

Ja'abari, Mufti Suleiman, 9
Jericho, Cairo Agreement (1994), 10
Jericho Conference (1948), 92

Jerusalem
  Anglo-Jordan treaty alliance, 93
  appointment of Mufti, 9, 16, 64, 92
  Arab–Israeli War (1948), 81
  Arafat's Johannesburg speech (1994), 12
  Armistice Agreement (1949), 8, 81, 82–3, 94
  belligerent occupation, 4
  British Mandate period, 8, 60
  bypassed by Napoleon, 42, 45
  Camp David Accords (1978), 5
  Capitulations of 1740, 34
  conquest by Allenby (1917), 54
  consulates, 80, 116
  corpus separatum, 72, 76, 78, 93
  cultural–religious status quo, 10, 112, 114–17, 120, 121, 123–4, 135–7, 139
  Declaration of Principles (DoP), 7–8, 12, 109, 129
  as a federal capital, 76, 78
  global/trans-territorial perspective, 2, 58, 124, 126, 131
  Hellenistic period, 26
  Herzl's proposal, 47
  importance of archaeology, 115
  international administration proposal (1916), 51
  as Israeli capital, 80, 83, 84
  Israeli decree (1948), 81–2
  Israeli Draft Resolution (1949), 86, 88–9
  Israeli policies, 81–2, 83, 84–90, 95–101, 121
  Israeli political sovereignty, 14–15
  Jewish Agency Plan (1946), 75
  Jordanian administration (1948), 92
  Jordanian position (pre-1967), 83, 91–3, 121
  League of Nations supervision and control, 73
  Madrid Peace Conference (1991), 6
  Morrison–Grady Plan (1946), 75
  Ottoman Empire, 34
  Palestine Conciliation Commission, 82, 86, 89
  Palestinian Authority jurisdiction, 11
  Palestinian Authority status, 10
  as Palestinian capital, 18
  Peel Commission (1937), 72
  Peres's letter (1993), 11
  permanent status negotiations, 7, 8, 9, 14, 109, 120, 125, 129
  PLO–Holy See Basic Agreement (2000), 22, 23, 135
  Pope's reference, 21
  Quartet Road Map, 125
  riots (1920), 63
  Roman period, 26
  special regime proposals, 73–4
  state/territorial perspective, 2, 58, 124, 131
  Sykes–Picot Agreement, 50
  territorial–political status quo post-DoP, 8–10, 12, 139
  Treaty of Amity and Commerce (1535), 33–4
  UN General Assembly Resolution 194 (III) (1948), 82, 87, 91
  UN General Assembly Resolution 303 (1949), 83

Jerusalem *(continued)*
   UN "Partition Resolution" 181 (1947), 78–80, 87, 89, 90, 116
   UN Resolution 242 (1967), 5
   UN Resolution 338 (1973), 5
   UNESCO World Heritage site, 116
   United Nations Security Council Resolution (1948), 81
   UNSCOP, 76–8, 80
   US position, 90–1
   Washington Declaration (1994), 13
   Woodhead Commission (1938), 73, 84
   see also Holy Places
Jerusalem Institute for Israel Studies, 136
The Jerusalem Times, 136
Jesuits, 43
Jesus Christ, 19–20, 37
Jewish Agency, 52, 73, 75, 78
Jewish community
   Balfour Declaration, 52
   British "Declaration to the Seven", 56
   British Mandate policy, 58–62
   establishment of the State of Israel, 81
   global/transnational perspective, 2
   Jordanian exclusions from Holy Places, 94
   migrants to Palestine, 46, 47–8, 52, 71
   Muslim/Jewish Modus Vivendi, 113, 114
   in Ottoman Empire, 32, 46
   riots (1920), 63
   Sykes–Picot Agreement, 51
   Western Wall disturbances (1925 & 1928), 65–6
   World War II refugees, 74–5
   see also Har Ha Bait/Haram Al Sharif; *yishuv*
Jewish Congress, 52
Jewish national movements, 46, 63, 71
Jewish–Christian relations, 1, 19
   Israeli–Holy See Fundamental Agreement (1993), 13, 18–22, 23, 101, 109, 113–14, 134
al-Jinan, 43
John Paul II, Pope, 19
Jordan
   administration of Jerusalem (1948), 92
   Anglo-Jordan treaty alliance, 93
   Arab–Israeli War (1948), 81
   expulsion threat from Arab League, 93
   Holy Places practice, 93–5, 121
   Interim Agreement, 8
   Islamic Holy Places, 13, 14–15, 16, 17, 18, 24, 109, 135
   Israeli Memorandum (1949), 86
   Madrid Peace Conference (1991), 6
   permanent status negotiations, 15, 134, 135
   position on Jerusalem (pre-1967), 83, 91–3, 121
   recognition of religious communities, 61–2
   Six-Day War (1967), 95
   UN membership, 93
   see also Israeli–Jordanian Peace Treaty (1994); Israeli–Jordanian relations; Transjordan; West Bank

Jordanian–Palestinian relations
   appointment of Mufti, 9–10, 16, 92
   Islamic affairs in Jerusalem, 16
   Jerusalem holy sites, 16
   Waqf administration in West Bank, 16
Al Jubeh, Nazmi, 132
Judaea, autonomy under Romans, 25
Der Judenstaat (Herzl), 47
June War (1967) *see* Six-Day War (1967)
jurisdiction
   defined, 138
   scope of state powers, 28, 29–31, 124, 138
jus gentium, 33
Justin Martyr, Saint, 19

Kahan, Justice, 97
Kemalist revolution, 44
al-Khalidi, Husayn, 71
Kidron Valley, 130
King–Crane Commission, 57
Kirkbride, Alec, 81
Kitchener, Lord, 49
Klein, Menachem
   Arab–Israeli War (1948), 81
   Arafat's Johannesburg speech, 12
   future of East Jerusalem, 10
   Israeli military plans for Jerusalem, 95
   Israeli recognition of Jordanian role, 14–15, 16, 18
   Peres's letter to Holst, 11, 12
   status of Jerusalem, 17
Kohn, Leo, 84
Kollek, Teddy, 102
Koran, 2, 31–2
Küçük Kaynarca, Treaty of Peace of, 35

Lake Tiberias, 51, 72
Landau, Justice, 110
Lapidoth, Ruth, 4
   Declaration of Principles (DoP) (1993), 8
   East Jerusalem, 8
   expression status quo, 114–15
   General Assembly resolution (1947), 79
   Israeli–Jordanian Peace Treaty (1994), 13, 15, 16
   Peres's letter, 12, 13
Latin Catholic community
   Canon Law, 108
   firman (1852), 36
   French protection, 35, 41
   Holy Places, 76
   Jordanian rule, 94
   Palestine Order-in-Council schedule, 61
   Sykes–Picot Agreement, 51
Latin Patriarchate of Jerusalem, 136
Lausanne Treaty (1923), 59
League of Nations
   British Mandate Annual Report (1923), 68
   British Mandate Annual Report (1924), 68, 69
   British Mandate terms, 52, 54, 56, 57, 58–62, 63–4, 65, 67, 72–3, 74, 80
   Covenant, 72
   Holy Places, 56, 63–4, 69, 71, 73, 137

mandate for Jerusalem, 73
Peel Commission (1937), 72
Permanent Mandates Commission, 70, 73, 74
recognition of Zionist Organization, 52
right to appeal, 60
rights at Western Wall, 66, 70
Special Commission appointment, 59
suspension of operations (1939), 74
Zionist Organization memorandum, 66
Lebanon
   Arab–Israeli War (1948), 81
   Arab–Syrian Congress (1913), 43–4
   British division of land (1917), 54–5
   expulsion of Jordan from Arab League, 93
   missionaries, 43
   religious conflict, 127
Lewis, Bernard, 53
Lie, Trygve, 79
Lloyd George, David, 50
Lombardians, 26
Lotus case (1927), 30
Luther, Martin, 105

MacDonald, John D., 90
McMahon, Sir Henry, 49–50
McMahon, Thomas G., 88
McMichael, Harold, 106
McNair, Arnold Duncan, 120
Madrid (El Escorial) Conference (1996), 136
Madrid Peace Conference (1991), 5, 6, 12, 20
Magnes, Dr., 84
Majali, Abdel Salaam, 17
Majid, Ahmad Issmat Abdul, 15
Mandela, Nelson, 11
Margiotta-Broglio, Francesco, 112–13
Maronite Christian community, 61
Marshall, George, 90
Marwan, Khalif Abd al Malak Ibn, 104
Mary (mother of Jesus), 19–20, 37
Mecca, 2, 51, 107
Medina, 107
Mediterranean Perspectives, 131, 132
Medzini, Meron, 4
Meeker, Leonard C., 91
Mejid, Sultan Habdul, 36
Melkite community, 61
Mersina, 50
Mesopotamia
   Arab–Syrian Congress (1913), 44
   foreign religious bodies, 43
Middle Ages, 26, 29, 127, 128
Milk Grotto, Bethlehem, 14, 37, 86
Millet system, 31–2, 36, 37, 46, 62, 72, 108
Minerbi, Yitzhak Sergio, 4, 20, 47, 50, 61, 67
Mingias, 28
Modus Vivendi/Status Quo, 18, 131
   extension of, 23
   Florence Declaration, 115
   on the Har Ha Bait/Haram Al Sharif, 13–15
   Israeli–Jordanian Peace Treaty (1994), 13–15
   in the Muslim–Jewish Holy Places, 101–4
   Peres's letter, 23
   PLO–Holy See Basic Agreement (2000), 24
   and the principles of freedom of religion and worship, 66, 112–14
   procedural and material norms 110–11, 114, 121
   Quartet Roadmap, 123–6
   Washington Declaration, 24
Mohammed Ali, 36, 42–3, 45
Mohammed the Prophet, 2
De Monarchia (Dante), 127
Moratinos, Miguel Angel, 130
Morocco
   Har Ha Bait/Haram Al Sharif, 130
   Islamic Holy Places, 18
   rights of US nationals, 118–19
Morrison–Grady Plan (1946), 75–6
Moses, 63
Mosque of Omar *see* Dome of the Rock (Mosque of Omar)
Mount Athos, 41, 150*n*
Mount Moriah, 1
Mount of Olives, 83, 86, 94, 130
Mount Scopus, 73, 83
Muasher, Marwan, 94
Münster, Treaty of, 127
Musallam, Sami F., 9, 10–12, 13, 16, 17
Muslim community
   British Mandate policy, 58–62
   curtailment of privileges during British Mandate, 58
   global/transnational perspective, 2
   Muslim/Jewish Modus Vivendi, 113, 114
   see also Dome of the Rock; Har Ha Bait/Haram Al Sharif; Holy Places, Islamic; *Umma*
Muslim–Christian Association, 63
Muslim–Christian relations, Nazareth Basilica, 14

Napoleon Bonaparte, 2, 42, 45
Napoleonic code, 44
Nara, Ibrahim, 17
Nasser, Gamal Abdel, 95
nationality, meaning of, 53
Navarro-Valls, Joaquin, 20
Nazareth
   access negotiations, 94
   Frederick William's memorandum, 36
   Holy Places, 36, 72, 73, 82, 107
   international administration proposal (1916), 51
   Peel Commission (1937), 72
Nazareth Basilica, 14
Nazism, 74, 75
Nebi Musa procession, 63
Netanyahu, Benjamin, 10, 101, 104
Netherlands
   Island of Palmas decision, 28
   treaty with Ottoman Empire (1612), 35
New Orient House, 9, 11
Nitti, Francesco Saverio, 57
Noble Sanctuary/Temple Mount *see* Har Ha Bait/Haram Al Sharif
Nonviolence, 136
Norway
   exchange of letters (1993), 10–13, 109, 134

Norway *(continued)*
  Interim Agreement, 8
  "Oslo channel", 6–7, 11, 16–17, 92, 128
Nostra Aetate, 19, 114
La Nuova Frontiera, 136
Nuseibeh, Hazem, 94

objective regime, 117–20, 124
Omar Ibn Khattab, 12, 50, 55
Orient House, 9, 11
Oslo Accord
  initialling, 7, 10
  see also Declaration of Principles (DoP) (1993)
"Oslo channel", 6–7, 11, 16–17, 92, 128
Osnabrück, Treaty of, 127
Ottoman Empire
  Arab rebellion, 49
  Capitulations, 32–5, 36, 43, 80, 118
  Christian community, 31, 32, 34–5, 36–9, 40, 110
  Christian Holy Places, 32, 34, 35, 36–45, 93, 107, 108, 110, 121
  decentralization policy, 64
  end of, 44
  firmans, 36–9, 40, 46, 66, 93, 110, 149*n*
  foreign and protected persons, 32–5
  foreign schools, 43
  and France, 33–4, 35, 40
  global/transnational perspective, 35
  and Holy See, 35
  introduction of state model, 42–5
  Islam, 31–2, 44
  Jewish community, 32, 46
  Millet system, 31–2, 36, 37, 46, 62, 72, 108
  missionaries, 34, 43
  Napoleon's conquest, 42
  nationalities, 53
  personal jurisdiction, 31–5
  Roman tradition, 62
  state/territorial perspective, 33, 35
  Status Quo, 2, 36–45, 107, 108, 121
  Sublime Porte, 32, 33, 34, 35, 38, 39, 44
  territorial jurisdiction, 31, 33, 44
  treaties with Russia, 35
  Treaty of Amity and Commerce (1535), 33–4
  umma, 64
  Young Turks *coup d'état* (1908), 43

Pakistan
  draft resolution to UN (1967), 96
  Jordanian actions (1948), 93
Paléologue, Maurice, 51
Palestine
  Arab–Israeli War (1948), 81
  Balfour Declaration, 52, 53–4, 56, 59, 63
  British "Declaration to the Seven", 56
  British White Paper (1939), 74
  De Bunsen committee proposals, 49
  defined by British (1917), 55
  Grey's suggestion, 48
  Harrison Report (1945), 74–5
  Herzl's proposal, 47–8
  international administration proposal (1916), 51
  Jewish immigrants, 46, 47–8, 52, 71
  "Jewish National Home", 52–3, 54
  Jewish World War II refugees, 74–5
  King–Crane Commission, 57
  Morrison–Grady Plan (1946), 75–6
  Napoleon's conquest, 42
  Paris Peace Conference (1919), 54–7
  Peel Commission (1937), 71–2, 73
  Samuel's plan, 48
  San Remo Conference (1920), 57
  Sykes–Picot Agreement, 51–2
  UN "Partition Resolution" 181 (1947), 8, 78–80, 81, 87
  Woodhead Commission (1938), 73, 84
  see also British Mandate
Palestine Arab Conference, Jericho (1948), 92
Palestine Conciliation Commission, 82, 86, 89, 91, 106
Palestine (Holy Places) Order-in-Council (1924), 60, 61, 67–71, 125, 133–4, 162*n*
Palestine Liberation Organization (PLO)
  appointment of Mufti of Jerusalem, 9
  Basic Agreement with Holy See (2000), 13, 22–4, 109, 135
  Christian Holy Places, 17
  founding of, 6
  Islamic Holy Places, 18
  jurisdiction in Jerusalem, 18
  Madrid Peace Conference (1991), 6
  New Orient House, 9
  Quartet Road Map, 125
  religious supervision role, 16
  restricted activities in Israel, 10
  status in Jerusalem, 10
  territorial–political status quo in Jerusalem, 9
  UN recognition, 6
  see also Declaration of Principles (DoP); Israel–PLO relations
Palestine National Assembly, 92
Palestine Royal Commission (Peel Commission), 71–2, 73
Palestine Zionist Executive, 52
Palestinian Arab Congress (1920), 63
Palestinian Authority, 6
  Christian communities, 61
  Department of Islamic Endowments, 16
  jurisdiction in Jerusalem, 11
  restricted activities in Israel, 10
  status in Jerusalem, 10
  Taba summit (2001), 130
Palestinian Council, 7
Palestinian nationalism, 42, 62–4
Palestinians
  Arab–Israeli War (1948), 81
  Declaration of Principles (DoP) (1993), 8, 12
  Guardians of Har ha Bait/Haram al-Sharif compound, 130
  Israeli–Jordanian Peace Treaty (1994), 16
  Jerusalem Holy Places, 18
  Madrid Peace Conference (1991), 6
  Palestinian Arab Congress (1920), 63

Peres's letter, 11, 12
post-Madrid bilateral meetings, 6
Waqf administration in West Bank, 16
see also Israeli–Palestinian relations;
    Jordanian–Palestinian relations
Palmas, Island of, 28
Paris Peace Conference (1919), 54–7
Paris, Treaty of (1856), 37, 39
Pawlikowski, John T., 19
peace agreements see Declaration of Principles
    (DoP) (1993); Israeli–Jordanian Peace
    Treaty (1994); Madrid Peace Conference
    (1991); "Oslo channel"
Peel Commission (1937), 71–2, 73
Peel, Earl, 72
Peres, Shimon
    Declaration of Principles (DoP) (1993), 7
    declaration to Knesset (1993), 100–1
    letter (1993), 11–13, 16, 17, 23, 109, 134
Permanent Court of Arbitration, 28, 44–5
Permanent Mandates Commission, 66, 70, 73, 74
permanent status negotiations
    Gaza, 6, 7
    influenced on international legal status, 4
    interim period agreements, 9
    Israeli–Jordanian Peace Treaty (1994), 135
    Jerusalem, 7, 8, 9, 14, 109, 120, 125, 129
    possible Jordanian participation, 15, 134, 135
    Roadmap provisions, 125
    state/territorial perspective, 131
    Taba summit (2001), 130
    Washington Declaration, 134
    West Bank, 6, 7
personal jurisdiction, 26–7, 28, 124
    defined, 29, 138
    in international practice, 29
    medieval Europe, 26
    Ottoman Empire, 31–5
    Roman Empire, 25, 31, 33
personal laws, 25–6, 44
Picot, François George, 50
Pieraccini, Paolo, 63
Piggott, Sir Francis, 47
Pinsker, Leo, 46
Pius X, Pope, 48
Pius XII, Pope, 91
Poland, Jewish migrants to Palestine, 46
Portugal, 118
Positivist School, 111
praetor peregrinus, 33
Protestant community, Frederick William's
    memorandum, 36
Prussia
    Berlin Congress (1878), 39
    Frederick William's memorandum, 36
    tripartite alliance (1841), 36

Qaddoumi, Farouq, 11
Quartet Road Map, 125–6
qubbat al-sakhra see Dome of the Rock
Al Quds, 1
Qureia, Ahmed, 6, 7

Rabin, Yitzhak, 7, 11, 16, 18
Rachel's Tomb, Bethlehem, 14, 55, 86
Rajoub, Jibril, 9
Ramon, Amnon, 95, 98, 103
Rau, Sir Benegal, 118
Ravenna, Felice, 48
Reiter, Yitzhak, 58, 63, 64
religion, as a central force, 126–7
research methodology, 3–4
Rockefeller Foundation, 136
Roman Empire, 1, 25–6, 31, 33
Roman law, 25–6, 27, 28, 33, 62
Romania, Jewish migrants to Palestine, 46
Rome Group for Arab Culture, 136
Rome seminars, 131–2
Ronzitti, Natalino, 92
Rosen, Rabbi David, 19, 20, 21
Rosenne, Shabtai, 106
Rothschild, Lord (Baron) Lionel Walter, 52
Rousseau, Charles, 30
Russell, Sir Odo, 70
Russia
    Berlin Congress (1878), 40–1
    Berlin Treaty (1878), 41
    calls for international administration, 51
    Constantinople Agreement, 49
    Frederick William's memorandum, 36
    French control of Syria, 49
    Jewish migrants to Palestine, 46
    nationalities, 53
    San Stefano Treaty (1878), 41
    Sykes–Picot Agreement, 51
    treaties with Ottoman Empire, 35
Russian Federation
    Declaration of Principles (DoP), 7
    Interim Agreement, 8
    Quartet Road Map, 125
    territorial–political status quo in Jerusalem, 10
Russian Revolution (1917), 128

Sabri, Sheik 'Ikrima, 9
Al-Sadat, Muhammad Anwar, 5–6, 9
Safieh, Afif, 6–7
St. Joseph University, 43
Saint Peter's Square, Rome, 129
Salisbury, Lord, 41
Samuel, Herbert Louis
    archaeology in Jerusalem, 115
    Balfour Declaration, 53
    disorganization of religious communities, 64
    as first High Commissioner, 59
    Holy Places policy, 49, 60, 67–8, 71, 72
    Palestine (Holy Places) Order-in-Council
        (1924), 67–8
    Palestine as "Jewish National Home", 49, 53
    partitioning of Palestine, 72
    plan to neutralize Palestine, 48
    Report for period 1920–1925, 59, 60
    restoration of Dome of the Rock, 60
    self-governing institutions, 72
    separation of Transjordan, 59
    tensions fostered in Palestine, 71
    visit to Vatican (1920), 57

Index

San Remo Conference (1920), 57, 63
San Stefano, Preliminary Treaty of (1878), 41
Sanctuary of the Ascension, 14
Saudi Arabia
  Arab–Israeli War (1948), 81
  expulsion of Jordan from Arab League, 93
  Islamic Holy Places, 18
  Palestine report (1947), 78
Sazonov, Sergey, 51
Scranton, William, 102
Second Vatican Council, 19, 114
Sèvres, Peace Treaty of (1920), 58, 59
Shapira, Moshe Haim, 95
Shapira, Ya'akov Shimon, 96
Sharett (Shertok), Moshe, 84, 88, 89, 91
shari'a, 42, 58, 64
Shaw Commission's Report (1929), 62, 65
Shaw, Sir Walter, 62
Shepherd's Field, Bethlehem, 14, 86
Sher, Gilead, 132
Shertok (Sharett), Moshe, 84, 88, 89, 91
Shuqeiri, Ahmed, 6
Silhab, Abd al-A'Zim, 9–10
Sinai Peninsula, 95
Singer, Joel, 12
Six-Day War (1967), 5, 95
  Jerusalem city limits, 4, 8
  territorial–political status quo in Jerusalem, 8–9
Slonim, Shlomo, 4, 76, 87
Sokolow, Nahum, 52
Solomon, King, 1
Solomon's Stables, 104
Sophronius, Patriarch, 12
sovereignty, 27–31, 124
  alternative definitions, 129–30, 138
  and authority, 27–8, 31, 129, 138
  etymological origin, 27
  and independence, 27–8, 31, 129, 138
  international law, 27, 28, 130
  public municipal law, 27
  in reference to states, 27
  subject of law, 30
  and title, 27–9, 31, 44, 129, 130, 138
  see also territorial sovereignty
Soviet Union
  Christian property in Palestine, 67
  Israeli Parliament opening ceremony, 90
  Jordanian actions (1948), 93
  Madrid Peace Conference (1991), 6
Spain, Jerusalem consulate, 80, 116
Spellman, Cardinal Francis, 91
Spinoza, Baruch, 27
state/territorial perspective
  Berlin Treaty (1878), 41
  British reluctance to adopt, 64, 69, 72, 125
  concept of nationality, 53
  cycles of Western history, 126–8
  definition of Holy Places, 105
  development of, 126, 127
  Holy Places, 2, 41, 42, 58, 105
  influence on local governments, 4
  Jerusalem, 2, 58, 124, 131
  limited by personal jurisdiction, 33
  and national-state identity, 42
  Ottoman Empire, 33, 35
  Quartet Road Map, 125–6
  range of exceptions, 31
  Status Quo talks, 131
  Western political elites, 32
  see also global/transnational perspective
Status Quo, 3
  Arab Report (1947), 78
  Berlin Treaty (1878), 14, 39–40, 41
  British Mandate period, 14, 40, 54, 58, 61, 64–6, 108, 125
  Catholic Church respect for, 21
  Christian Holy Places, 14, 22–3, 24, 36–45, 64, 94, 97–101, 107–9
  Church of the Nativity, Bethlehem, 14, 66, 86
  Custos of the Holy Land concerns, 76
  Cust's Memorandum, 14
  Declaration of Principles (DoP) (1993), 109
  defined, 110, 138
  distinguished from broad status quo, 114–15
  freedom of religion and worship, 112–14, 123
  global/transnational option, 131
  Har Ha Bait/Haram Al Sharif, 13–18, 86, 101–2, 103, 104
  historical analysis, 24
  Holy Sepulchre, 14, 65, 66, 86
  Islamic Holy Places, 14, 23, 64–5, 66, 101–4
  Israeli practice, 97–104, 108
  Israeli–Holy See Fundamental Agreement (1993), 18–19, 21–2, 23, 24, 101, 109, 134
  Israeli–Jordanian Peace Treaty (1994), 13–15
  Jewish Holy Places, 14, 23, 64–6, 101–4
  Jordanian practice, 93–4, 121
  Ottoman Empire, 2, 36–45, 107, 108, 121
  Ottoman *firmans*, 40
  PLO–Holy See Basic Agreement (2000), 22–3, 24, 109, 135
  procedural and material norms, 14, 104, 110–12, 120, 121, 123
  recognition by all rulers, 94
  state/territorial option, 131
  Western Wall, 14, 65–6, 86, 103–4
status quo, cultural–religious, 10, 112, 114–17, 120, 121, 123–4, 135–7, 139
status quo, territorial–political, 8–10, 12, 139
Stephan the Bourbon, 19
Straits of Tiran, 95
Sublime Porte, Ottoman Empire, 32, 33, 34, 35, 38, 39, 44
Suleiman the Magnificent, 33
Sweden
  Jerusalem Consul, 80
  UN "Partition Resolution" 181 (1947), 78
Sykes, Sir Mark, 49, 50, 52
Sykes–Picot Agreement, 51–2
Syria
  Arab–Israeli War (1948), 81
  Arab-Syrian Congress (1913), 44
  British "Declaration to the Seven", 56
  British division of land (1917), 55
  conquered by Mohammed Ali, 42, 45
  expulsion of Jordan from Arab League, 93

foreign religious bodies, 43
French intention to annex (1915), 49
independence (1936), 71
King–Crane Commission, 57
Palestine report (1947), 78
restoration of Ottoman administration (1841), 36
Sykes–Picot Agreement, 50
Syrian (Catholic) Christian community, 61
Syrian Orthodox Christian community, 61
Syrian Protestant College, 43

Taba summit (2001), 130
Tahboub, Hassan, 9, 16
Taliani, Egidio, 47
al-Tall, Abdallah, 92
Tauran, J.L., 20
al-Tel, Abdullah, 82
Tel Aviv, 80, 83, 84, 89
Temple Mount/Noble Sanctuary *see* Har Ha Bait/Haram Al Sharif
territorial jurisdiction, 26–7, 28, 124, 129
　custom as source of, 118
　defined, 27, 29, 138
　in international practice, 29–31
　Jordanian claims, 15
　medieval Europe, 26
　religious freedom obligations, 117
　restrictions on local governments, 117
　Roman Empire, 25, 31, 33
territorial perspective *see* state/territorial perspective
territorial sovereignty, 28, 124
　European model, 30, 126
　international law, 44, 138
　Ottoman Empire, 31, 33, 44
　spread in Middle East, 44
Thant, U, 96, 100
Theodoricus, King, 25, 146*n*
Thirty Years' War, 27, 127
Tisha b'Av, 94
title
　defined, 138
　and sovereignty, 27–9, 31, 44, 129, 130, 138
Toledo International Colloquium (1998), 136
Tomb of Jesus, 37
Tomb of the Virgin, 14
Tombs of the Patriarchs, 55
Transjordan
　British division of land (1917), 55
　establishment of, 59
　Holy Places of Jerusalem, 85
transnational perspective *see* global/transnational perspective
Truman, Harry S., 74, 75, 91
Trypho, 19
Turkey
　Jerusalem consulate, 80, 116
　Kemalist revolution, 44
　Lausanne Treaty (1923), 59
　Peace Treaty of Sèvres (1920), 58, 59
　see also Ottoman Empire

Umma, 12, 45, 64
UNESCO, 116
Uniate community, 61
United Nations
　Anglo-American Committee, 75
　Convention on the Civil and Political Rights (1966), 113, 122
　human rights, 112–13
　Israeli Draft Resolution (1949), 86, 88–9, 105–6
　Israeli membership, 85, 93
　Israeli Memorandum (1949), 86–7
　Jordanian membership, 93
　Palestine Conciliation Commission, 82, 86, 89, 91, 106
　Quartet Road Map, 125
　religious freedom, 112–13
United Nations Charter, 16, 27, 85, 89, 93, 112
United Nations General Assembly
　corpus separatum for Jerusalem (1950), 93
　Declaration on religious freedom (1981), 113
　Eban's statement (1969), 100
　Har ha Bait/Haram al-Sharif debate (1976), 102
　as material source of custom, 117
United Nations General Assembly Resolution 181 (1947), 8, 78–80, 81, 87, 89, 90, 91, 116
United Nations General Assembly Resolution 194 (III) (1948), 82, 86, 87, 91
United Nations General Assembly Resolution 303 (1949), 83
United Nations General Assembly Resolution 2200A (XXI) (1966), 122
United Nations General Assembly Resolution 2253 (1967), 96
United Nations General Assembly Resolution 3210 (1974), 6
United Nations Security Council
　Gold's remarks (1998), 101
　Har Ha Bait/Haram Al Sharif, 130
　Israeli expansion plans in Jerusalem (1998), 10
　Jordanian actions (1948), 92
　truce resolution (1948), 81
United Nations Security Council Resolution 54 (July 1948), 82
United Nations Security Council Resolution 242 (1967), 5
United Nations Security Council Resolution 298 (1971), 100
United Nations Security Council Resolution 338 (1973), 5
United Nations Security Council Resolution (May 1948), 81
United Nations Special Committee on Palestine (UNSCOP), 76–8, 80
United States
　Anglo-American Committee, 75
　Arab-Syrian Congress (1913), 44
　Camp David Accords (1978), 5, 6
　Capitulations of 1740, 34
　Declaration of Principles (DoP), 7
　endorsement of Balfour Declaration, 53

United States *(continued)*
  Harrison Report (1945), 74–5
  Interim Agreement, 8
  International and Inter-religious Commission for Holy Places, 58
  Island of Palmas decision, 28
  Israeli Parliament opening ceremony, 90
  Jerusalem consulate, 116
  Jewish immigrants in Palestine, 46
  Jordanian actions (1948), 92–3
  Madrid Peace Conference (1991), 6
  missionaries in Lebanon, 43
  Morrison–Grady Plan (1946), 75–6
  non-Christian Holy Places, 42
  Palestine as "Jewish National Home", 52–3
  Paris Peace Conference (1919), 55–6
  partition of Jerusalem, 90–1
  Quartet Road Map, 125
  rights of nationals in Morocco, 118–19
  September 11 terrorist attacks, 128
  Status Quo, 102–3
  UNSCOP, 76
  Zionism, 74
United States Supreme Court, 28
University of St. Joseph, 43
uti possidetis doctrine, 44

Vatican City, 111
Vatican II, 19, 114
Venice, 34
Verzijl, Jan Willem, 106–7
Vienna Convention, 13, 24

Wailing Wall *see* Western Wall
Wailing Wall Commission, 43, 46, 71, 110
Waqf
  administration in the West Bank, 16
  British Mandate, 58, 62
  control of Har Ha Bait/Haram Al Sharif, 13, 101–2, 104
  Israeli–Jordanian Peace Treaty (1994), 14
  post-1967 Israeli actions, 103
  restrictions on Israeli archaeologists, 104
  suspicion of Status Quo violation, 104
  Western Wall in Jerusalem Memorandum (1928), 65
Warhaftig, Zerah, 98, 99, 103
Washington Declaration, 13, 16, 18, 23, 24, 109, 134–5
Weizmann, Chaim, 55, 82–3, 95
Wellesley, William Robert, 72
Weltanschauung, 128
West Bank
  Anglo-Jordan treaty alliance, 93
  application of Geneva Conventions, 121
  Armistice Agreement (1949), 83
  British Mandate, 59
  control by Jordan, 6
  Declaration of Principles (DoP), 7, 8
  Interim Agreement, 7

  Israeli Supreme Court decision (1970), 97
  Jordanian citizenship, 92
  Madrid Peace Conference (1991), 6
  permanent status negotiations, 6, 7
  seats in Jordanian Parliament, 92
  Six-Day War (1967), 95
  Waqf administration, 16
Western or Wailing Wall in Jerusalem Memorandum, 65–6
Western Wall
  British Mandate period, 65–6, 67, 70, 103, 110
  disturbances (1928), 65–6
  Ibrahim Pasha's decree (1840), 43
  Israeli practice, 98, 102, 103–4
  Jewish prayer area, 15, 102
  Jordanian exclusion of Jews, 94
  riots (1929), 70
  significance to Jews, 2
  Status Quo, 14, 65–6, 86, 103–4
Westphalia, Peace of (1648), 27, 28, 127, 128
Wilson, Woodrow, 55, 57
Wingate, Sir Reginald, 55
Witkon, Judge, 116
"Women in Green", 11
Woodhead Commission (1938), 73, 84
World War I, 43, 44, 49, 58, 72
World Zionist Organization, 52, 56, 66

Yehoshua, Avraham, 126
Yemen, 44, 45
Yerushalayim, 1
yishuv, 46, 63, 81
Yom Kippur War (1973), 5
Young Turks *coup d'état* (1908), 43
Yugoslavia, religious conflict, 127

Zander, Walter, 4
  Berlin Congress (1878), 41
  Berlin Treaty (1878), 39
  Covenant of League of Nations, 72
  firman (1852), 36
  Holy Places, 36, 39, 71, 72, 78, 79, 93
  In Multiplicibus Curis, 91
  Jordanian appointment of Guardian, 93
  Palestine (Holy Places) Order-in-Council (1924), 70
  Peel Commission (1937), 72
  UN "Partition Resolution" 181 (1947), 79
  UNSCOP, 78
Zilberman, Ifrah, 16
Zionism
  American public opinion, 74
  British Government's sympathy, 52, 54
  Holy Places, 47
  Jewish colonization in Palestine, 52
  Temple in Jerusalem, 48
Zionist Congress (1899), 47
Zionist Federation in Italy, 48
Zionist national movement, 42, 63